THE BOOK OF THE MUTABILITY
OF FORTUNE

The Other Voice in Early Modern Europe:
The Toronto Series, 52

MEDIEVAL AND RENAISSANCE
TEXTS AND STUDIES

VOLUME 514

The Other Voice in
Early Modern Europe:
The Toronto Series

SERIES EDITORS Margaret L. King *and* Albert Rabil, Jr.
SERIES EDITOR, ENGLISH TEXTS Elizabeth H. Hageman

Previous Publications in the Series

The Other Voice in
Early Modern Europe:
The Toronto Series

SERIES EDITORS Margaret L. King *and* Albert Rabil, Jr.
SERIES EDITOR, ENGLISH TEXTS Elizabeth H. Hageman

Previous Publications in the Series

*In Dialogue with the Other Voice in
Sixteenth-Century Italy: Literary and Social
Contexts for Women's Writing*
Edited by Julie D. Campbell and Maria
Galli Stampino
Volume 11, 2011

SISTER GIUSTINA NICCOLINI
The Chronicle of Le Murate
Edited and translated by Saundra Weddle
Volume 12, 2011

LIUBOV KRICHEVSKAYA
*No Good without Reward: Selected
Writings: A Bilingual Edition*
Edited and translated by Brian James Baer
Volume 13, 2011

ELIZABETH COOKE HOBY RUSSELL
The Writings of an English Sappho
Edited by Patricia Phillippy
With translations by Jaime Goodrich
Volume 14, 2011

LUCREZIA MARINELLA
*Exhortations to Women and to Others If
They Please*
Edited and translated by Laura Benedetti
Volume 15, 2012

MARGHERITA DATINI
Letters to Francesco Datini
Translated by Carolyn James and Antonio
Pagliaro
Volume 16, 2012

DELARIVIER MANLEY AND MARY PIX
English Women Staging Islam, 1696–1707
Edited and introduced by Bernadette
Andrea
Volume 17, 2012

CECILIA DEL NACIMIENTO
*Journeys of a Mystic Soul in Poetry and
Prose*
Introduction and prose translations by
Kevin Donnelly
Poetry translations by Sandra Sider
Volume 18, 2012

LADY MARGARET DOUGLAS AND
OTHERS
*The Devonshire Manuscript: A Women's
Book of Courtly Poetry*
Edited and introduced by Elizabeth Heale
Volume 19, 2012

ARCANGELA TARABOTTI
Letters Familiar and Formal
Edited and translated by Meredith K. Ray
and Lynn Lara Westwater
Volume 20, 2012

PERE TORRELLAS AND JUAN DE FLORES
Three Spanish Querelle *Texts: Grisel and
Mirabella, The Slander against Women, and
The Defense of Ladies against Slanderers: A
Bilingual Edition and Study*
Edited and translated by Emily C.
Francomano
Volume 21, 2013

The Other Voice in
Early Modern Europe:
The Toronto Series

SERIES EDITORS Margaret L. King *and* Albert Rabil, Jr.
SERIES EDITOR, ENGLISH TEXTS Elizabeth H. Hageman

Previous Publications in the Series

The Other Voice in
Early Modern Europe:
The Toronto Series

SERIES EDITORS Margaret L. King *and* Albert Rabil, Jr.
SERIES EDITOR, ENGLISH TEXTS Elizabeth H. Hageman

Previous Publications in the Series

The Other Voice in
Early Modern Europe:
The Toronto Series

SERIES EDITORS Margaret L. King *and* Albert Rabil, Jr.
SERIES EDITOR, ENGLISH TEXTS Elizabeth H. Hageman

Previous Publications in the Series

The Other Voice in
Early Modern Europe:
The Toronto Series

SERIES EDITORS Margaret L. King *and* Albert Rabil, Jr.
SERIES EDITOR, ENGLISH TEXTS Elizabeth H. Hageman

Previous Publications in the Series

CHRISTINE DE PIZAN

The Book of the Mutability of Fortune

Edited and translated by

GERI L. SMITH

Iter Press
Toronto, Ontario

Arizona Center for Medieval and Renaissance Studies
Tempe, Arizona

2017

Iter Press
Tel: 416/978–7074   Email: iter@utoronto.ca
Fax: 416/978–1668   Web: www.itergateway.org

Arizona Center for Medieval and Renaissance Studies
Tel: 480/965–5900   Email: mrts@acmrs.org
Fax: 480/965–1681   Web: acmrs.org

Library of Congress Cataloging-in-Publication Data
This publication was submitted to the Library of Congress for cataloging. The catalog record was not
available at the time of printing.

ISBN 978-0-86698-570-3

Cover illustration:
Miniature of Christine in the Marvelous Room of Fortune's castle. From *Le Livre de la mutacion de
Fortune*, Bibliothèque nationale de France, fonds français 603, 127v, fifteenth century.

Cover design:
Maureen Morin, Information Technology Services, University of Toronto Libraries.

Typesetting:
Becker Associates.

Production:
Iter Press.

To my family

Contents

Acknowledgments

There were many moments during the course of this project when I felt, as so many of us do, as if I were toiling away alone, whether "*seulette*" in front of my computer or surrounded by others in a library reading room. In reality, however, that work represented a constant link with a vast community of scholars and students who share the range of interests swirling within and around *The Book of the Mutability of Fortune*. From feminist theory to medieval history, from mythology to morphology, from manuscript illumination to electronic lexicons—if Christine had any idea of all the people involved in all the disciplines in which she has become a focal point or a question mark over the centuries, her own self-perception as "*seulette*" would surely have to be re-examined. I sincerely hope that this project—the first start-to-finish incarnation of *Le Livre de la mutacion de Fortune* to appear in a language other than Middle French—not only does the poem justice, but does so in a way that makes it useful to the disparate and far-flung community for which this text represents a locus of encounter.

My thanks to all of the colleagues, mentors, and friends who have encouraged and inspired me in so many ways—Kevin Brownlee, Kathryn McMahon, Kristen Figg, Steven Taylor, John Block Friedman, Christine Reno, Christopher Callahan, and especially to Daisy Delogu for kindly helping to detangle some of the most resistant phrases. I fondly remember Charity Cannon Willard, who became my neighbor when I moved to the Hudson Valley; there was never a conversation that did not in some way affirm the magnitude of her contribution to the field of Christine studies.

I wish to acknowledge the colleagues at West Point who helped make my sabbatical possible—the time to focus made all the difference: Julia Praud, Charles Parsons, Scott Kutscher, Christophe Corbin, Ronald Hijduk, and Lawrence Mansour, for whom my absence meant that the load was a bit heavier for a while, and Gregory Ebner for his sustained support. Thanks also to Rebecca Jones-Kellogg, Marie Johnson, and Elizabeth Samet for so many enlightening and uplifting chats; to Professor Emerita Sheila Ackerlind for being a champion for research; and to Laura Vidler for her cherished friendship, for reading my scribbles, and for being a willing and insightful sounding board, whatever the issue.

I am very grateful to the editorial team of The Other Voice in Early Modern Europe series for so carefully shepherding the manuscript through the publication process. Particular thanks are due to Cheryl Lemmens for her many insightful suggestions.

Fond appreciation goes to my dear friend Nicolle Hirschfeld for contributing her expertise in Classical Studies to the cause; to Alison Thresher for making sure we never lost touch; to my first French teacher and lifelong friend, Gail O'Neill, whose influence on my professional path has been incalculable; and to Simon Barton for his help and encouragement, and for having the answers to so many questions.

Love and gratitude go to my family, with a special nod to Anita Smith and James Casey for reading sections of this with critical eyes. And above all, my deepest appreciation to Leslie Casey for being my almost-twin, most steadfast supporter, and closest ally since the day I was born.

Introduction

Christine de Pizan as "Other Voice"

Christine de Pizan stands out as the first professional woman writer in the French literary canon.[1] She presents herself explicitly as such, making her gendered authorial persona that of a carefully crafted "other," carving out a strong, at times controversial, place in a literary and intellectual landscape historically reserved for men.[2] She cultivates that persona through autobiographical references woven throughout her works, which persistently and often poignantly emphasize her identity as daughter, mother, wife, and widow.[3] Using her singular perspective as a platform from which to stage her writing, Christine's emphasis on her own gender pairs with an emphasis on women as subject matter. Deftly manipulating the dominant, historically masculine, discursive modes of her day—"courtly" and learned alike—Christine writes within and against them to assert a distinctively feminine voice anchored in a specifically feminine model of authority. As the term for a defined concept of feminism would not exist until the nineteenth century, it would be anachronistic to call Christine a "feminist" in the modern sense. It is quite safe to say, however, that hers is the first self-consciously polemical "proto-feminist" voice we hear from medieval France.

While Christine's life story and cohesive point of view were imprinted on her writing from the start, the most prominent and decisive moment in her establishment as a credible, authoritative "other" voice was her engagement in France's first public literary debate, the quarrel surrounding the *Roman de la Rose (Romance of the Rose)*. This voluminous poem, very well known in Christine's time, was composed by Guillaume de Lorris (lines 1–4056, ca. 1236) and Jean de Meun (lines 4057–21677, ca. 1270). It depicts a dream vision in which a lover pursues and ultimately ravages his love object, represented by a rose. This work would

---

1. The scholarly literature on Christine de Pizan is immense. In eleven cases where the documentation pertaining to a topic threatens to overwhelm the footnote apparatus, the reader is invited to refer to the Appendix. In this case, see Appendix/1: *Overviews of Christine's Life, Works, and Historical Context.*

2. See Appendix/2: *Christine's Self-Construction as a Gendered Authorial Persona.*

3. Notable examples are to be found in the first twenty poems of her *Cent balades (One Hundred Ballads)*, the prologue to *Le chemin de longue estude (The Path of Long Study)*, Book I of the *Mutacion de Fortune (Mutability of Fortune)*, and Book III of *L'avision-Christine (Christine's Vision)*. On Christine as an innovator with regard to autobiography as a genre, see María Angela Holguera Fanega, "Manifestaciones autobiográficas en *Le livre de la mutacion de Fortune* de Christine de Pizan," in *Las sabias mujeres: Educación, saber y autoría: siglos III–XVII*, ed. María del Mar Graña Cid (Madrid: Al-Mudayna, 1994), 203–11. Regarding autobiography and biography as focal points of Christine's writing, see James Laidlaw, "Writing Lives—Christine de Pizan," *New Comparison* 25 (Spring 1998): 25–39.

1

leave an indelible mark on French literature for its use of allegory, mythological and other learned references, and narrative structure.

Christine took issue with the *Romance of the Rose*, and in particular its second author, Jean de Meun, for his misogynist tendencies and vulgar language. The result was a public epistolary debate on the poem that unfolded from 1401 through 1402. On one side were Christine and her allies Jean Gerson, chancellor of the University of Paris, and Guillaume de Tignonville, Provost of Paris. On the other were Jean de Montreuil, provost of Lille and secretary to Charles VI; Gontier Col, also a secretary to the king; and his brother Pierre Col, Canon of Paris. The debate put Christine squarely in the company of a number of "heavy hitters," whom she likely knew through the circles of secretaries to the royal court that was her personal and professional milieu.[4] Not only did she hold her own, but she took a measure of control in the dispute by crafting the debate letters into a book at the end of 1401 and presenting them to Queen Isabeau of Bavaria and Guillaume de Tignonville. Ultimately, Christine's display of knowledge, wielding of a sharp pen, and deft self-promotion went a long way toward solidifying the author's reputation.[5]

Aside from her status as a professional woman author, Christine can be described as "other" in a number of ways, in that she was often a "first" for her time. She was the first woman among the wave of scholars who brought Italian humanistic thought and literary works to the French intellectual milieu.[6] With her *Livre de la cité des dames (Book of the City of Ladies)*, she became the first female writer to pen a substantive text in defense of women, which she accomplished by correctively recasting known texts to show that interpretations in favor of women were as viable as those that had been traditionally opposed to them. Her officially commissioned biography of King Charles V is extraordinary, as not only the first

---

4. Charity Cannon Willard, *Christine de Pizan: Her Life and Works* (New York: Persea Books, 1984), 47. Henceforth cited as Willard, *Life and Works*.

5. See Appendix/3: *The Debate of the* Romance of the Rose.

6. On Christine's humanism, see Susan Groag Bell, "Christine de Pizan (1364–1430): Humanism and the Problem of the Studious Woman," *Feminist Studies* 3 (1976): 173–84; Nadia Margolis, "Culture vantée, culture inventée: Christine, Clamanges et le défi de Pétrarque," in Eric Hicks, Diego Gonzalez, and Philippe Simon, eds., *Au champ des escriptures: IIIᵉ Colloque international sur Christine de Pizan, Lausanne, 18–22 juillet 1998* (Paris: Champion, 2000), 269–308; Margolis, "Christine de Pizan: The Poetess as Historian," *Journal of the History of Ideas* 47 (1986): 361–75; Earl Jeffrey Richards, "Christine de Pizan and Jean Gerson: An Intellectual Friendship," in John Campbell and Nadia Margolis, eds., *Christine de Pizan 2000: Studies on Christine de Pizan in Honour of Angus J. Kennedy* (Amsterdam: Rodopi, 2000), 197–208; and Richards, "Christine de Pizan, the Conventions of Courtly Diction, and Italian Humanism," in Richards, Joan Williamson, Nadia Margolis, and Christine Reno, eds., *Reinterpreting Christine de Pizan* (Athens: University of Georgia Press, 1992), 250–71.

"secular biography" written in France,[7] but as the first time a woman would be granted such an honor and responsibility—a rarity in any age.

Further, Christine was known to be closely involved in the commercial production of her works, highly unusual for writers in her day, and she even copied some of those texts in her own hand.[8] Charity Cannon Willard comments in reference to *L'avision-Christine* (*Christine's Vision*) that Christine "became the first woman to leave such an autobiography as a record of her evolution both as a writer and as a person."[9] Daniel Poirion goes a step further still, saying that *pour la première fois en France, nous ne pouvons pas séparer l'étude de l'oeuvre et celle de l'écrivain. Voilà, au sens qui deviendra classique, notre premier auteur, et cet auteur est une femme* (for the first time in France, we cannot separate the study of the work from that of the writer. Here is, in what will become the classic sense of the word, our first *author*, and that author is a woman).[10]

In sum, then, Christine was not just an "other" voice of the late Middle Ages, but also a forerunner with respect to modern concepts of authorship, in many ways redefining the relationship between writer and text. Christine's contemporary, famed poet Eustache Deschamps, called her "nompareille" (incomparable) in a ballad written for her, with the refrain "seule en tez fais ou royaume de France" (for your achievements, you stand alone in the French kingdom).[11] With some two hundred manuscripts of Christine's texts surviving—including the highest number of original manuscripts by any medieval author, many in the author's own hand[12]—she has lived up to that assessment, standing out as perhaps the most "present" of all late medieval French writers, of either gender, in our time.

Christine's Life and Works

While Christine's agenda was clearly a conscious engagement with the cause of women, she was not what we would call radical in her view of social roles. In fact,

7. Willard, *Life and Works*, 118.

8. See Appendix/4: *Christine's Involvement in the Production of Her Works.*

9. Willard, *Life and Works*, 160.

10. Daniel Poirion, "Christine de Pisan," in *Le Moyen Âge II: 1300–1480* (Paris: Arthaud, 1971), 206.

11. *Œuvres complètes de Eustache Deschamps*, ed. le Marquis de Queux de Saint-Hilaire (Paris: Firmin Didot, 1878–1903), 6:251–52; Ballad 1242, line 2 and refrain.

12. Gilbert Ouy and Christine Reno, "Le catalogue des manuscrits autographes et originaux de Christine de Pizan," in Bernard Ribémont, ed., *Sur le chemin de longue étude ... Actes du colloque d'Orléans, juillet 1995* (Paris: Champion, 1998), 127.

her "feminism," or lack thereof, remains a topic of debate to this day.[13] As Willard
wryly put it, "There still remains the problem of judging her as a woman as well
as a writer ... opinion has swung from admiration that she could have accom-
plished what she did at all to disdain for the fact that she did not do what she never
intended."[14] With respect to politics, morality, and social roles, Christine's views
were very much in line with the dominant thought of her day, particularly that of
the conservative world of the court. As a woman head-of-household, earning her
living through writing, she was a self-avowed anomaly. She observed more than
once that not only was she fulfilling a man's role, but in fact she had to turn into a
man to do so, as she graphically depicts in the most dramatic, explicit, and studied
of such references, found in the *Mutability of Fortune*.[15]

Christine's works are striking for their number and variety. She composed
love poetry. She wrote epistles addressed to readers real and imaginary, allegorical
dream visions, a world history, and a royal biography. She highlighted her faith
in religious writings. She shared her knowledge and entertained her tendency to-
ward didacticism through treatises on good governing, chivalry, and proper be-
havior for women.[16] Her patrons and dedicatees occupied the highest strata of
society, and included such luminaries as King Charles VI, Queen Isabeau of Ba-
varia, John of Berry, Philip the Bold of Burgundy, John the Fearless of Burgundy,
and Louis of Orléans. Christine's impetus to write professionally arose from crisis
in her life, and her ability to succeed at such a level was the fortunate result of her
studious nature combined with her unusual upbringing—an Italian transplant
who never lost her intellectual and emotional connection with her roots, and who

13. For a criticism of Christine's conservative stance, see Sheila Delany, "'Mothers to Think Back
Through': Who Are They? The Ambiguous Example of Christine de Pizan," in *Medieval Texts and
Contemporary Readers*, ed. Laurie A. Finke and Martin B. Schichtman (Ithaca, NY: Cornell Univer-
sity Press, 1987), 177–97. Christine M. Reno responds to Delany in "Christine de Pizan: At Best a
Contradictory Figure?" in Margaret Brabant, ed., *Politics, Gender, and Genre: The Political Thought of
Christine de Pizan* (Boulder, CO: Westview, 1992), 171–91. See also Beatrice Gottlieb, "The Problem of
Feminism in the Fifteenth Century," in *Women of the Medieval World: Essays in Honor of John H. Mun-
dy*, ed. Julius Kirshner and Suzanne F. Wemple (Oxford: Basil Blackwell, 1985), 337–64; and Douglas
Kelly, "Reflections on the Role of Christine de Pisan as a Feminist Writer," *Sub-stance* 2 (1972): 63–71.
For an early study of Christine's "feminism," see Rose Rigaud, *Les idées féministes de Christine de Pisan*
(Neuchâtel: Imprimerie Attinger Frères, 1911).

14. Willard, *Life and Works*, 222–23.

15. *The Book of the Mutability of Fortune*, English translation of *La mutacion de Fortune* published in
this volume, lines 1325–61.

16. On Christine's didacticism, see, for example, Roberta Krueger, "Christine's Anxious Lessons: Gen-
der, Morality, and the Social Order from the *Enseignemens* to the *Avision*," in Marilynn Desmond, ed.,
Christine de Pizan and the Categories of Difference (Minneapolis: University of Minnesota Press, 1998),
16–40; and Charity Cannon Willard, "Christine de Pizan as Teacher," *Romance Languages Annual* 3
(1992): 132–36.

was raised amid the people and resources of the French royal circle. From early on, Christine's work was well received in France, and thanks largely to the artistically attuned English noble, the Earl of Salisbury, whom she met at the French court in late 1398, she gained an audience in England as well.[17] Christine was also known in Italy, as a result of marriages between the French and Italian royal families around this time.

Christine was born in Venice in 1364 or 1365, where she stayed until ca. 1369, when her father Thomas (Tommaso di Benvenuto da Pizzano), doctor and astrologer to the court of King Charles V the Wise, relocated his family to Paris.[18] Christine was reared in the milieu of the intellectually-minded king, to whose extensive library she had access. Thanks to her learned father, Christine was exposed to more academic pursuits than most young people of her time, especially girls. Still, in her autobiographical reflections, she lamented that, having been born a girl, she did not receive the depth of education that a boy would have enjoyed, commenting that she was only able to gather the scraps from her father's table. Her writings, nonetheless, show her to have been extremely well read in the canonical texts known to the literati of her day, with the influence of such masters as Boethius, Ovid, Boccaccio, and Dante so prevalent that it is an important current underlying much of the scholarship on Christine and her work.

At age fifteen, Christine married Etienne de Castel, himself employed as a secretary to the king, and all indications are that she led a happy family life, which came to include two sons and a daughter. Christine's world would take a progressive downward turn, however. It began as early as September 1380, when the death of Charles V ushered in both an era of great turmoil for France and an immediate change in the fortunes of Christine's family. Suddenly, the standing and income of Christine's father suffered a precipitous decline, as would his health. After struggling with an illness that would strain his finances, Thomas died between 1384 and 1389, leaving little behind as an inheritance for his daughter.

Christine's troubles, however, were just beginning. Most catastrophic and life changing of all was the loss of her husband to illness in 1390. Now she was on her own, responsible for the well-being of her mother, three children, and a niece. Making matters worse, she was also thrown into the fray of lengthy legal battles to

---

17. On the dating of that encounter, see James Laidlaw, "Christine de Pizan, the Earl of Salisbury, and Henry IV," *French Studies* 36 (1982): 129–43.

18. For a study of Christine's roots in Italy, see Nikolai Wandruszka, "Familial Traditions of the *de Piçano* at Bologna," in Angus J. Kennedy, Rosalind Brown-Grant, James C. Laidlaw, and Catherine M. Müller, eds., *Contexts and Continuities: Proceedings of the IVth International Colloquium on Christine de Pizan, Glasgow 21–27 July 2000: Published in Honour of Liliane Dulac* (Glasgow: University of Glasgow Press, 2002), 3:889–906; and Wandruszka, "The Family Origins of Christine de Pizan: Noble Lineage Between City and 'Contado' in the Thirteenth and Fourteenth Centuries," in Hicks, Gonzalez, and Simon, *Au champ des escriptures*, 111–30.

settle her estate, gaining firsthand knowledge of the court system's corruption and hostility toward women. Christine's legal wrangling would drag on for more than twenty years, a trying and scary time to which she alludes in several of her texts, including the *Mutability of Fortune.*

It was during this period that Christine's literary enterprise began. Her first collection of poems, the *Cent balades (One Hundred Ballads)*, written between ca. 1394 and 1402, comprises primarily love poems, with the first twenty of particular significance for their autobiographical thrust. These poems depict Christine's recent widowhood and the terrible suffering it caused her. At this stage, Christine writes not just to make a living, but also as a refuge from her grief. Poem 11 of this sequence is the famous "Seulete suy" (A little woman alone am I). Here, Christine defines herself as a widow, with the end of line 1, "et seulete vueil estre" (and a little woman alone I want to be), affirming her resolve.[19]

Christine would experiment not only with ballads, but with the range of other fixed forms popular in her day—rondeaux, virelays, and lays. Christine's first long poem is the 827-line *Epistre au dieu d'amours (Letter of the God of Love)*, dating from 1399. The central theme of the *Epistre* is the negative side of romance, addressing as it does men's ill-treatment of women, with an emphasis on seduction, deceit, indiscretion, and slander — all so damaging to a woman's well-being and reputation.

While the initial phase of Christine's work focused on poetry and courtly love themes, even relatively early in her career she would take up weightier topics, seemingly compelled to offer advice where she had areas of concern. An early example is the *Epistre Othea (Letter of Othea)*, written in 1400. Known for its unique structure, combining verse passages with prose allegory and didactic gloss, the *Letter of Othea* draws on mythology for the lessons it contains. This work, focused on good morals and proper behavior for young men, is directed to Christine's teenage son, Jean de Castel. But copies were also given to Louis, Duke of Orléans, Queen Isabeau, Charles VI, and Philip the Bold, suggesting that Christine had

---

19. *Œuvres poétiques de Christine de Pisan*, ed. Maurice Roy (Paris: Firmin Didot, 1886–1896), 1:12. On this stance taken by Christine, see Lori J. Walters, "The Figure of the *seulette* in the Works of Christine de Pizan and Jean Gerson," in Liliane Dulac, Anne Paupert, Christine Reno, and Bernard Ribémont, eds., *Desireuse de plus avant enquerre ... Actes du VIe Colloque international sur Christine de Pizan: Paris, 20–24 juillet 2006: Volume en hommage à James Laidlaw* (Paris: Champion, 2008), 119–39. On isolation as a hallmark of Christine's literary persona, see Catherine Attwood, "The 'I' Transformed: The Poetic 'I' in the Works of Christine de Pizan," Chap. 5 in *Dynamic Dichotomy: The Poetic "I" in Fourteenth- and Fifteenth-Century French Lyric Poetry* (Amsterdam: Rodopi, 1998), 167–74; and Marie-Thérèse Lorcin, "'Seulete suy et seulete vueil estre....,'" in Kennedy et al., *Contexts and Continuities*, 2:549–60.

loftier aims for her text.[20] As it turns out, the *Letter of Othea* went on to enjoy the greatest commercial success of any of Christine's texts.

The years 1400–1405 would be a period of dazzling productivity, during which Christine composed the majority of her most substantial and important texts. We have already noted that the *Rose* debate of 1401–1402 represented a validation for Christine, establishing her authority in a new and public way, and galvanizing her place in the wider intellectual community. That event also marked a turning point in Christine's writing, as she began to engage more consistently in weightier topics such as history and governance, and to compose in prose rather than verse. While she did not abandon courtly love themes and poetry entirely, the overall trend as Christine's career unfolded was toward an expansion of her range of concerns and assertion of an ever bolder voice.

A major work dating from this period is *Le chemin de longue estude* (*The Path of Long Study*), inspired by both Boethius's *Consolation of Philosophy* and Dante's journey to the underworld. Written during 1402–1403, this is the first of Christine's texts in which she publicly expresses her concerns for her country's ills. The poem opens with a lament on the sad state of the world, and especially of France, where conflict is the order of the day. The Prologue is autobiographical, again emphasizing Christine's widowhood and the solace she takes in solitary intellectual pursuits. The poem goes on to recount an allegorical dream vision in which a sibyl guides Christine-the-protagonist on a voyage of discovery through which she visits many exotic lands, and then the heavens. She ends up observing a marvelous tribunal of sorts, where queens Wealth, Wisdom, Chivalry, and Nobility argue before Lady Reason over who is to blame for the sad state of affairs on Earth, and the best way to restore good governance and stability. The views of Christine-the-author are plain: Wisdom wins the argument, persuading Reason that the world needs neither the wealthiest prince nor the greatest warrior, but a philosopher-king, and that France is the rightful place from which to reestablish order. Christine-protagonist is chosen to bring the message about righteous governance and the responsibility of leaders back to France, which Christine-author indeed does by dedicating the work to the king and presenting copies to the dukes of Berry, Burgundy, and Orléans, three of the central figures in France's internal power struggles.

The *Path of Long Study* is contemporaneous with the *Mutability of Fortune* (to be discussed below). It is after that busy year of writing, and the success of the *Mutability of Fortune* in particular, that Christine would be commissioned by Philip of Burgundy to write his brother's biography, *Le livre des fais et bonnes meurs du sage roy Charles V* (*The Book of the Deeds and Good Ways of the Wise King Charles V*). It is Christine's first work entirely in prose. More than just the

---

20. Nadia Margolis, *An Introduction to Christine de Pizan* (Gainesville: University Press of Florida, 2011), 83.

story of the king's life, this is a treatise on kingship itself, with Charles V as the model. Christine extols Charles's virtue and intelligence, and expounds on chivalry and wisdom as qualities that a good king should possess. As Philip of Burgundy died in April 1404, he did not live to see the work's completion in November of that year. However, Christine began the year 1405 by presenting the biography to the king's brother John, Duke of Berry, on New Year's Day.[21]

Two of Christine's most important works would soon follow. In the prose *City of Ladies*, modeled on Boccaccio's *Book of Illustrious Women*, Christine recasts tales from myth, history, legend, and religious writings in a light favorable to women. The divine ladies Reason, Rectitude, and Justice appear to the naïve Christine-protagonist, confused and saddened by the condemnation of women that was so prevalent in writings of all kinds across the ages. Through examples of women whose accomplishments and character defy the negative judgments, Christine's visitors teach her to read in a new way, to trust in her own feminine experience, and ultimately to counsel and speak on behalf of all women. The metaphorical City of Ladies, of which the building blocks are all the examples that have comprised Christine-protagonist's education, will stand as a bastion in defense of women, with the Virgin Mary herself as queen.[22] Exemplifying Christine's pro-women agenda and highlighting her erudition, the *City of Ladies* has gone on to become the most widely read of Christine's works in modern times.

Christine's Vision, also in prose and also dating from 1405, is again structured as an allegorical dream vision. Part 1 is largely concerned with the history of France and its present-day ills, capped off by Christine-protagonist being charged with spreading the word to France's leaders about what must be done to get France back on track. In Part 2, Christine-protagonist moves on to the University of Paris to explore the implications of true wisdom versus opinion in one's understanding of life and the world. Part 3, the best known section of this complex and unusual work, contains the most extensive autobiographical passage in all of Christine's writings, in which she presents herself in terms of her dual status as ever-grieving widow and, by this point in her life, successful professional writer.

One of the last works to emerge from this flurry of activity is the prose *Livre des trois vertus* (*Book of the Three Virtues*), later renamed *Le tresor de la cité des dames* (*The Treasury of the City of Ladies*), composed in 1405–1406. This work, a follow-up to the *City of Ladies*, is a kind of how-to manual for the way women from all walks of life should comport themselves. As Willard points out, this work breaks new ground both by paying attention to women of all social strata and by

---

21. Willard, *Life and Works*, 132.

22. For a study relating Fortune's castle with this metaphorical city, see Julia Simms Holderness, "Castles in the Air? The Prince as Conceptual Artist," in Karen Green and Constant J. Mews, eds., *Healing the Body Politic: The Political Thought of Christine de Pizan* (Turnhout: Brepols, 2005), 161–75.

encouraging women to be proactive about their life circumstances.²³ Dedicated to Marguerite, the daughter of the Duke of Burgundy, who married the dauphin, Louis de Guyenne, in 1404, Christine's wise words on virtue and social behavior for all women undoubtedly held a message for the girl who was in line to become their sovereign.²⁴ Mindful of the future in the *Three Virtues*, Christine confronts the present in her 1405 *Epistre a la reine* (*Letter to the Queen*), pleading for a resolution to the conflict between the powerful rivals, the Duke of Orléans and John the Fearless of Burgundy, whose rift was so grave that it would fuel the catastrophic divide that defined the early years of fifteenth-century France.

Christine's rate of literary production declines after 1405, but variety remains a hallmark. Her *Livre du corps de policie* (*Book of the Body Politic*), from 1407, expounds upon what it means to be a good leader as well as a good subject. She addresses the formation of the ideal prince, followed by the desired qualities for nobles and knights, and finally those for groups making up the rest of society. In 1410, expanding upon themes present in Part II of the *Body Politic*, Christine would compose her military treatise, the *Livre des fais d'armes et de chevalerie* (*Book of Feats of Arms and of Chivalry*). Acknowledging up front that the topic is a surprising one for a woman author, Christine bolsters her position by calling out to Minerva, the goddess of chivalry and arms, in the prologue. She beseeches Minerva to support the undertaking, and aligns herself with the goddess by pointing out that "like you I am an Italian woman."²⁵ Christine clearly wished to show skeptical readers an example of another woman who dared to engage with the world of warfare, and succeeded.

On a very different topic is the *Cent balades d'amant et de dame* (*One Hundred Ballads of Lover and Lady*), also generally believed to have been written between 1407 and 1410. That text, which marks Christine's final foray into courtly love themes, has been considered her "swan song" to lyric poetry.²⁶ Her use of an innovative dialogic structure, in which she alternates poems in the voices of the man and woman in a doomed courtly love relationship, allows Christine to assert the feminine voice and point of view in ways that the traditional model of such debate sequences does not, presenting a harsh critique of the courtly love paradigm that can be so cruel toward women.

As different as these three works are, Christine's interest in teaching is present in all. If the *Body Politic* was primarily aimed at instructing boys and men as future leaders, and the *Feats of Arms* was a sort of manual for practitioners of mili-

23. Willard, *Life and Works*, 146.

24. That did not happen, as Louis de Guyenne died in 1415.

25. Christine de Pizan, *The Book of Deeds of Arms and of Chivalry*, trans. Sumner Willard, ed. Charity Cannon Willard (University Park: Pennsylvania State University Press, 1999), 13.

26. See Barbara K. Altmann, "Last Words: Reflections on a 'Lay Mortel' and the Poetics of Lyric Sequences," *French Studies* 50 (1996): 385–99.

tary arms and strategy, the *One Hundred Ballads of Lover and Lady* had at least the secondary aim of offering a moral lesson, primarily for girls and women.

In addition to the themes of politics, chivalry, and, to a lesser extent, love, Christine's writing from the second decade of the fifteenth century powerfully reflects her long-standing dismay at the tragedy of France's political infighting, expressed in works such as the emotional *Lamentacion sur les maux de France* (*Lament on France's Ills*) from 1410. The *Livre de la paix* (*Book of Peace*), from 1412–1413, would be Christine's last substantial treatise on good governance and her last attempt to appeal to the powerful elite. It is followed by the *Epistre de la prison de vie humaine* (*Letter on the Prison of Human Life*) from 1418, which directly concerns the suffering of women who lost loved ones in the battle of Agincourt in 1415.

In 1418, it is believed that Christine retreated to Poissy, about eighteen miles from the intense unrest of Paris, to the convent that her daughter Marie called home. Christine's last work, and lone major text to appear in the following decade, is the 1429 *Ditié de Jehanne d'Arc* (*Tale of Joan of Arc*). Written within the months immediately following Joan's victory at Orléans, this verse piece is simultaneously a glorification of "The Maid" who was responsible for the salvation of France and a plea for the acceptance of Charles VII as France's rightful king and great hope. Christine completed the *Tale of Joan of Arc* at the end of July 1429, as is indicated within the poem, after Charles VII's coronation on July 17, also referenced in the poem.[27] What is not known is whether Christine, who almost certainly died in 1430 or 1431, was alive to see the sad aftermath of Joan's triumph, the heroine's execution by the English in May 1431.

Historical Context

Christine's life coincided with the later phase of the Hundred Years' War, and specifically the period of transition from the relative peace and prosperity enjoyed under Charles V to the years of civil war, assassinations, rivalries among often ruthless power-mongers, and resurgent violence between France and England that marred the reign of Charles VI and beyond.[28] Christine's vantage point was

---

27. *Ditié de Jehanne d'Arc: Christine de Pisan*, ed. Angus J. Kennedy and Kenneth Varty (Oxford: Society for the Study of Mediaeval Languages and Literature, 1977), stanzas 61 and 49, respectively pages 37 and 40 (Middle French), and 48 and 50 (English).

28. On the relationship between Christine's works and the complex politics of her time, see Tracy Adams, *Christine de Pizan and the Fight for France* (University Park: Pennsylvania State University Press, 2014); Adams, "A Re-assessment of the Relationship between Christine de Pizan and Louis of Orléans," in Patrizia Caraffi, ed., *Christine de Pizan: La scrittrice e la città / L'écrivaine et la ville / The Woman Writer and the City: Atti del VII Convegno Internazionale "Christine de Pizan": Bologna, 22–26*

unique in that she personally knew and worked for a number of the key players at the highest levels—people whose actions and loyalties profoundly affected, indeed often determined, the events of this time. Furthermore, Christine wrote not only *for* these people; she wrote *to* them in her works addressing good governance and in her expressions of despair at the state of France. In fact, the copy of the *Mutability of Fortune* presented to the Duke of Berry contains notes, apparently in Christine's hand, highlighting certain passages on governance, and appear to be a direct message from Christine to the duke during that very troubled period.[29]

When Charles V died in September 1380, his successor was just eleven. Charles's brother Louis, Duke of Anjou, became regent, while another of the king's brothers, Philip the Bold of Burgundy, and the late queen's brother Louis II, Duke of Bourbon, took on the role of the dauphin's guardians. What ensued was not a smooth custodianship of power, but rather a sustained and vicious rivalry that would take its toll for decades. France's straits would go from bad to worse as Charles VI matured. In 1392, just four years after having assumed the reins of government, the king suffered what would be the first of many bouts of madness that would define his adult life. With no official regency reestablished, the rule of France became a political landscape fertile for continued infighting and instability. While Queen Isabeau was officially in charge during her husband's periods of incapacity, Philip the Bold was the principal power holder at this point.[30] Meanwhile, the king's brother Louis, Duke of Orléans, was nipping at Philip's heels.

The ensuing period was characterized by political maneuvering, strategic marriage arrangements, and shifting fortunes. The death of Christine's most supportive patron, Philip the Bold, in 1404, sparked an intense power struggle between Louis of Orléans and John the Fearless of Burgundy. The conflict exploded in November 1407, when Louis of Orléans was assassinated by partisans of his rival.

---

settembre 2009 (Florence: Alinea, 2013), 17–27; and Renate Blumenfeld-Kosinski, "Christine de Pizan and the Political Life in Late Medieval France," in Barbara K. Altmann and Deborah L. McGrady, eds., *Christine de Pizan: A Casebook* (New York: Routledge, 2003), 9–24.

29. See Christine M. Reno, "Autobiography and Authorship in Christine's Manuscripts," *Romance Languages Annual* 9 (1997): xxi–xxiv.

30. On Christine's views of Isabeau's role in governing at this time, see Tracy Adams, "Christine de Pizan, Isabeau of Bavaria, and Female Regency," *French Historical Studies* 32 (2009): 1–32; Adams, "Isabeau de Bavière dans l'oeuvre de Christine de Pizan: Une réévaluation du personnage," in Juliette Dor and Marie-Elisabeth Henneau, eds., *Christine de Pizan: Une femme de science, une femme de lettres* (Paris: Champion, 2008), 133–46; and Adams, "Isabeau de Bavière et la notion de régence chez Christine de Pizan," in Dulac et al., *Desireuse de plus avant enquerre*, 33–44. See also Daisy Delogu, "*Advocate et moyenne*: Christine de Pizan's Elaboration of Female Authority," in Dulac et al., *Desireuse de plus avant enquerre*, 57–67.

John, however, was pardoned by the king for his role, and his political victory was sealed when he was appointed governor of the dauphin two years later.[31]

France's troubles were far from over. In 1410, Louis's son Charles, Duke of Orléans, married the daughter of Bernard VII, count of Armagnac. Tensions crystallized as the family and its supporters, now known as the Armagnac faction, united in opposition to John the Fearless of Burgundy and his allies. In what may have been part of John the Fearless's propaganda counterattack,[32] Christine wrote her *Lament*, deploring the situation, envisioning catastrophe to come, and appealing to the French to find peace. There would be no such thing: in the summer of 1411, the Burgundians, with the help of the English, rode into Paris and established their dominance. The August 1412 Treaty of Auxerre reestablished stability, with John the Fearless in charge. But both peace and John's dominant position would be short-lived.

In April 1413, a pro-Burgundian butcher named Simon Caboche led a popular revolt in Paris (the "Cabochian uprising"), terrorizing bourgeois and intellectuals and rebelling against the Orléans faction. John the Fearless had initially encouraged the uprising, only to have the prevailing sentiment turn against the Burgundians when the extreme nature of the unrest proved distasteful to the populace. The dauphin turned to the Armagnacs for support when even his own family members and close associates became targets. Ultimately, the Burgundians were run out of Paris and the revolt was put to an end. Christine's *Book of Peace* both celebrates the Treaty of Auxerre and testifies to the terror of the violent times, while calling out for the dauphin to govern according to the highest ideals.

Stability continued to remain elusive. Taking advantage of France's tenuous state, the English under Henry V resumed aggression, resulting in the battle of Agincourt in 1415. The battle was catastrophic for France, and particularly for the Armagnacs. At the end of that same year, the dauphin Louis de Guyenne would die, leaving his brother Charles as the successor to the throne. In 1418, however, the English-sympathizing Burgundians again occupied Paris, attacking the Armagnacs and killing many of their partisans, including a number of pro-Armagnac intellectuals and Bernard VII himself, who was at that point Constable of France. Christine expresses her despair over the turmoil to Marie of Berry, Duchess of Bourbon, in her 1418 *Letter on the Prison of Human Life*.

Violence continued in 1419, when the Armagnacs exacted their revenge for the 1407 assassination of Louis of Orléans by in turn killing John the Fearless of Burgundy. That murder galvanized the loyalties of the Burgundians, under John the Fearless's son Philip the Good, toward the English king Henry V. France was all the more deeply divided, Paris was once again in a state of terror, and the

---

31. Willard, *Life and Works*, 183.

32. Willard, *Life and Works*, 187.

dauphin Charles's position as future king was in ever greater peril. In 1420, in an attempt to establish a measure of stability, Queen Isabeau negotiated the Treaty of Troyes, under the terms of which the French throne would be handed over to England upon the king's death. Two years later, in October 1422, that came to pass, and thus began a new phase of civil war between the partisans of the future Charles VII—that is, the side of the deceased Duke of Orléans and the Armagnacs—on the one hand, and the Burgundians, allied with the English, on the other. It was not until Joan of Arc's victory in battle at Orléans in May 1429 that the tide would turn definitively in favor of the dauphin, who was crowned King Charles VII in July of that year. After having commemorated that success in her *Tale of Joan of Arc*, Christine's voice would go silent, her own life coterminous with one of the nastiest phases of the Hundred Years' War.

While the Hundred Years' War was the defining factor shaping French society at this time, one must not overlook the other major cultural crisis in Christine's world, the Great Schism in the Catholic Church. Between 1378 and 1417, two popes vied for power, one in Rome and the other in Avignon, France. The rift had implications not only for the church, but for the politics of France, whose aspirations for supremacy were certainly not hurt by having the Pope in French territory.[33] An issue less prominent in Christine's immediate milieu, perhaps, than the civil war, the Schism was nonetheless disconcerting to a devout Catholic like Christine and served to exacerbate the political tensions in France and beyond. Christine laments this division in Book 3 of the *Mutability of Fortune*, calling for its resolution. In fact, in most of the illustrated copies of the poem, Book 3 features a miniature depicting two men vying for the papal throne, which serves to underscore the problem visually as well.

Such were the tumultuous times in which Christine lived and wrote, the trials of her own life resonating with the turmoil of the world around her. Through all this, in part because of all this, her "other" voice resonated and resonates still. As we will see, such parallels between the personal and the universal, and the immediate and the timeless, are put provocatively into play in the *Mutability of Fortune*.

Orientation to The Book of the Mutability of Fortune

In poem 7, lines 1–2, of her *One Hundred Ballads*, addressing her plaint to Fortune, Christine foretells the overarching theme of the *Mutability of Fortune* well before the time of its writing: "Ha! Fortune trés douloureuse, / Que tu m'as mis du

---

33. For a brief but useful overview of the Great Schism in Christine's time, see Barbara Wagner, "Tradition or Innovation? Research on the Pictorial Tradition of a Miniature in the *Mutacion*: 'Le plus hault siège,'" in Kennedy et al., *Contexts and Continuities*, 3:862–64.

hault au bas!" (Ha! Grievous Fortune, how you have put me from high to low!).[34] Indeed, just as the autobiographical thrust of Christine's earliest poems will set the path for her career, Christine's personal story will serve as a framework for the elaborate world history that is the *Mutability of Fortune*. Or, to put it in terms of Kevin Brownlee's succinct and often-cited description, the *Mutability of Fortune* is "a universal history framed by a personal history."[35] As Fortune lifted Christine to happiness and prosperity only to then throw her to the depths of despair and struggle, so has Fortune done even to the great civilizations of the world and their greatest heroes, over and over again, through the course of time.

The poem was completed on November 18, 1403, and was immediately placed before some very important potential readers. Of the first four copies of the *Mutability of Fortune* produced, one was presented to Philip the Bold of Burgundy, one to John of Berry, and a third was likely for King Charles VI.[36] With respect to Christine's professional evolution, the *Mutability of Fortune* can be seen as a milestone of sorts, as the initial copies of the work are more elaborate and of higher quality than the manuscripts her studio had previously produced.[37] The *Mutability of Fortune* also corresponds to the transitional period in Christine's career, when her emphasis was moving from lyric poems to prose and from love themes to history and politics. It is her first important historical text, and by far her longest work up to that point.

The *Mutability of Fortune* comprises 23,636 lines of octosyllabic rhyming couplets divided into seven books of unequal length, along with an interposed prose passage of some 3,500 words at the end of Book 4. Christine does not immediately launch into her retelling of the history of the world. Rather, she methodically leads up to it, setting the stage through the first three books and much of the fourth. In Book 1, Christine-protagonist describes her life, which happens to be that of Christine-author, in allegorized form. In this section, Christine explains how she came to be in the service of Fortune, and sets out her aims for the text to follow. Book 1 also boasts the most well-known and most commented-upon pas-

34. *Œuvres poétiques*, ed. Roy, 1:8.

35. Kevin Brownlee, "The Image of History in Christine de Pizan's *Livre de la mutacion de Fortune*," in "Contexts: Style and Values in Medieval Art and Literature," edited by Daniel Poirion and Nancy Freeman Regalado, special issue, *Yale French Studies* (1991), 44.

36. Willard, *Life and Works*, 107. The fourth copy was destined for an unknown recipient. Willard also points out (232n48) that the Duke of Burgundy's copy is the one designated as B (Brussels, Bibliothèque royale 9508), the Duke of Berry's is H (The Hague, Koninklijke Bibliotheek 78 D 42), and the other two are C (Chantilly, Musée Condé 494) and S (ex-Phillipps 207, private collection). For details on these manuscripts, see Gilbert Ouy, Christine M. Reno, and Inès Villela-Petit, *Album Christine de Pizan* (Turnhout: Brepols, 2012), 413–23 and 426–66.

37. James Laidlaw, "Christine and the Manuscript Tradition," in Altmann and McGrady, *Christine de Pizan: A Casebook*, 237.

sage in the entire work, Christine's transformation into a man following the death of her husband, a transformation necessary for her to handle the responsibilities and tribulations that her loss imposed on her.[38]

Book 2 elaborately presents Fortune's strange, marvelous, and forbidding castle, the paths leading to it, the different façades and doors through which one may enter, and the one door through which all must leave. She offers detailed descriptions of Fortune and of the figures guarding the doors and overseeing the crowds within the castle's walls. In Book 3, Christine discusses the masses of people who occupy the castle and how they are situated relative to each other, addressing all levels of society from the highest rulers of the secular and religious world to the lowest social strata. Overall, this section reveals Christine's critical view of the state of French society, with each group contributing in its own way to the erosion of social order and morality.[39]

It is in Book 4 that Christine-narrator begins her long account of the world history that she saw painted and written on the walls of the Marvelous Room of Fortune's castle. But first she expounds on the topic of the sciences and liberal arts, also depicted on the walls, where Philosophy rules over all. The world history begins with the stories of Adam and Eve and Noah. Christine then turns her attention to Babylon, with an account of Nimrod's arrogant and failed plan to build the Tower of Babel. Christine then shifts her focus to the history of the Jews, the only section of this text to be written in prose, which Christine attributes to an illness that sapped her ability to compose in verse (lines 8731–48).

Book 5 recounts the history of the ancient kingdoms of Assyria, Persia, Thebes, Crete, and Athens. In the course of these histories, we encounter, among others, King Ninus and Queen Semiramis, as well as Cyrus and his enemy, the Amazon queen Tomyris. We learn the stories of Oedipus, Judith, and Esther, and witness Theseus vanquish the Minotaur. Christine devotes Book 6 to the Amazons and the history of Troy. Among the tales included in this section are those of Jason and Medea, the abduction of Helen, the confrontation of Hector and Achilles, and the exploits of Ulysses. The seventh and final book recounts the history of Rome, including its founding by Romulus and Remus, and the war between the Romans and the Sabines. This section also includes the conquests of Hannibal and Alexander the Great, and the conflict between Pompey and Julius Caesar. Christine wraps up her poem with chapters on contemporary Italy, England, and France, in which she reflects on the exploits, failings, and virtues of a number of leaders from her time. The concluding chapter brings the tale back to Christine's

38. See Appendix/5: *Gender Transformation in Christine's* Mutability.

39. For a general study of Christine as a critic of her society, see Rosalind Brown-Grant, "Les exilées du pouvoir? Christine de Pizan et la femme devant la crise du Moyen Age finissant," in *Apogée et déclin*, ed. Claude Thomasset and Michel Zink (Paris: Presses de l'Université de Paris-Sorbonne, 1993), 211–23.

autobiography and immediate present, as she signs off from her self-imposed re-
treat into a solitary life of study.

The *Mutability of Fortune* draws upon a rich array of characteristically
Christinian motifs and stylistic tendencies. With respect to Christine's signature
ploys, one of the most fundamental—self-presentation marked by self-depreca-
tion—is liberally put to use in this poem. From the very first lines, she emphasizes
her limited intelligence, excusing herself for her inadequacies as she attempts
to tackle daunting topics and the often inexplicable nature of man's fate. These
gestures of humility, prominent throughout Christine's love poetry and learned
treatises alike, carry an inherent irony, especially as she makes her way through
her career with an ever-increasing body of texts to validate herself as an artist and
an intellectual. Also, further accentuating Christine's humble self-restraint, she
repeatedly acknowledges her sensitivity to her reader's experience of her text, with
many allusions to brevity and keeping her comments short so as not to become
tedious, again rather ironic in a text of this length and complexity.[40]

Another prominent feature of the *Mutability of Fortune* which is funda-
mental to Christine's approach overall is her extensive citation of Latin and Greek
philosophers, writers, and statesmen to illustrate and validate her points. Refer-
ences to Aristotle, Seneca, and Varro, to name a few, contribute to the impression
of learned, elevated discourse that Christine strives to cultivate, particularly in
her didactic works. Critics have long debated the extent of Christine's familiarity
with Latin, with the prevailing opinion being that her sources were largely French
translations and compilations available to her through the royal library. Through
such citations, Christine not only shores up her message, but demonstrates her
own vast erudition.

Yet another of Christine's "signatures" is, quite literally, her signature. She
weaves her own name conspicuously throughout her texts. The *City of Ladies*, for
example, is marked by the invocation of a formulaic "je, Christine," whose sheer
repetition, as Maureen Quilligan points out, "makes its distinctively idiosyncratic
frequency a signal mark of Christine's authority."[41] At times, Christine makes a

40. Christine's "humility topos" has been well-acknowledged by critics; one study focusing on that
theme and its gender implications is Christine Moneera Laennec, "Christine *Antygrafe*: Authorial Am-
bivalence in the Works of Christine de Pizan," in *Anxious Power: Reading, Writing, and Ambivalence
in Narrative by Women*, ed. Carol J. Singley and Susan Elizabeth Sweeney (Albany: State University of
New York Press, 1993), 35–49. On Christine's assertions of truth and concern for brevity, see Jeanette
M. A. Beer, "Christine et les conventions dans *Le livre de la mutacion de Fortune*: 'abriger en parolles
voires,'" in Liliane Dulac and Bernard Ribémont, eds., *Une femme de lettres au Moyen Age: Etudes au-
tour de Christine de Pizan* (Orléans: Paradigme, 1995), 349–56; and Beer, "Stylistic Conventions in *Le
livre de la mutacion de Fortune*," in Richards et al., *Reinterpreting Christine de Pizan*, 124–36.

41. Maureen Quilligan, "The Name of the Author: Self-Representation in Christine de Pizan's *Livre de
la cité des dames*," *Exemplaria* 4 (1992), 202. On Christine's signature(s), see also Laennec, "Christine
Antygrafe," 36–37; Didier Lechat, "Christine de Pizan, 'Dire par ficcion le fait de la mutacion,'" Chap. 4

game of it. In the 1402 *Dit de la Rose* (*Tale of the Rose*) for example (lines 647–49), she says that her name will be revealed to anyone "Qui un seul *cry* crieroit, / et la fin d'aou*st* y mettrait, / së il disoit avec une *yne*" (if he will say a single cry / then add the month of August's end / and if he says it with an een).[42] In the *Mutability of Fortune* (lines 375–77), she similarly identifies herself through an easily solvable riddle, while also playing on her name's fortuitous resonance with that of Christ himself: "le nom du plus parfait homme, / qui oncques fu, le mien nomme, / I. N. E. faut avec mettre" (the name of the most perfect man who ever was, and you must put I. N. E. with it). Throughout her works, Christine names herself as a means to assert her specificity, itself hinging on her status as simultaneously a woman and a learned author, all with repeated nods toward her Catholic faith as an underpinning of her enterprise.

The *Mutability of Fortune* is infused with a number of elements prevalent in late medieval literature more generally. The allegorical figure of Fortune, for one, with her two faces and her ever-turning wheel, had been a fixture in literature and the visual arts for centuries, figuring prominently in texts known to Christine, both ancient and more contemporary. [43] One notable example from near Christine's time would be Guillaume de Machaut's 1341 *Remède de Fortune* (*Fortune's Remedy*), which contains a nearly six-hundred-line exposé on Fortune's confounding ways.[44] Another example, more immediate to Christine, is ballad 1134 by her fellow court poet, Eustache Deschamps, the refrain of which stages Fortune declaring herself "mere de tous" (mother of all).[45] Fortune has a strong presence throughout Christine's own works as well, not the least of which would be the *Path of Long Study*, written at the same time as the *Mutability of Fortune*, in which the autobiographical prologue prominently features the narrator's suffering at the hands of Fortune. Fortune's malevolent manipulations also figure centrally in the autobiographical third book of *Christine's Vision*, composed two years later.

in *"Dire par fiction"*: *Métamorphoses du je chez Guillaume de Machaut, Jean Froissart et Christine de Pizan* (Paris: Champion, 2005), 441–44; Lori J. Walters, "Christine's Symbolic Self as the Personification of France," in Dor and Henneau, *Christine de Pizan: Une femme de science,* 197; and Walters "Signatures and Anagrams in the Queen's Manuscript: London, British Library, Harley MS 4431," *Christine de Pizan: The Making of the Queen's Manuscript* website (November 30, 2012) <http://www.pizan.lib.ed.ac.uk/ waltersanagrams.html>.

42. Citation and translation from Thelma S. Fenster and Mary Carpenter Erler, ed. and trans., *Poems of Cupid, God of Love: Christine de Pizan's* Epistre au dieu d'Amours *and* Dit de la rose; *Thomas Hoccleve's* The Letter of Cupid (Leiden: Brill, 1990), 121–25; emphasis mine.

43. See Appendix/6: *Discussions of Fortune in Medieval Literature.*

44. *Œuvres de Guillaume de Machaut,* ed. Ernest Hoepffner (Paris: Firmin Didot, 1908–1921), 2:33–54; lines 905–1480 <https://archive.org/details/oeuvresdeguillau02guiluoft>.

45. *Œuvres complètes de Eustache Deschamps,* 6:56–58.

For the *Mutability of Fortune*, Christine also draws from a number of specific literary works.[46] Her abundant use of myth, for example, is traceable largely, although not exclusively, to the *Moralized Ovid*, an anonymous medieval French translation and recasting of Ovid's *Metamorphoses*.[47] She refers to Ovid by name or by specific allusion to "the poet" no fewer than six times in the *Mutability of Fortune*. She also makes explicit mention of the *Romance of the Rose*, a work she may have made her reputation criticizing, but which is also recalled by her use of allegory, the figure of Fortune, and certain other motifs fundamental to her text.[48] Much of the history Christine uses is drawn from the anonymous *Histoire ancienne jusqu'à César* (*Ancient History up to Caesar*).[49] The thirteenth-century *Jeu des échecs moralisés* (*The Moralized Game of Chess*) by Jacques de Cessoles is strongly

---

46. On sources for this poem, see *Le livre de la mutacion de Fortune par Christine de Pisan*, ed. Suzanne Solente, 4 vols. (Paris: Picard, 1959, 1966), 1:xxx–xcviii. An early study of Christine's sources in the *Letter of Othea*, but also pertinent to the *Mutability of Fortune*, is Percy G. Campbell's *L'Epitre d'Othéa: Etude sur les sources de Christine de Pisan* (Paris: Champion, 1924). See also Louis-Fernand Flutre, "Eustache Deschamps et Christine de Pisan ont-ils utilisé les *Faits des Romains?*" *Cultura neolatina* 13 (1953): 236–40. On the influence of Boethius on this work, see Glynnis M. Cropp, "Boèce et Christine de Pizan," *Le Moyen Age* 87 (1981): 390–92; and Julia Simms Holderness, "Christine, Boèce et saint Augustin: La consolation de la mémoire," in Dulac et al., *Desireuse de plus avant enquerre*, 283–85.

47. See Appendix/7: *Christine's Use of Ovid*.

48. See Brownlee, "The Image of History"; Jane Chance, "Gender Trouble in the Garden of Deduit: Christine de Pizan Translating the *Rose*," *Romance Languages Annual* 4 (1993): 20-28; and Nadia Margolis, "The Rhetoric of Detachment in Christine de Pizan's *Mutacion de Fortune*," *Nottingham French Studies* 38 (1999): 177-78. See also Appendix/8: *Christine's Use of Allegory*.

49. Only portions of this text exist in modern editions, notably Catherine Gaullier-Bougassas, ed., *L'histoire ancienne jusqu'à César, ou, Histoires pour Roger, châtelain de Lille, de Wauchier de Denain; L'Histoire de la Macédoine et d'Alexandre le Grand* (Turnhout: Brepols, 2012), and Marjike de Visser-van Terwisga, ed., *Histoire ancienne jusqu'à César: Estoires Rogier*, Tome I: *Assyrie, Thèbes, le Minotaure, les Amazones, Hercule* (Orléans: Paradigme, 1995). Solente details Christine's use of this key source for more than half of the poem (*Mutacion*, 1:lxiii–xcii). Much of the material covered in the *Histoire ancienne* goes back to the *Histories* of Herodotus, dating from the fifth century BCE; for an English translation of Herodotus, see *The Landmark Herodotus: The Histories*, ed. Robert B. Strassler; trans. Andrea L. Purvis (New York: Pantheon Books, 2007). See also Catherine Gaullier-Bougassas, "Histoires universelles et variations sur deux figures du pouvoir: Alexandre et César dans l'*Histoire ancienne jusqu'à César, Renart le Contrefait* et le *Livre de la mutacion de Fortune* de Christine de Pizan," in "La figure de Jules César au Moyen Age et à la Renaissance (II)," ed. Bruno Méniel and Bernard Ribémont, special issue, *Cahiers de recherches médiévales et humanistes* 14 (2007): 7–28 <https://crm.revues.org/2556>; Franziska Huber, "*L'histoire ancienne jusqu'à César*, source du *Livre de la mutacion de Fortune* de Christine de Pizan: Etude comparative des récits sur Cyrus," in Hicks, Gonzalez, and Simon, *Au champ des escriptures*, 161–74; and Danielle Régnier-Bohler, "La tragédie thébaine dans 'La Mutacion de Fortune,'" in Margarete Zimmermann and Dina de Rentiis, eds., *The City of Scholars: New Approaches to Christine de Pizan* (Berlin: De Gruyter, 1994), 127–47.

present in Book 3.[50] The section of Book 4 on the liberal arts is closely borrowed from Brunetto Latini's *Book of the Treasure* and Isidore of Seville's *Etymologies*.[51] The story of Alexander the Great, found in Book 7, is traceable to a French translation of the Latin *Historia de preliis*.[52] Let us recall that in Christine's day, close and often undocumented borrowings were not only accepted, but were also a way for the writer both to demonstrate his or her own breadth of knowledge and to authorize his or her own text by inscribing it into a larger literary legacy. Christine does so abundantly in this sweeping poem.

Overall, Christine's devout Catholicism, her vision of a well-ordered world in which every social category plays its role with integrity, her moral teachings on the virtues of humility, patience, truth, and honor, all ring strongly in this text. Allegory serves as her vehicle, while history provides her with ample evidence with which to demonstrate Fortune's unceasing influence upon humankind.

Afterlife of The Mutability of Fortune

In the first book of this poem (lines 154–56), the narrator announces its title, couching it in the concept of future readership: "Et ce dictié vueil que l'en nomme / quant l'istoire sera commune: / 'La mutacion de Fortune'" (and when the story becomes known to all, I want this tale to be called "*The Mutability of Fortune*"). Two years later, in *Christine's Vision*, we see Lady Opinion remarking about Christine-protagonist's work, "Et le temps a venir plus en sera parlé qu'a ton vivant" (in times to come, more will be said of it than in your lifetime).[53] Such comments within Christine's works reveal that the author was keenly conscious

50. Solente demonstrates that Christine would have used the French translation from Latin by Jean de Vignai; see Suzanne Solente, "Le *Jeu des échecs moralisés*, source de la *Mutacion de Fortune*," in *Recueil de travaux offerts à M. Clovis Brunel par ses amis, collègues et élèves* (Paris: Société de l'Ecole des Chartes, 1955), 2:556–65.

51. Brunetto Latini, *The Book of the Treasure: Li livres dou Tresor*, trans. Paul Barrette and Spurgeon Baldwin (New York: Garland, 1993); and *The* Etymologies *of Isidore of Seville*, trans. and ed. Stephen A. Barney, W. J. Lewis, J.A. Beach, and Oliver Berghof (Cambridge: Cambridge University Press, 2006) <http://pot-pourri.fltr.ucl.ac.be/files/AClassftp/TEXTES/ISIDORUS/Etymologie/B1N8PWGetQy. pdf>. On the *Etymologies*, see Bernard Ribémont, "Christine de Pizan, Isidore de Séville et l'astrologie: Compilation et 'mutacion' d'un discours sur les arts libéraux," in Dulac et al., *Desireuse de plus avant enquerre*, 303–14.

52. See Solente, *Mutacion*, 1:xcii–xcvii. For an English translation of the *Historia de preliis* by the Archipresbyter Leo, see *The History of Alexander's Battles: Historia de preliis: The J¹ Version*, ed. and trans. Roger Telfryn Pritchard (Toronto: Pontifical Institute of Medieval Studies, 1992).

53. The original is from *Le livre de l'advision Cristine*, ed. Christine Reno and Liliane Dulac (Paris: Champion; Geneva: Editions Slatkine, 2001), 89. The English is from *The Vision of Christine de Pizan*, trans. Glenda McLeod and Charity Cannon Willard (Cambridge: D. S. Brewer, 2005), 86.

of the afterlife of her own writings—not just that they would be read, but with respect to their educational value and, one would imagine, the universal truths with which she sought infuse them.[54]

If we conceptualize the "afterlife" of the *Mutability of Fortune* as beginning with its reception immediately following its completion, we can start with the ways Christine gave the poem a presence in her own subsequent works, referring to it by name. In the 1404 biography of Charles V, she describes how John of Burgundy had graciously accepted a copy of the *Mutability of Fortune* in the previous year.[55] In the 1405 *City of Ladies*, Lady Reason reminds Christine-protagonist that she already knows stories about great women, as she has written about them in her *Mutability of Fortune*.[56] In Book 2 of the 1405 *Christine's Vision*, Lady Opinion admonishes Christine for having given Lady Fortune too much credit for her power over the world in her earlier text, explaining at length that in fact she, Lady Opinion, has had greater responsibility for what has transpired than Fortune ever has. She explicitly names the *Mutability of Fortune* three times during that come-uppance.[57] Ultimately, such allusions by Christine to her own texts serve not only as good marketing, but perhaps more importantly as a means for Christine to authorize her own writing and align herself with the countless other authors who figure so strongly throughout her works.[58]

Following her death, Christine's texts continued to be read, produced, and translated well into the sixteenth century. Two of the surviving manuscripts of the *Mutability of Fortune* date from that time.[59] Further, a comparative analysis suggests that the *Mutability of Fortune* served as a model for the sixteenth-century

54. See Appendix/9: *The Reception of Christine's Works*.

55. *Le livre des fais et bonnes meurs du sage roy Charles V par Christine de Pisan*, ed. Suzanne Solente (Paris: Champion, 1936–1940), 1:6–7; Book 1, chapter 2. For an English version of this passage, see the excerpt from *The Book of the Deeds and Good Conduct of the Wise King Charles V*, in *The Selected Writings of Christine de Pizan*, ed. Renate Blumenfeld-Kosinski, trans. Blumenfeld-Kosinski and Kevin Brownlee (New York: Norton, 1997) 113–16, at 115.

56. *City of Ladies*, Book 1, chapter 17. For the modern French edition of this passage, see *Le livre de la cité des dames*, ed. and trans. Thérèse Moreau and Eric Hicks (Paris: Stock, 1992), 73. For the English translation, see *The Book of the City of Ladies*, trans. Earl Jeffrey Richards (New York: Persea Books, 1982), 43.

57. *Christine's Vision*, Book 2, chapters 14–22. In *The Vision of Christine*, trans. McLeod and Willard, the poem is named on pages 74, 75, and 78. For the original Middle French, see *Le livre de l'advision Cristine*, ed. Reno and Dulac, where the poem is named on pages 75, 77, and 79. On this passage, see also Anna Slerca, "L'advision Cristine, Guillaume de Machaut, Boccace et le thème de la rétraction," in Dulac et al., *Desireuse de plus avant enquerre*, 315–16.

58. On Christine's strategy of auto-citation, see Kevin Brownlee, "Rewriting Romance: Courtly Discourse and Auto-Citation in Christine de Pizan," in Jane Chance, ed., *Gender and Text in the Later Middle Ages* (Gainesville: University Press of Florida, 1996), 172–94.

59. Manuscripts P (Paris, Bibliothèque nationale f. fr. 25430) and U (Paris, Arsenal 3172).

Labyrinthe de Fortune (*Fortune's Labyrinth*) by Jean Bouchet.[60] Even when medieval literature generally went out of favor in France between the sixteenth and nineteenth centuries, Christine and certain of her texts continued to receive more attention than most, relatively speaking.[61] The *Mutability of Fortune's* title appears in an article by Jean Boivin de Villeneuve, published in 1717 and hailed as the first substantial study of Christine and her texts.[62] The title is also noted in Prosper Marchand's 1759 *Dictionnaire historique* (*Historical Dictionary*), where his entry on Christine includes listings of works in the libraries of John, Duke of Berry, and the king of France.[63]

The content of the poem would not been seen again until the 1787 anthology by Louise-Félicité Guinement de Kéralio, *Collection des meilleurs ouvrages français, composés par des femmes, dédiée aux femmes françaises* (*Collection of the Greatest French Works Composed by Women, Dedicated to the Women of France*).[64] As an effort by a woman to champion the literary accomplishment of women throughout the ages, Kéralio's interests powerfully recall Christine's own. She is Christine's first female critic, compiling what is considered the first anthology of Christine's work, and it is here that several of Christine's texts first appear in print.[65] Among Christine's works, contained in volumes 2 and 3 of the anthology,

---

60. See Anna Slerca, "*Le livre de la mutacion de Fortune*, source du *Labyrinthe de Fortune* de Jean Bouchet," in Dulac and Ribémont, *Une femme de lettres*, 509–21. Further, Evelyne Berriot-Salvadore examines parallels between Christine's text and the treatment of fortune by sixteenth-century poet Clément Marot: see "La *Mutation de Fortune* de Clément Marot," in *Clément Marot: à propos de l'Adolescence Clémentine: Actes des quatrièmes Journées du Centre Jacques de Laprade tenues au Musée national du château de Pau les 29 et 30 novembre 1996*, ed. James Dauphiné and Paul Mironneau (Biarritz: J and D Editions, 1996), 91.

61. See Laidlaw, "Christine and the Manuscript Tradition," 231; Nadia Margolis, "Modern Editions: Makers of the Christinian Corpus," in Altmann and McGrady, *Christine de Pizan: A Casebook*, 251–70; and Earl Jeffrey Richards, "The Medieval 'femme auteur' as a Provocation of Literary History: Eighteenth-Century Readers of Christine de Pizan," in Glenda McLeod, ed., *The Reception of Christine de Pizan from the Fifteenth Through the Nineteenth Centuries: Visitors to the City* (Lewiston, NY: Edwin Mellen Press, 1991), 101–26.

62. Margolis, "Modern Editions," 253; Edith Yenal, *Christine de Pisan: A Bibliography of Writings by Her and About Her* (Metuchen, NJ: Scarecrow Press, 1982), 86.

63. Richards's "Medieval 'femme auteur'" is especially informative on Christine's reception in the eighteenth century. On this instance, see in particular page 105.

64. Kéralio, *Collection des meilleurs ouvrages français*, etc. (Paris: Lagrange, 1787) <https://archive.org/stream/collectiondesme00keragoog#page/n3/mode/2up>.

65. Kéralio planned to devote approximately thirty-six volumes to French women's writing, possibly to be followed with works by British and Italian women (1:vi and xv–xvi), but was interrupted by the French Revolution after compiling just fourteen. Volumes 1–5 contain works from Middle Ages and Renaissance, and 9–14 feature the letters of seventeenth-century aristocrat Mme de Sévigné; volumes 7 and 8 were not completed.

is a series of extracts (3:111-32) from the *Mutability of Fortune* linked together by Kéralio's commentary.[66] Some fifty years later, the *Mutability of Fortune* is briefly summarized in the first critical anthology devoted to Christine, Raymond Thomassy's 1838 *Essai sur les écrits politiques de Christine de Pisan* (*Essay on the Political Writings of Christine de Pisan*).[67] In 1842, A. Paulin Paris includes twelve short passages of the poem in his catalog of works held in the French royal library.[68] Marie-Josèphe Pinet would then include some forty short citations of the work in her 1927 *Christine de Pisan*. One understands that Pinet was not motivated to cite more, in light of her opinion that the poem was not only *trop, trop long* (much, much too long), but *si mal écrit que c'est à faire tort à l'auteur de le citer* (so poorly written that to cite it would be a disservice to the author).[69]

Although it may not have been universally admired, the *Mutability of Fortune* would have seen the light of day toward the early twentieth century had Maurice Roy, editor of three volumes of Christine's poetic works, pursued his intent to publish a fourth volume, which was to include this poem. Instead, he turned his intention to other projects.[70] As it is, the *Mutability of Fortune* was finally published in its entirety, in the original Middle French, in Suzanne Solente's four-volume edition, which appeared in 1959 (vols. 1 and 2) and 1966 (vols. 3 and 4). This remains the only complete modern edition.

Despite the power of this work, the impact it had when it appeared at the dawn of the fifteenth century, and the decades of intensive study (on certain sections in particular) by French- and English-speaking scholars, the complete *Mutability of Fortune* has remained confined to a relatively small world.[71] That being

66. Manuscript F (Paris, Bibliothèque nationale f. fr. 603) was Kéralio's base text. For closer looks at Kéralio's handling of Christine's works, see Claire Le Brun-Gouanvic, "Mademoiselle de Keralio, commentatrice de Christine de Pizan au XVIIIᵉ siècle, ou la rencontre de deux femmes savantes," in Dor and Henneau, *Christine de Pizan: Une femme de science*, 326–41; and Maria Giusepina Muzzarelli, "Louise de Kéralio Reads the Biography of Charles V Written by Christine de Pizan: A Comparison of Two Female Intellectuals who Lived Four Centuries Apart," *Imago temporis: Medium Aevum* 5 (2011): 101–15.

67. Thomassy, *Essai sur les écrits politiques de Christine de Pisan* (Paris: Debécourt, 1838), 122–23.

68. A. Paulin Paris, *Les manuscrits françois de la bibliothèque du roi: Leur histoire et celle des textes allemands, anglois, hollandois, italiens, espagnols de la même collection* (Paris: Techener, 1842) 5:136–48. The citations range from four to fifty-four lines, and total 263 lines.

69. Marie-Josèphe Pinet, *Christine de Pisan, 1364–1430: Etude biographique et littéraire* (Paris: Champion, 1927). Pinet's overview of the poem is found on pages 306–25; extracts range from one to twenty-eight lines, for a total of two hundred lines. Cited comment at 322.

70. James Laidlaw, "Maurice Roy: 1856–1932," in Campbell and Margolis, *Christine de Pizan 2000*, 247–49; Margolis, "Modern Editions," 261.

71. It bears noting that the *Mutability of Fortune* has either been the focus of or has figured prominently in a number of unpublished dissertations over the past several decades. They include Carole Ann Buchanan, "The Theme of Fortune in the Works of Christine de Pizan," PhD diss., University

said, a recent Google search uncovered a curious allusion to the *Mutability of Fortune* in the form of a ten-minute silent film, called "The Mutacion de Fortune: based on the life and works of Christine de Pizan," produced by a student in an unspecified animation class in 2010.[72] One would need to be quite familiar with the *Mutability of Fortune* and Christine's story to recognize some of the references to the text incorporated into this abstract depiction of Christine's loving marriage to and tragic loss of her husband, and her transition to writing. While the video may be a loose interpretation of a section of the text—a mutation of the *Mutacion*, so to speak—the very fact of its existence suggests that the life of this work goes on in unexpected ways. And the hope is, of course, that the present translation will contribute to its appreciation by a wider audience of modern readers.

Note on the Translation

A wise and seasoned scholar of Christine de Pizan, well experienced in translating her works, once said to me about the *Mutability of Fortune*, "It never gets any easier. You keep thinking you'll get into the swing of it, that it will go faster, but it just ... doesn't."[73] A lighthearted comment anchored by the weight of truth.

The *Mutability of Fortune* survives in eleven manuscripts, of which seven include the complete poem.[74] Solente's modern edition is based on manuscript "B" (Brussels, Bibliothèque royale de Belgique 9508). This single-text manuscript, apparently in Christine's own hand, was originally given to Philip the Bold of Burgundy in 1404. I have in turn used Solente's edition as the base text for this translation. There is no modern French version of this work, and while portions have been translated into English, the present translation, although abridged, will be the first start-to-finish incarnation of this poem in any language other than Middle French.

All texts present their own sets of hurdles, dilemmas, and challenges to those who seek to translate them. This one is no different. Among the most vexing

---

of Glasgow, 1994; Nadia Margolis, "The Poetics of History: An Analysis of Christine de Pizan's *Livre de la Mutacion de Fortune*," PhD diss., Stanford University, 1977; Marie-Josée Marquis, "'Une image vaut bien mille mots': Recherche sur l'iconographie des textes allégoriques de Christine de Pizan," PhD diss., University of Connecticut, 2014 <digitalcommons.uconn.edu/dissertations/632>; Andrea Tarnowski, "Order and Disorder in Christine de Pizan," PhD diss., Yale University, 1991; Delphine Videt-Reix, "Christine de Pizan et la poétique de la justice," PhD diss., Aix Marseille Université, 2011 <www.theses.fr/2011AIX10006.pdf>.

72. Sarah R. Lotfi's film can be found at <http://vimeo.com/38158445> (last accessed 1 September, 2016).

73. My thanks to Kevin Brownlee for this memorable conversation.

74. See Appendix/10: *Manuscripts Containing All or Part of* The Mutability of Fortune.

of those challenges is the first one encountered, and ultimately the most prominent: the title. The word "mutacion" is a tricky one, most commonly translated as "transformation" or "mutation." While both are valid, neither quite captures the ongoing nature of the transformations that Fortune effects, which is the unifying theme of this text, or the simultaneity of Fortune's shifting with the action of that transformation being lived out through its objects. "The Book of the Mutation of Fortune," "The Book of the Transformation of Fortune," "The Book of Fortune's Transformation/Mutation"—the grammar would allow for Fortune to be the transformer of things or to be the object transforming or having been transformed. In this work, the figure representing Fortune does not change. She has two faces—one evil, one kind. She stands with one foot in water, the other in fire. Her dual nature is constant, captured in a vivid description (lines 1911–54). Yet there is nothing more constant than the changeability of her whims. And the transformations that Fortune metes out on her "victims" are not stable or definitive themselves—up and down, high and low, the roller coaster does not stop until death for the mortals or the final crumbling of a society. And for the world as a whole it will never end.

Perhaps the English word that most fully captures what is portrayed in the text would be "vicissitudes," hardly a term one uses (or attempts to spell) every day. So, how to translate this deceptively straightforward, yet oddly elusive, title? The words "transformation" and "mutation" are too fixed, not fully capturing the constant morphing of Fortune or the perpetual action of her force. Worse, the word "mutation" carries an unfortunate overtone in vernacular English, something overly biological or evocative of science fiction. "Mutability," on the other hand, highlighting the notion of instability itself, the ever-present potential for change, and its implied ripple effects, avoids such drawbacks. All factors considered, and fully aware that there remains room for argument, I have therefore stopped the wheel at *The Book of the Mutability of Fortune*.

Wrestling with the title made it clear that if there were one concept at the heart of the decisions to be made throughout the text, it would be "balance." That problem, that goal, is surely at the heart of any translation. One area in which the question of balance was most evident had to do with the poem's length. How does one balance the practical matters of accessibility, appeal, cost, and time against respect for the totality of the work? How best to abridge it to suit the present purpose, keeping enough to provide substance and a sense of the work's imposing weight? Priority was given to the passages with the most powerful and vivid imagery, those essential to the flow of the story, and the sections that most strongly evoke themes and stylistic elements characteristic of Christine's corpus as a whole. All abridged sections have been summarized to keep the story line intact, and the line numbers have been indicated to give the reader a sense of the relative significance, in terms of lines dedicated to them, of the sections abridged.

Another challenge has been the sheer scope of this work, with regard not just to size, but also to subject matter. This poem is marked by the intensity of Christine's toil as she wrangled a world history into rhyming couplets, infused with didacticism and seemingly boundless erudition. There are countless references, some direct, others indirect, to myth, history, and contemporary society, sometimes complicated by Christine's tendency to customize stories or even confuse details herself. I have sought to support readers through judicious use of explanatory notes.

Our most significant and obvious departure from the original is the shift from verse to prose. That choice privileges meaning over style, in the hope of telling the story in a clear way, with its essence as close to the original as possible, unencumbered by the constraints that an attempt to replicate verse would have presented. The original contains a number of convoluted and sometimes "runaway" passages that give the impression that even Christine battled at times to keep control of the expression of her ideas in this form, or, at the least, got caught up in the fervor of the moment. The very opening of the poem, which one frank critic describes as *une seule interminable phrase de dix sept vers* (a single interminable sentence of seventeen lines)[75] is a harbinger of things to come. Further, the constraints imposed by rhyme and meter often lead to labyrinthine sentence structures, interjection of filler words, and vocabulary selection that can be unexpected or ambiguous. Many passages needed to be "detangled" in order for their sense to become clear, meaning that the sequence of some details in the translation may differ from how they are presented in a particular set of lines in the poem. As it is, several unavoidably complex sentences remain.

There were infinite smaller-scale decisions to be made throughout. For example, verb tenses can oscillate from one time frame to another depending on the exigencies of rhyme and rhythm. I have erred on the side of the integrity of the narrative where strictly keeping to the verb tenses used by Christine would be illogical. It is also worth noting that Middle French does not have fixed spelling, making the use of dictionaries and lexicons something of a scavenger hunt. Nor does Middle French require the use of subject pronouns, and Christine shows an often frustrating lack of concern for clear antecedents for subject and object pronouns alike ("Which '*le*' is this? 'He' the soldier or 'it' the castle?" or "Who just knocked whom off his war horse?"). In the name of clarity, for passages that would be unduly confusing otherwise, I have replaced some subject pronouns with the proper names or specific nouns to which they refer, or added a subject where a verb had none. Lastly, since medieval manuscripts include little or no punctuation, the modern Middle French edition is itself the product of a great deal of interpretation on the part of its editor. Merely bumping a period or comma in either direction can significantly affect meaning. Aside from eliminating abun-

75. Lechat, "Christine de Pizan, 'Dire par ficcion,'" 372.

dant commas and semicolons that clashed with the flow of the translation into prose, I also, at times, diverged from Solente's choices with regard to the division of verses into sentences where another solution seemed more apt.

Christine has been acknowledged for her rich vocabulary, some of which was already archaic in her time, some of which was more cutting-edge.[76] Nowhere is her lexical range more manifest than in Book 2, in her descriptions of the architecture of Fortune's castle and the passages depicting the textile manufacture, metalworking, and other trades flourishing within. Her familiarity with the personnel and ways of the justice system is evident as well. Generally speaking, however, I have used a wider variety of vocabulary than the more limited lexicon of Middle French, in order to try to capture the nuances of expression in a way that will be readily appreciated by modern readers. The risk here, of course, is that of the many possible senses of a given word, I may not have chosen the perfectly nuanced modern term. I have been sensitive to context in hopes of avoiding such self-inflicted wounds. When in doubt, the most literal translation of Christine's wording would prevail. Further, in attempting to respect the generally learned and serious tone of the original, with its occasional more lighthearted but not frivolous interjections, I attempted to avoid incongruously "modern" idiomatic expressions. As for proper names, especially those from Latin, Greek, and other sources, I have tried to stick with commonly accepted, recognizable spellings familiar to English-speaking readers. Biblical names are spelled according to the New King James Version.

The supporting apparatus has been structured primarily with nonspecialists in mind. This Introduction has been intended to provide the newcomer to Christine with the necessary context regarding her life and times. Notes to the Introduction are, in some cases, quite general, and suggest avenues of further exploration on topics not necessarily specific to the *Mutability of Fortune*. Notes within the translation are either explanatory or refer to studies focused on the moment in question in the text, such as Christine's use of a particular myth. With the vast and ever-growing body of scholarship available on Christine de Pizan and her works, the bibliography is, of necessity, selective.[77]

In sum, the goal of this translation is to make the *Mutability of Fortune* accessible for the first time to an audience beyond those familiar with Middle

---

76. See Appendix/11: *Christine's Use of Language.*

77. Several useful bibliographies exist: "Christine de Pizan," Les Archives de littérature du Moyen Age (ARLIMA) <http://www.arlima.net/ad/christine_de_pizan.html>; Angus J. Kennedy, *Christine de Pizan: A Bibliographical Guide* (London: Grant and Cutler, 1984); Kennedy, *Christine de Pizan: A Bibliographical Guide: Supplement 1* (London: Grant and Cutler, 1994); Kennedy, *Christine de Pizan: A Bibliographical Guide: Supplement 2* (Woodbridge, UK: Tamesis, 2004); Kennedy, "A Selective Bibliography of Christine de Pizan Scholarship, circa 1980–1987," in Richards et al., *Reinterpreting Christine de Pizan*, 285–98; and Yenal, *Christine de Pisan: A Bibliography of Writings.*

French, and at the same time useful to individuals further immersed in Christine studies. With no sibylline guide to lead the way, there have been infinite opportunities for doubt, and at times the feeling that the summit to Fortune's castle would not be conquered through any effort. Nonetheless, I pressed on so that this poem might live on in a new way, continuing to fulfill its own foreshadowing of future readership. And perhaps these readers, encountering history and myth, autobiography and allegory through "other" voices such as Christine's—some tales having been told and retold throughout the centuries, others unique and personal—will come away with new perspectives of their own.

Christine de Pizan
The Book of the Mutability of Fortune

I. *Here begins* The Book of the Mutability of Fortune

1–50

How will it be possible for me, simple and of little intelligence, to express appropriately what cannot be easily assessed or well understood? However much one has been able to learn, one could not fully describe what I yearn to write. That is because of the great variety of specific adversities and occurrences comprising the heavy burdens that the fickle influence of deceitful Fortune engenders. They are the result of her vast repletion, itself a veritable abyss of unfathomable depth. I cannot help but fall short in undertaking a work as vast as describing the envious nature of her deception. It would be difficult for me to speak of it adequately, given my limited intelligence, when many distinguished people have written about it and have been incapable of recording all that can be said about her.

I certainly will not give up, however. Fortune has dished out so many of her portions to me that I have grounds to speak about her. And I will not keep quiet about the good or bad that I may be able to recount, even though my understanding of her deeds might be subject to reproach. I learned about her maneuvers through various unfortunate incidents that happened to me because of her. They made my understanding much keener than it had been in the past. Without them, I would not have come to know so much about her ways. It is therefore right to reason that misfortune sometimes has a purpose, because it can teach at the same time. So I do not intend to tell lies to anyone who, without deaf ears, will rightfully be able to understand the true goal toward which I intend to strive.

II. *Here the person who wrote this book speaks of how she served Fortune, as she will explain in what follows*

51–88

Now I would like to tell of an occurrence which many may find impossible to believe. Even though some will disbelieve, it is proven truth, evident and fully experienced, and it happened to me personally. I was about twenty-five years old. When it happened to me, it was not a dream; I will truthfully recount a great wonder. No one should be surprised by it, however, because Fortune, who disguises everything, making and breaking at her whim, brought about the entire transformation I will recount here. Since it was her doing, no one should marvel at what happened. Although she knows how to deceive, everyone can clearly see

29

that she has the power to govern all that goes on in the world. Even though she is vain and impure, the entire world lies under her hand, as far as transitory things are concerned. She can dole out losses and victories, honor, possessions, and the contrary. She can, in surprising ways, bring about things that seem impossible, and wipe out things that seem possible. One sees her bring many things to their opposite conclusion, even unexpectedly changing the forms of bodies; that is an even greater marvel. The changes she effects are very widespread, and she has infinite power over all finite things.

89–122

I will recount how I saw Fortune, who is not the same to all people (even though she is invisible, she is plainly visible to the naked eye), and how I lived with her and tasted many a misfortune. She is a great crowned queen, more feared than anything ever born, with a grand and very powerful court where there are many different kinds of people. Whoever wishes to can learn a lot there, taking the good as well as the bad. One becomes wise by learning well, and gets ahead by serving. As Scripture says, for the one who strives to serve well, to serve is to rule.[1] Such a person rightly deserves praise and honor. By serving, one becomes master. It is therefore good to serve, if by serving well one merits good recompense and glory, or a good friend, male or female. But that is not at all how it turned out for me. I do not know if I made a mistake in serving, because I earned very little reward for it. I endured cruel suffering, many hard times, and tiresome and troublesome work, without anything getting any better for me. I am afraid that the fault lies with the master, however, because good recompense comes to one who serves a good master.

123–156

Now I will tell of how, by the will of those closest to me, I was placed at Fortune's court, where I stayed for a long time. I intend to explain to you where her strangely built dwelling is situated, and the strange and dreadful ways and deeds that I witnessed while I was at her court, where many a misfortune occurs. I will tell what I learned, what happened to me there, how Fortune did not forget me when she was moved to help me in my time of great need, and of the help she gave which barely sufficed for me.

To make my goal in addressing this topic more understandable, I will tell you who I am, I who speak, and who from female became male because of Fortune. Because she wanted it that way, she changed me, body and face, into a com-

---

1. Solente cites Psalms 101:23 as the source for this reference (*Mutacion*, 1:157, note to lines 103–4). However, both Mark 10:43–44 and Luke 22:26 resonate similarly with Christine's words, "est regner qui met sa cure / en bien servir" (Solente, *Mutacion*, 1:10, lines 104–5). Unless otherwise indicated, biblical references are to the New King James Version.

plete, natural man. I once was a woman; in fact I am a man. I am not lying—my ordeals are sufficient evidence of that. And while I may have been a woman in the past, what I am saying is the truth. Through a fiction I will recount the act of the transformation, how I turned from a woman into a man. And when the story becomes known to all, I want this tale to be called "The Mutability of Fortune."

III. *Here the person tells who her father was and what wealth he had*

157–210

If a person wishes to give a clear idea of himself, he must first say from what nation and of what extraction he is, who his family is or was, whether they were poor or well-to-do, and whether he is worthy of being known. And then he must also state his name. Therefore, it is right for me to say it: I was born near Lombardy, in a city of great renown.[2] Many pilgrims know the name! It was founded long ago by the Trojan people[3] and it is well and pleasingly situated. I was the child[4] of a noble and famous man, who was called a philosopher. He was rich and had great knowledge; his wealth was extraordinary! Many have heard tell of this, and I do not seek to hide his treasure, because such a possession is worthy of praise. It had such power, I dare say, that all the thieves ever born would never succeed in stealing one bit of it from him. Never did he have to fret, fear, tremble, or be afraid that someone would steal his wealth from him, as happens to many rich men who are slain and killed for it. Many are murdered for their fortune; they would be much better off having less! But this wealth I am telling you about is worth treasuring, because one is never troubled by it and it cannot be stolen by anyone.

2. Venice.

3. An origin legend that created a link between Venice and Troy; see, for example, Patricia Fortini Brown, *Venice and Antiquity: The Venetian Sense of the Past* (New Haven: Yale University Press, 1996), 12–14 and 41–42.

4. Curiously, Christine uses the word "filz" (son) here; on this, see Andrea Tarnowski, "Maternity and Paternity in 'La mutacion de Fortune,'" in Zimmermann and de Rentiis, *City of Scholars,* 116. On Christine as a daughter, both literally and with regard to her literary self-presentation, see Heather Arden, "Her Mother's Daughter: Empowerment and Maternity in the Works of Christine de Pizan," in Kennedy et al., *Contexts and Continuities,* 1:31–41; Leslie Abend Callahan, "Filial Filiations: Representations of the Daughter in the Works of Christine de Pizan," in Hicks, Gonzalez, and Simon, *Au champ des escriptures,* 481–91; Andrzej Dziedzic, "A la recherche d'une figure maternelle: L'image de la mère dans l'oeuvre de Christine de Pizan," *Neophilologus* 86 (2002): 493–506; Marie-Thérèse Lorcin, "Mère nature et le devoir social: La mère et l'enfant dans l'oeuvre de Christine de Pizan," *Revue historique* 282 (1989): 29–44; Maureen Quilligan, *The Allegory of Female Authority: Christine de Pizan's Cité des dames* (Ithaca, NY: Cornell University Press, 1991), 134–39; and Charity Cannon Willard, "Christine de Pizan: The Astrologer's Daughter," in *Mélanges à la mémoire de Franco Simone: France et Italie dans la culture européenne,* vol. 1, ed. Jonathan Beck and Gianni Mombello (Geneva: Slatkine, 1980), 95–111.

And there is even more good to be found in this wealth, I'm telling you for sure. That is because the more generously and constantly one who has it in abundance shares it, the more of it stays with him. There is no need for avarice stemming from fear of losing that wealth, because it is a flowing spring—the more one draws from it, the more it flows forth anew. Furthermore, this treasure is of such a nature that there is no question of anyone, if he is truly rich with it, ever lacking for wealth. Whatever misfortune may beset him, wherever he goes, and from wherever he comes, nothing could make him poor. He can open his treasure everywhere.

IV. *Here she tells of the precious stones that her father had*

211-258
My father was rich and satisfied with such wealth. He had plenty of precious stones, very noble and powerful, that he took from the fountain at Mount Parnassus, made by Pegasus's foot. That is where the nine Muses, who have guided many distinguished students, amuse themselves.[5] My father has kept the stones well since. He stayed at the fountain for a long time, and was so diligent that he gained the wealth I spoke of here, which is worth more than a county, along with many other riches that are abundant there.

Among the sumptuous treasures that my father had in his coffers, there were two precious stones of great value, which I prized. There is certainly no red garnet or fine ruby that holds their worth. One of them had such power that no king or emperor since the time of King Arthur has been richer. It shone in a magnificent way and was more luminous than a candle, its color like a star. It was beautiful and very elegant, and ever so precious. But it was very difficult to find. It may be difficult to obtain, but if a person were to put great effort into seeking it in the fountain, one of the Muses would give him a sign to show him where it is. That person would deserve great praise for it. Do you know what this stone is for? (Whoever has it should guard it dearly so as not to lose it). Whoever carries it with him has such knowledge that he can predict what will happen in the future. He who has rightfully found it is made celestial—this is not a lie—which allows him rise to the firmament and to heavenly abodes.

---

5. The Muses, goddesses of Greek mythology associated with knowledge and artistic inspiration, made their home on Mount Parnassus. The fountain referred to above, created when the winged stallion Pegasus dug the ground with his hoof, was sacred to the Muses, but was by tradition located on Mount Helicon. On this passage, see Shigemi Sasaki, "Fontaine de Pégase et 'chappel' de la poétesse dans *Le livre de la mutacion de Fortune*," in Dulac et al., *Desireuse de plus avant enquerre*, 265–76.

259–288

My father certainly had this stone, and he knew all its powers. He used it so well that he often informed princes who ruled the earth about great peace or war, about winds or torrential rains, death, and famine that were in the future, or the weather that was coming, according to what appeared to him. By means of this stone, he would dwell in the sky, where the planets turn. Thus he knew how they returned to their starting points in the zodiac,[6] and he perfectly understood the power and light of each, and how much higher one was than the other. He also knew all of the commonly occurring courses of the stars; he knew them by name. This made him so famous that everyone maintained that he lived in the heavens, for which he was honored and highly esteemed, praise God! He was welcome among princes, loved and held dear, thanks to the power of this stone, which is more valuable than gold, by St. Peter!

More on this same topic

289–338

As I just told you, my father had another stone in his treasury that was so rich and pure that never did refined gold or any other stone have its value. That one was worth a great deal to many, and it saved their lives. One should surely desire to acquire such a stone, but many are afraid to pursue it. It cures all maladies, even making the insane, whose hands and feet are bound, wise. It cures them entirely. Whoever knows how to use it correctly, without abusing its power, can cure all other maladies as well. I do not know what else to tell you about it, except that there is no leper so putrid that he cannot be cured by it. If someone knows its properties well and uses them correctly, there is no painful gout so severe or other variety of infirmity that cannot be cured by the stone. A person who knew perfectly how to use its powers, without faltering, could almost bring the dead back to life. My father had found this stone and put it to the test many times, thanks to which he saved many whom Death had nearly taken.

Why am I going on about this? It would be equally tedious to read or listen to if I were to list by name all the powers that my honorable father's jewels possessed. I am not saying this to praise him, but rather to tell the plain truth. My father drew all the stones from the very deep, clear fountain. I do not know why I would enumerate more of their qualities. I will sum it all up for you in one sentence: he was so rich with what he had that he would not give two cents for all

---

6. Christine refers to "zodiacs" in the plural: "si sçot comment elles retournent / par leurs zodiaques arriere" (Solente, *Mutacion*, 1:16, lines 272–73). This would seem to denote the starting point from which each planet begins its rotation through the zodiac.

the wealth of Octavian.[7] He more greatly prized the wisdom of Galen,[8] which he possessed, over that treasure. He desired no other.

V. *Here she speaks of her mother*

339–378

My mother, who was great and boundless and more valiant than Penthesilea[9] (God made her well!), in every way surpassed my father in wisdom, power, and worth, even though he was very learned. She was crowned queen as soon as she was born. Everyone is well aware of her strength and her power. It is plain to see that she is never idle. Without being belligerent, she busies herself everywhere with many different tasks. Her works can easily be proven—they are found everywhere, and she creates many lovely ones every day. Anyone who tried to count up all the deeds that she has done and that she does every day would never finish. She is old without aging, and her life cannot end until Judgment Day. God put her in charge of augmenting and maintaining the world ever since he made it, to sustain human life. She is called Lady Nature. She is the mother of every person; God calls us all brothers and sisters.

Now that I have told you about my very illustrious parents, I will tell you my name, whether anyone wants me to or not. Although it is little known, in order for my name to be stated correctly, take the name of the most perfect man who ever was, and you must put I.N.E. with it. No other letter is needed.

VI. *Here she tells how she gathered only scrapings of her father's treasure*

379–434

My father, of whom I have already spoken, had a wish and strong desire to have a male child who would be his heir, to take over his riches, which would not diminish through generosity, as he would say; I remember it well. He and my mother, in agreement, conceived me with that hope. But my father's aim was not realized, because my mother, who had much greater power than he, wanted to have a female child similar to herself. Thus I was in fact born a girl. My mother did so much for my father, however, that I resembled him in every way, right and truly, except only for my gender. As far as manner, body, face, even our nature, I was so like him that you would have believed we were the same in almost all respects.

---

7. The first Roman emperor, Augustus, born Gaius Octavius; he reigned from 27 BCE to 14 CE. Octavian acquired his wealth after his defeat of Antony and Cleopatra and conquest of Egypt.

8. Greek physician and medical scholar (130–200 CE).

9. Legendary Amazonian queen who joined the Trojans in battle against the Greeks; her exploits are recounted in Book 6, chapters 30–33.

Thus I was called daughter. My mother loved me very much and nurtured me in an atmosphere of kindness. She loved me so and held me so dear that she nursed me herself as soon as I was born. Sweetly she took care of me during my childhood, and I grew, thanks to her. There was no care or worry then, and I needed nothing but to play, as was typical, with the children of my age. But since I was born a girl, it was not the norm that I would benefit in any way from my father's wealth. More by custom than by right, I could not inherit the wealth that was taken at the esteemed fountain. If justice ruled, the female would lose nothing in this regard, no more than the son. But I am absolutely certain that in many places, customs reign over justice. Therefore, due to a lack of learning, I lost out utterly on this very rich treasure. That made me very unhappy with such a custom. If it were otherwise, I presume that I would have been rich, satisfied, and fulfilled with the treasure taken from the fountain, because I was very willing and still had a great desire to draw deeply from it. That is not something that just came over me yesterday.

435–468

I desired it more than anything on earth, but that did not matter at all; things could only go according to the custom, may it be cursed by God! Thus I am like the very passionate and desirous lovers who cannot see or hear what they wish to enjoy. I resemble them in this regard, because I desire what I do not have, which is the treasure that great knowledge gives to those who love possessing it. And even though I was female, which is why I could not have the wealth I spoke of, I had the inclination for it, because of my true nature and also in order to resemble my father. I could not refrain from stealing the scrapings and the little bits, the small pennies and the little coins that fell from the very great wealth that my father had in such bounty. And even though I have but little of it, considering my very strong appetite, the only reason I have any at all is because I took it furtively.[10] So I have amassed meager wealth, which is quite obvious in my work. What wealth I have benefits me greatly, however, and it does me good. No other wealth is rightfully mine and at least this has stayed with me, whatever I may have lost thanks to twisted Fortune. It will not falter until I die.

VII. *Here she tells how she was placed into the service of Fortune*

469–492

My mother, beautiful Nature, raised me until she deemed me a grown young woman. She wanted to consider my advancement carefully, because I had none of

---

10. On the food metaphor and Christine's "appetite" for learning, see Jacqueline Cerquiglini-Toulet, "Le goût de l'étude: Saveur et savoir chez Christine de Pizan," in Hicks, Gonzalez, and Simon, *Au champ des escriptures*, 597–608.

what is taken from the treasury of knowledge. In order for me to be able to manage, she wanted to place me in the service of a lady of high breeding. They were loosely linked by family, although they did not resemble each other. They were not made by the same measure; their faces, their deeds, their manners, and their natures were very dissimilar. That lady is a high and powerful queen, although she is of foreign origin. She is called Lady Fortune. And she has woven many a cloth so unyielding that many people would not know how to weave it or escape from it. My mother put me in Fortune's court at that time. Fortune was neither cruel nor harsh toward me. Rather, she received me well as soon as she saw me.

493–534

Thus I was placed with my lady Fortune, but I was not so importunate as to soon ask for favors. Since I was young then, I had no care but to play. I did not see, sense, or know, in any way I was aware of at all, how the court was organized, that place where joy and pleasure are very short-lived. Nonetheless, even if there is little joy at that court, there is no way to get ahead or prosper if Fortune does not arrange it. Therefore, I was put there and subjugated completely to her will.

I was raised there during my childhood, without being reproached or wronged. Then I began to grow up and to learn how I could serve the will of my lady. But my very good and tender mother, who was never harsh toward me, did not forget me in my need. Rather, she rushed very quickly to visit me, and recognized that it was necessary to think of my well-being. It was time for me to advance, to be married or betrothed. For that reason, my gracious, joyful mother wanted to make me pretty, so she gave me some of her jewels. There are none equal to them. They are even more select than those from the fountain I mentioned earlier, but whoever has both cannot lack for great knowledge. Together they are very beautiful. But the ones that she gave were a favor freely bestowed, it seems to me, without having to be sought; the others are acquired by great effort.

VIII. *Here she speaks of the crown that her mother sent her*[11]

535–566

The lady who did many very good things for me placed a noble and highly valuable crown upon my head. I love and cherish it more than any other. My mother took it, completely pure, from her goldsmith shop; it was rich in precious, fine gemstones. My mother, who gave it to me, finished it with many such stones and even more beautiful ones. It was so beautifully crafted, in my opinion, that it

---

11. Bernard Ribémont suggests that this crown may be seen as a metaphor for the entire poem in "Christine de Pizan écrivain didactique: La question de l'encyclopédisme," in Dor and Henneau, *Christine de Pizan: Une femme de science,* 80–82. Nadia Margolis also closely examines this crown and its properties in "Poetics of History," 104–8.

should have sufficed for me. Yet I certainly do not wish to imply that I would not have wanted an even better one, and even more of her wealth. Rather, I should praise her and express gratitude for her gifts and favors, because, God above, I thank her for all of her largesse. The crown that adorned me shone because of the stones. Since such a crown suits a young lady well, it made me much more beautiful, wiser and more thoughtful, and in every way more pleasing.

If I wanted to count all the stones and fully describe their wonderful powers, I would take a long time to do so. Therefore, I will briefly tell of the powers of only four of them, no more. I will name the main ones that are seen shining from afar, and which make the others shine.

IX. *Here is told of the properties of the stones on said crown*

567–602
The first stone, set in front, makes a person reflective, wise, moderate, and well-spoken, and it quells all anger. Whoever has it on him will never lose his sense, and in every respect will surpass others in goodness. To speak truly, there is no duchy or county, or rich realm or empire, that is in any way as valuable. Possessing all the wealth in the world would not make one any better off. The stone is called Discretion. Next, Consideration was set right in the middle of the crown and it sat well in its place. This stone is less valuable and more common, although like the other one, it is necessary to have. A thousand of them do not have as much value as the first one that I named, which is so greatly renowned. One cannot outbid another for this stone, because it is not too expensive for anyone. Rather, it appears in a variety of guises; not everyone has it in the same form. But Discretion is not everyone's friend—some people do not have it at all. And it is of little value to have Consideration without Discretion. A fool may have it, but he is the opposite of the wise man who knows well how to draw profit and honor from it. It seems to me, though, that whoever has these two stones together cannot be mistreated or lack wealth.

603–640
In front of Consideration, directly facing it, my mother had very deliberately placed another stone which cannot be praised too highly. That stone can be neither sold nor rented; my mother gives it. (A crown with such choice gems should be greatly loved!). This latter stone, which deserves much praise, gives the ability to retain what one hears, feels, and sees, and all that the heart conceives. Thus it has the name Retentiveness. Never can an overly hasty person rightly have this one, however well he might do what he is supposed to.

There was another stone on the back of the crown. It was very beautiful, and possessed great goodness. This stone makes one remember everything, whatever one may have heard, seen, heard spoken of, or read in the past, were it in science or history. Thus it is called Memory, where many an important thing is hidden, and often recounted. (It is not hated by any wise man!). This stone and Retentiveness are set well. If a clever person had both of them and did what he should, I believe, from what I see and sense about the stones, that one would see him acquire honor and wisdom. Those two go together naturally, and they resemble each other a great deal.

On this same topic

641–661

Now I have told you about the powerful and beautiful crown that my mother sent me, which has led me to many good things. Even though I may praise it, no one should think that I boast of having more of Nature's wealth than anyone else, or that I have the powers I named, which should be loved by all. I am well aware that I have but little of them. She gave me enough of her wealth, however, that at least I am eloquent and speak well, and I understand reason. It is not as much as I would like, or as much as I would need, but enough to allow me to use this wealth well and not abuse her kindness. I may not have a lovely or agile body, or the understanding of a sibyl, but this suffices for me as it is.

662–714

I thank God who made what I have and the powers I named. They are not disseminated everywhere. And although I just said that Nature sends them to us, in fact she does not give them to us at all, even though she is a mother and friend; rather, God gives them by his grace. Nature arranges the body and readies it to receive the soul, which can conceive of everything. But the soul is created by God himself. God consented to give Nature the power to make and undo true material form. The soul, however, is celestial, a light, invisible spirit, very knowing and attentive. These, then, are the working faculties of the soul, arranged in the body by Nature and given by God (no one could dispute me on this): understanding, memory, reasonable judgment, and other faculties holding a place there, all of which come from the soul.

So why do certain people have a greater abundance of these assets and virtues than other people, who have less? The only cause that we can identify, as far as I can understand, is that the body of a person who comprehends best, who has greater understanding, must be better arranged, denser, better devised, and of better proportions, although we may not know them, than that of someone who does not have intelligence. Thus I have proven my argument well: even though God sends the soul to the body, it is Nature who allows or disallows the soul's good faculties to function there, according to how the different tunings of the bodily instrument lead them.

It is time that I get back to the topic that I started previously. May God grant that it be advanced and completed according to his sweet will, the way it is or better, as is my desire!

More on the same topic

715–762

As you have heard, my good mother brought joy to my heart by giving so many of her jewels to me that they should well satisfy me. Still, she has better ones, more beautiful and opulent, worth more than rings or buckles, that she distributes among her children. She gives them out to the most beloved, without offending anyone, such that each has his share—more to some, less to others. They all pass through her hands. Thus she gave me this small crown, set on my curly hair. It was lovely and suited my station. I received it very gladly. Even though it was little, the stones on it were highly select. It would have troubled her if the crown were big, because it would have been too heavy for me to hold up, for I was young and did not need heavy responsibility. But what happens with the jewels given by Nature is marvelous, because their properties are such that as the body grows, their powers grow ever stronger. They get more beautiful and their light shines more brightly, provided they are not hindered or changed by an illness that ails and harms the body. The body is ruled by them, as is an empire or kingdom, even the entire world, for as long as it endures. And if that is not so, it should be, as God in heaven ordained it that way. For this reason, Nature gives out the jewels and hands them freely to everyone. But I believe that people often use little of the grace that God infuses in them, because virtues are often overturned and become vices. Nonetheless, we all have jewels, and if we do not use them, that is entirely our doing.

More on this topic

763–770

I was already past childhood when I was thus adorned. So I began to know reason, which made me wiser. Thanks to my crown, I was familiar with reason, which chides the unwise and was eager to teach me, and which protected me from much foolishness.

X. Here she tells of how Fortune sent her on one of her missions

771–816

Listen to how my lady Fortune, who saw that I had already started to learn and understand the ways of reason, put me to her use. In order for me to perceive and understand her ways even better, she wanted to charge me with one of her missions, even though I was still very young. Her consideration was a great kindness to me then, as you will now hear.

This lady has a fairly close relative, to whom many people go with good intentions. That is because, in order to augment lady Fortune's domain, my mother puts men and women to the test, so they will work to fortify their lodgings, which are not constructed of plaster. To keep people from losing their way, law and reason found a path toward that place, where I was sent and most remarkably guided. I will tell you surely that my lady, depending on whether she wants negative or positive things for people, divides up her assets, assigning and addressing good or bad portions, sending people either good or ill, sadness or joy.

That is where my lady wanted to send me. So she had a ship brought in and equipped with whatever would be needed for a long journey. She wanted to arrange my voyage fittingly with everything necessary for someone travelling by sea. The ship was soon ready because my lady, who had charged me with her mission, hastened the process. Then I took leave of my friends, who wept at my departure. I wept too, but I was obliged to accept my lady's order, as no one can refuse her. I had good and upstanding company with me, who were gracious, cordial, and harmonious. We took to the sea, along with honorable men and women.

817–850

We were soon far from the port. The sailors got to work to hurry the voyage, eager to reach land. They headed toward old Hymen; that is the name of the one I was going to see.[12] He was not bald or white-haired, yet he was very old. According to the words of poets, Hymen is a god who has many servants, from all social stations, at his court. There are numerous emperors, kings, and princes, and countless people of lower status, and they are all his servants. Some among them do not like being in his service, others are pleased about it. But any fault lies with those who act on bad advice, or with my lady who strikes them harshly, resulting in many arguments. As for Hymen, he is of good character and wants to do right by everyone. Everyone there serves him very attentively, but he has no use for people of the church; they would not take a step toward him. To be perfectly truthful, however, I did hear that he had some of those from Spain in his company. I never saw any at his court, though, nor did I see clergymen or priests among those who came. Hymen keeps them all far from him.

851–903

Thus we sailed day and night, without encountering anything that would harm us, until our ship arrived at the port. With joy and delight, and in great celebration, we thanked God who had guided us with no storms. Then the ladies who had brought me there instructed me well on how I should behave in front of the

12. God of Greek mythology, associated with marriage.

very wise god. They led me to a private chamber, where they dressed me richly, as befits a young lady. They put a splendid and beautiful crown, all gems and gold, on my curly auburn hair. I had a pristine white silk mantle with a train, lovely and elegant, joined with a clasp at the neck. I had a magnificent buckle at my chest, a belt, and all the accoutrements that go into the finery of a young lady who has such a mission to do, in accordance with her lineage. It was such that anyone who saw me would surely have deemed and declared that I looked like the emissary and dear friend of an exalted, beloved lady.

I was escorted by two barons and accompanied by noble people. You can believe that there were many ladies and damsels who were very grandly bejeweled and beautifully dressed. There were trumpets, minstrels, drums, and more than two pairs of horns that made everything resound. Without saying another word, we disembarked from our ship. From there we went toward Hymen's city. But since he already knew which people were meant to go to him, and was very joyous about it, he had left from his palace to come and meet us. This very worthy god knew how to conduct himself decorously. He brought elegant people with him, all wearing the same color, and everyone there expressed joy. There was a great resounding of instruments; it was very joyous to be in that place at that moment!

904–962

The god was standing right at the door. When we met (we were not yet inside), he took me by the bare hand straightaway and said to me, "Welcome! Daughter! From now on I will keep you in our court, that I oversee." I greeted him humbly and delivered my message very well, as I was charged to do. I believe that he was pleased with the way I dispatched it. He held a fine gold ring out to me, and in perfect love he put it on my finger. And I became his subject, because it is his way and his custom that when a woman goes to him on a mission, be she poor or rich, he puts a little ring on her finger if he wants to keep her in his court.

He had brought a handsome and pleasing young man with him. Then the god joyfully commissioned him with my care, commanding him to keep me, in health and sickness, without fail, and not to leave me for another, as long as I dwelled in Hymen's court and was considered one of his people. Then the young man promised me, by his faith, to be a true beloved, and that he would be my loyal companion, as was fitting. I held his company dear, because he was handsome in body and face. Then Hymen led me to his hall, where there was great rejoicing, and so many minstrels playing horns that one could not have heard God thundering. A prelate, who was not of that court, rushed to put on his vestments. He then sang the mass for us, and the people listened willingly. Then beautiful, rich presents from all over were spread out for me, and great and lowly alike paid honor to me.

After that, we sat at tables where there were many illustrious people. We were served numerous delicious dishes, with lovely and pleasing trimmings. I must joyously sing the praises of the occasion. Jubilant words were spoken. After the meal, very lively dancing began, with many new motets and instrumental arrangements performed. You could pick out the good dancers there!

963–981

Why would I make a long story of it for you? There is no need for me to tell you about all the little details and the happy things that went on there, because to hear everything would be tiresome. For that reason, I will tell you briefly that every person there was very joyous and everything went just as one would wish. I must therefore praise that place where Fortune chose to put me. I do not want to tell you at any greater length all that happened to me at that time. Thus, as I told you, I acquired a new master there. But all was under the authority of Fortune, who had brought me up in joy, pleasure, and comfort. My heart did not tire of being there for even one day; rather, to me the time was short.

982–1024

For ten years, Hymen kept me at his great court, where I had all pleasures and my share of desires. Hymen gave me capable people and a fine household, good and well-taught. My four squires and three ladies-in-waiting were considered handsome and lovely, which made me feel well provided for. But above all I was honored by the one who was charged with caring for me. He labored so much for me that I was at my ease and without distress at that court. He was such a loyal friend to me, and so good, that, by my soul, I could never sufficiently praise the good things that I enjoyed thanks to him. He was handsome, pleasing, wise, and courtly in every way. He loved justice and held nobility and knowledge dear. With his keen understanding of navigation, he knew how to steer a ship very capably in any season. The master was a highly capable boatman and knew well how to guide the ship, just has he should. He had learned this skill because it was necessary for him, since the land of Hymen, where many have had countless misfortunes whether they liked it or not, is near the sea. Whoever wants to rise in stature there must spend time at sea, know how to guide ships and galleys, and steer through good weather and storms. My master was so skilled in all of those things that he delivered me from many perils by his refined understanding of this great ocean, replete with ancient adventures.

XI. *Here is told of some miracles by gods, as related by Ovid*

1025–1056

It is now time for me to recount, as I promised at the beginning of this book where I put my name, the strange case, the extraordinary story, of how when I went back to Fortune's home, I turned from a woman into a man; it is a very astonishing thing. And it is neither lie nor fable to speak according to metaphor, which does not exclude truth, as Fortune certainly has the power over those under her authority to create even greater miracles than that. Often, when it pleases her, she makes beasts transform into lords so great that all welcome them favorably. And she can make knights turn into beasts when she wishes. That was quite apparent when, long ago, she made the seafaring Ulysses arrive at Circe's port.[13] Pretending to be friendly, Circe offered a drink to Ulysses's knights, which laid them out on the ground as if disabled, and they were transformed into pigs. My lady herself had prepared the drink that trapped them, and she made them arrive there willingly, in order to give them over to misfortune. She knows plenty about how to do such things, for which many endure harsh circumstances!

1057–1093

Fortune performs infinite marvels every day, even more incredible than those, without stopping. She can do that easily, because her workings are so much greater than those of the two snakes that Ovid tells us about in his book.[14] There he tells of a man, whom he names, who became a woman through an event that occurred. The case went like this, in my view: this man found two snakes coupling in a wood where he was frolicking. He took a stake and proceeded to strike them, as he feared that they could quickly kill him. But the one ill he suffered from it was becoming immediately aware of his whole body having been transformed. He was changed into a complete woman right then, and found himself to be in that state everywhere he checked. The young man, named Tiresias, was shocked. He stayed that way for seven years, during which he spun and toiled at the work that women do. At the end of that time, he went deep into the woods, and by chance he found the two snakes together, as the written text attests. He again took a stake, I believe, and said right then that he wanted to see if he could regain his previous form. He struck the snakes. His coloring and all his feminine feelings immediately changed, and his body turned into a man's as before, according to Ovid.[15]

13. Ulysses was the Roman name of Odysseus, the great voyager of myth and main character of Homer's *Odyssey;* Circe was a mythological sorceress known for casting spells on anyone who set foot on her island home. On Circe in this work, see Renate Blumenfeld-Kosinski, "Christine de Pizan: Mythographer and Mythmaker," Chap. 5 in *Reading Myth: Classical Mythology and its Interpretations in Medieval French Literature* (Stanford, CA: Stanford University Press, 1997), 176–80; and Ana Pairet, "'Circes l'enchanteresse': De l'*Epistre Othea* au *Livre de la mutacion de Fortune,*" in Danielle Buschinger, Liliane Dulac, Claire Le Ninan, and Christine Reno, eds., *Christine de Pizan et son époque: Actes du Colloque international des 9, 10 et 11 décembre 2011 à Amiens: Médiévales* 53 (Amiens: Presses du Centre d'Etudes Médiévales, Université de Picardie, 2012), 108–14.

14. The *Metamorphoses.*

15. Tiresias also appears in the *Odyssey.* Now dead and dwelling in the Underworld, he is visited by Odysseus (on the advice of Circe) and provides the voyager with the information he needs to return home.

1094–1131

We are also told of a king of Lydia[16] who hated women so much that he ordered his wife the queen, who was pregnant and about to give birth, that if she had a girl, she was to burn her or kill her in some ignominious way, on pain of death, because he did not want a daughter. But if it were a boy, she was to keep him, because there would be no wrong in that. The queen had a girl, and in no way did she abandon her to a cruel or bitter death; her maternal instincts kept her from that. Rather, she raised her as a boy and spread the word that she had had a handsome son. The king believed it. The girl had a perfectly lovely body and face. Her name was Iphis, a name that served for a girl or a boy. Soon she grew up big and strong, but under boy's clothing. Iphis's mother denied that she was a girl, for fear that the child's father would banish her. Instead, he wanted Iphis to marry without delay. The mother said it was too soon. After a long time, it was decided. Iphis's mother could not dissuade him from it. At that point, the queen was dismayed, and loathed her life, because she could not come up with any more tricks or ways hide Iphis. Thus she well feared being disgraced, and did not know how to hide the truth any longer. So she wept quietly, in secret.

1132–1158

She went to the goddess Vesta.[17] She knelt at the temple, wetting the floor with her tears. She offered gifts and oblations, altar candles, devotions, wax, incense and vows, and sacrifices of heifers and oxen. On bare knees, she struck her breast. She prayed and begged the goddess to come to her aid in this need, which had brought her to the brink of death. She prayed with such devotion that the goddess took pity on her. Vesta showed it clearly by making a sign. The queen took some comfort in that, and hurriedly left the temple. The preparations were underway for Iphis's wedding, which the king had hastened. There was joy and great celebration. This is how it came to pass: the goddess performed a great miracle, and the night filled the queen and her daughter Iphis with joy. Iphis had turned into a boy, thanks to the skilled goddess Vesta, who undid her woman's body and made her a son.

XII. *Here she tells how she lost the master of her ship*

1159–1192

Ovid recounts these miracles, but it is fitting that I tell you about my own transformation. I was changed by the visitation of Fortune, transformed from a woman into a man. I stayed at Hymen's place and put my energies into his works, and

---

16. A kingdom in western Asia Minor. In the *Metamorphoses*, the parents of Iphis are a poor couple, Ligdus and Telethusa, living in Crete.

17. Roman goddess of the hearth, associated with family life.

contentedly spent my life there. But I truly believe that Fortune was jealous of my great ease. So she considered it, and summoned me. Then I had to leave my great tranquility behind; I could not disobey.

Hymen then readied a well-equipped, large, and fast ship and entrusted it to my master. Hymen put my household, him, and me in it, and then, by Hymen's leave, we departed; we gave it no more thought. In a short time, we had embarked on the high seas, not encountering any hostile wind or storm. Or if we did, my master was so wise that he knew well how to pilot the ship in any winds and keep it straight. The wise captain thus steered us in the wind for several days. He knew well how to recognize the Pole Star and turn the sail, as was necessary to keep a straight course, such that we had no hardship or trouble. Thus we moved steadily forward.

1193–1222

Alas! It is time that I tell of the grief that attacked me at that point and overwhelmed my joy. I have not forgotten it for a minute since. As we were going along on our journey, sailing at sea, I saw the weather go dark and the clouds thicken, to the extent that we could hardly see anything at all. The master, who saw me fearful and frightened that a sudden wind or storm would harm us, climbed up on the stern to see from which direction the wind was coming toward us. He called out and summoned the sailors. One of them climbed up to the crow's nest to see whether we were near land, so that we could get away from the open sea, if possible, before a great storm hit. One shouted, the other asked questions. And the master exhorted and commanded another to pull ropes and mount the sail according to how the wind overtook us, or tie down or loosen the top, or let the sail out more or less, according to what his great skill deemed the best thing to do in the face of the impending storm, which was already upon us.

1223–1264

Ah! Good God! I do not know how to recount the pain that is always immediate to me, because tears and sighs trouble my heart and face, and the words recalling the incident that was so harmful to me double my sadness. But dragging this out would serve little purpose. Just as he was looking straight ahead, up on the stern of the ship, shouting for everyone to go straight and head toward the nearest land, at that moment a great wind suddenly rose up. The whirlwind twisted to and fro like a gimlet, and it slammed into the ship and knocked our good master so violently that it carried him far out to sea. I wanted to be dead right then! There was no way to help. The wind made our ship whirl around so that I really thought it would sink into the sea. But dying would not have been sad to me when I heard the yelling of the sailors who shouted loudly, crying out when they saw him plunge into the sea, he who was accustomed to protecting the ship, night and day, from all difficulties and troubles.

When I knew what I feared had indeed happened, I emerged from where I was under the stern, like a woman gone mad. I climbed up and would have thrown myself into the sea. I would not have failed at it—no matter who might have held me back, I would have jumped. Never did Alcyone jump so readily into the sea, when she lost Ceyx whom she loved so much,[18] as I would have done if people had let me. I was held back by the members of my household who shouted and came rushing to hold me, but my heart was ready to give out.

1265–1310

You would have said that the air trembled from the cries, shouts, bitter sorrow, lamentations, plaints, and wailing, mine and my household's together. Alas! For good reason we grieved the one who was our master. He was such an able captain that he protected many from death, and such a faithful beloved to me that there could never be another like him in any way. To see him perish in the sea that way, it was no wonder that my pain was unlike any other. And I truly feared that there would be no way for the ship ever to return to a safe port. Without doubt, I saw her almost completely lost in the storm many times. But the great madness I had because of him took away all my fear; my heart did not suffer from anything else. I lay there prostrate, wanting death. As I waited, I cried out so violently that you would have well believed that my voice pierced through the clouds and the sky; it did not go quiet. The loss tormented me so much that no comfort was worth anything. I was in that state for a long time, rejecting all pleasures, with no hope of ever having happiness or joy, to tell the truth.

Our afflicted ship was carried hither and yon. All winds were damaging to her, because there was no one skillful enough to steer her correctly. I well believed that I would never be able to return to any place other than the sea that separates grief from joy. I believed I would be there for my whole life, on the unfavorable side of good fate, which had taken a great hatred toward me, leaving me in a state of shock.

1311–1361

I did not stay that way, however. I have taken many steps on solid ground since then. To put it briefly, my grief was so intense and my eyes wept so many tears that even Fortune took pity on my hardship. As a good mistress, she wanted to do

---

18. In this myth, Alcyone, seeing the body of her beloved husband Ceyx washed ashore after a ship-wreck, joins him in death by drowning herself. On this episode, see Blumenfeld-Kosinski, "Mythographer and Mythmaker," 185–87; Judith L. Kellogg, "Transforming Ovid: The Metamorphosis of Female Authority," in Desmond, *Christine de Pizan and the Categories of Difference*, 183–89; and Jean-Claude Mühlethaler, "Entre amour et politique: Métamorphoses ovidiennes à la fin du Moyen Age: La fable de Céyx et Alcyoné, de l'*Ovide moralisé* à Christine de Pizan et Alain Chartier," in "Lectures et usages d'Ovide," ed. Emmanuèle Baumgartner, thematic issue, *Cahiers de recherches médiévales et humanistes* 9 (2002): 143–56 <http://crm.revues.org/76>.

me a kindness and help me in my suffering. But the help was extraordinary! I do not know if it was an even greater danger. At one point, as a result of being tired out from such extended weeping, I was languishing in a completely broken state. As if lifeless, I went to sleep early one evening. Then my mistress, who diminishes the joy of many, came to me and touched me all over my body. I remember well how she manipulated every limb and held them in her hands. Then she left and I stayed.

As our ship went along with the waves of the sea, it struck violently against a rock. I awoke, and things were such that I felt immediately and without a doubt that I was entirely transformed. I sensed that my limbs were much stronger than before, and my great despondency and grieving had faded somewhat. Then, completely bewildered, I felt myself. Fortune, who had transformed me this way, did not abandon me then, because she suddenly changed the great fear and doubt that held me in utter confusion. And I felt much lighter than I was used to, and my flesh was transformed and stronger, my voice much fuller, and my body harder and quicker. But the ring that Hymen had given me had fallen from my finger, which grieved me, as well it should have because I loved it dearly. Then I easily got up, and I no longer stayed in the sloth of weeping that had been increasing my distress. I found my heart strong and bold, which astonished me, but I felt that I had become a true man.

1362–1385
And I stood there, astounded by the occurrence. I lifted my eyes, by chance, and saw the sail and mast demolished. The powerful weather had similarly broken the ropes and tops as well. Our ship was severely smashed and cracked all over, and the seething water pushed its way in. The ship was already so heavy with water that had she not been protected by the rocks against which she had hurled herself, she would indeed have sunk to the bottom.

When I saw her shipwrecked that way, I undertook to repair her myself. With nails and mortar and a strong hammer, I rejoined the planks. I gathered moss from the rocks and stuck it in the cracks, in great quantity, in such a way that I made the ship sufficiently watertight. I rejoined the broken ends, and had the ship's hold drained. In short, I was very capable of making use of whatever was necessary to guide the ship.

1386–1416
As soon as I had learned to steer her myself, I became a good master of the ship. I had to be that way, by necessity, in order to rescue myself and my household, if I did not want to die there. Thus I was a true man—it is not a fiction—capable of guiding ships. Fortune taught me that skill, and thereby took me from that situation.

As you are hearing, I am still a man, and I have already been one for a total of more than thirteen full years. But it would please me considerably more to be a woman, as I was used to being when I would speak with Hymen. But since Fortune has taken me away from there, and I will never dwell there again, I will remain a man. And I will stay with my lady, even though I have encountered so many hardships in her service that I am ravaged by them. But I have to live there until death. May God deliver me from it, into salvation! I pulled myself from between those rocks, readied my ship, and headed toward the place from which I had embarked at the beginning of this part, where my lady had her dwelling. I arrived there in little time, even though I had had great misfortune. I was not soon at the end of it.

XIII. *Here she tells how she returned from her mission*

1417–1460

At that point I returned to the place I had left some time earlier, but I was able to observe its nature and what could exist there much more keenly than I had in my youth. And notwithstanding the great and bitter wrong I had suffered, my mother, who was always a friend to me, never forgot me. Because whether it was in sleep or in wakefulness, or through changes I may have undergone, or in difficulty or harm that Fortune caused me, or through long hardship or short-lived joy, or for any adornment that may have been made for me or crown that may have been placed on my head, my crown never left me. It was my share of my mother's wealth, and she had crowned me with it. It suited me very well, as I recounted earlier when I was telling of my mother and me.

But the stones have often been disturbed since then, and covered with the dust that flies on grief, which frivolous Fortune blows. But the stones were so much brighter then than ever before, and they grew greatly at the time I became a man. It is surely by their power that I came to port and learned how to steer ships and know the garden where Fortune lives, she who deprives everyone of great happiness. Then it was time for me to perceive the nature and know the ways of the court where I had been placed, better than I had in the past. So I will tell you what I saw there and all that I came to know of my lady's dwelling place, of her ways and conditions, and of her great transformations (she does not stay still even for an hour).

Here begins the second part of the book called
The Mutability of Fortune

I. *First, about the situation of the castle and how it is made*

1461–1506

There is a place on the sea known as Great Peril, where there is a high, icy[19] rock, marvelous and sharp. Atop a great metalled path sits a lofty square-shaped castle, perched most marvelously. It seems downright magical, because four chains hold the place up—I do not know if they are attached to something or nothing at all, but the roof is constantly turning, as if it were seated on a wheel that whirls around. This place does not stay still at all, and the top turns without stopping. No one has firm footing—whoever puts his confidence there is foolish! And because it is always moving, it often makes people dizzy, at least many who do not know how to hold themselves up or stay on their feet. Others have come to know the place better, and can steady themselves against the surrounding wall. But when I saw the turning and first noticed the changes I observed, I found myself so frightened that, without comparison, I would rather have been made a monk in a cloister than be put in such a place, even though I knew I had an important task there. But it seemed extremely perilous to me, very dangerous and bizarre, a place where much could go wrong. I always thought I was going to fall because the whole place leaned to one side, and there was no drawbridge or footbridge that was not set on a quagmire. It is never straight. And I declare for all to hear that the four winds blow constantly there, because it is perched so very high up that it will be very windy, in hot and cold weather alike, as those who have spent time there know.

1507–1565

The castle is precariously[20] situated there. I want to tell you about its construction; it should not be hidden. The castle has four great and wide façades, but the first

---

19. The vocabulary is tricky here. Christine uses the adjective "neÿve" (line 1463), which many, including Solente, interpret as "snowy" or "icy" for its association with the word "neige" (*Mutacion*, 4:227). Blanchard and Quereuil, among others, read it as "rough" or "natural" for its possible link with "naïf": see the *DMF: Dictionnaire du Moyen Français, 1330–1500: Analyse et traitement informatique de la langue française* (Paris: Centre National de la Recherche Scientifique; Nancy: Université de Lorraine) <http://www.atilf.fr/dmf/>. I have chosen the former in light of the description of the castle in the thirteenth-century *La Panthère d'amours*, one of Christine's sources. It includes the detail "elle siet toute sus glace / qui dure quel temps que il face" (lines 1963–64) [it sits entirely on ice that endures whatever the weather may be]; trans. and ed. Bernard Ribémont, *Nicole de Margival: Le Dit de la Panthère* (Paris: Champion, 2000), 99. Solente discusses the *Panthère d'amours* as a source for the *Mutacion* (1: xli–xlii).

20. The term here is "en l'empire" (line 1507), which would literally mean "in the empire." Thanks to its resonance with verb "empirer" (to worsen), the expression was used in word play conveying the idea of "going from bad to worse."

one surpasses the other three in beauty and size, just like the light and the great glow of the stars outshine little candles. Never was the castle of Ilion,[21] of which so much is said, or the beautiful Troy, or the highly renowned Rome, or the defunct Babylon, or any city, castle, or ancient gate ever as beautiful or as strong as the first façade of this castle. But a little storm completely wipes out its beauty, because its masonry is such that the walls are not good or sturdy, even though outwardly they seem to be. But clever Fortune, who deceives the world, made it appear invulnerable and very solid to passers-by. Its beauty and appearance are nothing but pure deception, however.

In the middle of this great façade, which pleases everyone at first, there is a marvelous doorway. (Whoever was bold enough to undertake such a work was very adept and clever!). It looks invulnerable. It is worked with such cunning that the edifice appears to be a very strong. And it is of such fine stonework that there is hardly anyone in the world so wise who, if he were not extremely astute, would ever say that he had seen or heard tell of one so magnificent; no one has since the time of Abel. It is exceedingly well carved, gilded, and enameled, with an abundance of apple-shaped finials and banners of more than a hundred thousand kinds. One could not look straight at it when the sun shone on it—the beam made the gold radiate for more than a hundred leagues. The whole stretch of country lit up from it. It is the main entry to the castle, so big on all sides and so high at the top that a thousand or more saddled war-horses carrying people with lances could walk straight in.

1566–1616

In the front, there are numerous drawbridges and strong barriers, and great, wide, and deep moats, deeper than an abyss. I could not describe for you one tenth of the strength and the defenses that this place appears to have, nor the great marvels of this castle, because never had there been any like them. I have never seen a building like this (the worker who did this was exceedingly skillful!), but I am relating it as best I know how. Inside on the wall, near the door, many unusual images had recently been painted, very richly done in gold and blue, to inform those who passed by along their way. My lady wanted the images to be seen, so the wanderers would want to go inside.

The seemingly enchanted castle has many visitors, because all the paths in the world, all rivers and the deep sea, head toward it. There is nothing to keep people from it. Everyone goes to that place on horseback, on foot, or by boat. They want to anchor their ships there, and all strive to enter the castle through the magnificent door. But no one enters if he is not favored, because the guard there is too daunting. Do you know who guards this doorway? A very famous lady named Lady Wealth. She does nothing for poor people. Her servants are well instructed

---

21. Ancient name for Troy.

in this regard, so well taught by her that they hold poor people in contempt. Lady Wealth is the sister of my lady, and she would not give one penny of her riches to anyone unless it were Fortune's will. Thus she is really just the guardian of the riches. My lady is the older one, because Fortune had already been around for some time before Wealth came to be. So she made Wealth her treasurer and the door-guard of this entryway.

II. *Here is told of Wealth's door*

1617–1658

Inside the doorway, Lady Wealth was seated on her throne, so golden and adorned with pearls, so richly decorated, that the whole place radiated from the great brightness emanating from the jewels covering it. They were worth a great deal of money. She had a crown on her head, but I would never come to the end of it if I set out to describe its tremendous value. Lady Wealth had many rings, buckles, and clasps to protect her from many evils, amassed in great quantity around her. She was not humble or compassionate, but arrogant in her ways and deeds, so haughty toward people that she barely deigned to speak to anyone.

She seemed stiffer than a post there, but do not think that she was alone. Rather, she was well accompanied, and do you know by what retinue? In no way was it servant boys or commoners who gather harvests, unless they were put there by the help of some good friends. There were rather kings and dukes, princes and counts. And in the chamber of accounts there were bishops and archbishops, along with cardinals and popes, earning their wages there. They all served Lady Wealth much better than they served God, I do not doubt it a bit. One can see why, because she is a great friend when she chooses to be, and gives extremely handsome and rich gifts. There were plenty of other prelates there. People of all kinds passed through that door, as long as they had gold and silver.

1659–1696

One thing was very distressing for me to see—Wealth had a practice that was highly contrary to reason. I saw her take great riches from her coffers, and she gave them (and still gives them) to the wealthiest people. And the more she gave them, the more she took of the poor people's meager assets. But no poor person could have any advantage or gift, favor or recompense at this court. You must also understand that Wealth takes no account of kindness, good sense, beauty, or strength, nor is she concerned about valor, goodness, or eminent qualities. To such people she is hardly a friend, and when she is, that situation usually does not last long. If it happened, unfortunately, that Fortune were to take their possessions from them, wrongly and very unreasonably, Wealth would never reason with them while they were in such a state. Whoever they might have been, whether prince or king, they would have to regain their status. She did not value their station at all, however much sense or goodness they might have had, as long as they were in poverty. Never was a poor person welcome there, and if one did manage to make it to that place, the devil would have brought him, and he would have been harshly knocked back down (he would be better off in Damascus or in India, at Saint Thomas's body![22]). He never would have escaped alive at that point, because there is nothing Lady Wealth hates more.

III. *Here is told of Fortune's two brothers who govern the castle*

1697–1750

I will also tell you who handles matters for those who wish to speak with Wealth and come inside. She and my lady have two very powerful brothers. Fortune made them castellans of this castle, to hear people's complaints and oversee this place where she reigns. And govern it they certainly do, that is to say, after a fashion, because they treat few people fairly. They take from some for no reason, and they give more than is right to others. They do not rightfully uphold justice; rather, it is badly mishandled and very perfidiously carried out. And they have their servants everywhere, their lawyers and doctors, who are nothing but people-eaters. No one gets to them without money. But if someone softens them up with gifts, he will have his affair well addressed, and a person who has committed a misdeed will be very easily pardoned and freed of it. I do not know why the earth does not crumble beneath those who carry out such justice. But my lady keeps them in power (the two brothers I am telling you about), here where the throngs are greater than in Rome, but where the path is not sure.

One brother is named Luck, the other Mischance. They govern this place, which is greater than any kingdom, but they do not share the same function. Mischance oversees my lady's justice, and there is no rightfulness in it at all. And Luck, who is appropriately pleasing, keeps company with Wealth, because he is of her lineage. He stays in front of the door to answer whoever comes up. Standing there, he holds a green laurel crown in his hand, and he places it where he sees fit. Not all get it, it seems to me. He also goes to the garden. He is called when my lady wants to raise someone's worth, because no one is knocked down by him.

---

22. St. Thomas is reputed to have spread the Gospel as far as India and to have been buried there. Before traveling to India, he is said to have spent time in Damascus, where the Bab Tuma ("Thomas Gate")—one of the gates of the ancient city walls—was named after him. Christine makes similar allusions to Thomas in lines 11–12 of Ballad 55 of the *One Hundred Ballads* (*Cent ballades*), in *Oeuvres poétiques*, ed. Roy, 1:56 and in lines 1477–78 of the *Path of Long Study* (*Chemin de longue étude*), ed. and trans. Andrea Tarnowski (Paris: Livre de Poche, 2000), 174–75. This phrase has the idiomatic meaning of "far away."

IV. *Here is told of the ways of one of Fortune's brothers*

1751–1804

I will tell you about the ways of the brothers. I believe they were from two fathers, because they do not resemble each other. They differ from one another in many ways. Luck is small in size, well put-together, not very wise, pale, and white. He has green eyes. He is not proud or cruel. Although he has a thoughtful countenance, he is not inclined to speak much. He has a shifty look in his eye and he does not move at a speedy pace, but when he commits, he is so generous that he gives over body and possessions. He willingly keeps himself well dressed and the place in nice shape, because wherever he is looks good. He very willingly dresses in green. He also brings good news and is pleased by new things. He is a knight of great nobility, closely resembling his sister Wealth—both were of the same womb. Lady Wealth is never without him. He goes in front, never harming anybody. Luck is greatly loved by all; he is elegant and well dressed. He truly seems to be of royal lineage. He dearly loves his sister and her household. Luck has much goodness in him.

I certainly would have esteemed him highly if he did not require so much currying favor and were not so difficult to get to know. But whoever can gain his friendship will never lack for wealth. Whoever has it can consider himself quite clever—Luck is a friend to few people. His favor is acquired with great difficulty, and one loses it easily without knowing why. He has many friends who never deserved it, or who well and loyally served. He has a bad habit of this, and I consider him much less wise for it, because sense and prudence are of little value in acquiring his friendship; it is nothing but pure chance and a short-lived joy. In that respect, by my soul, he resembles Fortune, his sister and lady. He is as changeable as she is, and his love is fleeting.

V. *Here is told of the ways of the other brother*

1805–1840

Now I will tell you about Mischance. He is the exact opposite of Luck, even though they are brothers. I do not know if he resembles his father or his mother, but his ways are replete with all manner of fault. He is big, rough, and thick-set, with a dark hairy body; I remember it well. His face is ghastly and grimacing, his head bristly and disheveled, his expression horrible, and when he talks he seems to hiss hideously, like a snake. He has a great beard that hangs nearly to his belt. I truly believe that never had such an ugly creature ever been created, nor one more feared or less loved!

Even though he may be very heavy, you can know for sure that he is not slow to spring into action. He is so mobile that he seems like a veritable devil to see running around there, because he goes very quickly in and out, now on the road and then on the path, then up high, then low where wind does not blow, with a big crowbar at his shoulder. He has neither a game nor a joke, and he seems as if he is about to go wild. He wants to correct everyone unjustifiably, and he makes such a ruckus that it seems as if everything there goes downright topsy-turvy. He is never at rest, and he is not lazy. He is not this quarrelsome without reason.

1841–1910

And do you know with what business this devil always occupies himself? Doing harm and taking away my lady's favor, which is not ample for those who want it and wish to acquire any wealth. The evil one who turns my lady's wheel hinders them in that, and he places them in such a tough spot that everything goes badly for them. Indeed, all those who pass through his hands, and there are many of them, are maltreated by him, and turned from the highest point to the lowest. There is no pity in him at all, nor faith, loyalty, or friendship. And aside from how ugly he is and how everyone holds him in disdain, his clothing is extremely bizarre (I do not know if it was designed by the tailor who made it), but it has a very disagreeable and ugly cut. It is made entirely with long stitches that are not pretty or elegant, and it is trimmed along the tails with horrible serpents' tongues. The fabric is black in color, signifying all pain. And this robe suits him well, because he takes joy from many.

This brother stays close to my lady, to know whether she wants to do harm to someone. He is always ready to dash from here to Brest or England or elsewhere, day or night. There is no country so far away that in well under a week he would not have gone there and promptly devastated it, if my lady had cursed it and condemned it to be destroyed. When such a thing is ordered of him, either to do harm or obstruct, know that he does not wait to be summoned. Rather, he jumps very quickly to the place, as long as he knows it pleases her. But inasmuch as he cares about himself, he would not dare to approach it if she were not angered first. When she directs her wrath against a person or a land, however, or she wants to harm one of the sides in some war, then Mischance will not leave until he has annihilated everything, and he no longer finds anything there to ruin or harm. This treacherous one (God curse him!) knows how to undertake this, because he has mistreated many a person, without cause and very wrongly. I have good reason to complain about him myself, because he did me a great deal of harm. Because of the way he acts, I endured great hardship, and I am not yet at the end of it. Never did Luck do me as much good as Mischance has done me harm; it is his occupation. I cannot make friends with Luck.

VI. *Here is told of Fortune's outward appearance*

1911–1954

I want to tell you what the lady, who heralds many bad things, looks like—that is, just as she appeared to me. She has shown herself to others with a different form, as a number of people have written in many a text. Some have depicted her according to the image that appeared on high to Nebuchadnezzar,[23] her head entirely of precious metal. Or one may find the feet and other limbs of her body made of iron, brass, lead, or clay. But I have a different memory of her, as you will hear me describe her, and I know how to tell it accurately.

Fortune had two faces, which she knew well how to use. The one in the front was very beautiful—smiling and white, fresh and smooth—even though there was nothing sincere about it. The one in the back was ugly and dirty, black, shadowy, horrible, dark, and ominous to see. She had a very strange crown. The part surrounding the beautiful face was of shiny gold, with lovely stones. The back, over the hideous face, had a much different appearance. It was made of swords and sharp knives with poisonous edges. In her right hand, Fortune held a pleasing and lovely crown. In her hidden left hand, she had a sword at the ready, morning and evening, to throw at anyone. This is how I saw that lady. She held her right foot in water and the left one in a great fire. She kept her wheel nearby, which Mischance turned sometimes, and which was sometimes turned and handled by Luck.

VII. *Here is told of Luck's role at the door of Wealth*

1955–2018

Now I have told of the brothers and of the lady in whom there is no goodness. And I will tell you more about Luck, which I did not tell you earlier: his purpose at this door. You can know for sure that people bring him requests from all over. People make pious offerings to him, more vows and gifts than to God, aiming to be granted entry into the dwelling of Lady Wealth, the duchess of the proud. Seeing people arriving there from far and wide and striving to enter through the enceinte[24] would remind one of the practice one must uphold in France when pursuing money. People who have to do that know this practice and everything one must do to pursue the officials.

Different kinds of people arrive from all sides, even though they are jostled by the large crowd there. Everyone is very eager to have his matter handled well. And indeed the officials are watched so that they do not go out by the back door, and then hither and yon when they leave. And when someone believes he may be very close to having completed what is required, he is served with another delay,

---

23. Daniel 2:31–33.

24. The enclosure, usually a stone wall, surrounding a castle or fortification. Cf. Book 6, chapter 9.

or new ordinances are passed and more information must first be heard by our lords, who work for the most important people. Thus, often, when one has pursued and followed them for a long time, one has accomplished nothing; it has to be redone, or it is necessary to make another order—this one is outdated. You can understand that whoever gets that response is very dejected! And he would like very much to have an ounce of that of which he had hoped to have a pound, just to be free from their grasp.

I know this, I experienced it. I can speak of it from proven fact, because I pursued them for a long time and followed them to many places, with a valid royal order—not for a gift, but for debt legally owed me. I was in an awkward situation and in great need, but in doing so I was pursuing my own best interest. I will say nothing more of it, because that is enough. And I do not say it to reproach them, or so they might make themselves less likeable. This may be how they make people waste their time, but they do enough to justify themselves, because they could not resolve everything that people come to ask of them.

VIII. *Here is told how people try to enter through Wealth's door*

2019–2061

Luck thus pursues people, and all the possessions that they bring him are put into Wealth's coffers. He gives of it only to his friends, because he himself carries the keys. He stands at that door where all kinds of people adore him, all for money. All great lords arrive there, the eldest and the youngest. They have money, they want more of it, and they say that they are accustomed to having more. There are great throngs of knights, bourgeois, church people, clerks, merchants, upper-crust, ladies, poor people, great mistresses, and people of all social status. All arrive there in great numbers. They all come seeking Luck and to ask for his help. One comes to present his letter. Another promises to serve Luck in every way, as long as he is granted all or part of what he is deeply concerned about, and Luck is his friend in need. Another says he has served well and deserves great recompense. Another says that he has never stopped pursuing arms since the time he was a child, and has sold and pledged his land for war to serve the king, so Luck should do something substantial for him in the form of either wealth or honor. All who travel this way, the greater and the lesser, are thus seeking Luck's help, because no one else leads them to Wealth by any path. Whoever wants to amass great wealth must pass through this door; without Luck, no gain is realized.

2062–2108: *Luck is fickle and toys with those who pursue his favor. Christine criticizes him for doling out wealth unfairly, often to those who least deserve it.*

2109–2164

Thus Luck is but a game of chance, because the person who happens to have pursued him all his life will be chased far from him, yet Luck and all worldly goods will soon come to the one who does not remember him. But that is not rightful wealth, to tell the truth, because there is much to reproach about it, and it is quickly made and quickly unmade. There is only one perfect asset: eternal heaven. May God lead us there in the end! There is no security in any other outcome, nor is there any other happiness.

But Luck has the greatest multitudes because of the base desire that people have for worldly possessions. For that reason, all men and women run there faster than fallow deer, seeking Wealth, which is gained through Luck. A person would be greatly deceived, however, and the outcome would be less than good, if he were to claim and maintain that knowledge or learning a profession is of no use to anyone who wants to become rich. And that to be sure of having wealth, all one needs is Luck, which happens entirely by chance, and therefore no one would need to learn a skill. But that view deserves a lot of criticism, because one should do one's duty in hopes of having wealth, even though Luck brings a great deal of it; we see this happen to many, by rights. Where there is more knowledge and goodness, there should be more good fortune, because those who have sought it well have already found it by acquiring that great knowledge.

Luck spreads wealth in many ways, although I have only mentioned here what the emotions desire immediately, nothing more, and what results in reaching Wealth more readily. That is what should be called "Fortune's favors," for we see her trick often: the most deserving people are not the best served by her. We should fault those who allocate the goods and split them up so inappropriately. And since those shares are badly apportioned and unfairly allocated, one can say that Mischance takes them from us and Luck gives them.

IX. Here is told of the ill that Mischance does

2165–2193

Thus everyone chases after Luck, and there is a great crowd at his door. Some are chased away, and others are pushed inside. He is there during workdays and holidays. People make many requests of him. He refuses more of them than he accepts, and very few people pass through. But whoever enters that way can amass great wealth. Since Luck will have put him there, he will be a friend of Wealth. If he is a clerk, he will have a fine office in the castle, or great favor, however little he may know, because Wealth will pull him in. And he has no reason to worry about leaving there if my lady's front guard does not chase him away. But Mischance, who sees hardly anything there, is very often the enemy of the people Luck takes as friend. And as soon as Mischance attacks them, Luck also immediately abandons them and turns his back on them completely. Then their repose turns into great suffering, because Mischance, bit by bit, breaks down all the good that Luck had done, and takes away Wealth's love.

2194–2211: *People who are attacked by Mischance lose their fortune, friends, and reputation.*

2211–2282

Slanderers will spread the word everywhere that the wretches should be hanged for having spent so much on luxurious things, follies, or pretty baubles. They say that those miserable people have met with harm thanks to their great greed, dice games or ribaldry, or some vile excess. "One should by no means follow such people. They do not deserve to live, because they have spent what they had or they lost it by misfortune. One should not pity them, because it is all due to their bad behavior." And they say no one should feel sorry for them. Thus Mischance makes people complain about the poor who have done no wrong, but have always done the best they could, and who enjoyed such good grace when they were prospering. They were in good standing then, and now they are worth nothing! Dear God! Now the good is cast away! Their state is even worse still, because since they look bad, anyone among their friends and family would consider it a burden to lodge them for a week. The rich take no account of their poor relatives; rather, they are ashamed to see them badly dressed. The poor do not count for even two strands of straw, however good or upright they may be. Their goodness is worthless now. Since they have nothing, it is but rubbish.

Wherever such people may be found, the rich say that their lives go on too long and that they devour more goods than everyone there and in the households where they are lodged. They scorn and yell at such a person, and complain about everything he eats—a little wine, bread, or salt pork. If the poor man is old or broken by illness, he will be scorned even more. And Mischance makes things even worse for the old and withered, and the young alike, because thanks to him, their moaning to their families is met with contempt. Few find comfort there. And when they fail their friends and are cut off from their possessions, they become so distressed that there are some who, in despair, crumble and abruptly kill themselves, or do something by their own hand that gets them hanged the next day. Thus many a good man is treated, without cause. No one knows the burden of the ill that arises because of Mischance. May God protect us from him, because whoever runs into him has very bad fortune and is not secure. And whoever encounters Mischance upon rising might just as well go back to bed, because I believe he will need to if Mischance plays his tricks on him.

X. Here is told how those with good fortune despise the unfortunate

2283–2372: *Wealthy and contented people believe that they are worthy and secure in their position. The powerful are also flattered and feared, and thus feel free to commit affronts against others. Luck and Fortune, however, can turn against them at any time, exposing their misdeeds, humiliating them, and throwing them into the depths. Once abased, those people will in turn be objects of scorn and blamed for their own downfall.*

XI. Here is told of the second façade and door of Fortune's castle

2373–2410

I have described the magnificent first façade. Now I will speak of the next one, which does not closely resemble it. Rather, there is considerable difference in beauty and appearance. It is not durable, and it is neither painted nor gilded. It is made of more pieces and the masonry is weaker. And while it is not as exquisite as the first façade, it is even less durable than it looks. From the outside, it appears lovelier, better, and stronger than it is. Like the first façade, it has a door in the middle, but this one is easier to pass through. The doorway is handsome and pleasant enough, but it is not durable, and the door is not plastered. The entry is larger than on the first side, about three times as big, and it seems like those who arrive at this side will never be able to enter in a timely way. I do not know how they live, because there is such a crowd trying to get in, and they all smother each other so much that I do not know how they do not suffocate, or how they manage to get inside. The door-keeper there is more courteous than the other one. Whoever goes to the door that this one guards, as long as great poverty does not keep him from it, can enter without difficulty and easily find lodging in the castle according to his status, although it is not to everyone's liking.

2411–2458

Now I will tell you about the door-keeper who is noble of heart and perfect for her type, gentle, compassionate, and without pride. I want to tell you about her manner, ways, and behavior that have made many hearts rejoice. She is a very high princess, a powerful queen and a grand mistress, and she is of grander stature than any other so great or wise, with lovely broad shoulders, a wide lower back, and low hips, generous and well formed through the sides. She is not at all misshapen in her clothing, but nor is she elegant. She is dressed in a large tunic, blue intermingled with gold, flecked with several colors. Her adornment is very appealing, simple, pleasing, and respectable. She has a nice-sized and very well formed face, without a doubt, white and blushing like a rose in May. When she looks at people directly, her expression lifts them from their troubles. They have no reason to fear ill, because she protects them from harm. She has a very pleasing

expression, and her sweet countenance well shows that she is a friend to all, be-
cause she laughs with everyone all the time. She attacks no one. Rather, she wants
everyone to have what he desires, right or wrong. And no one will ever fail at that
because of her—other people's wishes please her at every step.

She is called Lady Hope, and she is greatly loved by all, loved! And who
would not love her? People would be lost if she did not exist. They could not live
without her. She delivers them from evil, and does immense good. Nothing else
in the world comforts people so much. Many would be dead from grief and would
die every day if she did not exist.

2459–2508

She constantly comforts people, without resting, and bolsters hearts with joy. She
consoles the sick, for whom foods are bland, promising them she will cure their
illness very quickly and assuring them that they will not die. And she makes the
dying, who aspire to God's grace, hope for paradise, asking for mercy for their
misdeeds. He who does not have Hope will never go to heaven. She reassures
all people. She promises gold and silver, honors, status, and fiefdoms. She makes
chivalrous exploits happen, has great esteem accorded to great lords, and makes
people take on difficult, seemingly impossible challenges. Because of her, people
bear troubling situations lightly and with great joy, and undertake long journeys.
She also makes them fight over the lands of lords and start wars, and she promises
the best to all.

Lady Hope concerns herself with everything, high and low. She does not
forget the enterprising, and she gives courage to the brave, but she hates the cow-
ardly very much. She finds nothing impossible to do. She brings many significant
and difficult things to a positive conclusion, at great hardship, hoping to bring
them to fruition. It is a marvel—whatever people do, it is Hope who makes it
happen. But whoever believes in her completely often buys much more on credit
than he could repay; there are few people who have yet to try that. One would do
well to value Hope, who allows a person to lead a pleasant life, even if he has little
possibility of doing so. But her strongest promises are often lies, and many find
themselves deceived by the path on which she has set them. Many have become
aware of it too late, having made such bad decisions that they wound up dead or
ruined because of it.

XII. *Here is told of the lady who guards the second door*

2509–2560: *All who come to the castle rely on Lady Hope, and she refuses no one
passage. Evil Mischance can still turn people away, however, at his whim. Lady Hope
does not stay at her door, but moves among the people, comforting them and prom-
ising them good fortune, which she cannot in fact guarantee.*

XIII. *Here is told of the poor people who are at the third door*[25]

2561–2584

Now I have told what, in my view, I saw at the two beautiful façades, and of the construction of the two doorways, which were not made by masons. I will tell you about the third. I sighed when I saw it, because never in my life had I seen anything I could have desired less. It has no handsome wall, no attractive wood. Rather, it is uglier than anything, very dilapidated and cracked, old, split apart, and in ruins. The wall is low and demolished, broken in many places, replastered with new plaster, but the whole thing is worthless! It has one door right in the middle that suits the place well enough—it is very ugly, black, and broken (and there is nothing that reeks so much when sniffed), but it is extraordinarily big and wide. Many a wretched vigil is held there, where poor people who have no bread, wine, or money gather.

2585–2626

A lady guards the door, and she has no fear of thieves. Poverty is her name; she is loved by no one. She is very ugly and pale. She seems utterly weakened by destitution, cold, and hunger, and she cannot help but tremble. I do not know how the cold does not kill her in winter, because she is very meagerly dressed in thin clothes, and has no cloak or garment but an old, flimsy dress, all ripped to pieces. And she does not have any underclothes. Through her chemise, her flesh appears to be withering all over, dark, dry, and very close to the bones. And I believe that she gets little rest—whether she accepts it willingly or not, she has only a little straw under a stair to sleep on, no other prepared or valuable bed. The house is wretched and smoky, with a little fire creating a lot of smoke. There is nothing but poverty.

    She has such a bad reputation, with all her other adversity, that anyone would rather nearly lose his head than visit her. I have no doubt that no one would want to frequent that place; rather, they would flee it more than an epidemic that

---

25. On Christine's attitudes toward the lower social strata, see Giovanna Angeli, "Charité et pauvreté chez Christine de Pizan," in Hicks, Gonzalez, and Simon, *Au champ des escriptures*, 425–38; Angeli, "Figure della povertà da Boezio a Christine de Pizan," *Rivista di letterature moderne e comparate* 49 (1996): 143–60; Susan J. Dudash, "Christine de Pizan and the 'menu peuple,'" *Speculum* 78 (2003): 788–831; Dudash, "Christine de Pizan's Views of the Third Estate," in Kennedy et al., *Contexts and Continuities*, 2:315–30; Dudash, "Christinian Politics, the Tavern, and Urban Revolt in Late Medieval France," in Green and Mews, *Healing the Body Politic*, 35–59; Otto Gerhard Oexle, "Christine et les pauvres," in Zimmermann and de Rentiis, *City of Scholars*, 206–20; Pierre André Sigal, "Christine de Pizan et le peuple," in Kennedy et al., *Contexts and Continuities*, 3:811–28; and Brian Woledge, "Le thème de la pauvreté dans la *Mutacion de Fortune* de Christine de Pisan," in *Fin du Moyen Âge et Renaissance: Mélanges de philologie française offerts à Robert Guiette* (Antwerp: Nederlandsche Boekhandel, 1961), 97–106.

terrifies many. Poverty is feared even more still because nothing frightens anyone as much. Many people wind up in hell because their fear of being poor pushes them to acquire numerous ill-gotten gains. Thus they kill themselves with their own two hands, because it is better to have less or to be poor for a little while than to lose paradise forever.

On this same topic

2627–2666

Ancient Poverty is the guardian of this door. But this place and this door-keeper are so hideous that no one would go in that direction or would pass through her door if Mischance did not push them in there with great force, by the order of my lady, who spares no one in this situation. Mischance does his hunting there, and you must know that he, his aides, and his servants chase all kinds of people to this place, people of all social stations, noble or not, and many an important person of great renown. He batters them so much, and makes so many people wind up there, that unless one already knew it, one would not believe that there were so many poor people in the world. And still new ones are made every day. Those who do their whim the best on earth[26] chase them to this place and pursue this for them. The people arrive there in forced marches, with their clothing all in disarray, and they have no small change or coin, bread or wine, grain in the granary, or clean place to lodge. They dearly need the hospitals that, fortunately, were created by good rich people in spite of Mischance, to accommodate the lowly, poor, naked, indigent masses. And may God wish to lodge them in heaven, all those who established those hospitals back then and who saved for charity! Such wealth reserved for God was well earned.

On this same topic

2667–2700

This door is besieged by people whom the world despises. They are the disparaged poor, and there are some with maimed and injured limbs, completely out of their senses. There are those people, and there are great numbers of the sick, pale in color, the blind and crippled, others shrunken with illness, widows, and orphans, who have no money, ovens, or mills, no granary, land, or dwelling. (Mischance took everything from them, leaving them worth less than two crumbs.) And their fathers were once well employed and of high standing. There are masses of such people who have entered into poverty, even well educated clerks. Many go there on crutches. Acquaintance with such people is valued little; they are but vermin. Should one give them a coin or some change, they consider themselves

---

26. That is, Mischance and his cohorts.

well paid—they are satisfied with very little. All who arrive there pass through Poverty's very unfortunate door. There are many who strive not to go through it, but Mischance carries them there, whether they like it or not, and drives them in, even many who had been rich!

2701–2730

But do not think that Hope, who pushes the enterprising forward, forgets the poor people there. Rather, if they are not handsome or pleasing, she comforts them first. Their suffering would be too harsh if she did not exist, and she comes to console them and chase away their ills. She serves them according to their status. She does not make them hope for high social standing, great riches, or great wealth, but only to live near the rich and have some leftovers from their tables. Without having to put themselves to great pains, they will be able to beg today as they did yesterday, and thus live day to day, with well-served Wealth sending them a little bit of her portion. And Lady Hope will guide the richest, even if they are stingy or miserly now, making whoever gives alms or does something good for the poor hope for heaven. In that hope, by having such an aim, the rich will do good for the poor. And thus the poor are often encouraged and reassured by Hope, making their misfortune much less painful to bear.

XIV. *Here is told of the fourth façade and doorway of the castle, and of the doorkeeper*

2731–2770

Now I will speak of the fourth façade. But I do not know how I can describe its appearance precisely, because no one would be able to express the frightening horror of the place. It is so terrible that people passing by would be rendered paranoid and put completely out of their senses if God, in his great mercy, did not extend them the kindness of keeping them in his faith. All would be driven to unbelief, as this façade is so horrible and gloomy, terrifying and shadowy, that nothing so dark is of human creation. And the wall there is so very low, and the building so degraded that it barely holds itself up, and it often happens that the wall falls into large and small pieces. And the people who pass that way are naked; one sees them wearing nothing. The place would quickly collapse on this side, but Nature rightly keeps the castle in the desired state, maintaining it by her power, and rebuilding it often. But with a little wind, it all falls down. Yet the whole castle is propped up on this side, and entirely leaning on this façade that erases worldly glory. There is a narrow door in the middle of the wall, so low that many have moaned, lamented, and wept at the horror of passing through it. There is no other small passage through which it would be so distressing to go.

2771–2810

As terrible as this place is, there is an equally horrible door-keeper. Never before has there been anything more terrifying to see, and this is no fable, nor anything that would naturally horrify any creature so much. Her appearance is very odious. I can never fully describe it, nor am I skilled enough to precisely depict every one of her characteristics, which are replete with horrible traits. Her body and her aspect are utterly horrifying to see. It is not that her body is deformed at all; it is just as Nature made it. But it is so terribly loathsome compared to how it once was that nothing has ever been so weak or so pallid. She has a face the color of dirt, the mouth open with the teeth overlapping one on top of the other, the lips pale and dry, the eyes murky and crossed, half open and rolled back, the nose ashen and pointy, the face anguished and sullen, showing signs of great suffering. She is all discolored and dark in color, and so skinny—bony, I dare say—that in the whole body there is nothing but bones, and the skin is so tight that one could count them, without miscounting. She has a high, bony chest. And since there are no bones there, it seems that someone sewed the skin from her belly right to her back. It is very empty, flat, and caved in, and it collapses more and more every day.

2811–2853

This creature lies there, and she has no dress or cover, only a single thin garment, however cold the weather may be. She lies outside the door, which is misshapen and twisted. She is paid by the tax that one must render at this passage. The door-keeper is called Atropos, to speak in a metaphorical way; that is what the poet named her.[27] This is the place that puts an end to everything. It is the very last door of the castle and the main exit, but no one makes it through there without sweating from the anguish of doing so. No one can use this passage to enter the castle, however. No panniers, parcels, or people, be they dressed or naked, enter there. No one has ever entered through this door, but all, male and female, from wherever they are, leave the castle this way.

Everyone owes the tax there, and neither king nor prince has an advantage. All people are in this servitude, however great an effort one might make to put off the day. Every creature born must leave by this door, even though everyone attaches greater importance to this displeasure than all others, because one must pay and settle accounts. It becomes clear there who has saved and toiled profitably, because in passing through that door, one takes away only the good that one has done, nothing more. He who has committed many misdeeds has a lot to worry about, because if at this end point he does not gain forgiveness, it will be too late.

---

27. One of the three Fates, associated with death. The poet is Ovid.

2854-2874

Some believe that they will be granted grace just in time. But they may fail in that and leave through there suddenly, without the luxury of making reparation for their misdeeds and asking for pardon. The time spent there is not pleasant, because no one knows what day or at what hour he will have to pass through the door, where a man carries away nothing but his deeds. For fear of death, it is a good thing to live as one would want to die! People go out through this place, frequently and quickly, completely naked, taking nothing with them when they leave. One can well divide up their wealth, because they will never use any of it. Whoever departs from there abandons it all. There are people leaving the castle from that door at all times, but the departure is arduous for anyone who does not have God on his side!

XV. *Here is told how the beautiful façade of the castle is constructed*

2875-2910: *Christine turns her attention back to the first façade. There is a great and extraordinarily beautiful courtyard, with high buildings around it, in which people are lodged according to their status. Many marble stairways lead upward.*

2911-2937

There are beautiful windows on all sides, large, wide, and well carved. All are crafted with sculpted leaves and large, paneled circular embellishments over paned windows. There are towers and turrets in abundance, galleries and attic lofts, well equipped with barbicans. More than one hundred thousand chimneys dot the houses, I believe, and none so beautiful have ever been seen. There are crenels, galleries, and very beautiful private rooms, gilded apple-shaped finials that are just right, and emblazoned banners on the houses, fluttering in the wind. I do not believe that anyone has ever seen as many as are there, or any as beautiful, or so many new blazons. Why am I telling you about it? I would more easily have dried up a river by drawing water than I would have fully described and informed you about the magnificence and the appearance of this place. In short: there is no greater beauty in this world, nor earthly goods so plentiful.

2938-2959: *The palaces differ in beauty and value, but none compare to one in particular, notable for its high keep.*

2960-3004

There has truly never been a more exquisite structure to see, because it was built with such great skill and so finely made that it seemed to all people, great and lowly alike, that the highest point touched the clouds. It is so high that one cannot see the top at all if the sun does not shine just so. Still, even someone who tries can barely get a good look at it. Because of the castle's great height, its shadow is seen more than a thousand leagues away when the sun cloaks it. And while it may be high, handsome, and straight, most of all it seems strong, and of unfailing and sure durability. Even if I were not to stop speaking, I would not have the power to describe the magnificence of the stonework, design, workmanship, architectural motifs, and lovely gilding, because they are nothing if not miraculous. It is greatly renowned because Wealth dwells there. It is right that she be well lodged, because such a castle is suitable for no one but this lady. There is incomparable beauty here (what a shame that it is not lasting!). From this side, the castle is extremely pleasant and agreeable. Yet there is no one who would perceive from this side, however keenly he might examine it, the incomparable marvels at the castle, or the edifice which is well behind it. That is because of the great and tall buildings that Wealth had very well laid out there (not for the poor), that block the view of the lower ones.

XVI. Here is told of the four paths to climb to the heights of the castle and what they are called, starting with the first one

3005–3044

In that great court described above, where only the rich can live, there are numerous winding staircases—just as I said, because I saw them—and enough steps to climb to the high palaces. But I want to tell you about the names, construction, appearance, height, width, and features of the four principal ones. The first is called Great Pride. It is very close to the door where Wealth entertains herself. It is marvelously big and wide, and so high that there is no lodging that it does not reach, even in the highly prized castle keep, all the way to the highest one. Wealth had this path made, and it is evident that she lives there, because the steps are all of fine gold from the foot to the end.

This stairway is often climbed by those who have first been placed on it by Luck, which makes many feel overly secure. There are multitudes of such people, and they are often heard complaining about climbing to the highest levels. But whoever climbs up there descends again. There is a vast throng at the departure, and an even greater one at the descent, because it happens that this path has a very strange nature: anyone able to climb this path high enough to reach ever-higher palaces, provided that he does not falter, would justifiably believe himself so highly placed that everyone would be beneath him and completely subjugated to his will.

3045–3072

But one thing turns many of these climbers away: when the wind shifts. That is because my lady has another sister, aside from Wealth, who cannot on any account witness good coming to anyone (she has a very evil nature!). She has such tremendous jealousy toward those who lead a good life, and who are rich, satisfied, and fulfilled, that she cannot see them clearly—thus she is called Envy. She has plotted, arranged, and carried out many a treachery. She can create a bad ending, because there is no hardship she will not cause, and no good or peace that she does not erase. Her ways are very contemptuous and her nature pitiless. I am not looking to describe her otherwise, or to tell you more about her appearance. Ovid depicts her well, accurately, and notably in his great, renowned book called *The Metamorphoses*. Whoever would like to know about her appearance and her manner can read of them there, and will find her in the fable of Mercury, if he cares to.

3073–3108: *Allied with Mischance, Envy looks unfavorably on the climbers and relishes making them fall down, never to emerge from the depths.*

XVII. *Here is told of the second path*

3109–3136
I saw another path to the left, but whoever wants to climb up that way and go by that path has to be a master of Great Malice! That one is marvelously covered, not by branches, not by leaves, but by an obscure covering, so hidden that if one did not know of it already, one would perceive it barely or not at all.

Good God! How strange that path is! All the steps are scattered with worms and serpents with crests of gold, or with three heads, along with a great deal of strange vermin. So whoever travels that way to get to the highest levels must take great care and be wise, and must place his foot correctly, or else he would be better off being run through by a pike. No man has ever run there quickly. Rather, it is necessary to climb very calmly and carefully. This path is less frequented than any other by half. Lady Envy is the fore-guard of it, and keeps a close eye on the climbers.

3137–3153: *Many undertake to climb this dangerous path because it can lead to the highest point.*

3154–3180
This path, where treachery often lies, is called Great Malice. Many seeking to climb to the castle keep make use of it, with unfortunate consequences—they are often knocked down lower than diving loons (it is true!). For those who use treachery, no good can come of it in the end; one sees it happen often. But whoever can climb high by Great Malice does whatever he wants, as long as Luck is helpful to him and Lady Fortune kind! The two paths just mentioned, called Great Malice and Great Pride, which are so high, grand, and extraordinary, go along the whole extent of the first two beautiful façades and descend to the latter ones. But that is by a dangerous path, more slippery than any parchment. One cannot climb high from the two shadowy façades that are black and gloomy, but one descends

there in one fell swoop, because there are wide and open paths exclusively for descending.

XVIII. *Here is told of the third path*

3181–3213
Far from the others, on the right-hand side, there is a path where many endeavor to climb, night and day, in order to reach higher levels. But passing there is not easy, because this custom is in effect on this side: one must subdue, with great difficulty, a very wild, fierce, exceedingly formidable, and terrifying serpent. It is the one once subdued by Cadmus at the fountain at Thebes.[28] It has left many dejected and contrite. If this serpent is not subdued, the loser will never have the power to climb up that way. Whoever vanquishes the serpent, however, finds this path so agreeable and pleasant, so delightful and appealing, so sweet-smelling, so lovely, that there is no melancholy so deep that the traveler would not forget it there. It is neither too hot there nor too cool. The grass grows green, fresh, and beautiful, along with many new flowers of white, violet, vermillion, blue, and many other colors, fresh roses, and fleurs-de-lys. All delights and all elegant things are found there, even precious stones that give off great light.

3214–3242
Any bad tree is pulled out, and all good plants are cultivated. There is no precious, newly grafted fruit tree that is not there expressly, and the balsam tree grows there as well. It is an extremely delightful garden. There is none in the world so remarkable, and there are so many stairs that it climbs to the highest heights. In short, what can I tell you about the place? It seems like an earthly paradise. The springs there are gushing, with a great abundance of streams emanating out over the whole world. I believe, may God grant me pardon, that nothing more pleasant or better arranged exists in this world. This path is very sure. Mischance cannot obstruct it, nor can evil Fortune or Envy. As long as it exists, this path will guide whoever climbs it to the highest buildings. This one is called Great Knowledge. It is of very noble renown, but it is hardly frequented at all, because of the evil magic serpent that deprives many of the passage. Whoever goes that way must be wise.

XIX. *Here is told of the fourth path*

3243–3287
There is another path, even more perfect and made by the hands of God. He shaped it with his right hand, and it rises all the way to the highest place in the

---

28. Cadmus was the mythological founder of Thebes, credited with having slain a terrible serpent which itself had killed several of Cadmus's men.

castle and runs through it, penetrating through the very highest summit. It even pierces the sky, rising to such a height that anyone taking it sees God face to face. This path leads all who climb it up to heaven, guiding God's favored ones along with the holy chosen saints. This path is the highest one of all, and the most beautiful and valuable, because there is no earthly thing or worldly adornment that would make a place comparable to the beauty of this stairway. But Jesus, who climbed up there himself and rose above all things, deliberately made it narrow.

The eye has never seen anything so beautiful! It is more brilliant than the sun, brighter than a star or light. Nothing in this world is as precious, dear, or dignified, nor is anything so sweet to see. It is the Path of Paradise. Saint Peter and the pope of Rome climbed up that way in the past, along with others whom I will not name here for the sake of brevity. But they endured a great deal of pain in doing so, because no one can imagine how narrow this path is, even though it is high and straight. It is not ugly or horrifying, but it is so steep and difficult that there is hardly anyone who strives to climb that way, because everyone so fears the struggle that the climb would entail.

3288–3314

Still, one hears few people complain about climbing this path. Alas! Whoever willingly accepts the arduousness of this stairway for a while is filled with joy. One does not attain great goodness at no cost, and he who wisely seeks to progress must pay a high price for that which elevates his worth so greatly. This path has a name: Just Life. Too few people desire it. And even if one does many praiseworthy things, one would be unable to do enough to buy or rent this passage. Whoever does not go that way is imprudent! Prelates once climbed by this path that I am telling you about, even to my lady's castle keep. But nowadays, no one climbs up there. The Holy Spirit led the Holy Church then, and guided the pastors, who did the will of God, up this stairway. Many popes, and other prelates who occupied the seats of the prelacy, climbed that way by true and holy intention.

On this same topic

3315–3344: *Many other paths stem from these four, leading to the middle and lower levels, as Fortune and Luck see fit. Christine will now turn her attention to the second side of the building, toward which Hope always urges people, from all the paths. Some endure hardship as a result, because Hope makes things look easy even if they are in fact very difficult.*

XX. *Here is told of the building on the second side*

3345–3364: *Those who enter through this door find a large space, agreeable but less extravagant than the surroundings of Wealth. There are common areas, as well as lodgings at different levels, with stairs to climb to them.*

3365–3390

Sects and faiths from many walks of life are there, along with great cloisters and abbeys for all religions and from all regions. There are fine and beautiful abbeys for all sorts of nuns who do God's service, each according to her office, as well as chapels, temples, and monasteries. I could not even tell you a fraction of it. There would have been still more of them, if everyone were to do his duty. There are cloisters with priests and canons, and priories for all monks, greater and lesser, and for all brothers and sisters. There are archpriests' houses, cloisters, presbyteries, cells, and hermitages of all kinds, rough, cramped, and simple. There are humble little houses, but they are very pretty and clean, harmoniously arranged and very nicely constructed, some poorer, some richer, and others that are not worth two crumbs.

3391–3420

There are also very lovely manors that are handed down from heir to heir. Anyone else who possesses one does so wrongfully. These houses are not all adjoining, nor do they resemble each other. They are actually very dissimilar. Whoever built this made a very diverse place, which should please anyone who is content to be lodged according to his status. But do not think that it satisfies anyone, because the very wide path of Great Pride is there, just as it is at the dwelling place of Lady Wealth, who made it. But as much as tin is worth less than gold, this path does a great deal more ill on this side than on the other. That is because it is not as well gilded or rich, or as highly esteemed, because the steps there are of mud, adorned with deception and grimaces. There are great crowds of people climbing and descending, very cramped. Great Malice is very wide there, along with Great Deception, that protects it. Great Knowledge is hardly known there, because the serpent repels too many, and Just Life is hidden, even though it may hold much goodness.

XXI. *Here is told of the building on the third side*

3421–3462

The castle gets worse from this point. From here on, I can describe the two ugly façades. I sigh in doing so because it would fill happy hearts with rage just to think about them, as it would any living person who would pass by the miserable door of Poverty. That is how horrifyingly ugly these façades are. The Fifteen-Twenties,[29] with their badly oiled shoes, are not far from there. They are blind, in poverty, and they suffer a great deal of hardship! Some poor people have it even worse, with ailments in the body and chest. Miseries are manifest there.

The houses there are uncovered, dark, black, and oozing, low, ugly, and collapsing, cracked and replastered, with low and wretched entryways. They are ugly in back and front, and the wind comes in from all sides. They are without doors, without windows, and without hinges. And there is no oven there, no fire iron, nothing made to warm people. In lieu of a fireplace, one sees a miserable pit in a niche. But with the wind coming in from behind, a little smoldering from straw or a tiny bit of coal fills the house completely with smoke. So there is nothing good in there. Thieves cannot do harm in that place. There is nothing to drink or to eat, save perhaps a few scraps of what other people do not want. There is little to put on one's feet or to wear as clothing, and there is much suffering to experience. And God knows, it is terribly cold in there as long as winter lasts, because a person so badly attired must certainly feel the frost.

3463–3494

And there is worse, because the sun is always setting there, non-stop. On no day does it shine fully, on hill or plain. The place is damper as a result, bad for sciatic gout. There are miserable streets, wretched houses, little children, women, old men, maladies, sicknesses, all painful ills, and all hardships. The great path of Pride comes to an end there. Great Malice has little welcome, and Knowledge is in little favor. But Just Life is found in such a dwelling, in many places, however poor and old the place may be! Why would I go on telling you about it? I would bore you as you read if I were to recount all of their ills. It is displeasing to many people to hear it described, but not for the pity they would have because of it. Rather, they are convinced that by rights they have wealth, gold, and silver, so poor people are of little concern to them! But one should have pity for the poor, and, for God's sake, show them friendship, because they are flesh just as we are, our fellow women and men. And God himself commands us to do it and proclaims it in Scripture: "Blessed be he who does good for them and who will offer them alms!"[30]

---

29. Reference to three hundred blind people residing at the *Hospice des Quinze-vingts* (Hospice of the Fifteen-Twenties) in Paris, established in 1256 by the charitable King Louis IX (Solente, *Mutacion,* 1:162, note to lines 3429–32). This institution still exists today as a national ophthalmology center.

30. Solente cites Ecclesiasticus 11: 23–24 (Vulgate <http://vulgate.org/ot/ecclesiasticus_11.htm>) as the source for these lines (*Mutacion,* 1:162, note to lines 3492–94). Other equally possible sources could be Proverbs 22:9, Psalms 41:1, and Acts 20:35, all of which stress the virtue of giving to the needy.

XXII. *Here is told of the fourth side of the building*

3495–3526
Now comes the last door, which takes away all things. The hand of the flayer is there, and no cheater's deception counts. All must leave this way, often without the chance to get old. It is the door of Atropos, where there is no joy or repose. This is the castle's exit, where everyone leaves his property. There is no pleasant place, no handsome lodging. Rather it is so black and dark that one cannot see anything at all there. The lodgings are miserable, in ruins, and demolished, so low that whoever passes through there on foot could not remain standing, as one might expect. And it is also so bitterly cold that a person becomes stiff as marble there in a short time, blackened and dark like a blackberry. There is no one who does not freeze from cold there, because it always rains, snows, and ices over. And everyone's eyes have a hard time, because neither the sun nor the moon shines, and one does not know where one is going because it is impossible to see even one bit. The place is so dark and murky that all vision gets blurred. The place is horrifying, more dreadful than anything.

XXIII. *Here is told of what people are lodged in these buildings*

3527–3538
And now it is fitting for me to relate, according to what I best came to understand, who and what are housed in these abodes and lodgings, and what dwellings are inside, even though they may be collapsing in areas. I will speak of the first two at least, and leave aside the other two, because talking about them too much can be more bothersome than rain after good weather. It makes the heart rejoice very little, and therefore it bothers many to hear it.

3539–3560: *The castle keep houses a great number of rooms of various sizes, adorned with the finest furnishings and décor.*

3561–3600
The greatest lodgings are there, for the highest lords, popes, emperors, and kings, for their accoutrements and their retinue, for prelates of the Holy Church, and for all princes, some higher, others less so. But all of their lodgings are, at the least, big, wide, and spacious, splendid, lovely, and luxurious. All the princes who have lived, who live now, and who will always be are all very richly lodged there—of whatever faith, from wherever they may be, whether they be pagan or Saracen,[31] or of another religion, however savage it may be, from all countries, of all languages. Prester John of Greater India is there, as well as the great Khan who is keen to

---

31. "Saracen" denoted an Arab or Muslim, particularly during the Middle Ages.

bring down Christianity, and the Sultan (who will never have salvation!).[32] They possess great property there, as do the kings of Media and Persia, and many others from different lands. Their dukes and all their military commanders are there, and all princes like them who are spread out around the world, for as long as the world lasts, be they on this side of the sea or beyond (surely it is not necessary for me to name them all). All the princesses, empresses, noble duchesses, and great crowned queens are there, all arranged according to a similar order as the princes. Their lodgings are organized by level. Thus the rich domains are all taken by these noble people, and each one is lodged according to his station.

3601–3658

But these princes of whom I speak here, who are held in great esteem in the world, did not climb recently to my lady's high castle keeps (by my soul!). Rather, they were born there, and their ancestors reigned there in great honor. I do not know who led them there, but many have been there since ancient times. And others (I do not know who) were put there by Luck, who was their friend. Whoever was willing climbed there by one of the above-mentioned stairways. That was according to how it pleased my lady to choose, at her will, to put a certain one in the high places, and to dismiss another. She does that very often; fools and wise men should know it. That was often the case for the prelates' seats, because she seats many, high and low, as it best suits her; I remember it well. She does it more now than ever before—the Holy Spirit no longer works there! It is up to her to bestow the places and to arrange the whole thing, and many climb there by the path of Great Pride or by the hidden Great Malice, at her will, not for their just deserts.

But even though many princes, reigning in many regions, were born in these places and not led there by chance, should they not all keep in mind that they are often vilely dismissed and reduced to the very lowest low? Because my lady, who made and established the edifice, very maliciously set it up so that it is very dark in places, and even though the wooden floors are very rich and expensive, and all seem to be seated on vaults without a bad crack or underground pit, there are big openings in them. One does not see holes, doors, trapdoor, or trap, until one finds oneself at the hatch, because they are obscured by covers that one notices only by chance. If Mischance guides a person to that place, the person might as well give away whatever possessions he has, because he will never see them again.

32. "Prester John" was a legendary Christian leader of a kingdom said to have been in India or Ethiopia. The "great Khan" refers to the Central Asian conqueror Timur (reigned 1370–1405). The Sultan of Egypt in Christine's day was Nasir-ad-Din Faraj (reigned 1399–1412, with a two-month interruption in 1405 when his brother temporarily took power); see Solente, *Mutacion,* 1:162–63, notes to lines 3577, 3578, and 3580.

3659–3694

Even a prince of high lineage will never have any advantage here. Because if he sets his foot on an opening, he will fall to the depths of the tower as if he were smitten by a pike, and he will have no way to get out. He will be led to prison by my lady, and so mistreated by Mischance, who holds the keys, that he will never leave from the door. He will be so afflicted that he would want death one hundred times more. And thus it happens, without reason, often by betrayal. Another takes his place, thanks to Luck, and my lady will offer that one many benefits and allow him to dominate for a certain time. But just when he most believes he can exercise control over his throne according to his will, he will come shamefully tumbling down by Great Pride, by which he had risen to begin with. And he will no longer be guided by Luck, who will have sent him packing; rather, Mischance will accompany him back. There were often such people on the path of the two ugly doors, where all joys are dead. There, one is put in the prisons of Poverty by great misfortune, or ignominiously chased out of the castle in grief and damnation by the rear door, where no daylight or light are seen.

XXIV. *Here is told how the safest place is in the middle of the castle-keep*

3695–3726: *While the middle of the keep may be the most secure place, still it shakes and sways violently in the wind. A fall from that high place would be extremely perilous. A fall from lower down would be less so, but the lowest part of the tower has its own problems—dark and damp, its crumbling walls ooze moisture.*

3727–3740

The place is cold and harsh because it is close to the sea. Nevertheless, it endures and holds its own. It is often necessary to do masonry work, because the wind or the great tide from the sea, which batters against it and gravely undermines it, would otherwise knock it all down. However, the prophecy announcing the coming of Christ says that this castle will be completely burned and struck by fire all over. It will all be set to fire and flame, sparing neither man nor woman.[33]

XXV. *Here is told of the crowds comprising all the people at the second door*

3741–3756: *Christine returns her focus to the area where Hope receives the crowds and keeps them occupied.*

3757–3782

That place is very crowded, even though it is not small or narrow, because many people are there from all walks of life: multitudes of knights and nobles, clerks

---

33. Isaiah 9:19.

and bourgeois of all sorts, merchants of all goods, provosts, bailiffs, and officers, judiciary from all kinds of courts where plaintiffs have recourse, and a greater community of academics than were ever in any town or country, whichever it may be. Lady Hope willingly receives municipal police, bailiffs carrying ceremonial batons, court officers, officers of all functions, and others who have benefits off which some live bountifully, others meagerly. But she disappoints more than a third of them. Thus the poor and the rich are there, and many who do not have assets valuing two crumbs but who lead their lives here, there, and everywhere. And all these diverse and very different kinds of people want the best situations.

3783–3820

People of all occupations are found there, and there is a need for them. The great power of those who forge money from gold and silver with various stamps, and who stamp works of various metals into coins, is essential there. There are numerous stalls for all occupations—forging, goldsmithing, blacksmithing, and for armor-makers and harness-metal workers who beat iron to make nails and other small items. And there are others who lath the houses and hammer without stopping, and carpenters who cut up wood. Masons and roofers who make houses toil there in all seasons. There is a great need for that, because this place is not fully intact.

Silk fabrics are worked there, as well as fabrics of gold and silver, and all jewels with which people adorn themselves. There are many very lovely ones, and every single day more are made, in beautiful new styles. There are sendals,[34] rich twill silks, precious silk-cotton moiré cloth, and all fabrics used to make sumptuous, luxurious, and elegant silk clothing. There are more there than in Constantinople. All works of silk are made there, embroideries and fabrics with open stitch-work, gold-embroidered trim, fringes, ribbons, and cloths. And fine fabrics are woven, top-quality colored fabrics, fabrics with needlework, tapestries from Arras[35] with images on them, tablecloths, fine-textured cloths, and heavy ones for household use.

3821–3852

There is tableware of gold and silver, rich jewels that are lovely and elegant, fancy clasps and crowns, hats, rings, fine belts, clothing trimmed in gold that is demanded by the rich, sumptuous and fine furs of vair,[36] gray squirrel, and ermine, and of other highly valuable pelts, and rich fabrics of great worth. There are miters,

34. Sendals: Fine silks used to make ceremonial robes and church vestments.

35. Arras: Town in northern France famous as a center of the medieval wool industry; the word "arras" came to denote a hanging tapestry or wall covering made of rich fabric.

36. Vair: Fur from a variety of squirrel which was blue-gray on the animal's back and white on its underbelly. Pelts were often sewn together in a pattern of alternating colors to form the linings of cloaks,

staffs, and clothing luxuriously made of gold, pearls, rubies, and other stones, and handsome adornments to decorate altars. No one would believe what they were like. There are reliquaries worked in gold with well polished stonework, crosses, censers, pyxes, plates of gold and silver, flat and raised images on gold plate, with many rich stones, innumerable other church accoutrements with great designs, dedicated to the service of God (those are put to the best use), and treasures of all kinds. Gold and silver extracted from mines are brought to this place, and Wealth sets them aside. She will hide them in her coffers, because she is accountable to my lady for them.

3853–3874: *Incalculable treasures are doled out by Wealth in varying portions, not always justly.*

3875–3904

Thus each has his part of the assets that Wealth apportions, because they are all distributed by her. As a result, many live in difficult situations and cannot gain any wealth even if they are good and wise. Above all, it is the great landowning lords who have more authority over this wealth than other people. Gold and silver pile up for them, because everyone, great and small, is bound to pay them tribute, and each person owes the lords a portion of his assets, by the right of prince and lord. All the greatest princes should therefore keep their people in peace, uphold justice and right, and defend their subjects from all enemies. Fortunate is the country, and happy are the people, who have a good and attentive lord, hardworking in every way, diligent in caring for his people with the counsel of the eldest, but sustaining wars with the young who can tolerate the difficulty better than the old. The counsel of the old is of greater value, however.

3905–3952

Praise belongs to such a prince, who loves his people and keeps them in peace. He should well be loved and called a righteous lord by his people, because one who is hated by his men is no lord to his country. The truth of this can be seen and understood through living examples. It is a true thing that to a good lord goes the great glory of having good subjects who love him, and who safeguard and revere his honor. It is security, it is a great assurance; whoever believes in this rests well assured. It is a strong and lasting tower, and an invulnerable castle. There is nothing in the world as strong as people who are loyal toward their lord. It is a passage that enemies will not penetrate. And because it is a wall too strong to break through, no one could breach it.

---

or mantles; the resulting design was adopted in heraldry. Vair is also mentioned in Book 3, chapter 8, lines 5537–38, stressing the material as a marker of status.

The lords have their treasurers and officers there, receiving agents and controllers, their tax officers, notaries, those who deliver, take, and receive what the lower people owe them. If they faithfully execute their functions, without treating the lesser needy people too roughly, and they are diligent and painstaking in doing their duty at all times, they should be praised and rewarded for it. But if they do otherwise, they lose their way, and are condemned by the wealth that they keep.

Thus is the wealth of the world, but it is not all in one heap. Rather, it is divided in different ways. And if there is a lot of it there, you must understand that all the treasures of all the princes who have died, whether they were Trojan or Roman, or others who had no fewer riches, or Saracen, Jew, or pagan, and even the wealth of Octavian, have all been transported here and set aside in several places.

XXVI. *Here is told of the perils and misfortunes at the castle*

3953–3985

In this place that is common to all people, where wise men, fools, and madmen are all received, great and considerable marvels and incomparable occurrences often take place, because there are many extraordinary parts of it where everything is topsy-turvy. The Place of Chance is there. Whoever escapes from it safe and sound is fortunate! This is the castle where justice is lacking and danger is everywhere. There lies also the Perilous Abyss of the sea, so terrible that it swallows up any ship that heads toward these parts. Everything that goes near that abyss perishes. Everything sinks there, and all falls down into the deep sea, or completely smashes against hard magnetic rock that attracts iron and draws all the way to hell. There lies the great ocean, the Red Sea, and the Mediterranean, where many dangerous passages and difficult, harsh routes are found. The dangerous Charybdis is there, along with the terrifying Scylla, sea monsters and great whales, the passage of Circe and the Sirens, and isolated places hidden between rocks, where the wind shoves many ships that never set forth from there again.[37]

3986–4023

It is necessary for men to go out on the sea. They want to be protected, but many have perished there. There are islands with great horrible giants, and lands with terrible, big, and fierce serpents of many kinds, with many strange forms. There are dangerous savage monsters and frightening men with highly extraordinary bodies (their appearance is so strange it would be very difficult to describe them,

37. In Greek mythology, Scylla and Charybdis were sea monsters living on opposite sides of a narrow strait; the seductive Sirens reputedly caused ships to wreck by luring them to their island shores with music. Odysseus was able to make it past both dangers by heeding advice that he had received from Circe.

and so we will not attempt to). There are pygmies in a clearing in the forest, who are as small as a child at birth. They apply themselves well to pleasing works, and live for a short time. There are people of many teachings, and some who have ugly wide faces on their chests. Others have eyes like shields, a single eye in the middle of the forehead, and others have only one foot which they use to protect themselves from the sun (but nonetheless they move well on foot). There are frightening savage beasts and countless treacherous snakes of many kinds. There are so many such adventures, they are innumerable in this place that passes like a shadow. I do not know what more to say to you about it. I could no more tell you all about it than I could have drawn all the water from the sea since yesterday. The marvels of the world are found there, and whoever reads the *"Mirror of the World"* will find a great deal about it.[38]

4024–4042: *Mischance is found at this dangerous vortex where all the waters of the world converge, and where people are always at risk.*

4043–4088
This is the place of murder, war, and confusion, of rumors and great battles, of deceptions and lies, and of great hidden betrayals and terrible fights, of all ills and vices. There are very few naïve people there. Rather, they all put their efforts into knowing how to deceive one another. The path of Malice is hidden there under a deceptive furred cloak, and Great Pride has no bounds. The person without a penny who climbs there never thinks he will arrive fast enough. There is a great throng of climbers who ardently aspire to displace princes from their seats and take their place. Thus the climbers go there to assail them and are convinced they will destroy them. Wars are waged over this and many deadly captures are made. Even the most important men undertake them, and they often kill and capture each other, along with their close friends and their people. And they are zealous in their claim to those places that are so much lighter than corks.

There are violent rebellions of people prouder than lions, disloyal in deed and will. Rising up on Great Pride, they rebel against their princes. They want to dismiss and depose them, and elect others. There is no tumult like the wrath of a rebellious people. No more than mad dogs do they maintain rhyme, reason, harmony, pity, or mercy. They do not fear doing wrong. Good God! Such great destruction and dreadful devastation by people so worked up and stirred up against their prince!

---

38. *L'Image du monde* or *Mappemonde,* written by Maître Gossouin, also known as Gautier de Metz, in 1246: see Oliver H. Prior, ed., *L'image du monde de Maître Gossouin: Rédaction en prose* (Lausanne and Paris: Payot, 1913), and for this passage, see in particular 112, 130–32.

4089–4128

But such things often happen, and they generally go badly for those who act that way, because they so disgracefully misbehave. That is because there is no greater crime than a people against a lord, especially those who have lords by birth and not through tyranny, lords who treat them well and humanely, without cruelty, and to whom the people owe fealty according to the ancient rights of nobility. Such a prince should love his people and take up arms for them. If anyone wanted to attack them, he should be eager to defend them, like the shepherd would his sheep, without cruelty or unfair taxes.[39] Such a prince governs all of his people well, great and small. To pursue ill against him would be to seek their own destruction. But in many places, they do not uphold righteousness. Whoever dealt with them correctly would burn them, or cruelly destroy them with an ignominious death. But God holds punishment for them, and even though he may delay revenge, at least he defames them for it. They are forever labeled "bad," called "proven traitor," and hated and scorned by all. (And may God punish their physical body for their misdeed, according to the situation! May God pardon the soul!). No one should have any pity for a traitor who is the instigator of such wrongdoing. But now I will lay this aside, to focus on hastening my work.

4129–4158

There is no marvel that one does not see there. Some people are seen climbing up by a strange path, others descend. The one who is the lowest of the crowd is often situated at the highest point, even though it must be ill-suited for him. Luck and my lady place him there. And the one who does not have a bit or a dram of sense, or goodness of any sort, will often be raised highest of all. The person who is good, loyal, and wise, and who should be put ahead, will be dismissed and placed at the very bottom. At the same time, one sees servants becoming lords by being very diligent, and masters being demoted to the lowest condition. Thus the cloak is often turned inside-out, in summer and winter alike! Laments of great despair are heard—one because someone lost his possessions, another for some unfortunate circumstance or illness. Whoever has only one misfortune has no business complaining, as there are many who have several, or who suffer them because of cruel bad luck. So they cry, shout out, and lament for the very grievous torment they feel.

4159–4245: *Some use their skill to gain money, while others resort to deception, flattery, or thieving. The virtuous and the wicked, of all ages and estates, mingle in that place. The good people are what hold God back from sending another Flood, or plagues as in Egypt, but sudden vengeance could happen at any time. After all, Sodom and other cities were destroyed for their unrepentant sinning.*

---

39. This recalls the parable of the Good Shepherd, who "gives his life for the sheep" (John 10:11–15).

4246–4272

It once pleased God to announce through his prophet in the city of Nineveh,[40] which was of great nobility and which was rich, grand, and joyful, that "the city would be destroyed, and the people killed and wiped out for their ugly and horrible sins and their impermissible, base morals." But the king, who heard that sentence, repented deeply for his misdeeds, and prayed so much to God and cried out for mercy from his heart, with fasts and prayers, that God had pity and mercy on them. (All the people who heard it came out of their houses, each one holding his hands out to the sky, crying to God for mercy). Dressed in sackcloth, ashes on their heads, and fasting, they and their animals were very contrite and were so devoted that God, in his kindness and compassion, had pity on them. He told them through the prophet that they had made peace with him.

Explicit the second part of this book.

Here begins the third part of the book called
The Mutability of Fortune, *which talks about the places*[41]
and conditions of those who are lodged in the castle

I. *Here is told of the highest place*

4273–4308: *Having described the castle and the crowds gathered there, Christine wants to speak more about the inhabitants' situations according to their levels of status, from highest to lowest. She starts with the very top of the edifice, where Saint Peter had once ascended via the path of Just Life.*

4309–4334

This place is so narrow that two people are very cramped there, because it was only made for one. But in fact two occupy it.[42] So they are not comfortable at all.

---

40. Ancient capital of Assyria located on the site of present-day Mosul, Iraq. God's threat to destroy Nineveh, and the people's subsequent repentance, are the subject of the Old Testament Book of Jonah.

41. The word here is "siege," and its meaning is vague. Most literally, it means "seat." Christine also uses it to mean, more generally, position, place, or situation, often with the underlying notion of status. On the thirteenth-century *Jeu des échecs moralisés* (*The Moralized Game of Chess*) as a source for Book 3, see Solente, "*Jeu des échecs moralisés.*"

42. A reference to the Great Schism. The rival popes in place at the time Christine wrote this poem were Boniface IX in Rome and Benedict XIII in Avignon. On the Schism in this work, see Nadia Margolis, "Culture vantée, culture inventée," 299–304; Margolis, "The Rhetoric of Detachment in Christine de Pizan's *Mutacion de Fortune*," *Nottingham French Studies* 38 (1999): 170–81 <http://www.euppublishing.com/doi/abs/10.3366/nfs.1999-2.008>, at 178–79; and Gianni Mombello, "Quelques aspects de la pensée politique de Christine de Pizan d'après ses oeuvres publiées," in *Culture et politique en France*

In spite of their discomfort, however, the place satisfies and pleases them so much that neither one wants to hear talk of leaving it or going down to a lower position. Although each one knows that only one can sit there, neither of them would want to leave, and each one says that he has a right to it. I do not know whether the Holy Spirit put them on this level, or by which path they climbed, or how they situated themselves in there. I am waiting for what comes of it. But I know well that much ill arises from this. Thanks to the dispute between those two, there is such harm and grief that many people are angry, for the church should be but one. And this Schism makes people stray further from the tithe.

4335–4381

I see more than twenty-six people seated at the lower positions where the Apostles, who were agreeable to people, sat in the past. Each of the two above had placed some of them up there, at his will and desire, regardless of whom he would have pleased or hurt. And thus those two who lead the world astray had their people there, with their entourages and retinues, by the approval of certain kings who are in great conflict because of them. Some princes would like very much to enter into an accord, but there can hardly be an end to this if God, by his grace, does not see to it, because the wisest person can scarcely see his way clear!

As for their retinue, seated high and low on several levels, I do not know if I have ever seen more perfidious people than some of them. Of such servants one makes shepherds, who are really wolves and keen to devour flesh. Many of their servants are the sort who know well how to shear ewes at any time, indeed skin them. They have shepherd's clothing but they are lynxes, striking greater blows than clubs. And rumors circulate full-tilt about their being filled to overflowing with all manner of ambition, vice, evil sin, baseness, sacrilege, and simony, by which the whole world is dishonored. There are many among the counselors of princes who are fuller than cellars with wines and all excess of gluttony, debauchery, and all the deadly sins. And such people are the leaders of the world! It is no wonder that the limbs are deformed, twisted, and crooked when the high head is completely poisoned. One should not be shocked if the body beneath is of little value.

4382–4466: *Rapaciousness, cruelty, and murder are the order of the day. There are many such people in high places. Christine mentions the cases of Pope Urban VI and*

à l'époque de l'humanisme et de la Renaissance, ed. Franco Simone (Turin: Accademia delle Scienze, 1974), 75–80. Regarding miniatures depicting this section of the poem, see Millard Meiss, "Christine de Pisan: *La mutacion de Fortune,*" in *French Painting at the Time of Jean de Berry. The Limbourgs and Their Contemporaries* (New York: Pierpont Morgan Library, 1974), 1: 11–12 and 2: figures 23–28; and Barbara Wagner, "Tradition or Innovation? Research on the Pictorial Tradition of a Miniature in the *Mutacion*: 'Le plus hault siège,'" in Kennedy et al., *Contexts and Continuities*, 3:855–72.

the counselors of England.[43] *She questions the thinking and faith of people who damn themselves for money or glory, when life is short and hell is eternal. And these are the people who should be showing others how to do good and serve God! Christine does not speak of this in order to defame the "very noble angelic order" (4449–50) or anyone individually, but in hopes of shaming the guilty ones.*

4467–4480

There are surely many good people who are displeased that true unity and good morals are lacking this way. They are worthy, thoughtful men, who gladly serve God and place their hope in him. They lead a pleasant and good life, and ardently wish for the Schism to be eliminated, peace to be established, and this calamity to end. In fact I have heard mention of such good people, whom one should love— may God complete them in all good and grant that peace be made by them!

II. Here is told of the second place

4481–4514: *The second highest place was vacant at the time that this poem was written, and Christine had seen but one powerful prince there in her lifetime.*[44] *Christine condemns the lack of heart among potential leaders who could seize this throne and take charge. Meanwhile, many on nearby thrones have been troubled by Fortune.*

III. Here is told of the places toward the Orient and Africa, and others

4515–4554

There were several strange-looking places oriented directly toward the East, situated high up. I am not looking to take great account of their ways and their natures because they are not our concern. Closer to us, I saw a high seat, at the height of grandeur in the past, but Fortune had tormented and oppressed it with great battles. Long ago, Constantine in Byzantium held that throne in his power, but now it is greatly diminished.[45] I believe that is because its neighbors grew in a bad way. I have seen many places with much less value than they held in the past. Those who were seated there had little security; grieving and bewildered, they were often shoved aside by other people who climbed over them. But I am not

---

43. Urban VI (Bartolomeo Prignano), Pope 1378–89, was known for his vicious temper. The second reference is to the dethroning of Richard II (reigned 1377–99), by his cousin Henry of Lancaster; Richard died in captivity the following year (Solente, *Mutacion*, 2:335, notes to lines 4400 and 4401–2).

44. This refers to the throne of the Holy Roman Empire, which was not filled after Wenceslas of Bohemia was deposed in August 1400. The powerful leader alluded to here is Emperor Charles IV (reigned 1346–78), who preceded Wenceslas (Solente, *Mutacion*, 2:335, note to lines 4481–84, and 2:336, note to lines 4499–4502).

45. Constantine I the Great lived 272–337 CE.

thinking about discussing every one of them—I must move along to complete my work, because I would take too much time to finish it.

In a place surrounded by the sea, I heard about a knight wearing a crown who was highly reputed for voluntarily taking up arms.[46] He was praised for prowess. Indeed he was said to be a veritable Lancelot in feats of arms and battle. Nonetheless, Fortune made great trouble for him for more than a year, so much that I believe for certain that even his own people held him in prison, although I do not know why; I have thought little about his situation.

4555–4598

Toward Africa, there was also a place that was sent from the top to the bottom by many vessels armed with Roman forces.[47] I have not heard any glorification of any princes in renowned positions from among those people, who were little loved. Nor have I heard of them having great sense or truly loving chivalry and feats of arms. But I have certainly heard that some were accustomed to being governed by their wives. Since Hannibal stopped leading wars for them long ago, no such man has ever come from them.[48] Fortune, who never sleeps, made many strange things happen there, and made relatives kill each other to depose them from their ranks. She knows how to do that very well when she sets out to ruin a place. Let no one say anything against me about this, however—I am not saying that there are not numerous valiant people, diligent in their pursuit of arms. I have certainly seen many who have earned great glory in deeds of arms, who persevere, and who love and follow all good things.

The place where Venus was once queen[49] is now in great ruin. The person who had power over it, whom everyone esteemed for his generosity and considered good, was put to death by his own blood, in treachery and great wrong.[50] The place has hardly regained its power since. In the castle where Fortune dwells—she who knocks many down from high to low—there are plenty of such places where pleasures are erased. But in the interest of brevity I will pass on the topic of their joy or suffering.

---

46. A reference to Richard II (Solente, *Mutacion*, 2:336–37, note to lines 4541–54).

47. A reference to the defeat of Carthage (Solente, *Mutacion*, 2:336–37, note to lines 4555–72).

48. Hannibal, the Carthaginian military leader (247–182 BCE), is the focus of Book 7, chapters 13–23.

49. Venus, the Roman goddess of love, is said in one legend to have been born off the coast of Cyprus.

50. Peter I of Cyprus (Pierre I de Lusignan) was killed by his brothers in 1369 (Solente, 2:337, note to lines 4583–92). Christine recounts his life briefly in Book 7, chapter 54.

IV. *Here is told of the place of Italus*[51]

4599–4642

Oh, what will I say about the marshland where Italus once reigned, beyond the high Alps? Where once the proud commander lost an eye because of the great cold of its everlasting snow?[52] There are calamities in this wide and vast place, because the people are always very keen to kill each other. There is no lord or great sovereign who would know how to put a limit on the people, however well he might go about it. All vie to kill each other. Evil impulse inspires them to battle against each other. Between the Guelphs and the Ghibellines,[53] they know no other motivation than to kill each other for no reason aside from one saying that his entire lineage was always Ghibelline and he too is Ghibelline, and the other saying that his side is from the ancient Guelph lineage, and that the Ghibellines had always done harm to the Guelphs. That is why they must hate each other and kill each other in the same town from which they come. More than one hundred thousand have killed each other for this sole reason. They kill each other, and hastily knock each other's houses down to the ground. It is a singular curse to destroy each other in such a way! It is a shame and a pity because it would be a very glorious country if there were amity between them. But the princes and inhabitants there are so hostile that they are always at war. There are very angry people in many places, but they are clever and cunning. It is a great shame that such a bad custom prevails among them!

4643–4691

Their own authors have told of it and reproached them in many different works. The distinguished poet Dante of Florence, who lost all of his wealth because of this harmful dispute, spoke of it in his lovely and very important book, strongly condemning them.[54] So did another author named Cecco d'Ascoli—on this he was in full agreement with Dante and other Italian scholars, very great authors. Cecco tells of the Bolognese in his book,[55] relating it in these words: "Oh, Bolo-

---

51. Legendary ancient king reputed to have given Italy its name. On French attitudes toward Italy in Christine's time, see Patrick Gilli, "Politiques italiennes, le regard français: c. 1375–1430," *Médiévales* 19 (1990): 109–23 <http://www.persee.fr/web/revues/home/prescript/article/medi_0751-2708_1990_num_9_19_1192>.

52. This is a reference to Hannibal.

53. Historic rivals for power in medieval Italy. The Guelphs supported the Pope, while the Ghibellines favored the Holy Roman emperor.

54. Italian poet Dante Alighieri (1265–1321), author of the *Divine Comedy*. This is a reference to *Purgatorio* (Part 2 of the *Divine Comedy*), canto 6.

55. This writer lived 1257–1327. The book mentioned here is *Acerba*; the quotation is from the start of Book 2, chapter 15.

gnese! Souls of fire! You destroy yourselves little by little. Your crimes and lusts will surely send you suffering." He spoke similarly of Pistoia and other cities. And Dante, speaking to Florence, where he resided, mockingly told it to "rejoice and laugh, because on land and sea they beat their wings, and even hurl themselves all the way to hell, in which house there are multitudes of its people."[56]

I have seen Italus's place stained by many other evil sins. I have seen lords commit wrong toward their people by taking too much, by extortion, by infinite charges, forbidden by God and justice and not enforced at all in other places. And they pillage and devour everything. I have seen ugly, hideous cruelties among many shameful lords, and I will keep quiet about the rest. May God establish peace everywhere! Toward the place of Silvius,[57] I have seen a custom of another kind, which greatly amazed me. They hold up white and red roses, by which they undo themselves as Guelphs and Ghibellines do—the one holding up a red rose gets revenge against the one who holds up the white rose. This is surely devilry!

4692–4752

The place of Janus[58] destroyed itself with this madness for a long time. But as I understand it, a good remedy came along. It pleased God that the place of Italus would be entirely subdued, and the bad practice was taken away from them. The person whose intelligence, chivalry, and virtue brought an end to that madness should certainly be praised for it![59] If the people did not abandon the practice in their hearts, at least it did not progress as much, whoever might have dared to rebel on either side. They should truly praise God, who gave them courage, for wanting to save them, for their greater good, in giving them such a noble prince and having them brought into good order by a wise and prudent deputy. He deserves praise and reward for it. They were saved from that evil fire, which inflames others so much that they continuously annihilate each other out of great wrath.

Thus that nation has seen many changes in lordship. There is no prince, however wealthy he may be, who would be able to keep them in peace for long. And whoever goes there to take hold of the place commits a great folly, because even assuming that one could conquer them, no one has ever managed to keep them tranquil for long. They quickly have another lordship, as it pleases them, as soon as the first one is destroyed by rebellion. It is a thing that cannot be hidden. "Long live the conqueror" is their motto. Foolish is he who enters into conflict against them! One can observe it in Roman warfare, in that the powerful Romans could never conquer the people there, even if they inflicted many torments on

56. Dante, *Inferno* (Part 1 of the *Divine Comedy*), canto 26.

57. A son of Aeneas; the region referred to is Lombardy (Solente, *Mutacion*, 2:338, note to line 4683).

58. Legendary first king of Latium, the region of central Italy in which Rome was founded.

59. A reference to Azzone Visconti, lord of Milan from 1329 until his death in 1339 (Solente, *Mutacion*, 2:339, note to lines 4711–12).

them. The people would very quickly rebel, just as soon as the Romans were going to do them harm. This diabolical and ruthless society would cruelly and furiously rebel over any misfortune. But just as the authors mentioned above describe their fiery ways and point the finger at them, it distresses me, because by nature and birthright I should surely love these people. It displeases me that they fail, because I have had friends die there. And if I could implement a solution, I would put all my efforts into it, without a doubt!

4753–4781

But praise God, I see an extremely beautiful place there.[60] That magnificent, peaceful place is situated just like the rose enclosed by thorns. People do not lose control there, for which everyone should love it. Situated in the middle of the sea, it was founded long ago by the Trojans, who, in order not to pay tax and tribute to any living man who would be able to pursue them, had no desire to establish their dwelling-place on land. So they founded it in the sea, and then little by little they improved it. Since then that place has grown so much bigger that no one has defeated it in war or by force. It has won very great sovereignty, and not by a circuitous path. And I believe that God maintained it that way because there are many righteous people there. It is the treasury of many riches from foreign lands, but the places are well guarded. Justice is upheld for everyone there, and nothing that should be done quickly is delayed at all.

4782–4826

The people there govern themselves in such a way that no one can quarrel with them or admonish them for wrongdoing. They are good people, gentle and peaceful, although they seem less than sensible about honors and flattering ceremonies, which dishonor people. But they are wise in their deeds and perfect seafarers, and they are wealthy, well-off, and satisfied. Beggars are not seen out in the open there, because the place is overflowing with wealth, and it is very well populated. Their frigates go far by sea. They are not Guelphs or Ghibellines—all have equal rights. They govern themselves collectively, by the oldest families, where there are very wise people. So it is my opinion that this place which I am not naming governs itself quite in line with how Rome used to, as one finds in many texts, because there the public good is well protected, so that it suffices.

Thus this place sits amidst the flames without burning or destroying anyone, even though the lands of the other princes all around are in great wars, all because of the above-mentioned custom that puts many to an abrupt death. Quite close to there is the resting place of Antenor the Elder,[61] who once went there from Troy with many people. He founded and kept the place and region where he

---

60. Venice.

61. A Trojan counselor. According to the *Aeneid*, Antenor was buried in Padua, which he had founded.

lies, where there is a lovely entry. It seems to me, and I have oft heard it said, that the place about which I speak so much is worthy of great praise. And I have not lauded it this much just because I was born there, moved by partiality to speak in error, because the truth about this place is also proven, and easily verified.

V. *Here is told of the place of Brutus*[62]

4827–4846: *Christine will not write at length about the land from which Brutus chased the giants, as it has been treated elsewhere.*[63] *King Arthur no longer reigns there, nor do his qualities. People there pretend to be gentle, but they are treacherous.*

4847–4862

They well showed it to Actaeon, who was killed there by his own dogs, as soon as he turned into a stag; more than twenty people know this.[64] But in my opinion, staring Diana in the face is not the reason it happened. Rather it was done by Mischance and my lady, who set many places to fire and flame. But the hunter who so very dishonorably made dogs mistreat their master, by sounding his horns and his hunting cries, should beware. Because if my lady were to turn a little bit, I well foresee that she would do him ill. Because from doing evil comes evil (foolish is he who does not remember that!).

4863–4910: *The people there are in conflict because they are not from one lineage— the Phrygians*[65] *were first, and later much of the land was conquered by the Saxons, as Fortune saw fit. The Saxons were at war with the lineage of Corineus,*[66] *who had come from Troy.*

---

62. Brutus, the legendary founder of England, was said to be a descendent of Aeneas.

63. For example, in the twelfth-century *Roman de Brut (Romance of Brutus)* by Wace.

64. In this myth, the hunter Actaeon spies Diana, goddess of the hunt, as she is bathing. She reacts by turning him into a stag, and he is killed by his own dogs. On this myth in the *Mutability of Fortune*, where it hints at a warning against political disloyalty, see Renate Blumenfeld-Kosinski, "Christine de Pizan and Classical Mythology: Some Examples from the 'Mutacion de Fortune,'" in Zimmermann and de Rentiis, *City of Scholars*, 11–12, and Jacqueline Cerquiglini-Toulet, "Sexualité et politique: Le mythe d'Actéon chez Christine de Pizan," in Dulac and Ribémont, *Une femme de lettres*, 83–90.

65. People of Phrygia, an ancient region of Asia Minor.

66. Legendary warrior, reputed founder of Cornwall.

VI. *Here is told of the place descended from Friga*[67]

4911–4950

Now I do not wish to get off track any further, or distance myself from where I am, to speak of far-off places. I will speak of one. I will tell of the third-highest seat at the castle, which I saw situated near the first two. I saw that it was of high origin, its lineage having descended from King Friga. Oh, God! How magnificent it is—high, glorious, powerful, famous, feared, and formidable—even though it has been struck many times by bitter Fortune. Yet she is a good mother to it. It is much more unified than elsewhere, the body not separating from the head. That is mainly what sustains this noble place and keeps it in peace, along with the gentle blood of the inhabitants and the princes there. Cruelty is not very common there, as it is in many places. The people seek God's help in their great hardships, and I believe they are avenged by him. One writer, criticizing cruel and merciless princes, says that princely cruelty is particularly destructive to a kingdom, and it ends badly for the prince himself when all is said and done. That became clear to Nero[68] and to many other great barons, so hated for their cruelty that they were fatally attacked because of it.

May it now please God for this place to be rid of vices and for everyone to be ignorant of the kinds of misdeeds that I believe make their situations worse, because truth is hardly found anywhere these days.

4951–4964: *Christine laments the rampant dishonesty here, especially among nobles whose word was once their bond.*

4965–5008

Does one not read about Alexander, who would rather deign to appease his great wrath than go against his word, when he swore that he would not do what his teacher asked?[69] Alexander knew well that the scholar wanted to ask him, on behalf of the scholar's homeland, not destroy it at all. But because the place was enemy to Alexander, Alexander intended to destroy it and do the scholar wrong. But the wise scholar entreated Alexander to destroy the entire city, without favor and without ever rebuilding it at any time. In order for Alexander to keep to his vow, therefore, he had to leave the city completely in peace. Alexander preferred

67. That is, France. King Friga, founder of Phrygia, is said to be the ancestor of the French, linking France's history with that of the Trojan civilization (see Book 6, chapter 4).

68. Roman emperor (reigned 54–68 CE), blamed for the Great Fire of Rome in 64 CE and for executing his own mother, among other atrocities.

69. Alexander the Great, conqueror and king of Macedonia (356–323 BCE). In the episode referred to here, Alexander's former teacher, Anaximenes, was sent to plead with an angry Alexander to spare the city of Lampsacus. Alexander is the focus of Book 7, chapters 45–52.

to uphold truth than to appease his heart by getting revenge against the city. And the good master Quintilian[70] said that it is not at all suitable for a prince to be unable to swear, in any situation, to be as truthful to any man as he would be to a prince, and to hold perfectly to his oath.

Alas! It distresses me even more to see things go so badly that justice is ill-respected in that place. It is very often delayed by favor or by the taking of great gifts; few have yet to learn that! Ah! well armed Justice, how truly you were loved by the good! Does David not say in his Psalter, in teaching the right path to kings, that to protect justice from criminals and their vice, "you will rule them with an iron rod"? He also says in this gloss, "You will bend them and shatter them like vases."[71]

5009–5050

Since princes were not made solely to be arrogant and gain glory by their deeds, without serving some other cause, we can now take as apropos what Varro seeks to impart. He says: "Not all messengers were created to be frivolous, that is, only to travel. Nor was man made only to talk a great deal, or just to live on earth, or for the purpose of being born. Rather, man was created so that during his lifetime, he would apply himself to making his life a totality of beautiful and worthwhile things that would be beneficial forevermore."[72] David, the true prophet seen by God, also says that righteousness befits a prince very well; wherever he finds himself, "righteousness will go before him, and will put itself along his paths so that he will not stray. And it will ready the path for him."[73] Seneca said, "righteousness is the throne of good fortune in a prince, which makes him shine and lead in all virtues."[74]

Ha! Good God! I am indeed extremely ashamed of certain covetous people, when I hear foreigners told that there is a great deal to reproach in them. A wise man offered some notable words to Alexander, which I would like very much for those people to keep in their memory: "If you are a man, routinely consider that

---

70. Spanish rhetorician (ca. 35–100 CE).

71. Psalms 2:9.

72. Marcus Terentius Varro, Roman scholar (116–27 BCE). The source of this quotation, and those by Seneca and the "wise man" in this passage, is the *Jeu des échecs moralisés*; see Solente, *Mutacion*, 2:341, notes to lines 5014–24, 5033–36, and 5042–50.

73. Allusion to Psalms 84:14 (Vulgate <http://vulgate.org/ot/psalms_84.htm>).

74. Lucius Annaeus Seneca, Roman Stoic philosopher (ca. 4 BCE–65 CE), tutor of the emperor Nero, who forced Seneca to commit suicide. For a study of stoicism in Christine's writings, see Charles Brucker, "Mouvement et fragilité humaine dans quelques oeuvres de Christine de Pizan," in Jean-Claude Mühlethaler and Denis Billotte, eds., *Riens ne m'est seur que la chose incertaine: Etudes sur l'art d'écrire au Moyen Age offertes à Eric Hicks par ses élèves, collègues, amies et amis* (Geneva: Slatkine, 2001), 161–80.

you are mortal, and you should not want ill-gotten property. You should not burden yourself with covetousness, because it enflames people. Covetousness kills a man and pushes him toward many vices."

5051–5078: *Christine condemns taking from others, as well as the excessive monetary gifts often bestowed upon undeserving people.*

5079–5103

How many worthy men, very intelligent people, or truthful, knowledgeable clerks do we see advanced or exalted without flattering someone? If one sees them climb high, it is by chance, because wisdom and great learning are valued little, along with truth that flatters no one and knocks deception down flat. Nonetheless, we can see that God has allowed some of those people to sit high in worldly society, because they were governed by wise and capable teachers. Aristotle[75] thus taught Alexander good ways, to believe those who were wise and reasonable, to draw good men toward him, to let no one enter into his counsel who was not taught in wisdom, and to value those in whom there was prowess. Thus he did it back then. And I would say as much about the Romans, who gained because of it.

5104–5130: *One can judge an individual by the behavior and character of his friends and valued servants, because people surround themselves with others who are similar.*

VII. *Here is told of the place of nobles*

5131–5184: *In the area around that seat, there are many high lords, some admirable and others prone to bad behavior. Christine tells of this not to speak badly of anyone, but to expose some troubling vices she observed, such as excessive drinking, foul language, and indulgence.*

5185–5226

Ha! Perverse Gluttony! Must your excess overturn the reputation of those who should be unfailingly governed by excellence? Ha! Good God! Likewise, when I think about it, I cannot imagine how it is that knights and noble people nowadays are so very zealous about bodily delights! I certainly recall that all the ancient texts, written by good people, say that the meritorious ones were not delicate at all; rather, they were used to crude provisions and hard beds. Creature comforts did not matter to them anywhere. But anyone who now sees the nobles pursuing their pleasure in eating and drinking, and the great caprice that some have for being self-serving, would say that nothing in the world would satisfy them, whether

---

75. Greek philosopher (384–322 BCE), tutor of Alexander the Great.

they had gold or silver, even though there are limits everywhere and foolish is he who goes too far! I am not talking about their finery, because according to many passages of Scripture, at the right time and season, rich clothing is reasonable and fitting for noble people who strike blows in defense of the common good. But as for comforts, I know well that excess is not good. There are many who exceed the limits! At what hour would they get up in the morning if their fire were not just right in winter, their outer garment were not warmed, and if there were not great numbers of servants around to attend to them?

5226–5236: *That is the case for many who, in Christine's opinion, should be satisfied with less.*

5237–5273

Is it suitable for them to play out of greed this way, at dice or other games? Certainly not! I have no doubt that anyone who can argue differently is someone who throws himself into gaming too much, indeed loves it. He loses praise because of it, and often loses his possessions and advances little as well. And should the most bellicose noble people be proud? Well, truly I think not, however much prowess they have and however high their name. One reads about Julius Caesar,[76] who was so valiant and distinguished, but who never in his life said a proud word to anyone, nobleman or commoner. Nor did he insult anyone if it were not in an act of war. It was well known to all. One can also ask about Hector,[77] who was so gentle, humane, and full of great affection that he held out his hands to all people. He even received the vanquished with pity when they surrendered. Vegetius[78] says that people should act that way, and neither pride nor self-importance has any place in a noble heart. Yet many will be quick to call a Christian "dirty vile dog" for something that matters little, or they soon strike great blows, kicking him all over, for no reason. Such people are degenerate and do not know what nobility is, and it does not bother them. Excessive comfort is what makes them act up this way.

---

76. Roman political and military leader (100–44 BCE).

77. Trojan prince. Hector is a central figure in Book 6, especially chapters 7–21; see Kevin Brownlee, "Hector and Penthesilea in the *Livre de la mutacion de Fortune*: Christine de Pizan and the Politics of Myth," in Dulac and Ribémont, *Une femme de lettres*, 69–82, and Liliane Dulac, "Entre héroïsation et admonestation: La matière troyenne chez Christine de Pizan," in *Conter de Troie et d'Alexandre: pour Emmanuèle Baumgartner*, ed. Laurence Harf-Lancner, Laurence Mathey-Maille, and Michelle Szkilnik (Paris: Presses de la Sorbonne Nouvelle, 2006), 106–9. On Hector in Christine's works more generally, see Lorna Jane Abray, "Imagining the Masculine: Christine de Pizan's Hector, Prince of Troy," in *Fantasies of Troy: Classical Tales and the Social Imaginary in Medieval and Early Modern Europe*, ed. Alan Shepard and Stephen D. Powell (Toronto: Centre for Reformation and Renaissance Studies, 2004), 133–48.

78. Fourth-century Roman author Flavius Vegetius Renatus.

5274–5306

What should I say about the ones who are slanderers, in word and deed? Is it right for a noble man to get carried away like that, with base language? I would surely dare to wager that if someone, young or old, had a reputation for slandering, even if he were as worthy as Hector and had as much wealth as Octavian, his company would be held less dear. And he would be praised much less because of it, regardless of how people acted toward him. There is hardly any stain worse! What does it matter if one is good at arms but not constant and firm in morals, abandoned to ugly vices that are even admonished in fools? One should put such people as it were on a perch, or on reserve in a box or a chest, until such time as war comes, if there is nothing good to be found in them aside from skill at arms. It is a different matter entirely when nobility is involved, because one good quality should attract another, and put an end to the opposite. But it is even worse when they speak badly of women. Good God! What shame it is for nobles to defame the great, the lesser, and women, whoever they may be! Whoever hears them despises them!

5307–5352: *People who associate with vile gossips are foolish, as they too will surely be victims of badmouthing. Some nobles also feel entitled to take women, possessions, or land from others.*

5353–5393

Those who say such evil things to women as the filthiest churl in the empire might say, are they courtly or are they dishonored? What do I mean, "say"? Some actually treat women that way, and they commit a terrible wrong! I heard about one, whom I do not know, who not three months ago beat a woman he greatly despised, on the bridge of Paris. Although he is said to be a famous man, I do not know his name. He had his fill of beating her with a piece of alder and with his hand, in front of everyone, because she did not want to do something for him that should not be allowed done to any woman who is virtuous and does not have a dishonorable reputation. Good God! How he made it lovely to see! Whoever would like to place honor on someone, it would be well set on him, because he is distinguished and calm!

But thank God, they are not all like that! I know it well, because there are some who would rather lose their possessions than have such vile acts attributed to them. On that side, I know of a famous person of high repute. He is quite well known by many, but among all the good qualities that he can and does possess, above all things and in every situation, he defends women against defamation, by word and deed.[79] He would in no way tolerate any kind of slander being spoken

---

79. Solente believes that this refers to one of Christine's supporters, Charles d'Albret, Constable of France in 1401–11 and 1413–15 (*Mutacion*, 2:342–43, note to lines 5379–94).

about a woman, noble or lesser, and he could forbid it thanks to his reputation. I knew of it and saw it with my own eyes. May God grant him joy for it!

5394-5486: *There are other good people whom Christine does not know personally, but whom she feels compelled to mention—the Lord of Chastel, for example, along with an unnamed Picard who shuns pride, some of the Bourbonnais knights,[80] and others from outside France.*

5487-5504

It was not my intention to defame the noble class, who should be loved, but rather to reproach vices that are ill-suited to nobles. When they have vices, they become worse for it. In that place, I saw many courtiers of base ways, extorting the poor people, and they stirred up disputes which displeased many. And God knows the very unclean life of a number of them! There are those whose sole desire is to do evil, yet they have great favor. They are proud of that. Many bad reports come to the judges about their conduct, but no one dares to seek justice for it.

VIII. *Here is told of the seats of the counselors who were there*

5505-5536: *All around these places, occupying more than ten levels, Christine saw the counselors, scribes, and deputies of great lords. Some among them might have been learned, but not all were good.*

5537-5563

I believe I saw a number of odious people there, even though they may have been dressed in vair, whose innermost thoughts were known only to God. I feel firmly that they can be very clever and wicked in finding ways to get money; where it came from did not matter to them, provided that they could get hold of it. And one finds in the authentic and true histories of Rome that the counselors of Rome, where there were good knights, were typically poor, because they never took anything from anyone. The common good sufficed for them, and none aspired to personal wealth. As long as the Romans acted that way, they conquered kingdoms and empires. But once they strove for their own good, they put an end to their greatest honors. Many wicked counselors did not guard against this—may fire burn them!—and I saw high esteem accorded to deceitful people who were more

---

80. Guillaume du Chastel was a chamberlain of Charles VI and the Duke of Orléans (Solente, *Mutacion*, 2:344, note to lines 5437-54). Christine also celebrates his reputation for courage in battle in *Autres ballades*, 29-31, in *Oeuvres poétiques*, ed. Roy, 1:240-44. Solente speculates that the anonymous Picard may have been Jean de Hangest, lord of Heuqueville (d. 1407) or Raoul V de Gaucourt, lord of Argicourt (d. 1417) (*Mutacion*, 2:345, note to lines 5459-72). The Bourbonnais knights were members of the Bourbon family, whom Christine admired for their chivalry (Solente, *Mutacion*, 2:345-46, note to lines 5477-80).

diligent at acquiring personal profit than at seeking common gain, but who acted as if they had virtue.

5564–5580: *Such treacherous people skillfully hide their malice, making it difficult to protect oneself from them.*

5581–5623

One must never put on a false appearance, more deceiving than a thief stealing, in the guise of Mendicants or Jacobins and brothers who wear sandals, as Meun once did in the *Romance of the Rose*, telling about a lover.[81] In the castle, deception was at its most perfect in words and deeds, and surely much more dangerous there than among people who have no involvement at all in worldly administrations, for whom one would do very little. But the people there were in fact involved in government, where they concocted fake contracts and great villainies using their very deceiving appearances. In their infinite wickedness, however, they knew well how to cover up their acts, which has caused many a person to be ruined and dishonored. They pretended that they did everything for the best and that they despised all bad contracts. They acted that way in front of princes, but the people who spent time with them and had some dealing with them knew more about their behavior, because they were fleeced there, coming and going, without conscience or regard for pity in any deliberation. Since Scripture says (and it is not contradicted by proverb), "honors should only be brought to those who have good morals,"[82] you can believe that it harmed and displeased me terribly to have to show great respect to those people of such deceptive character, genuflecting when speaking to them, and calling them "my lord"! And God knows what account they took of poor people, when the poor went there for some dealing with them!

5624–5653: *They delay the cases of the poor and make them jump through hoops for a year or more. Interested in their own gain, these people serve the rich with feigned virtue.*

5654–5677

Happy was the official who could do the pleasure of the richest people, whether they wanted it or not. The official would do it for nothing, without profit or salary, purely because of the wealthy person's reputation for being important. It is a

---

81. The term for "false appearance" in line 5581 is "faulx semblant." In the *Romance of the Rose* by Jean de Meun, that is the name of the character False Seeming, who is dressed as a monk and represents deceit and hypocrisy. "Mendicants or Jacobins and brothers who wear sandals" refers to religious orders such as the Franciscans and Dominicans, whose followers were dependent on alms and often went about barefoot or in sandals.

82. Ecclesiasticus 10:31 (Solente, *Mutacion*, 2:347, note to lines 5611–14; Vulgate: <http://vulgate.org/ot/ecclesiasticus_10.htm>).

strange oppression that impels such foolishness, where one pays homage to the wealth of others without receiving any of it at all. Ha! Good God! What horrible liars I saw there, who made all vice grow! And they were people of great authority. Indeed, one never heard the truth come out of their mouths, but rather lies, without fail, in every case. It was so common among them that there was not one truth there, not in pledges or in oaths, but rather shameless public perjury in every case promised. I do not know how such people were put in the high places where I saw them. I swear to you, they did not possess goodness or truth of any kind.

5678–5749: *Lying is a terrible vice because the known liar is not believed even when telling the truth, and he cannot trust others. While Christine is impressed by some learned people there who lead others back to the right path, it is impossible to describe all of the misdeeds that go on. People go to any lengths to obtain money— ruses, selling possessions, borrowing at interest—in order to stay in proximity of the highest lords.*

5750–5760
I saw plenty of such people there, and I also saw worthy men who love loyalty and righteousness, and who would not be swayed against justice for any amount. I have heard them strongly debate about doing away with some of the customs or ordinances that were not good. If those people were heeded, I believe that everything would be better for it! I have seen such things in many places.

IX. *Here is told of the preceptors of the children of princes*

5761–5788
I saw counselors of young people there, companions and valets of the children of several very powerful people, who were not of good quality or skillful, but counselors of bad judgment. I have seen many foolish undertakings carried out by them and at their will. Ha! Good God! What teachings one hears such people give to the children of lords! They were responsible for numerous great offenses that harmed many, with respect to honor, possessions, or some other damage. Often, to flatter the children, the preceptors set out to goad them with their ideas about women, by making many comments to them, saying: "That one is the most beautiful! My lord! It is high time that you loved, because you will be fifteen or sixteen years old in no time." Thus, with such language, to please the young people, they set them on the path of desire. And if someone follows that path too far, a shameful outcome often ensues.

5789–5802: *Once young people go astray, it is difficult to bring them back to the right path.*

5803–5862

Preceptors and masters of such children should have a high standard of behavior themselves, so the young people they instruct never see in them an example that can lead them astray in any way. A child watches nothing more closely than the ways of the person who has charge of him. So the masters should not approve of everything the children do, but give examples of all good things, and remind them often of the manners that all worthy people should have, in word and deed. They should tell the children about the deeds of courageous, sensible, and honorable people. And as one finds in many tales, the sons of princes were brought up that way in the past, with learned, intelligent, prudent masters, and older knights who were noble and famous. They would do nothing if not for their teachers. That was evident in Alexander's situation, because when his father, King Philip,[83] saw his son born, the one who would be the leader of the kingdom, he immediately sent a message to the very wise Aristotle. He informed Aristotle that he had a male heir, and that he rejoiced even more because Alexander was born in Aristotle's lifetime. That is because Philip hoped that Alexander would be led by Aristotle toward good morals and suitable works. And thus he was, because from then on Aristotle was Alexander's master.

Thus children born of kings and princes should be educated by wise men, not by perverse meddlers who, to flatter the children, tell them the opposite of the truth and inflame debauchery. They should teach them appropriate pastimes, and not take up others. And do you know what happens when such a child grows up? He remembers the ways of his master, and if the master was of like mind, allowing his charge to indulge in foolishness, he is dissatisfied with the master for it, and with all those who encouraged him to do ill and told him stories of violence or drew the naïve ones to vices. I do not doubt that there are many good masters, wise in every situation, and whoever fulfills such a role well has no small burden!

X. Here is told of the Church's courts of justice

5863–5876: *Christine has seen many people's rights abused at court, some even wrongfully condemned to death.*

5877–5896

Oh, what devilry is the norm in many courts! It is difficult for me to pass on the court of the Church because it surpasses the others in very wicked deceits. That court is extremely hostile toward poor people, who are often harmed there and eaten up. One could not exploit people better, if they are rough around the edges, than to summon them to that court. Let us not doubt that, because the bearers of summonses, often lacking in honor, will summon them on a failure to appear in

---

83. Philip II of Macedonia (382–336 BCE).

court, or on two or three, when there are none. That is their right. And the default must be paid, notwithstanding that the poor person had been summoned but one time. But all goes to the profit of the place, which endures.

5897–5926: People may be excommunicated for no clear reason and have to pay to be absolved. Such deceits are the way of the court. Christine leaves the topic now, as going on would be tedious.

XI. *Here is told of the lay courts*

5927–5965
And what could I say of the lay courts? It is my view that they get completely carried away at the castle, where righteousness is lacking. I saw a great dearth of it everywhere! A judge should be utterly without bias, however, just toward every person, and refuse if someone gives him something in order to sway him. He should not be fickle, or bend for kinship or out of deference to rank. The words of Anacharsis, who lived as a philosopher,[84] apply readily to things I witnessed on several occasions: "Laws here resemble spider webs, great like sails, that do not take bumble-bees, big flies, or swarms of harsh, stinging wasps. But they do not fail to catch little flies with weak wings that fly around them. Those are taken in the net, not the queen bees." Thus I have seen lowly people taken, tied up, and condemned by many court officials. But such law held no sway over the important people. Another justice was applied to them, because they surely gave handsome gifts. Such people would know how to defend themselves against those who would tear the bread out of their hands. But God knows the terrible harm and punishment the lowly suffered, since they could be taken in by some trick or language!

5966–6014: With corruption and manipulation rampant, people can buy favor from the court officials, even in the case of executions. People without means are the most abused.

6015–6028
If a lowly person were to speak loudly against the officials, or were not to give them goods for such a matter, the officials, as it pleased them, would say that there had been fraud. I have seen that with my own eyes from some, but they are not all like that. There was harm; it is unnecessary, and a pity that people of bad conscience would have such complete power and such license. No one could tell you the falsehoods that would be seen there if someone cared to pay close attention, or how justice is upheld in that place.

---

84. A Scythian philosopher of the sixth century BCE.

XII. *Here is told of some who were called clerks, but were not*

6029–6074: *While Christine has seen some wise and just people working with integrity at all levels in the courts, corruption abounds. A number of people are called clerks, even though they devote themselves not to wisdom, but to making money. They are ignorant and prone to faulty reasoning.*

6075–6119

Their opinions are more foolish than I have heard from little old ladies, because they do not care about knowledge. And they would not strive to know something if it were not an applied science. They place little value on the theoretical, where understanding is perfected. (Thus it is plain to see that the enemies of knowledge are those who do not have a bounty of it!) Such people do not value a noble soul either, nor a learned man or woman, unless he or she were rich and well dressed. They do not take virtue into account. And when they are carousing, if anyone were to recall the words of a worthy or renowned person who was not known to be rich, they would say, "Those are all worthless things, and there are plenty of lies and folly in those writings and big words, and in the yammering of philosophers. And such people, who reputedly did not care about money, were really stupid fools!" People like that hate the wise, and mock them at their gatherings. There are many such deceivers. God knows, they talk about many at their dinners and their tables! You would hear fine sayings blathered in many places! There is no neighbor, wrong or right, or woman nearby, be she unattractive or beautiful, about whom they do not tell a story, often ugly and coarse, be it truth or lies. Of whom do these lords not take their accounting when they are comfortable, well fed, and full of wines and hippocras?[85] They would not spare dukes, counts, kings, or queens, because there they fear them no more than a handful of straw!

6120–6142: *Fortune may place vain and ignorant people in office, but Christine does not consider them clerks.*

6143–6166

Other good and worthy people are not called clerks. High and low, morning and evening, they seek out books on good government, and stories of valiant people who were valorous and made an effort. And they conduct themselves with good and prudent morals, wisdom, and maturity. Such people, who love and seek knowledge, may well call themselves "clerks," even if it happens that they cannot acquire it in spite of their diligent efforts. I saw more than a thousand other good people who were not qualified in science, but who would in no way want to treat anyone with derision. If they have a clerk's office, they manage their affairs well

---

85. Hippocras: A type of spiced wine.

and wisely. I never hear at all about the ones who have it in their hearts to do all good things. I speak only of the mockers who hold all people in contempt, except themselves, where there is no value.

XIII. *Here is told of the people who were involved in finance*

6167–6201: *This "place full of disorder and perverse improprieties" (6169–70) teems with people seeking to curry favor with the officers in charge of money.*

6202–6229

I saw a number of people receive very small compensation, and I should know plenty about that! I heard malicious acts attributed to some officials. I do not know whether their accusers were deceived, but they said that a number of officials conducted many bad affairs and harassed people with delays, people who were following them and pursuing their money with painstaking effort. And the people pursuing money complained a great deal, in distress, saying that the officials committed a great mortal sin, harassing them that way and causing such torment. In their opinion, all people would consider themselves better satisfied if an official were to give them a firm date, even if it were far off, instead of so many meaningless short deadlines, provided there was no default at the time. That would be better than specifying one day after the other and treating people that way day and night, making them spend their assets to pursue them. And the officials themselves would have less of a crowd of people than they do now.

6230–6247: *The officials should not string claimants along with vain hope. Meanwhile, the money-handlers get rich.*

6248–6272

You will very often hear the claimants curse at the treasurers, saying quite loudly: "We are very displeased with such people! They do not have any money (so they say), except to purchase houses and put up masonry. They indeed have piles of money, and there are some with cellars full of fine wines, and thoughts full of money for their expenditures. And not ten years ago they were so poor that they borrowed from everybody. From where, evil Devil, would such wealth spring forth, if they did not take it from somewhere, rightly or wrongly? One certainly could not put enough aside from the wages they earn to support the very high situation that they maintain." Many people say these things, often cursing the money-handlers. They say that they are amazed that lords do not remove officers like this from their posts, because everyone complains about what they do.

6273–6320

But I think that one can speak of this as the noble Julius Caesar once did in his empire. He was asked why he did not quickly remove from office the officials who were maligned everywhere for the way they ran things. He replied that the people could have worse. He remembered a time when he was concerned about a man who was covered in wounds and badly mistreated. The man had a great number of flies on him, whether he was outside or in. Julius Caesar, out of pity, shooed the flies away, but this kindness did not please the sufferer one bit, and he said to Caesar in an impatient way: "You are going to way too much trouble for me when you shoo away flies full of my blood, because soon others will come back and will bite me more than these big and happy ones here, already gorged on my blood." "It is similar regarding these people," Caesar said. "Even though they may not be good or kind, they are sated and rich with wealth, because they have held office for a long time. So they do not need to covet as much as poor newcomers would, because the newcomers are completely devoid of riches. It would therefore be better to leave the plump ones than to place skinny, needy officers in there to fatten up, craving to acquire wealth."

I do not say such things to reproach anyone, because I should love many of those officers who took pity on me, by right and true kindness, and who advanced my cause. And thus, I believe in fact they are charitable toward many. But in a deep place, completely filled with many treacherous things, it is inevitable that there will be some hateful and bad ones! It is a true thing and Scripture also affirms it.

XIV. *Here is told of the merchants*

6321–6368

Did I not see other people? Yes, I did. Joyous and pensive people seated at the end, in the middle, and all over, as it happens because of Fortune. I remember well seeing one group of people who bought and sold. They gained and lost often. Those people were called "merchants"—there were more of them in towns than in fields! I saw many sorts among those who lived off commerce. And even though it is suitable for a merchant to uphold truth and good faith in all his acts, I saw that not all were perfect in that place. Rather, I saw them play a lot of tricks on many people, not nice ones, in selling, buying, and in many false dealings. There were so many that I would not know how to say which deal was the worst: bartering merchandise and exchanging bad for good; deluding with flattery and oaths; promising that something could not be better when it was bad, counterfeit, and made entirely to deceive people; or selling on terms with false contracts. I saw tanned skins and cloth, jewels, dishes, mercery,[86] goods sold by weight, spices,

---

86. Mercery: Fine fabrics such as silks and linens.

and all other things likewise falsely arranged there, usurious contracts and loans under many strange arrangements that were condemnable and counter to reason. I saw multitudes of such merchants going out in search of merchandise on sea and on land, rapacious with greed, some greater, some lesser, roaming through hills and valleys, except for horse-traders. Ironically speaking, I saw them to be trustworthy in this place. They did not sell horses groomed to look like something they were not—they would never do that!

6369–6412

I saw plenty of other false and bad merchants, I promise you, impelled by cupidity as much as avarice, to which they are given. They are so strongly attached to evil gains that it may cause them to lose one of these days, if God does not remember them. But Cicero[87] speaks in this manner about the vice of avarice: "Avarice is the desire to acquire and take wealth with no fear of doing wrong, to possess it and hold more than is necessary to provide for one's needs, beyond reason, to hold onto dead treasure." And Seneca says in a book that "avarice makes people drunk, and makes them dry out from thirst. It is without a doubt the foundation of all ills and vices, and the intention behind all ugly misdeeds." But even though it is defamed by all authors, it is loved by the inhabitants here, where integrity has little place. The frauds and underhanded deceptions that I saw among merchants, hidden and in the open, would all be too long to recount. Talking about them less can suffice. Nevertheless, I have seen few of them become rich without great deception, because a man can hardly acquire great wealth without taking that of others. I believe without a doubt, however, that there are many good and trustworthy ones in that group, truthful people of honor, who have honestly acquired what they have and who are charitable, good, and noteworthy. They fulfill a necessary function, and it must be the same in all places. No one can deny that, so one really should pray for them!

XV. Here is told of the common people

6413–6432: Christine has seen untold scores of common people there. They are loyal to their leader; she can only hope that they are as loyal to each other. These people are prone to gluttony, which holds them back from a better life.

6433–6461

I see workers of all trades there, drinking to excess. You will find them in the taverns every day, relaxed, drinking all day long. Or as soon as they have done

---

87. Marcus Tullius Cicero, Roman philosopher and politician (106–43 BCE). The quotations from both Cicero and Seneca are from the *Jeu des échecs moralisés*; see Solente, *Mutacion*, 2:349 and 2:350, notes to lines 6376–84 and 6385–90.

their day's work, many must go drinking. They spend more than they earned in the whole day there, this is true. Or if they have saved up during the week, all will be drunk on Sunday. Their throats will never have their fill of gobbling food and overindulging. There is no need to ask if they fight when they are drunk—the civil authorities have registers filled with fines for that, all year long. Plenty of them are found in there! And in order to carry on such drunkenness, it does not concern them how they cheat people, as long as they can pull in money. So you would find enough swindling there to provide for their households and carry on their drunkenness. They have to use trickery, and often even get themselves hanged and killed for their excessive spending, which ultimately brings them suffering.

6462–6518: *Christine criticizes lazy drunkards, condemns gluttony, and reproaches men and women given to base acts. That said, she acknowledges the good, hardworking people she saw there as well.*

XVI. *Here is told of the people of the village*

6519–6546

I also saw people of villages there, fed on beans and dairy products, cultivating arable lands. I believe that of all living people there is none, in whatever state he may be, as my mind conceives of it, in whom there would be less to admonish or who commit fewer offenses. That is, even though one may see them do wrong, which to my mind is a great shame. I am speaking of the people who are out and about; I do not hear about others. It is a very righteous and blessed life. Thus we find in many writings that at the time of the golden age, our first ancestors were of their ranks. God was more honored then than he is now, and Covetousness had not yet been brought to the world. Covetousness uncovered the striking distinctions among the traits displayed by non-nobles and noblemen. We all came from one father, notwithstanding that great prestige befits the well cultured rank of nobles if they conduct themselves according to the values that go along with their nobility.

6547–6580

Of the laborers, I have seen many who were indolent, debauched, no-good, apathetic on others' farmland, and doing a lot of dishonest work to finish their task more quickly than they should. And be it in the vineyard, the farmland, or in other small fields, it did not bother them to go late to work and leave early, as long as they had money. And another steals the hay from his neighbor's field, or his wheat or grapes, or does him some other harm. It is my opinion that such a disposition is now human nature, and hardly does one see a being without a serious flaw. Even Scripture, which loves our salvation, says it. There are many good laborers who lead their lives faithfully and strive greatly to make their living and get ahead, and truly always want to work in good faith. They merit heaven that way, because they work painstakingly to make the goods prized by the rich and that support everyone's life. And no one should want to harm such people in any way. Rather, pray to God that he would want to save them, because their labors are more necessary than other business. He who does wrong to such people for no reason truly commits a great sin!

XVII. *Here she apologizes for the things she said*

6581–6616: *Christine explains that if she has been critical of what she has seen, it is not because there are more vices at the castle than elsewhere. Rather, she is like the person who cares for a friend—the friend's burden may be but a splinter, but it seems larger than that of a stranger who carries a great timber. Thus are these faults to her, and she wishes to help, in spite of her own imperfections.*

XVIII. *Here is told why women were not remembered here*

6617–6674

Some who hear my words might wonder why, when I talked about these varied situations, I did not mention feminine morals in the mix, and the vices of some women of foolish ways. I did not do that because in my opinion, whatever women's shortcomings may be (because there is no one without vice) their greatest misdeed or malice surely does little to worsen the state of the world. Although they are not all pure, in general they are little involved in the essential dealings of government. Therefore, even the most contrary of women cannot do much harm. And they would always be slowed down because their spun work and their distaffs are their greatest occupation. Notwithstanding, many authors have talked about them in their books, making an ounce of badness into two pounds. But even though the authors have talked about them, I believe overall that anyone mindful of the evil that happens in the world can see, if he really looks, that it generally does not come from women. It is apparent in justice, which is hardly put to use because of women; they are of little detriment, it is a proven thing.

It is certainly true that I would advise no one to follow debauched women, or those completely cut off from honor, or wicked, evil, or perfidious women of perverse ways, or women who offer dangerous counsel. Anyone who may become foolishly enamored of such women could lose body and soul, and give up all wealth by pursuing and trusting them. Nothing is more unseemly than a foolish and unpleasant woman, and there is nothing more pleasing than a sweet and peaceable one. Such a woman is a great comfort to a man when he finds himself upset. And even though many have heatedly reproached women's morals, I believe that there many good and lovely ones, and great numbers of those who maintain virtue in all circumstances, and who love reason and right. That may be lacking in some, but rare is the rule that has no exception. And I believe that the majority of women are free of perverse and ugly morals.

XIX. *Here is told what Fortune is and whence she comes*

6675–6714

Now it is time to turn from the above toward another topic, because it is not needed or necessary to focus exclusively on one theme. I had it in my mind, from the very beginning of this poem, to talk about Fortune—how she is well known to harm some people and treat them quite badly, while it pleases her to help others. I named this book about the cases she provides us "The Mutability of Fortune," because she is more changeable than the moon. We must pay attention to the things that have to do with her, things that one can rightfully call "unfortunate," because not everything that ends badly should be called "unfortunate." Rather, let us see if we can observe or know to some extent what Fortune, who so changes people's state, can be, for she has no form or body, and her disposition also varies a great deal.

It seems to me that she is an influence linked with the movement of the sky, according to the angular distances between the planets. She comes to many places according to people's birth, via the far reaches of the ill-fortuned planets or the fine, pure good ones ascending at the time a person is born of his mother. According to the configuration of the constellation, I believe that one's fortune will either have less goodness in it or be more fulfilled and replete with joy and good health.

6715–6742

But one could ask me, "How does it happen that an empire, a country, or a kingdom can be seen as fortunate or unfortunate?" and whether Fortune is a friend or enemy to it. That is not at all a matter of birth. Rather, I say, as many stories tell it, that every earthly region is subject to the high power of the course of the sky governing it, by the same action and astrological zone as is the body of a man. The body, for its diversity of form, is called a true image of a small earth, where all strangeness abounds. And as for what Fortune gives us at a given time, good or bad, I understand this very thing: the sky arranges everything down here by diverse constellations—some good, others adverse. That is according to the changes in the courses of the planets' rotations, which are either favorable or contrary for us. And they have to do with the affairs of the countries where they are more influential, relative to what each planet dominates.

6743–6796

Notwithstanding that this subject is not to be taken lightly, in no way does it necessarily follow that Fortune chases one toward good or bad, or that it has to be that way. Whoever believes otherwise deceives himself, because God, who can help all beings, is higher than Nature. And I contend that one can sensibly resist bad fortune sometimes; it is a known thing. This applies to some circumstances because, may God keep me, it would very great foolishness to say that the vengeance and anger of God, with which he punishes the sins that stain the world, should be called Fortune. Because such vengeance is hidden, God's secret, until it happens. Whoever says that such a thing arises because of Fortune is sorely mistaken, because our Lord consents to all this by very rightful, unbendable justice. If one deserves to be hanged or put to some other torture, and he is, that is not Fortune. The case of whoever says the opposite is therefore outrageous. Similarly, if someone deserves to have good, and good comes to him, one should know that Fortune does not give it to him; rather his good work makes it happen.

But when something comes out of the blue, a sudden incident that leads to death by a very strange event, or something good happens unexpectedly, or one easily comes into wealth, I say that such cases come from Fortune, in an extraordinary way. Thus Fortune does not give peace and tranquility at all (she is not such a good friend to people!). Those come from divinity. But it is certainly true that God allows Fortune to be so powerful that she can divide up and distribute worldly goods as she wishes, because such goods are of no account to him. I tell of Fortune because she causes the world to suffer when she does everything according to her will.

XX. *Here is told which people are unfortunate and which are not*

6797–6848

Would it be more appropriate to describe Fortune by saying that in every kingdom, one is "fortunate or unfortunate" depending on what occurs by chance? Fortune is this—a person puts all his effort into doing good, strives to maintain his possessions and honor, and so fears dishonor that he would rather die than do a bad thing. Along with that, he serves and fears God, and prays with all his intention for God to help him in his need. He would in no way wish to be a lord and leader of people and commit base sins. And if he is pleasing, has good sense, and controls all his appetites well, he can truly be learned and very wise. And then everything turns against him, and he expends all his effort in vain, unable to accomplish anything, however well he may conduct himself.

If he is a prince who holds great land, and he loves peace and upholds right, war will arise against him for no reason, and may take all his honor and inheritance from him. Harm will always come to him, or his people will rebel or treacherously abandon him, or pursue some trouble (this did not start yesterday or today!). So it goes, from misfortune to misfortune, until Fortune has completely finished him off, killed or ruined him, because she set out to torment him. If he is a duke or a military leader, he may be very adept at arms and know how to use them, and he may be prudent and wise at every turn, but he will still be unable to bring anything to fruition if Fortune is against him. Everything will turn out badly for him, even though he does not falter a bit in organizing his battles and governing his people well. If Fortune does not shape the game of arms, he will have the worst of the battle.

6849–6900

If he is a simple knight who works diligently to acquire honor and praise, and he is unfortunate, I dare say that he will get the exact opposite of what he wants. Nothing he may do will ever benefit him because Fortune will destroy whatever he may undertake. If he is a clerk possessing great knowledge, and Fortune goes after him, he will need to be patient, like the worthy Boethius[88] once was, when he lost all of his wealth and was ruined by ill-counseled Romans. If he does not stubbornly resist her, she will quickly mistreat him. If he is an honorable man and holds a position where he must maintain justice, and if he rightly wants to safeguard it, he will need to protect himself. That is because if Fortune attacks him, Envy, who never sleeps, will burden him with such harsh situations that she will finish him off or ruin him.

If he is at court and serves lords, and by serving well he deserves to be better off in every way, the rumblings of the jealous will awaken bad fortune. The jealous ones will alert the lords, alleging that he had committed some wrong or misdeed against his lord's interests, with respect to possessions or honor. He would not know where it was coming from, as he would never have thought of such a thing. Although he may be more worthy than his accuser, however much he apologizes for it, he will not be able to be heard. Thus he will be pushed out of his place, not knowing why, and will have to keep completely silent. People serving at the great courts are often treated with such trickery. That is why common parlance says that "service is no legacy." Anyone who would become prideful is foolish, because one who always believed he reigned there goes out in shame and soon sees his glory end.

6901–6942

If someone pursues a position or function with lords, even if it were destined to be his, it will be denied to him, because Fortune will get in his way. She will dry up all his aid, because if such a person has any friends who could smooth the way for him, they will happen to die or leave the country, or he himself will be gripped and taken by some illness. Someone else will have the position he was striving for, with little difficulty if Fortune led him, even if it were not destined

---

88. Roman philosopher (ca. 480–524) who wrote *The Consolation of Philosophy* while in prison. Boethius's influence is visible in Christine's writing; see Cropp, "Boèce et Christine de Pizan," and Holderness, "Christine, Boèce et saint Augustin."

to be his. And if someone is of middle status, a worthy bourgeois or city-dweller, a good and honest-living gentleman, Fortune may take all his possessions from him out of spite. And she surely will, because he will be blamed for having made some false contract or error in the past, for which his assets and his situation will be undone, whether he is a lesser man or a great master. Or he will be done in by fire in his house, or for some other strange reason, or because of some business on sea or land. There are so many causes, it would be real drudgery to look for them all. Foolish is he who does not fear Fortune! On the contrary, the good side of Fortune gives plenty of great benefits, as we see come to many every day. We see people who are not very virtuous achieve notable honors and status as a result. But Fortune guides them there and also very quickly brings them back to a low point when she turns and knocks them down, making them dejected and sad.

XXI. *Here is told of the misfortunes of women*

6943–6974

Since it seems to me that very unfortunate fates often befall the feminine sex, it is fitting for me to incorporate into my account a bit about ill fortune that plunges women into ruin. Nature and pity draw me to this, and make me lament the women's martyrdom. Ha! Good God! What painful things happen to a woman, and go on for a long time, when Fortune saddles her with a bad husband who wants to beat her. And not only does he want to, but he often does it. He shows up acting woeful for little reason, and thinks about how he will be able to do ill to his wife, by coming up with infinite quarrels. It cannot go on if he does not quarrel or play the jealous man, or if he actually is jealous, such that whatever he sees displeases him. That is no small misfortune! Whoever has such luck has not won! Or when he gambles everything at dice, or is frequently filled with wine, then gets angry and grumbles and wants to beat on everything, and the children wail in the hall. Ha! Good God! What a sweet paradise that is! And it is necessary to be in fear all the time, because that is what completes the torment that this subjugation imposes.

6975–7005

Other women will be wrongly blamed by some deceitful rapacious gossiper, for little reason. May evil fire devour them all! Thanks to them, many dishonorable things are attributed to men and women who were never guilty of them. Rather, they are untrue stories. Alas! But what bitter fortune and misery attack a woman when she loses a good and peaceable husband, who honorably and wisely kept her near him, and who held her dear! She rightfully shows a despondent countenance over it! Then she can say that Fortune had attacked her, because lawsuits will immediately spring up at her from all sides. If she has relatives, they will plead to the wretched woman for a share. If they succeed, there will indeed be nothing left of what the woman had. Creditors will come forth, and wicked liars, and they will say that her husband owed them, that he may have borrowed something of theirs, although there will be no proof. Thus the sad widow will be summoned and subpoenaed to several courts and misled by frauds and trials sought against her, denied and stripped of inheritance and land.

7006–7052

And at the time that her husband was alive, and held an important and fine situation, another man flattered and fawned over her many times, doing her honor and showing generosity in every way. Now he turns his back on her, and may impute many bad things to her in devious ways. He may insinuate that her husband, whom that person had loved dearly, was deeply indebted to him, and that her husband maintained his status by borrowing money from him. And the man needed to get it back, and prove it by some pretext. The simple woman, for fear of entering into a lawsuit and to avoid conflict, will settle it by paying. What is more, the bad fortunes that widows endure come in a thousand guises, but the women's comfort is weeping and tears. Even if I must speak beyond my own area of expertise in this case, God knows of it—may he wish to ease the women's suffering!

If it happens that women have to get involved in a case in order to pursue their own benefit, what friends will they find in the many places they must go? Is this a time when kings, dukes, or counts support girls, ladies, or any women, and sustain them in their just cause? Not at all. That is lacking now. And justice, which should be favorable toward women, no longer lasts for them if they do not have the means to pay up. But they will be told good stories in secret! If they have lovely bodies or pleasing ways, or simply are young, they will be well and notably counseled. But I do not advise any of them to believe in such counsel, because advice with a shameful consequence is not credible in any situation. Thus they find charity dead. Those who experience this know it!

Explicit the third part of The Book of the Mutability of Fortune.

Here begins the fourth part
of The Book of the Mutability of Fortune

I. *Here is told of the room in Fortune's castle and what images are there*

7053–7096

I have spoken a great deal about that place where many lots were cast by Fortune, in whom there is no certainty at all, as my simple intellect allows me to perceive and describe it. It is now fitting that I turn back to the high tower, to better get at my topic, because I have not yet talked about everything I observed at the castle; there are many subjects and I cannot say everything at once. In that tower, where Fortune has issued many an edict, there is a marvelous room.[89] Never were there as many marvels in the Perilous Guard, which Lancelot's romance says belonged to him after he conquered it,[90] as there were in this room. Nor did leaves of aspen or birch ever tremble or shake in such a way, because it seems that everything is always falling and leaning to one side. This is the palace of adventures, some pleasant, others harsh, but I am not looking to tell you everything—it would be a long process to recount all that I saw happen there. I would keep you for too long. I will tell you the essential things and be quiet about the rest.

It is no lie that the room, where the wind blows without stopping, is longer than an archer could ever shoot. And anyone who took its dimensions would find it circular and very high at the top. It is certainly marvelously beautiful—bright, great, and high, and of seemingly sturdy workmanship, even though it trembles all the time.

7097–7133

In one hundred years I could not describe the wealth, great riches, adornments, and magnificent objects there. I would not know how, nor would anyone else, no matter how wise he may be, because all the finest works in the world are there. It is very richly painted in gold and blue, all around and on the well-crafted pillars. The deeds and conquests of the great princes, and all kingdoms that they acquired, are written there. They conquered them thanks to my lady, who at first seats them in the high tower, and unseats at least some of them when it pleases her. The lives, situations, and ways of every emperor, prince, and king are portrayed there, as are their appearance and every one of their adventures. One sees how each one first came there to serve Fortune, how they were accustomed to succeeding with her help, and how she was favorable to some for a time and then changed, turning all their good into bad. In a nutshell, you can know for sure that there is no prince who does not serve in her court. There is none so great that he would not be keen to serve her and earn her favor, because they hold that level of authority and power thanks to her.

89. On Christine as "guide" and interpreter of the images in this room, see Kenneth Varty, "Christine's Guided Tour of the *Sale Merveilleuse*: On Reactions to Reading and Being Guided Round Medieval Murals in Real and Imaginary Buildings," in Campbell and Margolis, *Christine de Pizan 2000*, 163–73.

90. The castle conquered by Lancelot was called the "Dolorous Guard." Solente suggests that Christine's name "Perilous Guard" ("Garde Perilleuse," line 7070) is the result of conflating "Dolorous Guard" with the name of another place in Lancelot's story, the Perilous Forest (*Mutacion*, 2:351, note to lines 7070–74).

7134–7172

She has the capacity to put them there and to cut them off from it too. She has so shrunken the wealth of many, even though they might have been great, that none of it remained. Just when they thought they were the most secure, she would knock them from their place. And upon the death of the princes who serve her, and who in serving her become her subjects, she has their stories portrayed in remembrance. The stories of those worthy of renown are there, as well as the stories of the ones who have a bad name for having committed great cruelty and treacheries in kingdoms or empires. The best and the worst are there, and all others whose fame should be spread far and wide.

I will tell of the people whose portraits I saw there. I will not describe all of them, because that would take too long. Rather, I will tell of the principal important lords who were the greatest because of Fortune, holding an empire or kingdom and reigning thanks to her, and others worthy of memory, as it comes to my mind. Then I intend to talk about those who, during my lifetime, served this lady to whom man and woman are truly subject when it comes to worldly assets. But I will leave out the elevated forms of wealth, which are granted to us by God and sent by his great grace. Those are the highest riches of the soul that Fortune takes from no one.

II. *Here is told of Philosophy*[91]

7173–7205

To make my work more complete, rather than pressing on further, I will set aside the topic started earlier for a bit, to tell of other things that I am keen to point out about the place. I well imagine that I will come back to my subject after that.

At Fortune's residence, in the well decorated room filled with unusual images, I saw all of the sciences given by God, neatly arranged in lovely rows. It would please me to talk about them a bit, even though my limited intelligence must rise to address such lofty things, as I surely did not fully understand their great subtlety. But I will tell a little bit of what I noted about them, as best I can, even though I may have a fool's intelligence. I saw Philosophy placed very highly, in such a way that she seemed very much like a high mistress and the guide for all the others. I understood most of the purpose she serves and what she does, and I

91. Much of Book 4, chapters 2–17, is closely borrowed from Brunetto Latini's thirteenth-century *Book of the Treasure* and Isidore of Seville's seventh-century *Etymologies*; see Solente, *Mutacion*, 1:l–lix, for a comparison between Christine's poem and those sources. On this section of the poem, see Glynnis M. Cropp, "Philosophy, the Liberal Arts, and Theology in *Le Livre de la mutacion de Fortune* and *Le Livre de l'advision Cristine*," in Green and Mews, *Healing the Body Politic*, 139–59; and Anne Paupert, "Philosophie 'en forme de sainte Théologie': L'accès au savoir dans l'oeuvre de Christine de Pizan," in Dor and Henneau, *Christine de Pizan: Une femme de science*, 43–46.

will tell you just a little bit about that. I will add nothing of my own. My mind was transported and captivated by the writings that I saw.

7205–7272: The divine, the natural, and the human are the three areas in which one seeks truth through Philosophy. When humans, who at first lived in an animalistic way, became aware of their ability to reason, they began to seek understanding. Under mother Philosophy, there are three branches of science by which one explores these questions.[92]

III. *Here is told of Theory*

7273–7292
The first is Theory. This true discipline reveals the first question to us: how to be fully familiar with the beautiful things of both celestial and terrestrial natures. But in that the former are very obscure and different from the things of a weighty nature, like material objects, and are not located among them, it was very reasonable that the apt science of Theory would divide its body into three more sciences, to demonstrate the three natures that I just stated. These renowned sciences are thus each named as follows.

IV. *Here is told of Theology*

7293–7319
The first is Theology, which is very highly placed. It pierces through the sky and shows us the things without bodies. It demonstrates that which is not touchable or found among bodies at all. It illuminates it in such a way that, through Theology, we know God, his light, and the Trinity. In three we confess one single God and the true Catholic faith in an apostolic church. Theology teaches us all that has to do with faith, and from Theology comes the intellection and mindfulness that we have of divine essence. This is the super-celestial science, which, through its line of inquiry, shows us the high and merciful divinity. This one is more worthy than another, in light of its lofty subject where all of science is contained, the grandeur of its style, and its absolute and subtle necessity and fitting aim. This one deals only with what is connected with God, in whom all things end.

7320–7400: One looks to Theology for the liberal arts. Through Theology and the other subdisciplines of Philosophy such as Grammar, Rhetoric, Arithmetic, and Music, one can understand the Trinity and other divine concepts.

---

92. These three are Theory, Practice, and Logic. While Christine refers to the three branches here, she omits Logic from the discussion to follow.

7401–7456

The sovereign Geometry is there, by which God wanted to put everything in its place through measure and order. The line cannot go astray from striving for God; the triangle is exactly even at each angle. The square figure is there, closed just right; it is the holy, indivisible soul. The beautiful, sapient sphere is heavenly God; it is the world from which he wants us to answer to him. There is the true Astronomy, of which the sun is an integral part. It is the eternal son of God, a very luminous and lasting circle. His birth, which came earlier, is the sunrise, and his death is the sunset, which renders us learned and knowing. And the moon is the holy Church. The saints, in whom God's grace is placed, are the very pleasing stars shining in the sky.

The sovereign Physics is there. The doctor and practice of it is Jesus, the benevolent physician. The sinner is thus the sick one. The acute fever is debauchery. Quartan malaria,[93] which lasts a long time, is avarice and covetousness. Destructive paralysis is the greedy desire of gluttony. Crazed delirium is pride. The medicine is penitence. The diet is temperance, fasting, and contrition undertaken through great devotion. The supreme and true science of laws is to defend widows and orphans wisely, comfort the poor with a tender heart, know the law of God well and carry it out in all places, spurn falsity and vice, defend favorable truth, and open your mouth virtuously, without covering yourself in falsity. Thus you will immediately be a true and complete theologian, learned in all sciences. Therefore, this one would be first, with all other knowledge pushed to the background. And because it is the highest, I spoke less hastily about it.

V. Here is told of Physics

7457–7468

The second branch of Theory is Physics, which teaches us and engages us in understanding less obscure things. It is the nature of all bodies that are found around us. The bodies, we will say, are people, beasts, birds, fish, rocks and bushes, plants, grass, and all things that possess a form and body, that all coexist and are perceptible to people here below.

VI. Here is told of Mathematics

7469–7483

The third is Mathematics. This truth-telling science also shows us the nature of things that have no visible evidence of a body but are all around material things. Four different kinds of noble and highly valuable sciences are integrated, delim-

93. Quartan malaria, or malariae malaria, is characterized by a recurrence of paroxysms every four days.

ited, and included in Mathematics: Arithmetic is one of them, Music another better known one. The third is Geometry, and the fourth is Astronomy, which in my opinion is superior.

VII. *Here is told of Arithmetic*

7484–7544: *The first mathematical discipline is essential to all the others, and even to understanding holy Scripture. Christine underscores the symbolic value of numbers (e.g., four is perfection, the forty days that Moses fasted); no such concepts could be grasped without arithmetic.*

VIII. *Here is told of Music*[94]

7545–7594

The second here is Music, which teaches us and engages us in making lovely sounds with loud and muted instruments, to sing in rhythm, and to play church songs in time with a sweet sound, on the organ or other kinds of instruments. Music is composed by Muses, and was first established and created by Jubal, who did not leave it aside for one day. Jubal descended from Cain, who offended God. But he later invented Pythagorean tuning[95] from the sweet memory of the sounds of hammers striking stretched strings. Music was known and common among people long ago; they all used it universally. They, even the kings, made their songs and laments using the sounds of instruments or human voices.

Without Music there can be no measure in any being. Even the world is composed of a pure harmony of sounds. Also, the whole sky turns, keeping its order in the manner of a sweet and lovely harmony, in rapid modulation.[96] Music moves the sensibilities, and stimulates the senses and intentions in various ways. In battles and tournaments, the sounds of trumpets inflame and call to the combatants, and the more loudly the horns are blown, the more effort they put into the fight. Music gives comfort to the despairing and fills the miserable and afflicted with joy. It appeases angry hearts and furious diabolical rages. That was seen when David cured King Saul with the sound of his tuned harp.[97] Birds and beasts are attracted by well-played Music, and commotions are calmed.

---

94. On this passage, see Nadia Margolis, "'Où celestiel chimphonye chante … ': Voyage encyclopédique d'un terme musical devenu moral de Macrobe à Christine de Pizan," *Cahiers de recherches médiévales et humanistes* 6 (1999): 187–203 <http://crm.revues.org/935>.

95. A system of musical tuning based on mathematical ratios between sound frequencies.

96. The ancient concept of *musica universalis*, or "music of the spheres," on which Boethius expounds in *De institutione musica* (*The Fundamentals of Music*).

97. 1 Samuel 16:14–23.

IX. *Here is told of Geometry*

7595–7630

The third is Geometry, thanks to which we have the art of proportions and measures, to construct houses straight and make everything even, precise in length and width. By this science, the wise men of ancient times strove to use intelligence to determine the magnitude of the sky and the earth, and the vertical distance between them, as many a writer tells it. And they arrived at the proportions of many other things.

Geometry was first created and verified by the Egyptians. The primary reason was because of the Nile River, that once overflowed and rose so much that it damaged the region a great deal. Because of that, when the water retreated and was back in its place, the inhabitants could not recognize the boundaries or the limits of their fields, which were touching each other. They then established measures and lines, with which they measured their lands. For this reason, Geometry was called the art and skill of measuring, because "geos" means earth, and "metrie" surely means measure, it seems to me. And thus these two words together formed the name of this beloved science.

7631–7659

After a long time, thanks to keen intellects, many measuring tools and compasses were invented. And little by little, the wise and educated worked so much at it that they invented measures and marking instruments, markers, lines, and proportions, with which they measured everything, even the sky, air, earth, and sea. They wanted to calculate the dimension of the earth by measuring the spaces and heights, as the writers tell it. By this science they wanted to try to discover what distance and space pass between the sun and the moon, between the earth and the moon, how much bigger one is than the other, and to what extent the sun, in rising along its axis, is distant in the sky at the summit. One puts a number to it using this science, and in just that way, by provable and true reasoning, the Egyptians designated the distances in the sky through considerable evidence, as well as the perimeter of the world, that is not small, by the number of stadia.

7660–7672: *This discipline of lines, distances, and numbers is itself divided into four branches of plane and solid geometry.*

X. *Here is told of Astronomy*

7673–7720

The fourth mathematical science is Astronomy, which is a friend to intelligent clerks. This one teaches the arrangement of the sky, the movement of the firmament and the stars, and the courses of the seven planets. It teaches their courses' perpetual movement through the twelve beautiful rising signs of the zodiac, their influences and their natures, from which come heat and cold. However, it is called by different names, which are suitable to it. It is called Astronomy, and it is a friend to us, because it comprises the rotation of the sky, how it appears to us, the rising and setting of the noble and valuable star, the movement of the planets that it alone makes happen, the course of the sun, the moon, and the stars together, all other forces that regulate time, and the changes caused by the natural rotation.

It is similarly called Astrology. It is in part natural, and converted into an invented superstition. The latter part is not approved by some.[98] And practitioners of Mathematics[99] also follow it in its applications, which combine with predictions, according to the diverse movements and courses of the wandering stars. They arrange the signs of the sky by sections in their tables, divided into the soul and the limbs. They prognosticate about the future, how it should come, and the ways and conditions of people by their station or their birth, according to the movement of planets on various courses. Abraham, according to Josephus, discovered it, if I was reading well.[100] The Chaldeans[101] later established the predictions, which they found valid.

XI. *Here is told of Practice*

7721-7740
Practice is the second science of the pleasing Philosophy, which shows us what one should do and what is not permitted. Its application and nature can be divided in three ways. One way is to do good things, keep away from bad ones, and eschew what is not good. That is to say, to govern oneself first and foremost and to behave well. Another way calls for governing one's situation with regard to household or heritage, one's possessions and home. Another way is necessary for leading a people or a kingdom, or foreign people in peace, war, and through all perils.

7741-7755: *The ancient sages divided the science of governing oneself and others into Ethics, Economics, and Politics.*

98. On this, see Edgar Laird, "Christine de Pizan and Controversy Concerning Star-Study in the Court of Charles V," *Allegorica* 18 (1997): 21–30; and Willard, "Astrologer's Daughter," 105–6.

99. Christine uses the word "Mathematiques" in line 7703 as a personification of the science (Solente, *Mutacion,* 4:150). The translators of the *Etymologies,* Christine's source for this, have substituted the term "astronomer" for "*mathematicus*" (*The* Etymologies *of Isidore of Seville,* 99).

100. *The* Etymologies *of Isidore of Seville,* 99. Abraham: biblical patriarch; Josephus: Jewish scholar Titus Flavius Josephus (37–ca. 100 CE).

101. People of a small nation that existed between the tenth and sixth centuries BCE in southern Babylon (the region of modern-day Iraq). Chaldeans were renowned for their skill in astrology.

XII. *Here is told of Ethics*

7756–7764
The first of these sciences is Ethics. Ethics holds us back from vice and teaches us how to govern ourselves first, to live well and honestly and do virtuous works, because no one could demonstrate or teach others about productive works without taking them on themselves.

XIII. *Here is told of Economics*

7765–7774
Economics is the second, which teaches us through lovely eloquence to manage our households and instruct our children and our people, be they strong or weak. It teaches us how to increase our wealth and property, manage our possessions and uphold our residences, give and hold back appropriately, and maintain our status.

XIV. *Here is told of Politics*

7775–7802
The third, called Politics, is the highest overall. And in that it reaches higher, it teaches how justly and reasonably to govern an entire country, big or small, foreign or local, noble and bourgeois, kingdom and city, be it in peace or adversity, at all times and in all seasons. Similarly, it teaches all the arts and trades, which are universally necessary to the lives of men. They are identified and made known in two ways: one is through acts, and the other reveals itself in words. The way of acts means the occupations of those such as artisans and carpenters, and all the manual work necessary to human life—these public trades are called mechanical works. And the work that is in the form of discourse, which the mouth says and speaks, is three perfect sciences, undertaken with very great study: Grammar and Dialectic are two of them; the other is Rhetoric.

XV. *Here is told of Grammar*

7803–7831
The first is the foundation and origin of the others. This science teaches us to speak with wisdom, read and write without fault, barbarism, or the defect of solecism or sophism, which puts many a schism into an argument. I will now say what Isidore says with regard to this in his first agreeable and notable book, *Etymologies:* "This is the science and discipline of speaking with proper discourse, as it would be the foundation of the sciences, to be exact, and of the liberal arts. Among the disciplines that come to us, Grammar was invented after letters, so

that those who already knew letters would be more clever, and they would conceive of fine ways of speaking, through proper, well-ordered speech."[102] And it seems to me that within Grammar there are four principal parts, divided in the following manner: letter, syllable, oration, and diction. It is necessary to arrange all Latin discourse according to them.

7832–7880: *The letter is the foundation of text; the syllable is the assembly of letters; diction is words made of one or more syllables; oration is the assembly of words. Christine cites Quintilian's* Institutio Oratoria,[103] *which affirms the importance of grammar, essential for acquiring knowledge.*

7881–7892

And in several places, Saint Gregory recommends it among all the arts,[104] saying that "there is milk in three breasts, which is not allowed to dry up at all. In one there is the milk of orthography, which means to spell well. In the other is the milk of prosody, that is devoted to the study of pronunciation. And the third is syntax, that makes speech correct and well ordered. Grammar, who nurtures and instructs her children, gives them these three milks."

XVI. *Here is told of Dialectic*

7893–7974: *Dialectic teaches one to assert and prove a statement through effective argument. Christine cites Varro's metaphor of the human hand,[105] in which dialectic (that which holds words together) is like the closed fist, while rhetoric (which disseminates words) is the open hand. She notes that the term comes from "dya" (two) and "logos" (word), referring to the back-and-forth of argument and questioning.*

XVII. *Here is told of Rhetoric*

7975–8058: *This discipline teaches one to arrange one's words well and argue prudently. Cicero asserts that this art sets us apart from the animals, and is a necessary skill that has led to more great works than arms ever could. Once again citing Isidore of Seville's* Etymologies *by name, Christine explains that Rhetoric is divided into*

---

102. *The* Etymologies *of Isidore of Seville*, 42.

103. A twelve-volume text concerning rhetoric, dating from ca. 95 CE.

104. Solente points out that this passage does not come from Saint Gregory, but that it resonates with Alexandre de Villedieu's *Doctrinale puerorum*, a grammar in verse composed ca. 1200 (*Mutacion*, 2:353, note to lines 7881-92).

105. The text containing this metaphor is cited in the *Etymologies* (Isidore of Seville, 79), but it has since been lost; see Marcia L. Colish, *The Stoic Tradition from Antiquity to the Early Middle Ages* (Leiden: Brill, 1990), 321.

five parts: invention, disposition, elocution, memory, and pronunciation, with the
ultimate goal of persuasion. A skilled orator is a guide among men.

8059–8070

Now I have told, in part, how Philosophy is divided into several branches and
sciences, according to the very diverse manifestations of certain properties. And
speaking briefly, I have told how all sciences are born of and developed by her. She
is their mother, their nursemaid. There is none that does not come from her. She is
the fountain and the source from which the others originate. But from here I will
pursue my topic, first moving toward the origin.

XVIII. *Here is told of the beginning of the world*

8071–8120

In the very first part of the long and wide room of which I spoke, were found rich-
ly painted depictions of how God made the sky, the earth, and everything found
there; how he put the moon and sun in the firmament just right, and adorned it
with stars; how he separated night from day; and how it pleased him to make an-
gels marvelously beautiful. But Great Pride destroyed this beauty, because thanks
to their great disloyalty, presumption, and grave sin, the angels were knocked
down from the sky to the depths of hell. Their prince was named Lucifer, and is
still called Lucifer. But now he is ill-named, and his name should be criticized, be-
cause while Lucifer means "carrier of light," he is now tremendously ugly instead.
Because they wanted to be like God, the ones who had been angels became devils.
And thus God pays the prideful, although he may wait! May no wise man count
on pride, therefore, because it is too great a vice. God hates it and renders justice
for it. But then almighty God made other angels and placed them in the sky, from
which they never fell, and they could not sin.

   All of this is portrayed in the room I mentioned. After that is vividly de-
picted how God first wanted to form man from the mud of the earth, and make
him in his image without seeking any other aid. He made him more virtuous and
wise than any other earthly creature, and of a better nature. God wanted to give
him the power over beasts, fish, and birds of all kinds, so that man could have free
use of them.

8121–8176

God then made Adam sleep for a while, and from the man's rib he fashioned a
beautiful woman, who had the form of a complete human and a soul endowed
with reason, and was similar to the image of God. When the man awoke from his
sleep, he looked at the woman in the flesh, and he loved her very much and held
her dear. God said that because she was made from Adam's bones, it would be
fitting for the woman to accompany man in work and at rest. Then God led them

through earthly paradise, and he gave over use of the whole place to them, along with all the fruits, except that he forbade them to eat the apples from one single apple tree in the orchard.

But the devil was jealous of man, who would possess paradise after his life, from which the devil had fallen in the past. Because of that, the devil wanted to place an obstacle there, and he did not slack in acting upon it, first taking the form of a snake. He came to Eve and told her that she should taste of the forbidden fruit and urge her husband to eat of it; they could be confident that they would immediately have knowledge of good and evil, and they would be equal to peerless God.

Eve, who did not imagine malice there, naively believed the devil. She took the apple to her husband. She ate of it, and so did the man, which brought them little reward. They immediately started to be ashamed of each other, and hid themselves. They pulled leaves off a fig tree and covered their private parts with them. At that time they recognized that they had greatly transgressed and had lost the state of innocence, for which they were deeply ashamed. At that point our Father came to them and called Adam by name. Adam, who heard God's call, responded in shame and said to him fearfully: "Father! I am hidden here because I know that I have sinned." Then he used the woman as an excuse and blamed her for his misdeed.

8177–8222

Our Father chased them out of paradise and then said to them: "Because you have transgressed my command, you will have pain and torment as long as you live on earth, and you will die an agonizing death. And you, Adam, remember that you will labor with great sweat from your body in order to sustain your life, as will your descendants! And woman, you will carry and give birth to your children with severe pain, and your children will be stained with the sin that you committed in disobeying!" He said to the snake, very angrily, "On earth you will go on your belly, hated by all. Because of this, you will hide, for all men will attack you when they see you!"

Now you hear of such a fate! Fortune, because of whom all good leaves us, was thereupon born, and was complicit in the whole affair. She did this because of her fickleness. And I believe her to be the daughter of the devil because I do not find any writing or text—not prose, not verse—that says or proves that God, who makes all good, beneficial works out of nothing, ever formed or loved Fortune. So I believe that the devil made her, so that she would undo all good and put man in servitude, because there is no shame, damage, or misfortune that does not come to man because of Fortune (may all remember that!). And she does even greater harm to the best than to the worst, night and day. Her disruptive influence will not be short-lived; rather, her control will last until Judgment Day. Thus it was all portrayed and meticulously written in the room.

8223–8244

From that point, Fortune began to reign and control everything, elevating some on her wheel, and throwing others into the mud. Envy was born with her, I believe, on the same day, as was Mischance, who resembles her. Those three were all born together, and they have hatched many a bad plan, because they are always working at it. And it was very well depicted there how, before the world had existed for a long time, Cain took Abel's life because of Envy, for which God cursed him in great anger. I do not plan to tell everything that the Bible attests for us; I would undertake too big a task! And I do not intend to talk about what does not pertain to Fortune, who is the master of everything, and who fabricates and brews up many great misfortunes.

8245–8278: *The earth was populated by the offspring of Adam. The first age of the world lasted for 1,656 years, beginning with Adam and ending with Noah. The world was stained by sin, which made God want to drown all creatures in the great Flood.*

8279–8337

God almost regretted that he had ever created man, so much did he see men driven to all evils, but he had no desire to destroy humanity. So God ordered Noah to make a very beautiful ark, in a certain place, and to bring aboard a male and a female of all useful beasts and of all flying birds. God placed Noah in the ark, along with his wife and children, who had committed no offense against him. The text tells us that they were no more than six to restore the human race. They loaded themselves and their provisions into the ark, with no other retinue, and they closed the ark up tightly. God blessed them and protected them from the Flood that lasted so long it drowned the whole world, because the sea crested with such a great wave from the rains that did not end for forty days, drowning every living thing on earth. When God had satisfied his vengeance, he parted his great clouds, and the sun spread its rays. A rainbow then appeared in the sky for the first time. Noah knew by that sign that God had appeased his wrath. Thus peace was made from the conflict. Nonetheless, the water stayed on the land for 140 days, without getting back on its course.

Then Noah took the crow, in order to learn by watching it whether the land was uncovered. He put it outside the ark, which he had opened, but the crow was in no hurry to return. Rather, it landed on carrion, on which it lived. Noah cursed it when he saw that it did not return to him. He sent out the dove. It flew faster than a sparrow-hawk and brought back an olive branch. It was apparent that the earth was uncovered. Noah devoutly praised God. Fairly soon after that, the ark carrying Noah and his household settled on top of a high mountain in Armenia.[106] God wanted that, so Noah would come out there. Noah thanked God, who had saved him from being killed in the Flood. Thus the matter came to an end.

8338–8412: *The earth was repopulated by descendants of Noah. The second age, from the Flood to the time of Abraham, lasted 1,072 years, during which time the Tower of Babel was built. The third age, from Abraham until David, lasted 942 years. During that age, Troy was burned and the Bible was written. The fourth age, from David's time until the migration from Babylon, lasted for 612 years, although Christine acknowledges disagreement regarding that number. The 585 years from the Exodus to the arrival of Jesus is the fifth age. The sixth age, starting with Jesus, is still going on. Christine decides to get back to her topic, as she has not yet even reached the middle of the depictions on the wall.*

8413–8442

So that I may complete my work and omit nothing from it, I will extend my discourse just a bit more. I will be quiet about the things that Fortune brings up, then down, in many domains. But I will touch upon the ancient and true histories of the Jews, because I do not at all attribute their deeds, their prosperous times, or their great adversities to Fortune. Because God, who held the religion as a friend, punished and rewarded them according to their deserts, putting them high or low depending on their vice or merit, by his justice. As far as I can say, I believe our Lord granted that Fortune would send them gains or losses as deserved. Just as a judge consents to the executioner drowning the sinner, he also consents to the opposite: to the good, give reward. I will therefore touch briefly on the Jews, and align the lordships of those who held the world in joyous triumph with the context of their times; they will be discussed later.

XIX. *Here is told of Nimrod and the founding of Babylon*

8443–8563: *The giant Nimrod, great-grandson of Noah, was the first king after the Flood. Prideful and with no concern for God, he forbade his people to worship anyone but him. Ignoring the objections of the wise people of his lineage, he decided to go to war against God. He set out to build a tower so high that he could conquer heaven, and also be safe from any flood that God might send.*[107]

---

106. Mount Ararat (Genesis 8:4), today located in eastern Turkey.

107. The biblical story of the tower is told in Genesis 11. Nimrod's involvement in the project is not mentioned there, but can be found in Josephus, *Antiquities of the Jews*, and in the *Histoire ancienne jusqu'à César*.

8564–8603

At a suitable place along the Nile, which is a very great river passing through Egypt and descending to the sea from Armenia, Nimrod had the new tower erected. The foundations were great and deep, to last a long time, because to complete such a great work it was necessary to make strong foundations. The giants themselves scoured the earth and did the work, because it required such strength that other people would not have had the power to erect such a sturdy structure. Nimrod, who governed them all, dictated how fired clay was to be made, polished, and whitewashed, and how they would make the mortar and prepare the cement to seal the hard stones together at the joints. Then Nimrod came up with all the instruments and tools necessary for making buildings. First, to make strong masonry, by his cleverness he invented the rules and measures to erect the buildings and keep the stones straight. There was no idleness, because each giant did the job that Nimrod chose to assign him. He had ladders and machines built to bring the stones up high, along with everything a worker needed to do the masonry. And thus the giants built the tower, and then left from it in shame and confusion, as I will tell you in the conclusion.

8603–8642

But first they worked so much that they built the tower very high. I will tell you how big around this tower was. Hardly would any man believe, by any account, the breadth, thickness, and height that had already been reached when God wanted the nefarious project of the giants, who already lived inside, to be entirely undone. The Tower of Babel was begun five hundred years after God, who judges all, had sent the Flood. It was so far along that it was already three leagues and 460 feet high when God, who watches over everything, in his wisdom made the work stop. The wall was handsome. That was the height of the Tower of Babel. This tower that Nimrod hurried to build was perfectly square. It contained forty leagues of arable land, ten on each side. And there were thirty-one very strong doors of brass or copper on each side. This tower was built with very hard stones, and so solidly made that the walls were fifty cubits thick. Anyone who sees it even now, although it may be in ruins, can see that the tower of fired clay, hard and strong, sealed with cement, was great, wide, and quite high then, as I said. At around noon hour, the shadow is visible seven leagues away. Never was there such a high wall!

More about this

8643–8692

As you are hearing, the giants, working as quickly as they could, accomplished so much that they raised the beginnings of the tower to the noted height. They were hoping to reach the sky, but they could not. At that point, God, who confronts pride, by his divine providence, took away any hope for their plan. He suddenly put such variability in the language they spoke that when the masons wanted to ask for lime, stone was brought to them, or someone went seeking cement for them. Or if they asked for a rule or a hammer, the others did not understand them for anything and gave them the very opposite. Then their labor and the goal they were striving for failed, because they did not understand each other. At that point, they considered themselves tricked (and you know that many were bewildered by this occurrence!). Now they knew that no being could fight against God. Foolishness made them strive for it!

Then they completely abandoned the project, parted from each other because they spoke different languages, and went to different countries. For the havoc that God, by his promise, sent there because of their pride, the place was henceforth named: "The Tower of Babel." That is to say, "confusion," because our Father sent confusion there, which disoriented all the workers. And the construction stopped. The seventy-two strange and diverse languages that are spoken everywhere in the world were first found in those structures. Previously there had been only one language, Hebrew, that Jews spoke by custom and nature. None of the others are worth that one, because God himself invented it, and it is the most authentic language.

8693–8730: *Nimrod was furious that his plan, impelled by Great Pride, had been thwarted. Many gods were worshipped in his kingdom, which prospered for a time.*

XX. Here is told of the Jews[108]

8731–8748

Now it is necessary for me to make a little excuse here, because I cannot amuse myself with rhyming, due to a sudden fever that has overpowered me and from which I am suffering. I must let the rhyming be for this passage of the text. Instead, to speed up my work, I will turn to prose in order to write word for word

---

108. On Christine's attitude toward the Jews, see Thelma Fenster, "The Fortune of the Jews in the *Mutacion de Fortune*," in Buschinger et al., *Christine de Pizan et son époque*, 80–87; Jean-François Kosta-Théfaine, "Christine de Pizan et la question des Juifs: Problème d'orthodoxie, d'hétérodoxie ou simple (in)tolérance?" *Speculum medii aevi* 3 (1997): 39–52; Nadia Margolis, "Christine de Pizan and the Jews: Political and Poetic Implications," in Brabant, *Politics, Gender, and Genre*, 53–73; Earl Jeffrey Richards, "Christine de Pizan, Tolerance and the Plea for Equal Protection under the Law: Revisiting the Question of Her Attitudes toward Hierarchical Justice, the Jews, Widows and Rape Victims: A Close Reading of the *Livre des fais et bonnes meurs du sage roy Charles V*, 1.23," in *Tolérance et intolérance: Actes du Colloque international des 1er, 2 et 3 mars 2011 à Amiens*, ed. Danielle Buschinger (Amiens: Presses du Centre d'Etudes Médiévales, Université de Picardie-Jules Verne, 2011), 108–14; and Richards, "Poems of Water without Salt and Ballades without Feeling, or Reintroducing History into the Text: Prose and Verse in the Works of Christine de Pizan," in Richards, ed., *Christine de Pizan and Medieval French Lyric* (Gainesville: University Press of Florida, 1998), 206–29.

everything in the above-mentioned room, where I found the Bible written. May that not be taken wrong, because I am not in full health, which is troubling my mind somewhat at the moment. Whoever takes on the task of rhyming well has no small charge, especially abridging histories in true words!

On this same topic[109]

1—Starting with the time of Nimrod, who founded Babylon, the lordships of the Hebrews were governed in several ways. Their government first had the Patriarchs. Then they were governed by Judges, third by kings and by dukes. Abraham, the great Patriarch who lived at the time of Ninus, king of Nineveh,[110] governed them first. He first created the Hebrew letters, and lived for 180 years. In his time, the five cities of Sodom and Gomorrah were burned by fire from the sky.[111]

Christine then lists six succeeding Patriarchs and notes how long they lived, some of them contextualized with respect to events of their times.

2—After this begins the time of the Judges who, over the span of 818 years, held the lordship and government of the people of Israel. Joshua, otherwise called Jesus,[112] was the first Judge to have authority over the people after the death of Moses; he lived 110 years. In his time, the river Jordan dried up and the sun stopped for a span of two days. After him came Caleb who, at the time of Joshua's death, was already one hundred years old. In his time, the musician Orpheus prospered, as did Saturn and Jupiter, as well as Solinus, Varro, and the first Sibyl,[113] who was from Persia.

From the second half of section 2 through section 5, Christine continues to list the succession of Judges, ending with Samuel. Next came the time of Kings.

6—The first king was Saul, who reigned for twenty years. In his time, David killed the great giant Goliath, and Codrus, also known as Codros, seventeenth king of Athens, had his reign.[114] In his time, the kingdom of the Corinthians also began,[115] and Aletes reigned first. King Saul had several battles against the

---

109. The prose section, which begins here, comprises approximately 3,500 words divided into fourteen sections (2:156–70).

110. King of Assyria and Babylon, credited with founding the city. On Nineveh, see also note 40.

111. Sodom and Gomorrah, along with three other cities, were known as the "cities of the plain" in the region of the Dead Sea. They are said to have been destroyed by God for their rampant vice (Genesis 18–19).

112. Referred to as "Jesus, son of Nun" to avoid confusion with Jesus Christ.

113. Orpheus was a musician of Greek myth whose playing had supernatural powers. Gaius Julius Solinus was a Latin linguist and geographer from the third century CE; for Varro, see note 72. The Sibyls were women of Greek myth believed to be endowed with the power to predict the future.

114. Eleventh century BCE.

115. People of Corinth, a Greek city-state, rival of Athens.

Philistines;[116] he was victorious several times and defeated several times. After him, David reigned for forty years in Jerusalem. Homer reached his prime during his time.[117] The people had several battles then, sometimes victories, sometimes defeats, which were always caused by transgression of the law, idolatry in particular.

From the second half of section 6 through the first half of section 13, Christine elaborates on the succession of kings, again alluding to historical events of their times. Regarding defeats and tribulations suffered by the Jews, Christine blames "the people's mistaken idolatry, toward which they had a strong inclination, and the cruelty of the kings" (section 10).

13—[…] the Jews had kings of their lineage all this time, until Herod,[118] who reigned at the time that our Lord was born. He was the first foreign king to reign in Judea, because he was not a Jew. Rather, he was Idumean and acquired the kingdom of the Jews for the Romans, to whom the Jews were entirely subjugated since Pompey, a prince of Rome, had taken Judea.[119] Starting with Herod, the Jews did not have kings of their lineage. Rather, the land of Judea was always governed by foreign agents ordered by the Romans.

14—Forty-two years after the death of our Lord, the kingdom of Judea completely failed, and Jerusalem and the country were destroyed by Titus and Vespasian, emperor of Rome.[120] Those who remained gathered together and established some dwellings in Jerusalem. But a long time later, that is to say the year 119 after the incarnation, the emperor of Rome, named Hadrian,[121] subjugated them and drove them out. He rebuilt Jerusalem in such a configuration that the sacred places of the Passion and Resurrection of our Lord, which had previously been outside the city, are now within. And because of his name, Helius, he called Jerusalem "Helya." Starting then, the Jews were wandering and unstable, without country and without a lord, in punishment for the sin that they committed in crucifying our Lord.[122]

Explicit the fourth part of the present volume.

116. People of Ancient Palestine.

117. Greek poet of the eighth century BCE, author of the *Iliad* and the *Odyssey*.

118. Herod I, or Herod the Great (ca. 74–4 BCE).

119. The Idumeans were the people of Idumea, or Edom, a region south of the Dead Sea. Gnaeus Pompeius Magnus, Pompey the Great (106–48 BCE), was a Roman political and military leader who subjugated Judea in the Siege of Jerusalem (63 BCE).

120. Vespasian was emperor of Rome 69–79 CE. His son Titus succeeded him, reigning 79–81 CE.

121. Emperor 117–38 CE.

122. The prose section ends here.

Here begins the fifth part
of The Book of the Mutability of Fortune

I. *First, about the first kingdoms that ruled the world, and about the nobility of Greece*

8749–8778
Thank God! The malady that troubled my thinking and weakened my body is now cured. So I will rhyme, as I am used to doing, following my initial style. Let it be in the name of God almighty! At that time Covetousness, which inflames the human heart to acquire honor, started to spread. The great wanted to subjugate and dominate the lowly, and therefore they sought to oppress each other by wars and battles. That was the beginning of the calamities and ills that caused painful troubles for many. Because there was little order among them, all nations wanted a king and princes who would exact rightful payment from great and small, and be their chief and leader. So they made the most powerful, strongest, and most illustrious among them king, all of common will. Thus the princes have carried on from heir to heir since, aside from those who were stripped of their lands by Fortune, treason, or war.

II. *Here is told of the beginning of the kingdoms of Assyria and Babylon*

8779–8837: *Belus was the first king of Assyria, followed by the powerful Ninus, who named his capital city Nineveh. That city had been founded by Assur, a grandson of Noah and the person for whom Assyria was named. Ninus set out to conquer Babylon. The Babylonians—strong, proud, and hot-tempered—were ready for him.*

8838–8894
At that time, there was no armor of iron or steel, which weighs down heavily, nor helmet, shield, or target, only boiled leather. Without having girded themselves with sharpened swords, they were dressed and prepared for battle. They were not otherwise armed. In place of swords and lances, they had big, gnarled clubs of wood. The men had distinctive marks on them, as a sign and to be distinguishable from one another. They still rarely went on horseback because they were so big and strong that they had little need of horses. They could sustain great exertion on foot, without another beast carrying them or hurrying their journey even more. They waged war that way. At the start, the princes had rapid wagons made, and loaded them with whatever they needed to defend themselves and attack their enemies. The wagons were equipped with rich accoutrements, and the princes and kings were fitted out in very great array.

They had bows and arrows then, which they shot very well. And the princes were seated in wagons with five or six of their people who served them best or who had highest standing. Horses clad in leather pulled the wagons where the princes sat. But there was a well known custom in those days, whereby neither the wagon-driver nor the horse would move if they were not first struck by someone or attacked. Then the princes fought and brought down everything before them with shots from crossbows, spears, or slingshots, making deep and deadly wounds in whatever they struck. Battles were like that then. Thus Ninus, with his people, attacked the Babylonians and battled violently against them. But the Babylonians did not fall short at all. Rather, they received him harshly and fought confidently, like strong, hot-tempered, hardy people. I do not know what more I can tell you about it!

8895–9050: *With Fortune on his side, Ninus won the bloody battle, and the Babylonians retreated within the city's impenetrable walls. Ninus, who wanted the city, was ready to resume fighting the next morning. The Babylonians fled the city, however, allowing Ninus to seize it and populate it with his people. Ninus married the noble and warlike Semiramis,[123] and together they conquered many kingdoms. Ninus had a great temple built, where the people worshipped a golden image of his father Belus. Ninus reigned for fifty years, continuing his warring ways, acquiring Chaldea, Asia, and Scythia.[124] He started the practice of collecting taxes and tribute from those whom he subjugated.*

9050–9086

But listen to the trick of Fortune, who upsets everything, how she ambushed Ninus when she had seated him at his highest, and how Mischance burdened him with violent hardship in order to put an end to his pleasure. After he had attacked and taken Babylon, Ninus happened to be struck by a very strong arrow. I do not know who shot it, or whether he was watched or betrayed, but he was so severely injured that he deteriorated to the point of death. Thus he no longer pursued arms, unless he went to war in hell, because on earth he could fight no more. Then the world had peace from him.

That is how Fortune treats those she elevates, all of a sudden striking them with a blow of misfortune. And as it happens, she will have protected them in greater perils a hundred times, without their perishing. But when they are not on their guard, at the point when they think they are protected and can reign happily, then they perish in some way, without seeing it coming. We see this happen often! It is thus a true thing that the joy and glory of people, which matters little, lasts a short time and costs too much. Fortune takes it away in a moment!

123. Amazonian queen.

124. A region of central Eurasia, now known as the Pontic-Caspian steppe.

III. *Here is told of Semiramis*

9087–9142

Ninus was put in the sepulcher. His wife, the powerful queen Semiramis, then ruled. The kingdom and lordship did not fall to ruin under her. Rather, after the death of her lord, she subjugated many kingdoms by her feats of arms and prowess, and took them into her hands. Indeed she dominated even more than before, because she conquered all of Ethiopia. Then she entered India by force, and won so much through arms that she took it into her possession. No one else had ever accomplished that, however much he might have tried and however keen he might have been to do so, except Alexander the Great, of whom I will speak later on.[125] But this lady, who had very great sense, strength, and power, brought it, along with many other regions, under her authority, because she had many legions of warriors serving her and following her into all countries, to gain profit and honor.

Never had a lady been born on earth with greater generosity, or with more wisdom to command a powerful army, because she kept nothing secret and held nothing back. Rather, she gave each person his or her share of the property she acquired. In that way, she conquered a great deal by force of arms and people, and by giving gold and silver. Semiramis was very feared and loved by her friends. She comported herself valiantly in arms. She built up her kingdom and kept it in peace. She founded many castles, towns, cities, and burgs. All of her efforts always went toward acquiring lands and gaining power, and she conquered and held plenty of them. She was the first to have trenches made to fortify cities, and the first to erect palisades, fortified castles, and many clever defenses against enemy attacks. Semiramis had Babylon completely enclosed in trenches, which was surely a tremendous work.

9143–9174

This lady had many virtues, but many reproached her because she had married her son. She justified doing that, however, because in no way did she want him to have a wife or lover who would be crowned queen. She did not want any woman born, besides herself, to be called lady in her kingdom, whether she was feared or loved. There were no laws or writings then, aside from the law of nature, and according to that, people were allowed to do whatever pleased them most and indulge in whatever would bring them the most pleasure. Therefore, Semiramis was not actually to be reproached for taking her son, because I truly believe that if there had been a law then, she never would have married him.

---

125. This allusion points to the shifting demarcations of this area over the centuries; Alexander did not conquer all of what we now recognize as India.

This lady kept the domain in great prosperity for forty-two full years, and she acquired nearly a third of the world through her chivalrous might. Semiramis had very powerful help from Fortune, who was exceedingly gentle and kind to her. But although Fortune helped her, in the end Fortune was bitter toward her and attacked her. Fortune did not help Semiramis in her need, because they say that she met a violent death.

9175–9200: *Babylon was then besieged and burned by Arbaces, a lieutenant of King Sardanapalus of Media, whom Arbaces went on to unseat.*[126] *The renown and authority of Assyria and Babylon were lost to the supremacy of Media, in another example of Fortune's doing.*

9201–9224

All these things that I have recounted were portrayed in the room of Fortune's castle. I must pass, however, on many great princes and other people, because I would be burdening myself too much if I were to relate everything I saw on the wall and what the images I saw there revealed to me about Fortune's tricks. If I wanted to write everything, I would never complete it. It suffices, therefore, for me to tell only how the greatest lordships came and were then destroyed, as examples of how Fortune changes in an instant. That is why one should not have faith in her, because she pays more than she owes, but the pay is often harsh. Still, one must endure it. And thus the reputation of Assyria was destroyed, which had been the most favored over all the empires of the world, and had lasted for thirteen hundred years.

IV. *Here is told how Arbaces transferred the authority and honor of Babylon to Media, and about his heirs*

9225–9258: *The heirs of Arbaces reigned after him. One night Astyages,*[127] *the sixth king of Media, dreamt that a vine issued forth from his daughter and surrounded the kingdom. According to the soothsayers, the dream foretold the birth of an heir who would threaten the king's rule.*

9259–9308

Because of the strange dream, and to eliminate the possibility of its coming true and of anyone remembering it, the king married his daughter off lowly and quite poorly. That way, the heir would have neither the power nor the opportunity to make it happen. But his stratagem and what he did to implement it hardly worked to his advantage. As I understand it from history, almost no time had passed be-

---

126. Arbaces was a prince of Media, a province of Assyria, of which Sardanapalus was king. The time frame for these events would be the seventh century BCE.

127. Reigned 585–550 BCE.

fore the woman had a handsome son by her husband. That angered the king, and he swore and vowed that he would have his grandson killed, so he would be safe from the whole thing, and from Fortune and Mischance. To do that, he thereupon summoned his provost and ordered him in complete secrecy to kill the child. While the provost did not dare to contradict the king, he did not kill the baby. Rather, he quickly had him placed in the forest, out in the cold.

The child was found there by chance, by a shepherd who heard him crying.[128] The shepherd saved the boy from a big, fierce hunting dog who was nursing him and who protected him from other animals, from fierce wild beasts, and from snakes and vermin. The shepherd was very surprised by that. He put forth such an effort that he rescued the baby. But first the dog suffered many blows, which afflicted her greatly. The shepherd, who did not underestimate this marvel, took the child to his house (that was surely right!). The boy was well cared for there, because the shepherd's wife immediately fed him as if he were hers, or as if she were receiving great recompense for it. The child was a very lovely creature of noble appearance, so gracious and pleasant that there was nothing more agreeable. The shepherd's wife, who loved him dearly, named him "Spartacus."

9309–9356

When the child had grown up a bit, having always thought that the shepherd was his father and that the shepherd's wife had carried him, he led their animals to pasture every day. But Spartacus reverted to his true nature, because in his ways, body, form, behavior, person, and condition, he seemed very much like the son of a king. And he had such a very proud heart that all the shepherds of the woodland elected him to be their king, and made him their lord and master. Spartacus, who was king of the children, punished offenses according to what the misdeed was. He punished them all, without sparing brother or sister. He kept them in line with great rigor, and all obeyed him and did as he ordered.

He had already punished more than twenty children when this case arose: a shepherd, cutting a cake, lost his little knife. Another, sitting by his side, had stolen it from him. The shepherd complained to the king, but there was no way for the king to know the truth about the knife. Therefore, he had all the shepherds undress, and thus the truth was proven. The knife was found on the belt of the shepherd's son, Spartacus's brother, by mother and father. The guilty shepherd believed that their family tie would make a difference. He had no advantage, however, because Spartacus himself hanged his brother in the wood. And when the shepherd heard that Spartacus had hanged his son, he would have killed Spartacus immediately, but the shepherdess, looking at her child, kept him from it. This event was not kept secret, and it was soon known far and wide that the shepherds had a king, even if he were dressed in coarse cloth.

128. Cf. the story of Romulus and Remus, a king's grandsons raised by a shepherd, in Book 7, chapter 2.

9357–9386

Astyages heard the news. The event was very surprising to him, and he summoned the shepherd. Wanting to know the truth, he inquired about it and it was told to him. He also learned from where the child had come, and how the shepherd had found him naked in the great forest and immediately took him away to his house and cared for him, so that he would not die or be killed. The king looked at his grandson, who pleased him greatly, and asked him why he had punished the children, who had taught him to do it, and who had designated him king. The child started to talk frankly to the king, with very wise words and a bold expression. He told the king that the shepherds, who take care of cows and bulls, sheep, ewes, goats, and billy-goats, had elected him above all others to be their king and master. For that reason, he wanted to be equitable and uphold justice for all, otherwise he would not be suited to be king, to reign over shepherds, or to govern.

9387–9402: *Realizing Spartacus's true identity and seeing that Spartacus had already established his own "kingdom," Astyages no longer feared that the dream warned of a threat to himself.*

9402–9421

The king kept the child at his court to learn honor and the custom of taking up arms. He committed Spartacus to the authority of his provost. But the king wickedly took cruel vengeance for the provost's having disobeyed him by not killing his grandson, because the king had the provost's own child cooked and made him eat the flesh. That meal was later sold to the king at a high price, because for that great cruelty and many others, the king lost his royal power. Thus it went. And the provost talked about it so much to the barons, in fact, that Spartacus was made their king. Thus the predictions were proven true.

9422–9436: *Spartacus and his army would go on to attack Astyages and his assembled troops. Spartacus spared his grandfather's life and granted him lands, even though Astyages was greatly despised.*

V. Here is told how Spartacus, who was later called Cyrus,[129] **was made king of Persia, and how the authority of Media was transferred to Persia**

9437–9486: *Spartacus asserted his power in Persia, where he was called Cyrus, meaning "right and powerful heir" (9454).*[130] *He continued his conquering ways, gaining Scythia, Asia, Assyria, Chaldea, Syria, and Babylon.*

VI. Here is told more about Cyrus and his conquests

9487–9534: *Conquering Babylon took extreme effort, as the city was protected by the fast and deep Tigris River. Cyrus assembled a great number of workers to dig the earth, in order to lower the water level enough that a woman could ford the river without lifting the hem of her dress. He left Darius*[131] *in charge of that area as he went on to conquer Lydia.*

VII. Here is told of how Cyrus was killed by Tomyris, queen of Amazonia[132]

9535–9658: *Cyrus wanted to conquer Amazonia, where Tomyris was queen. He entered her land, and had his rich tents set up and a great feast laid out. Knowing that the Amazons would soon attack, Cyrus was fearful in spite of himself. So he came up with a ruse. He and his men fled the site on horseback. Seeing this, the approaching Amazons, led by Tomyris's beloved son who resided in Scythia, believed that Cyrus was fleeing out of fear, and they pursued him. Once the armies of Amazonia and Scythia chased Cyrus and his men far enough away, they returned to pillage Cyrus's tents and enjoy the sumptuous provisions, thinking that the danger was gone.*

9659–9702

It was night. They were asleep when the Persian army sprung upon them and attacked them with great troops, killing them blindly, such that none of them would remain. The son of Queen Tomyris was killed by a sword there, which saddened her heart. It was a pity and a shame, because he was a worthy and wise young man. The queen had grief beyond measure over this defeat and over her son, whom she loved greatly, and who had feared her so! And she swore to her gods, in great fury,

---

129. Cyrus the Great, founder of the Persian Empire (ca. 600–ca. 529 BCE); on Cyrus in this poem, see Huber, "*Histoire ancienne jusqu'à César.*"

130. This is just one of many possible meanings ascribed to the name "Cyrus" over time and across languages.

131. Darius I, called Darius the Great (550–486 BCE), king of Persia as of 522 BCE.

132. According to Herodotus, 1.201–05 (*The Landmark Herodotus*, 107–11), Tomyris was actually the ruler of the Massagetae, people of Central Asia. The founding of the Amazon kingdom of warrior women is the focus of Book 6, chapter 1 below.

that as soon as Cyrus left the empire, she would make him pay for the grief that closed up her heart, or she would die trying.

Tomyris, who was very smart, carefully considered a great ruse. Before showing any signs of fighting Cyrus or doing him ill, she allowed him to enter further into a narrow passage in the mountains. She had three ambushes set in place: two in the ancient forest, the third on the rough rock by the passage that Cyrus would have to traverse when he came through there. When Cyrus had made his way between the mountains and away from the fields, and his whole army had entered the passage, he was abruptly met with an ambush in that byway. Never had so many wasps issued from a nest, or sparks from a fire, as arrows flew from the women archers there, who had sold the lives of their good friends too dearly to the Persians, who killed them. By their misfortune, the Persians had put themselves in the hands of such extraordinary women, who took the Persians' souls from their bodies.

9703–9732: *With arrows and rocks, the Amazons massacred the trapped Persians. The valleys echoed with the Persians' cries, blowing horns, and whinnying horses. Fortune had turned her back on Cyrus.*

9733–9758
The valiant Tomyris, who had more beauty, strength, vigor, and daring than Paris,[133] was there. She fought fiercely. The memory of her son made her put all the Persians to ruin and grievous death by arms and piercing arrows; blood ran from them in great streams. King Cyrus was taken and very closely guarded. It could be no other way, because Fortune, who had remained good and gentle to him for a long time, had promised that ultimately she would put him to the death that she had destined for him. When the battle was over, the princess Tomyris, mistress of the other queens, had her trumpets and horns sounded loudly, such that one could hear valleys and hills resonate with them. There was no louder blowing of horns in the whole world! Then the troops of women all came and gathered there.

9759–9802
They traveled so much by fields and furrows that they came to their tents, where they celebrated very joyously, in great honor and victory. Tomyris, loved by her people, disarmed at the tent and changed into rich clothes. Cyrus, who tried very hard to gain mercy through eloquent pleas, was then pitifully brought before the lady. Tomyris thereupon said to him with a high and proud heart, "Oh you, king filled with great cruelty, who has caused so much bloodshed! Whoever would hang you at the gallows and bring you even greater misfortune would not sufficiently avenge the human blood shed because of you. But I will make you drink

133. Trojan hero; a central figure in Book 6, chapters 11–29.

from such a cup that you will have your fill, because you will drink blood, which never satiated you before. Now you will drink your fill of it!" She then had his head cut off, and had a great wash-tub, deep and round, brought near him. It was full of the blood of the barons whom she had had killed in his presence, to make him suffer even more. To settle the score, she had his head thrown into it, saying, "Oh you, Cyrus, who craved human blood night and day, now you can drink of it copiously from a vessel much larger than a glass!" Thus King Cyrus died because of Fortune, who was not done until she had finished him off completely. He truly believed that he had been born to conquer the whole world. But folly made him seek out that which Fortune gives and takes away, and changes at all times!

VIII. *Here is told of Cambyses, the great king of Persia, called Artaxerxes or Nebuchadnezzar the second*[134]

9803–9836

King Cyrus had one son, valiant at arms and of keen intelligence. He reigned after his father, who had met his end through bitter fortune. He was Cambyses, called Artaxerxes by many, and he reigned for eight years. In that time he conquered many countries, because he was very valiant, chivalrous, and diligent. He accomplished a great deal by his feats of arms, conquering such great lordship, wealth, and treasure that he was called Nebuchadnezzar the second by some. The story of Judith tells of him and his ways. He vanquished the Egyptians and put them to shame, as they had rebelled and stopped paying him the tribute that his father had gotten from them. So he paid them grievous recompense. In Egypt, along the Nile, he established a beautiful city that was called the new Babylon,[135] and he made it very strong. He erected many a sturdy tower and gate there, and it was enclosed in solid walls. He put great treasure in there, and he populated it abundantly. At present there are very many people in that city, which is still strong and powerful today.

9837–9865

Cambyses already held Assyria, because his father had made him lord of it during his lifetime, and he inherited the city of Nineveh. For that reason he was then called Nebuchadnezzar the second. Arphaxad reigned in Media at that time, exercising absolute authority and power over the country. He was rich with people and wealth. He set out to conquer countries, foreign kingdoms, and nations by force of arms and war. His armies had already entered many countries when Nebuchadnezzar heard of him. Nebuchadnezzar thought he would go mad with anger when it became clear that Arphaxad would no longer, for any reason, pay him

---

134. Cambyses II, King of Assyria and Persia, son of Cyrus the Great; reigned 529–522 BCE.

135. In what is now part of Old Cairo.

tribute from Media. Nebuchadnezzar said he would remedy that. Then he had such a great army assembled that the country should have trembled from it. But Arphaxad knew about the whole thing, and said he was not afraid of Nebuchadnezzar. He believed he would well take revenge against Nebuchadnezzar, were he able to approach him. Arphaxad rose up in great pride, and then left from his city of Ecbatana.[136]

9866–10030: *Arphaxad set off with a great army. The two sides met in violent battle, where Fortune favored Cambyses (Nebuchadnezzar). Cambyses, ever more prideful, sent messengers far and wide to demand tribute from other lands and threaten war should they not comply. When many refused, he made good on his threat, putting Holofernes in charge of the war.*[137] *Cambyses ordered that statues of himself be erected and adored in every land that Holofernes conquered. After Holofernes dominated Mesopotamia and Cilicia,*[138] *other lands surrendered to him without a fight. He replaced their idols with images of Nebuchadnezzar.*

IX. *Here is told of Holofernes*

10031–10052
Holofernes, who went about conquering all and ravaging countries, then wanted to go against the Jews, who fled into towns and strong towers because they greatly feared his attacks. They were all frightened of him and pitifully lamented to God, in great prayer, asking him to enable them to escape Holofernes. They asked that Holofernes not be able to capture them, and for God to protect his holy religion, so that Holofernes would not take it over and destroy it with his frivolous, vain, and false idols. They were in a very difficult situation in the city of Jerusalem, because of their fear of that great army. It was God's will to protect them from it and defend his holy religion, which no one had the right to harm!

10053–10072: *Although small in number, the Jews set up defenses at a narrow mountain pass. Holofernes heard about their resistance.*

10073–10111
Duke Holofernes then wanted to know the whole truth about the Jews. He was told what faith they practiced, where they were from, and from where had come the sons of Israel, who would have just one God and honor no others. Moab,

136. Capital of Media; the site of modern-day Hamadān, Iran.

137. A general under Cambyses, beheaded by Judith (see chapter 10 below).

138. A region in southern Asia Minor.

Achior, and Ammon[139] gave Holofernes a great discourse on the Jews. They said that when the Jews served their God, by true and good intention, no one would have any hope of harming them, because their God would protect them well. No one could do damage to them, however much force they might put into it. But when they were not striving to serve their God, ill would often come to them. Otherwise, things did not go badly for them. They therefore advised Holofernes to learn whether the Jews had lately incurred the wrath of God. If yes, he should attack them. If not, he should pull back from there, because in no way would it be advantageous to wage war against them. It would be foolish to attack! Holofernes was very angry at this discourse, and he started to say to Achior, out of great indignation, "You know that I do not deign to esteem the god of which you speak, and that all gods besides Nebuchadnezzar are trifling. I want you to go to the Jews right now, and you will be hanged and killed when I overtake them." Then he had Achior, to whom he did not want to listen, taken by his sergeants and brought before Bethulia.[140]

10112–10148

There was a castle near the mountains, right at the edge of the countryside, where Holofernes had dug in and held siege. The sergeants left Achior there, tied to a tree. The people in the castle, seeing him tied up, ran there to learn what was going on. He told them everything. They untied him, raised him up, and led him inside the castle, where he told them all about the event. They thanked God, and prayed devoutly that God would not forget them. The Jews greatly honored the man they had untied, and he praised God for it, turning to that religion, which made him more virtuous. Holofernes, who was outside with all his armies and troops, cut off the water from those inside (it came to them via conduits), which frightened them terribly. The deprivation lasted so long that to have water, a number of the Jews became agitated and said to the elders who governed them that they would be better off surrendering to Holofernes rather than being taken and hanged by him or moaning there in distress. Ozias[141] then calmed them, telling them that they would suffer for five more days, praying to God every day, and that God would send them help and guide them best.

139. "Moab" represented the Moabite people (Solente, *Mutacion*, 4:155); the kingdom of Moab was located in what is now western Jordan and was partly bounded on the north by the kingdom of Ammon. Achior was a general of the Ammonites, or "sons of Ammon." Both the Moabites and Ammonites descended from Abraham's nephew Lot, according to Genesis 19:36–38.

140. Biblical city saved by Judith.

141. Leader of the Jewish people of Bethulia.

X. *Here is told how the valiant lady Judith killed Holofernes*[142]

10149–10210

In the city there was a widow, a very beautiful and virtuous lady. She was called Judith. She was wise and of high repute. She was of the lineage of Reuben, the son of Jacob,[143] and she rejected earthly things. She considered the troubles and great perils of the Jews, which put them in danger of being destroyed. She had tremendous pity for them, so she entered into a very risky undertaking: to save the people of God, she would put herself in great peril. But she had great trust in God, and she prayed and crossed herself so that he would help her in this great need and always support her. The lady adorned herself richly and dressed in elegant and well-made clothing, arranging herself so well that she seemed to be a goddess or a fairy; she was so lovely and well attired! She and her most trusted servant, no one else, left from the city and went straight toward the area where Holofernes's army was located.

It was already dark, because it was nighttime. When the men of the army noticed the women, they immediately ran there. They looked intently at Judith by the light of the moon. Those who kept watch to guard the army marveled greatly at her beauty. They led her before Holofernes, who said that he had never seen a woman of such beauty. And he asked her, in good faith, what had brought her there. He received her grandly, with a great feast and joyous welcome. He said that he dearly cherished her arrival. The lady, who hid her thoughts well, then replied to him: "Lord! Your very great merit brings me here. Know that all the Jews will be taken by you, because they have transgressed against God, served him badly, and committed sins. God cannot suffer misdeeds for long without punishment. Because of this, with God against them, you will achieve your goal. You will soon be able to do your will to them, this I know well. And if you wish to believe my counsel, you will in fact take them all, and you will learn how from me. I will surely not delay in telling you the hour and the day, where and how."

10211–10245

The duke greatly rejoiced upon hearing those words, because the lady pleased him so much that he believed whatever she said. She seemed to him a very honorable lady, more gracious and beautiful than other women. And when he looked at her more intently, he coveted her more in his heart. He presented her with great treasure, rich jewels, silver, and gold, and a fitting place for her lodging. The lady said that her custom was to worship God by night, and to separate herself from people. It was therefore necessary for her to come out from the tents, if he would

142. On Judith in Christine's works, see Claire Le Ninan, "La veuve et le tyran: L'exemplum de Judith dans l'oeuvre de Christine de Pizan," in Caraffi, *Christine de Pizan: La scrittrice e la città*, 75–82.

143. Jacob: biblical patriarch.

be willing to allow her to do that. He said that it pleased him well. The lady was lodged near the duke's tent. He asked what she wanted someone to bring for her meal, and said that she should request whatever food would please her. But she replied that she would transgress her religion if any mixture or preparation of food were made for her by a stranger who was not of her faith. For that reason, her servant had brought her all of her provisions in a small wooden basket. It was bread and cheese, wine, oil, and other dairy products. She did not wish to ask for any other food.

10246–10265: *Judith stayed there for four days, revealing her plan to no one, and praying nightly to God for the courage to carry it out and save her people. One evening, a drunken and desirous Holofernes summoned her.*

10266–10318

Prudently, she went there, saying that she would do his wish and surely not oppose him over it. Holofernes, who was drunk, went to bed. The lady hardly hurried to join him. Rather, she delayed, praying to God all the while, because she trembled all over from fear. Meanwhile, the drunken duke went into such a sound sleep that he felt nothing. Judith called him, and tugged and pulled at him, in order to know whether he was sleeping soundly. She prayed to God for his help. The duke had had the tent emptied, so there was no chamberlain, valet, noble, or lowly person. He so wanted to be alone in private with Judith. The lady had the front and back guarded by her chambermaid, so that no one would come upon them and make things go badly for her.

Holofernes had a great sword at the head of the bed, and she went to seize it. She took it out of its sheath and approached Holofernes. She gave him such a blow that she cut off his head. And then by force she pulled away a bed-curtain of worked gold and green silk, and many rich stones, which had covered the entire bed. She took it, calmly, and wrapped the head in it. She left from there, and by divine grace she got away, past the army. She and her servant went so far that they came to the gates of the city with no difficulty or adversity, safe and sound in body and soul. Then the lady started to cry out "Open! Open! God is with us! Come to me! Save yourselves! Because by me, woman, God has saved the whole land of Judea!" Then they opened the doors to her. And when they saw the duke's head, they expressed great joy inside. They led the lady in front of Ozias, who received her with great honor when he learned of the deed.

10319–10366: *Ozias, the elders, and priests honored Judith for having saved their people. Holofernes's head was displayed over the wall. When Holofernes's men saw the Jews exiting the city, they ran to alert him, and found his headless body. The roles now reversed, the Jews routed the Persians and were free of them, as the Bible says.*

10367–10400

Then the Jews returned, and for thirty days did not finish gathering up the great spoils. And they ordered that every year, without fail, this day would be celebrated solemnly and without frivolity, in remembrance of this God-given victory. They gave lovely gifts to Judith and brought her to Jerusalem. Joachim, who was bishop, along with all the clergy, came out toward Judith. They received her and her people with great joy, and they went straight to the temple to thank God (that was right and just!). They held a great celebration there, and kept it up every year, giving God and Judith the glory for their victory. Judith then went back to Bethulia, where she stayed for the rest of her life, with no desire for anything but to serve God who had made her in holy, perfect widowhood. She lived for 110 years. She was mourned by her family and all others after her death, because she had been such a fine woman all her life, without misdeed or blame, and very loyal to her spouse. Never after was she beside anyone but him.

10401–10418: *Christine turns back to Cambyses (Nebuchadnezzar), who was distraught over the fate of Holofernes and his men. He vowed revenge and prepared to attack.*

10419–10432

The situation soon changed, because God flailed Cambyses with a multi-strapped whip as soon as he left. He was struck in such a way by a severe illness in the limbs, body, and brain, that he could not be saved, and he ultimately died from it. Kings, dukes, and counts carried him away on their shoulders and then buried him in Damascus, where he had died. He did not go any further. It is true what many say: "Many a fool's intentions go undone!"[144]

XI. *Here is told how Darius Hystaspes[145] was made the king of Persia by his cunning*

10433–10556: *Out of greed, King Cambyses had secretly killed his brother Smerdis, and only Patizithes[146] knew about it. It was said that Smerdis was alive, but sequestered in a chamber, as was the custom, and would take the crown when he was old enough. Patizithes married Cambyses's daughter, a rightful heir. Patizithes soon fell ill, but before he died, he convinced the barons that his own brother was in fact Smerdis, and the young man was crowned.*

---

144. Christine's text (line 10432) reads, "Des pensers du fol moult remaint!" (Solente, *Mutacion*, 2:230), a variation on the proverb "Moult remaint de ce que fol pense" (*Mutacion*, 2:361, note to line 10432).

145. Darius I, the Great; see note 131.

146. One of the Persian magi, called "Hermïedés" in Christine's poem.

Among the seven most powerful barons in Persia, called "satraps," was one who was very suspicious of the new king's legitimacy. He had his daughter marry him so that in the night she could surreptitiously feel his head to see if he was missing one ear. If so, that would prove that he was actually the brother of Patizithes, who had lost an ear in childhood. The trick worked, and the barons then killed the king. In order to decide who the next king should be, they agreed that all seven of them would go to the temple on horseback. Whoever was sitting on the horse that whinnied would be deemed the divinely chosen successor.

10557–10592

One of the satraps was Darius, whose father was Hystaspes. He was a very wise knight, valiant at arms, strong, and nimble. He was neither ignorant nor naive. He devised a very dirty trick, for he was nothing if not covetous. By the dark of night, he had his finest steed led before the temple where the event was to take place the next day. He had a mare brought there to make the steed whinny more readily. The steed copulated with her there, without fail. Then Darius turned the steed around.

In the morning the satrap got on that horse. He was with his companions, who were not such sleuths that they would notice the deception. They would not have put up with it if they had known. When they came to the stated place, no sooner had they reached it than the steed on which Darius sat whinnied so loudly, whomever it might displease, that it could be heard from far away. This made Darius's heart rejoice, because he well knew that this whinny would make him the high king. All believed that it was a miracle that the steed had whinnied that way, and that the gods, who had made the steed whinny, had chosen Darius to be king. But it was the mare who had made the miracle because she had caused the horse to whinny so much. Darius was crowned by the barons, and nobly ordained king.

XII. *Here is told more about King Darius*

10593–10802: *Darius had previously chased the Jews from their temple. He made good on a vow to their God that if he were to become king of the Jews, he would make amends by rebuilding the temple and returning treasure to the Jewish people. Darius went on to fight against the peoples who rebelled against Persia, restoring authority in Assyria, Babylon, and Chaldea. He then set his sights on marrying the daughter of Arthur, king of Scythia. When her father refused him, Darius attacked Scythia, only to be fended off. Darius went on to conquer Asia and Macedonia. He took to the sea to defeat the Ionians, and then invaded Athens. Aided by the Laconians[147] and other allies, the Greeks routed Darius, because Fortune had decided to work in*

---

147. People of a region of southern Greece, whose chief city was Sparta.

favor of the Greeks. Darius then amassed a huge army, but he fell ill and died before he could again enter into battle.

XIII. Here is told of Xerxes, king of Persia,[148] son of Darius, of his great power and bad fortune

10803–10961: *Bent on revenge, Darius's son Xerxes amassed the greatest army and flotilla Persia had ever seen. Well provisioned, they set off. Xerxes arrived at Sparta, where Leonidas was king. The small Spartan army ambushed the over-confident Persians at a narrow pass, severely harming them. Eventually, the Persians' great numbers managed to wear down the exhausted enemy. Leonidas pulled his men back, paid his foreign mercenaries, and remained with a few of his most loyal men.[149]*

10962–11002

Leonidas had only six hundred worthy and proven knights left with him, and he found all of them to be good, loyal, and valiant. They would never leave him, ever—they would die with him! That night, Leonidas reflected. He decided that they would not wait for day. Rather, they would go and attack their enemies that very night. He put himself and his men in great danger. They made their way through the fields, in tight formation, until they arrived at the tents where they found the Persians all sleeping, because never, ever, would the Persians have expected the Greeks to dare to attack them this way.

The army had no watchman, and no sooner did the sentinel sound the horn than the Greeks attacked. At that point they did not hold back. Rather, like impatient men, they killed the Persians in great numbers. The Persian army was very rattled. Many entered the fray half-armed, others naked. Some hid themselves between the tents, while others crouched among the narrow furrows in the ground. Still others ran away, and the Greeks gave chase, shouting at them, killing them, and cutting them to pieces, without the Persians' getting revenge in any way. They were utterly overwhelmed, because they all believed they were doomed. There was such a great multitude of dead that one could not pass because of the bodies, and they continuously killed, without pause. Nobody could imagine the havoc or the massacre there!

11003–11054

The terrible suffering and horrible defeat, in which many lost their lives, lasted until noontime the following day. All the Persians were killed, except only the ones who saved themselves by the dark of night. But the day brought harm to those who were found alive. King Xerxes, who had experienced Fortune's fluctua-

---

148. Xerxes I, who reigned 486–465 BCE.

149. This section is a somewhat distorted reference to the battle of Thermopylae in 480 BCE.

tion, could lament her influence. It had harmed him severely. He fled from there in haste, with as many men as he could. He abandoned all tents and possessions and secured himself in his ships, where his misfortunes did not let up. Since Fortune was against him on land, where she made him suffer many bad things, he wanted to wage war with his enemies by sea, to see if he would fare better there and succeed in vanquishing them. He had little advantage there, and instead he came to even greater harm. That is because Themistocles, a duke of Athens,[150] was not overwhelmed. Rather, thanks to the aid that the Greeks and Ionians gave the Athenians at sea, he had had great multitudes of ships and barges armed against Xerxes, which reined in Xerxes's violence. Queen Nitocris,[151] along with more than twenty galleys, came to the aid of the king of Persia. She was put on the front line against the hostile side. They attacked each other head-on, at which point arrows flew more abundantly there than flashes or sparks of a burning fire. Ships and small boats sank to the bottom from Greek fire and cannons. There was no civil law, church canon, faith, love, or law in force aside from that of the naked sword or axe, the two-bladed axe, or sharp steel lances. They cleaved each other's brains and spilled each other's guts.

XIV. Here is told of the pitiful death of King Xerxes

11055–11079: *As the Persians got the worst of it, Mardonius[152] urged Xerxes to flee because Fortune was clearly against him.*

11080–11107

The king secretly hid like a thief, and left from the fray by night, taking just a few people with him. He traveled so much, without coming across anyone, that he arrived at the fortified castle of Abydos,[153] on a high shore situated above an arm of the sea called Hellespont. Xerxes, who was hiding, had previously had a timber bridge built over this sea, which he believed was still there. But it was destroyed, because it had been broken into pieces in the rough weather that occurs at sea. The king then began to reproach the harshness of Fortune, because of whom he endured too much misfortune (he had plenty to be distressed about!). However much trouble he might have gone to before, if he wanted to pass through to save

---

150. Lived ca. 524–459 BCE.

151. This refers to the Battle of Salamis, 480 BCE. In Christine's text, this woman is called "Nido," whom Solente identifies as Nitocris, queen of Egypt. While there was an Egyptian queen by that name, she existed centuries earlier than the time frame for this episode. There was also a Nitocris of Babylon, who lived in the sixth century BCE, and therefore a century before this battle. The woman in question here would likely have been Queen Artemisia of Halicarnassus, a city in Asia Minor.

152. A military leader during the Persian Wars; died 479 BCE.

153. Ancient city in Asia Minor.

himself then, he had to enter in two fishing boats, because he could find no other. That filled his heart with great anger. He also gravely feared a storm, because of the weather at sea.

11108-11140

Let us consider here the false nature of deceitful Fortune, how she is violently changeable, when one who was accustomed to lording over all and having wealth, whom the whole world feared, and with whom one counted a million men in battle, was now accompanied by no one! He was taken to the point at which he had hardly anyone to serve or accompany him, this man who knew so well how to lead campaigns that he made the whole world tremble! Now he fled alone to evade those who hated him. Before he would get to his country, Fortune dealt him so many bitter blows that few people remained with him, in light of the many cruel, grave, and difficult misfortunes that came his way.

Mardonius, who had stayed in Greece, besieged a fortress and took it by force. Still, he tried very hard to make peace with the Greeks, if possible, provided that there be some tribute from them. But he was not able to achieve that. When he saw that, he did not want to stay in the country. Instead, he left. But first he set fire to the outskirts of Athens from all sides.

11141-11191: *Athens sent one hundred thousand reinforcements. The Persians were defeated in a fierce battle, losing their ships and a huge amount of treasure. Meanwhile, the Asians rebelled against Xerxes. When Xerxes's men, who were fighting there, heard of the fate of Mardonius and the Persians in Greece, they were so disheartened that they were easily defeated.*

11192-11243

Thus the Persians, who were accustomed to being more esteemed than any other renowned kingdoms, lost honor, reputation, life, and possessions. They were no longer revered or loved because so much misfortune had come to them so many times. Thus the great power of the Persians declined. Their sense and wealth no longer enjoyed prestige. They became poor, destitute, and naked, because they had ill-advisedly spent their wealth on the great wars that they sustained for a long time. Now you can see how Fortune set out in various ways to ruin and completely destroy those people! That is her way! Once she starts to do harm, she will not stop finding ways and means, through many disputes, to abase the good and the worst alike, in every way, be they kingdoms or empires. Once she sets out to do harm, there is no remedy against it.

Once again Fortune, the very deceitful one, did not grow weary. Rather, it suited her to bring King Xerxes to an end through great calamity. He grieved so much that he nearly died, with more and more torment and grave misadventure coming his way. Thanks to his terrible misfortune, he was hated by his own people. He found himself greatly troubled, because news came to him every day of lands rebelling against him. He had no troops to send there or force to use against anyone. He was hated and considered contemptible, supported by no one, to the extent that he was hardly considered king, even if he was portrayed on the wall of his people, who held him in great scorn.[154] In the end, he was done in by one of his own villainous and dirty provosts,[155] who had contrived and plotted to kill Xerxes in his room and take on the reign for himself. But he only lasted for seven months.

XV. Here is told of Artaxerxes and other kings of Persia

11244–11264: *Artaxerxes reigned for forty years. During that time, Ezra of Judea received the Jewish law from God. Then Sogdianus reigned for seven months, followed by Darius, called Nothus. Upon his death, his son Artaxerxes, called Ahasuerus, reigned with great renown.[156]*

XVI. Here is told of King Ahasuerus, named Artaxerxes

11265–11295
King Artaxerxes, called Ahasuerus, was the greatest of the kings of Persia. Fortune was not harsh or hostile toward him, in peace or in war, because this king held more land than any Persian king ever had. The kingdom was well rebuilt then, because 127 different countries were defeated by the Persians and brought into tribute. Thus the Persians' kingdom grew bigger day by day, until they ruled over all of India and Ethiopia, conquering all by the sword. As history tells us, King Ahasuerus was very powerful and increased his might every day. He displayed his glory in his principal city called Susa,[157] which was highly renowned for its might and beauty. It should well have been powerful, because it was surrounded outside by high towers and strong walls. And within, it was constructed such that never before had a living creature seen an edifice more beautiful, rich, or well laid-out.

11296–11324
King Ahasuerus had a very rich palace built there. It was made to sparkle up high with gold and precious stones in very pleasing arrangements, like the sky is illuminated by planets and stars. It was brighter than candles thanks to the red garnets all around the walls, so extremely fine that I could never fully express it. No duke or king has ever had more lavish! Because, for as impossible as it is to

---

154. Xerxes was known for the emphasis he placed on public commemorations of his reign—for example, the Gate of All Nations at Persepolis, on which his name is engraved in three languages.

155. Artabanus (not to be confused with Artabanus, the uncle and advisor of Xerxes).

156. Artaxerxes II Mnemon, who reigned 404–358 BCE.

157. City in the region that is now Iran; the modern town of Shush is located near the site of Susa.

believe, the stones, gold, silver, and ivory that were assembled in this place amply showed that Ahasuerus, who made it, was overflowing with wealth. He erected columns of silver, decorated with flowers of gold bedecked with stones, on which the vaults of this high and bright room were supported. And in the dark of night, the artfully set garnets that shone there would make a light greater than a hundred torches. Of course! No one would believe me if I told of all the magnificent riches and splendors of this place! For that reason I tell you, in short, that there is no place like it in this world!

11325–11416: *After reigning for three years, in order to cultivate his renown, Ahasuerus assembled his highest barons. They celebrated with an extravagant feast lasting 170 days. One day, Ahasuerus decided to send for the queen*[158] *to show off her beauty, but she refused to come. Angered by her disobedience, Ahasuerus exiled her and sought a new woman to crown queen.*

XVII. *Here is told of how King Ahasuerus married the noble woman Esther*

11417–11476
Then the beautiful, esteemed, and wise Esther was brought to the king. She was of Hebrew lineage and of God's chosen religion.[159] She is greatly praised in the true holy Scripture. She was a very lovely creature, worthy, prudent, renowned, and loved by all people. This maiden was so beautiful and attractive to Ahasuerus that he chose her above all others. Maidens, lovely of body and face, wise and of noble lineage, were paraded before Ahasuerus, for him to choose the most refined and the one who would best please him. He said that he would leave all the others aside in favor of this one, who was such a beautiful, humble, and courtly maiden. So the king set Vashti aside and married Esther. She behaved and conducted herself so prudently toward the king that he granted her whatever she asked for, seeking nothing but her peace and happiness.

This is how it happened, as holy Scripture, which recounts the whole story of this event, affirms for us. One of the Lenten liturgies, recited about the noble Esther in the holy Church, also tells us of it. King Ahasuerus had one provost who despised the Jews with mortal hatred. Without the queen's knowledge, he criticized them harshly to the king. He said that their annihilation would be good and favorable for the king, that they had a religion peculiar to them, full of nonsense, and that they did not want to adore idols like other people. He said it should please the king to have them taken by his soldiers in every country, and destroyed

158. Queen Vashti, referred to by name below. The story recounted here follows the Old Testament Book of Esther.

159. As instructed by her uncle Mordechai, however, Esther did not reveal her religion or family background to the king (Esther 2:10).

and hanged at the gallows! King Ahasuerus was pleased by this, and approved of it being done without delay. Thanks to the perfidious advice of his treacherous provost Haman, he granted it and wanted it done, because then he would have the Jews under his power, in servitude. And to bring that situation about, he agreed with Haman.

11477–11522

He gave Haman the ring from his finger, and put him in charge of the whole affair. He said Haman should go wherever he had authority—in the land of Judea, in the city of Jerusalem—and write, seal, order everywhere, and have it declared throughout and commanded of all the provosts, that the Jews were all to be summoned on the third day of the month. At that time they and their law would be destroyed. They would be burned, killed, hanged, and stretched on great crosses. The order was made everywhere, and indeed even commanded in the city of Susa, which anguished the Jews deeply, because there were great multitudes of them there.

When Mordechai heard about this, he went to his house woeful, dejected, and full of rage. Mordechai was very wise, of the greatest lineage of Jews in the land of Judea. He had raised the queen in her childhood, because she did not have a father. Mordechai was her uncle; she loved him greatly. He sent this harsh news to the queen without delay, and said that if she did not do something about it quickly, and in a very short time, it would be too late. She should complain to the king about this offense and the harm that Haman had brought upon them. As a noble and wise person, she should deliver the people from this terrible servitude (because God had deliberately placed her in this position, in order to do that), or else she would incur his wrath. When the queen heard about this development, she thought about it a great deal and it troubled her deeply.

11523–11610: *As no one dared to address Ahasuerus without being summoned, and he had not summoned Esther for some time, she had to devise a plan. One day, she beautified herself and dressed in a luxurious garment, and went to an orchard upon which the king was known to gaze. Seeing Esther looking so beautiful and kneeling in humility when she saw him, he called her to him. He offered to grant her any wish. Her sole wish was to dine with him the next day, with only Haman in their company.*

11610–11641

They had sufficiently amused themselves at great leisure, eating and drinking to their pleasure for several days, before Esther requested anything at all from the king. One day, the king feted her greatly, telling her and firmly commanding that if she had any request, she should boldly ask him. Whatever it may be, she would have it at her feet. And then the queen threw herself at his feet, and loudly crying and weeping, she begged for his mercy, asking that he not wish to make the Jewish people perish and die. She said to him: "Oh you, powerful king! Please, may you desire to alleviate the great pain in my heart! And may you not wish to estrange me from all joy, because in the end, if I should see my people perish this way and come to a terrible end, no honor, gold, or silver would bring me comfort! Because of this, I will not stop weeping, nor can I ever be soothed from it! I pray not to be so abased by you who chose me, unworthy, to be queen and the lady of your royal retinue! May you not wish for me to bathe myself in such tears and feel such grief forever more!"

11642–11692

Esther thus lamented before the king, who was shocked by what she told him. He responded: "Noble lady! Who dares to undertake such a great affront against you? Because I promise that you will well be avenged against him and relieved of your mourning." "Haman, who is here, does this," said the queen, "and does not cease tormenting us. By his great perfidy, he wants to take the life of Mordechai, who is a relative of mine, tied to me by lineage, and who saved you from death in the past, when he sensed the treachery of those who once wanted to kill you. They desired it intensely.[160] He made them known to you, and you found that it was true. Never did he have praise or reward for it. And this disloyal heretic wants to kill him; he seeks nothing else. The cross where he wants to have him killed immediately, if he does not fail in his intent, is already built in his court."

At that point, Haman was frightened, seeing himself so hated by the king that he did not know what to do. Then the king commanded that he be taken to die ignominiously. Thus God wanted to save his people by Queen Esther, who was so gentle that no one could ever seek a better woman in all the world. And the Jewish people were overjoyed to be out of servitude thanks to the noble and wise Esther, who arranged it such that they would be the greatest of the country and have authority over all of it. There was great joy throughout all of Judea. Mordechai, the friend of God, was then put in the place of Haman, and was greatly honored by the king. The Jews then praised God, and every year celebrated a feast for the granting of this request.[161]

---

160. Esther 2:21–23. Mordechai exposed two of Ahasuerus's chamberlains, whom he had overheard conspiring against the king.

161. The feast is Purim, which comes from the word "pur," meaning "lot." As told in Esther 3:7, a lot was cast in Haman's presence to determine the day and month on which the Jews were to be massacred.

XVIII. Here is told of King Artaxerxes, named Ochus, the one who destroyed the king of Egypt, Nectanebus[162]

11693–11728: *Artaxerxes, also called Ochus, reigned for twenty-six years after the death of Ahasuerus. He defeated Nectanebus, king of Egypt, and waged many other great battles during his life. Alexander the Great was born in this time. After Ochus came Arses, and then his son Darius, who would be killed by Alexander, marking the end of Persian power, as Fortune wished it.*[163]

11729–11748

Everything I have recounted was written on the wall of the room where Fortune lives, she who does grave harm to many. And I will tell you about some parts of several other occurrences, while keeping quiet about others, because I cannot tell everything. That could become very tedious. Rather, insofar as I have told how Fortune, who often overturns things, allowed authority to be held and passed from Chaldea to Media and Persia—in that order, since the beginning of the world—I would like to tell of other kingdoms and how they were governed. I began this work and have advanced it this far in order to bring to mind the turns that can often be seen with the naked eye.

XIX. Here she begins to speak of several kingdoms, firstly of Greece

11749–11764

Before I go any further, to avoid leaving it out and to better craft my work, I must go back in time to talk about other kingdoms, how they started and ended in various nations, through many persecutions, during the time that the things I have spoken of took place. I will also tell about people who held many other foreign kingdoms that were also led by Fortune in various ways, and about their origins. So I will leave the topic of Persia, bringing it to a close.

About Greece

11765–11980: *Christine begins her account of the noble and powerful land of Greece. At the beginning, this place was called Sicyon, and Aegialeus was the first king. His heirs ruled for nearly one thousand years. It was later called Peloponnesus. The city*

---

162. Artaxerxes III Ochus, King of Persia (425–338 BCE); Nectanebus, or Nectanebo II, pharaoh of Egypt, who reigned 360–343 BCE. For the story that Nectanebo II was the father of Alexander the Great, see Book 7, chapter 45.

163. Arses reigned 338–336 BCE. Solente notes that he was a cousin, not the father, of Darius III, who lived ca. 380–330 BCE (*Mutacion*, 4:112). Nor was Alexander the person who killed Darius, although Alexander was pursuing him at the time Darius died; see Book 7, chapter 47.

of Argos was greatly renowned. Inachos was its first king. Argos would prosper for 564 years, until it was conquered by Perseus, for whom Persia is named. Inachos's son Phoroneus established a system of justice, as well as marketplaces for commerce. His wise sister Io went to live in Egypt, where she taught the people how to work the land. She would later be worshipped as the goddess Isis.[164] Phoroneus's son, Apis, who would later be known as the god Serapis, was said to have invented the science of surgery. He founded the new Babylon, then called Memphis,[165] along the Nile (some fifty days' distance from the Babylon founded by giants along the Tigris River in Chaldea), which would be greatly expanded by the pharaohs who ruled after him.

11981–12016

Right around this time, a very wise lady, beautiful and arrayed in finery, marvelously appeared on a Greek lake. She was called Minerva, and she invented many new ways to make armor.[166] In this kingdom, she first invented shields and targes, coats of mail of fine steel, and helmets. And she invented a variety of other good, strong, and sound armor and many practices for battle. For this, the ignorant-natured people called her a goddess. They adored her and named her goddess of chivalry, battles, and armaments. They also called this lady, whom they so loved, Pallas, for an island named Pallene, where she was born.[167] This lady was from the country of Thrace.[168] She was so well educated and learned in great science that no one has ever surpassed her. This lady invented many more things that proved to be good, profitable, and wise, as well as how to make works of silk thread, with some effort. She invented and imparted the entire art of spinning wool, weaving, and making such works. For this, in truth, they called her Pallas, goddess of wisdom.

12017–12068

It seems to me that Prometheus, who knew well how to join wood, also lived right around this time. The foolish people said that the clever master caused people to be born of wood. That is because he beautifully carved out of wood great and lovely images of people, animals, and birds. And thanks to his skill, by some clever means, he made them move when they were completed. So the people thought

---

164. Associated with maternity, magic, and healing.

165. This should be Cairo, not Memphis.

166. Minerva, a Roman goddess, is often identified with the Greek Athena, one of whose epithets is "Pallas Athena." On Pallas/Minerva in Christine's works, see Blumenfeld-Kosinski, "Mythographer and Mythmaker," 210–12; and Andrea Tarnowski, "Pallas Athena, la science et la chevalerie," in Ribémont, *Sur le chemin,* 149–58.

167. On Christine's source for this detail, see Percy G. Campbell, *L'épitre d'Othéa: Etude sur les sources de Christine de Pisan* (Paris: Champion, 1924), 149–51.

168. Region of southeastern Europe on the Balkan peninsula, north of the Aegean.

the carvings were alive. He was very clever and quick, and he created the first rings to put on the finger, setting them with precious stones. At that time he did not make rings of gold or silver to adorn people; rather, he made rings of iron or steel. He said that the ring should be on the smallest finger of the left hand, because a vein comes from the heart to that finger, and it was more fitting to wear a ring on that finger than on the others. One should wear an elegant and beautiful ring on one's finger, with rich stones, to signify authority and worth.

In Crete there was also a very wise and learned lady who devoted herself to devising many trades. She taught the Greeks the practice of working the lands and plowing, and how to measure out wheat and grain with vessels used for measuring volume. Previously, they knew nothing at all about that, and measured grain in piles; they had no other measure. This lady was named Ceres, by whom the arable land in Greece was plowed, sowed, and burned so that it would become fertile. She was esteemed and loved, and throughout Greece was called Ceres, the goddess of grain, because thanks to her they had it in abundance. Now I want to tell you about another city in Greece that was powerful and then came to an end through a very strange fate.

XX. Here begins the story of Thebes[169]

12069–12107: *Christine's focus turns to Thebes, a city mistreated by Fortune. Cadmus founded the city, and was followed in power by Athamas and Pentheus. Later came Laius, of their lineage. When Laius's wife, Jocasta, was pregnant with their child, Laius dreamt that he would have to kill the baby in order to protect himself from a bad destiny. He thus ordered his newborn son killed.*

12108–12158

To carry out the king's order, the servants carried the baby into the forest, but they refrained from killing him, because they were too kind. They had pity for the child, who laughed at them out of affection. They hung him by his swaddling clothes. But first they split his feet, to be able to recognize him if he were to grow up. The huntsmen of King Polybus of Mycenae[170] found the child, which was a good thing for him. The king had him cared for until he could run and play with other children. The child was praised for his beauty, his ways, and his pleasing manner. Polybus believed the child was the son of a king, as well he should have. Because of that, the king held him as dear as his own son, and wanted to make him his heir because he had no other child but him. Fate would play out differently, however.

---

169. City in central Greece. On this episode, see Régnier-Bohler, "Tragédie thébaine."

170. Ancient Greek city in the northeastern part of the Peloponnese.

Oedipus was his name, and he was handsome but too proud. He grew big and restless, and wanted to dominate the children. Another child, out of extreme anger over some offense (I do not know what), started to say as a reproach that Oedipus had no reason to be prideful, when he did not know any parent, father or mother. He said that they took out great vengeance against Oedipus when they put him on a tree, hung by his swaddling clothes. The child was sure that Oedipus was in no way the son of the king. Oedipus was dismayed and enraged over this. He went to the king, saying that the king should tell him the truth about this, for God's sake, and not refuse his question. Polybus was very sad about this, but in the end, he told Oedipus the whole truth. The king was very reluctant, but Oedipus had pleaded with him so much that he told him. Oedipus went away crying, wanting to seek the truth: who could his parents be?

12159–12215

Oedipus immediately went to Delphi[171] to ask the god Apollo to reveal where he could learn more about his situation. Apollo answered his request, directing Oedipus to make his way toward Thebes; he would come to it that way. Oedipus had hardly journeyed far when he came upon a domain called Phocis[172] along his route. He immediately headed to that place. On that day, there was a great, stately celebration at the castle, where young knights were making merry and putting themselves to the test in a number of games of strength, with everyone trying his very best. Because of Fortune, it happened that Laius, the king of Thebes, had come in noble array to watch the games with his people. He was the father of Oedipus, whom bitter chance had led to that place. The spectators became disturbed by a dispute; I do not know what it concerned. It reached the point that the adversaries had to fight. Laius, who saw them fighting, was troubled, and intended to calm their anger and make peace among them. He approached to separate them. I do not know if he knocked against Oedipus in passing, or what he did, but Oedipus quickly drew his sword and cut off his father's head. Indeed he killed him, I know not for what misdeed!

Oedipus went away and headed toward Thebes by an unusual path along the side of a mountain, because he feared that someone would catch up with him. He left the metalled road, but he had not traveled far when a dangerous, frightening, and terrible monster came down from the mountain, so quickly that Oedipus heard its steps. This beast was very fierce and strangely put together, because it had the body of a lion, the feet of a serpent, and the hands and head of a disheveled maiden; that is how it was put together. It was extremely horrible and cruel. It was called the Sphinx by the people throughout the country.

171. The Temple of Apollo in Delphi, on Mount Parnassus, near the Gulf of Corinth.

172. A region in central Greece.

12216–12280

Upon this encounter, the Sphinx cried out to Oedipus (who would have liked very much to be elsewhere!): "Now, handsome master! I advise you to respond quickly to my demand and expound the question that I will pose, and if not I will kill you before you leave from here! So be very careful not to fail, because according to an edict that I established, anyone who does not know how to respond to my words must die for it; nothing would be able to save him." Oedipus said, "I concur! As long as you keep this agreement for me: I may silence you if I answer your question." This arrangement was agreed between the two, and the Sphinx asked Oedipus this question: "Now tell me, I command of you, what beast is it that comes out from its mother by great bitter pain, and is then so frail that the smallest thing hurts it? In no way can it stay upright on its feet by itself, because it is not able to. And then it grows so much and gets stronger, so that it needs to go on four feet, then on three, then on two. Now make a guess about it, if you wish, because later, the beast reaches such a state that it must go on three, then it goes with great difficulty on four. Now will you tell me what this is about? Can you determine the beast? You must, in order to save yourself."

Oedipus replied: "Ha! Churl! The beast is the human being, who is weak at the beginning and does not stay upright at all. Then it grows stronger and reaches the point where it can hold itself up on feet and hands. Those are girls and little boys, who pull themselves around on all fours. Then, before they know how to talk, they are made to go on three feet, with the help of a little stick. Thus go the little children. When they are big, they go on two feet. Later when they are old, on three—that is, on two feet and a cane. And then old age strikes a man so much that he has to go on two crutches, thus on four feet, for sure. Now are you taken aback and confounded? The question by which you have killed more than six tricked men will have been sold to you at a high price!" Then Oedipus cut off the Sphinx's head. I do not know whether the monster defended itself. Thus, as the book tells us, the country was rid of the Sphinx. The country may have been delivered of the Sphinx, but it was given over to grief as a result.[173]

12281–12334

This event was witnessed from the high walls of Thebes. Oedipus brought the head, and was received in the city with great celebration. There would have been more joy if their king were not dead, for which they were suffering. Nonetheless they came before Oedipus, bringing him great honor, as they should because they were joyful about what had happened. Oedipus stayed in the city for several days, where he was served, honored, and esteemed by many. They were almost assuaged thanks to him. They went to Jocasta, who was mourning greatly. They told her to dispense with grieving and celebrate the knight who had earned great praise for

---

173. That is, because of the events to follow.

delivering the country from the one who had brought them so many misfortunes, and whose head they could see. She received Oedipus as well as she could, and welcomed him with joy. After that, the barons made such an effort and so strongly urged the queen, who was very troubled about it, that in fact she married Oedipus, taking him as her husband and lord. Now the ill was even greater for the one who killed his father and then married his mother! Fortune, who uses many tricks to fool people, had arranged things such that she combined husband and son. In Thebes, there was great celebration over this marriage, but the celebration turned harshly for the worse.

They were indeed together for so long, I do not know how many years, that the queen had four children, two boys and two girls; the boys were handsome and the girls lovely. The first son was named Eteocles, and the second Polynices. The elder daughter was named Antigone and the other Ismene, with the fair face; she was later a very wise queen. The boys, who had many bad qualities, gained strength and grew. They were wicked and combative, and fought each other all the time.

12335–12379

A day came, by chance—because everything falls into its rightful place—when the king was in front of his bed. Because of the warm weather, his feet were bare, and he had stretched them out on the ground. The queen thereupon noticed his split toes, and thought of her son. She had heard her servants being told that the king's men "had left him in the great forest, without killing him, his feet split, and hung by his swaddling clothes." She became extremely upset, because her heart told her in complete certainty that it was her son she saw before her, who had killed his father and married his mother; that was she. Thus was explained the dream that she and the king had simultaneously dreamt as they slept, when she was pregnant with Oedipus, and which brought her great suffering. She was so alarmed that she could not say a word, but sighed very deeply from her heart and was very troubled. Oedipus saw that she was weeping and wanted to know the cause. She told him the whole truth. She asked him, pleading ardently, to tell her the truth about himself, by his oath, from what family he came, and in what country he was born. They continued their discussion until each one knew the whole truth about the affair. As they came to understand it, never had two people felt such grief. Oedipus was so sad that he did not wish to live anymore. Thus he thought he would kill himself with his sword. But the grieving queen, who pitifully lamented her painful misfortune, snatched it from his hands.

12380–12420

This affair was very difficult for Oedipus, who felt sullied by such an evil sin. He went into a temple in great sadness, and spent his life there in mourning and grief. And in the end he was in such a wretched state that he was scorned by all. To add to the misery, his two sons, filled with bad qualities, with hearts that were far too hard, mocked and derided the suffering father in his old age. The woeful Oedipus lamented to the gods, weeping, and complained about Fortune who tormented him so. (Never had she tormented a man more!)

His two sons inflicted such humiliation on him, from bad to worse, that the father became so violently angry one day that he completely tore up his face, and ripped his eyes from his head (that was a great misfortune!). He threw them in his sons' faces, and the evil-natured ones trampled them underfoot and kicked them back and forth in great cruelty. One can now imagine the great suffering of the miserable father and mother! But the two evildoers in no way left it at that. Rather, beating on their wretched father, they lowered him down and threw him into a filthy hole, where he did not stop weeping, until he passed away in great suffering. The tormented queen, who had carried those children of evil extraction, also carried great grief for all her days. And her two children were not done yet—they were born for her grief!

XXI. Here is told of the great quarrel between Eteocles and Polynices over which of them would reign

12421–12590: *After their father's pitiable demise, Eteocles and Polynices settled their rivalry by agreeing that each would reign for one year at a time while the other was off on adventure. Eteocles, the elder of the two, took the first year. Polynices made his way through storms to sail to Argos, where he took shelter for the night in a castle portal. Another weary, rain-soaked voyager, Tydeus,*[174] *asked to share the space for the night, and the two ended up fighting. Meanwhile, Adrastus, king of Argos, dreamt that he broke up a fierce battle between a lion and a wild boar, and gave his daughters to them in marriage. Awakened by the sound of the men fighting, the king intervened. Upon learning who the two men were and what had brought them there, he welcomed them into the castle with great honor, and indeed had them marry his daughters. News of the event spread to Eteocles, who had no wish to hand over the kingdom at the end of the year, and who was perturbed that Polynices would now have allies should he attempt to go against him.*

XXII. Here is told of the great army that King Adrastus assembled to attack the city of Thebes

12591–12806: *When the year was up, King Adrastus discouraged Polynices from going back to Thebes because of the danger. Tydeus volunteered to go in his stead, to negotiate with Eteocles. Tydeus arrived in Thebes, very nobly greeted the court, and*

---

174. One of the "Seven Against Thebes," commemorated in the tragedy by Aeschylus (fifth century BCE), a group of champions on the side of Polynices in the conflict with Eteocles.

requested that Eteocles step aside so that Polynices could take his rightful place. Hid-ing his anger, evil Eteocles said that his brother was welcome to continue to amuse himself elsewhere. Recognizing what that really meant, Tydeus left in anger, and Eteocles sent ten knights to kill him. Tydeus single-handedly killed all but one of them, whom he sent back to Eteocles to report on the failed attack. Eteocles killed the messenger. Tydeus, injured and exhausted, arrived at Argos, to the simultaneous joy and consternation of Adrastus, who was sad and furious to hear what had hap-pened.

XXIII. Here is told of the great armies that were assembled to attack Thebes

12807–12888: *In Argos, the army prepared to attack Eteocles. Informed of this by spies, Eteocles assembled many soldiers. Amphiaraus, a wise clerk of Argos, foresaw the devastation about to happen, and predicted that he himself would be swallowed up by the earth. He hid in order not to bring misfortune with him. The king, unwill-ing to leave without him, found him and ignored his warnings.*

XXIV. Here is told of the great slaughter in front of Thebes

12889–13026: *The Argives arrived at Thebes in spite of many hardships that Fortune sent their way en route. As the people of Thebes did not want war, Queen Jocasta entreated her son Eteocles to honor his agreement. He pretended to give in, on the condition that he hold hostages. It soon became known that Eteocles had changed his mind, and the battle began. Violent fighting raged for days.*

XXV. Here is told how Amphiaraus the sage was swallowed up

13027–13086: *As foretold, Amphiaraus's chariot, led by four horses, was swallowed up by the earth. The war continued, as Fortune wanted it, "and no one but God can keep her from doing what she wants" (13061–62). Tydeus was among the countless knights to die there.*

XXVI. Here is told how Eteocles and Polynices killed each other in battle

13087–13136

It happened one day, through bad fortune and in a highly extraordinary event. The two sides battled on a field where many trembled in fear that day. (They should well have trembled, engaging in combat in such a mortal place where there was so much killing. Never since has anyone heard of people so evenly matched dying in such great numbers!). The two brothers, born of their mother out of bad fortune, chanced to encounter each other in battle. Never has anyone seen a goshawk at-tack prey more violently than the two brothers bitterly attacked each other. The battle was surely very harsh because they hated each other intensely. They lusted to kill each other.

Polynices attacked his brother so ferociously that his entire worn-out body was tainted with blood. Polynices knocked him down from his war horse. Polynices descended to kill him, but Eteocles, who felt himself mortally wounded, then came up with a very clever ruse, thinking of how to give his brother such a blow that he would kill him. Thus he said piteously: "Dear brother! Too late I have decided give myself over to your mercy. But before I die here, I beg you to be willing to pardon my misdeeds and give me one single kiss, in a sign of true friendship." At that point Polynices, who truly believed that Eteocles repented fully for this war, was moved by great pity. Weeping, he lowered himself toward the ground, over his brother, to kiss him and ask for his mercy. He gave Eteocles back his sword, and said that he forgave him. Eteocles thereupon gave Polynices such a deadly blow from below that he abruptly killed him there. Thus the two brothers died in bitter, evil death.

13137–13164

The men of the army were so shocked by it that they fled from both sides. But there were already so many dead that the bodies made it impossible to pass. That day was harsh for them! That day rose for their bad fortune! Few of their barons remained, because all were left dead on the field. Both sides expressed great grief, and no man born would know how to recount all the mourning that they expressed in transporting the remains. The queen tore her flesh in great chunks, like a mad woman avenging herself. Cursed be the hour she was born, and her sad fate at having ever borne such children! She nearly destroyed herself with grief. In the city, they went into deep mourning for their friends who had died. They wept, cried, lamented, and rued the war. Adrastus and those from outside lamented over the death of their friends. The king grieved and mourned for his progeny, and cursed the hour of the war.

XXVII. *Here is told how the ladies of Argos came into the army to help their husbands*

13165–13320: *King Adrastus sent a messenger to tell the women of Argos of the great losses his army had faced. With no men left in Argos to send, the tormented women set out for Thebes themselves to avenge their men. At the spectacle of the women arriving, King Adrastus was so anguished that he nearly killed himself, but was stopped by his countryman Capaneus.[175] The women unsuccessfully sought a truce so they could bury their dead. It happened that the duke of Athens was in the area, and he came to the aid of Adrastus, at which point the battle began anew,*

---

175. Another of the "Seven Against Thebes."

*with the ladies working to sabotage the wall around Thebes. The good Capaneus
died there. The wall finally gave way, and the Argives entered the city, pillaging and
killing. Thebes was set afire and destroyed. The Argives undertook the gruesome task
of disposing of their dead, the women mourning piteously.*

13321–13356

But then a great marvel occurred. I do not believe there has ever been anything
like it. When they burned the two brothers in two fires, the smoke that issued
forth from their bodies battled high up in the air, and the flying sparks were hos-
tile toward each other, a sign of the deep root of their mortal hatred. When all
was done, King Adrastus and the ladies took leave of the good esteemed duke of
Athens, thanking him for the kindnesses that he very willingly did for them. Then
the great host of women returned to Argos, where they did not celebrate or amuse
themselves! The king's daughter, who had married Tydeus, had had a very fine son
with him. He was an exceedingly handsome child, and the heir to Argos. He was
useful to the Greeks then, because he was a valiant and wise knight, full of prowess
and noble qualities. He was called Diomedes, and was loved by many people. The
history of Troy recounts a number of his good deeds, because he performed many
valiant feats of arms there—it was an activity that he favored. This is the end of
this story, as I found it memorialized in Fortune's room, written on the wall that I
described above.

XXVIII. *Here is told of Crete and Athens*

13357–13382: *Ion, king of Thessaly, established Athens 385 years before the fall of
Troy. The first laurel tree was found there.*

13383–13409

After the city of Thebes had been destroyed by adversity, as I understand it, and
a good 540 years before Rome was founded and well guarded by the Romans, a
fierce battle arose between Crete and Athens. It had a very strange beginning.
Through very deadly animosity, they fiercely attacked each other in battle by land
and sea. They fought that way for a long time, but the people of Crete defeated the
Athenians, and took very cruel and evil tribute from them. The Athenians had to
draw lots, and the person chosen met with very harsh misfortune, however much
prowess and praise he might have had, because he had to go to Crete. No further
discussion was needed. There, he would be given to a fierce monster that would
kill him. The monster was called the Minotaur.[176] This lottery only applied to the
young males of the city.

---

176. The Minotaur, said to have been born of Queen Pasiphaë (wife of King Minos) from a sexual
encounter with a bull, had the head of a bull and the body of a man.

13410–13456

The Minotaur had already devoured more than a thousand of them when the noble Theseus, son of the king, pulled the lot. It was hopeless; he had to go. He would die there if God did not remedy it, and great mourning was expressed for him. The lad was brought to Crete. Ariadne, the daughter of the king, fell in love with his appearance, because he was very courteous, proper, and handsome of body and face. She wished to love him, and wanted to save his life. So she taught him what he had to do in front of the evil monster.

Theseus was put in the prison of Daedalus.[177] His adversary believed he could kill and attack Theseus, but Theseus strove so much that by his valiance and courage, he killed the monster in the cage. His lady had given him a ball of thread. He certainly did not fail to keep hold of the end of it, because otherwise he would never have succeeded in getting out of the prison. The lady with no character flaw at all held the other end of the thread that she had spun. Thus Theseus exited. He would have been maltreated there if she had not helped him, but she appealed to Cupid on his behalf, and so he was spared from death. They left together and he later married her. Thus the custom of that cruel tribute, from which too much harm had come, stopped at that time. Theseus was a very noble and distinguished knight then.

In Thessaly, the Thessalians and the Lapiths,[178] who wanted no good for each other, also battled one another and fought fiercely. As a result, there were great numbers of dead, as long as that period lasted.

Explicit the fifth part of the present volume.

---

177. A labyrinth built by Cretan architect Daedalus to hold the Minotaur.

178. Christine writes "Sabïen" (13453), which Solente points out as inaccurate (*Mutacion*, 4:170). The Lapiths were a legendary people of Thessaly.

Here begins the sixth part
of The Book of the Mutability of Fortune,
which speaks of the Amazons and an abridged history of Troy

I. *Here is told of King Vexones[179] and how the kingdom of Amazonia began*

13457–13534: *At this time, Vexones, king of Egypt, wanted to conquer the world. He chose to attack Scythia first. The Scythians defended themselves fiercely, causing the Egyptians to flee. The Scythians followed them back to Egypt, where the Scythians prevailed. After that great victory, the Scythians spent the next fifteen years conquering foreign lands. The youth of Scythia decided to join their fathers.*

13535–13583

All of the youth left the country, but they utterly failed in their goal, because they were all killed. Their mothers, hearing of it, were deeply grieved and tormented. Then the women determined among themselves that they would let go of all the mourning and arm themselves to go and avenge their men. From then forward, as long as they lived, they would never have princes, lords, or husbands. Since theirs were dead, they wanted to be independent. There would be no king or master in their land, nor would they be beholden to anyone. They would maintain and defend their kingdom against all men. Never at any time, for any sum, would they put up with a man holding their kingdom or coming to it. They pledged to all of this by an oath, and then they also killed all their male children. They did not ever want to see any man there.

Among them were two ladies, the most noble of all the women. The women elected them their queens and installed the queens as sovereign over them. One was named Lampeto, the other Marpesia. The dignified, renowned ladies armed themselves nobly. They set off in a great army, entirely of ladies and maidens, and they put such great effort into it that they arrived in their enemies' land. They ravaged it and stayed in the country long enough to well avenge their men. They subjugated many great countries entirely to their dominance. Now they had well attained their goal! Thus the women started to carry arms, and they advanced in very great renown. They were victorious in many armed expeditions, and accomplished many great missions.

13584–13612

Among them they established a law dictating that in order to have descendants, they would leave from their kingdom and know men elsewhere. The highest la-

---

179. More commonly known as Sesostris. In his edition and translation of *Orosius: Seven Books of History against the Pagans* (Liverpool: Liverpool University Press, 2010), at 63n203, A. T. Fear suggests that Sesostris could be the pharaoh Senwosret III, who reigned ca. 1878–ca. 1841 BCE.

dies had high barons as lovers, and the other ladies had lovers suitable to them, without any promise of marriage, each according to her rank. And thus their lineage grew. When they gave birth to male children, they sent them to their fathers. They nurtured females, however, with great care. They would dry up the nobles' right breast, but they would deprive non-nobles of the left one[180] as soon as they were born, so that the breast would not hinder them in easily shooting arrows, which they knew better how to use than other people, as I see it. In order not to impede them from wearing a shield, they took the right breast from the nobles. Since these women thus had their breasts removed, they were called *Amazons,* which is what that means in their language, as I have heard it, and their great and extensive kingdom was called Amazonia.

13613–13704: *Lampeto and Marpesia conquered land in Europe and Asia, and founded Ephesus.*[181] *Lampeto returned home, but Marpesia was killed in battle. Marpesia's daughter Sinope was crowned, and went on to avenge her mother and subjugate many more nations. Antiope and Orithyia, who would later be the mother of Penthesilea, stayed in Amazonia and were crowned.*

II. *Here is told how Hercules went with a great host against the Amazons*

13705–13742

The ladies' great renown, how they would conquer lands and lay waste to many regions, had already spread through all countries. In Greece they heard the news of the women, and it did not please them! In their country, they feared that the Amazons would invade. At that time, the noble and strong Hercules, who conquered so much by his efforts and accomplished so much with arms that his renown endured forever after, was in the flower of his youth and at his greatest prowess. He heard about those women. He wanted to go to their country to conquer and destroy them, so they would not come to do harm in Greece. They had already approached Greece, and had knocked down castles.

Once this was known throughout Greece, Hercules's valiant friend Theseus came and set off with him, along with a great army and large fleet. They then sailed across the sea more quickly than an arrow, traveling so far that they arrived at Amazonia. But Hercules did not dare to enter the port by day. Rather, without a long delay, he would surprise them by the dark of night, without their knowing what was going on. He said that if the Amazons were surprised that way, the Greeks would quickly have them all killed or taken. But coming to that place by

180. Curiously, this is the opposite of what Christine says in the *City of Ladies* (Book 1, chapter 16; in English, trans. Richards, 41; in modern French, ed. and trans. Moreau and Hicks, 71).
181. An ancient city in present-day Turkey and an important center of early Christianity.

day could certainly go badly for the Greeks, because the women were fierce and powerful, strong and skillful in every way.

13743–13778
Thus the Greeks, who so feared the Amazons, invaded them by night. Indeed, they went about killing them everywhere. When the Amazons became aware of the deliberateness of the Greeks' actions, the cry quickly went out throughout the land. The women rushed to arm themselves as best they could, and they all ran toward the sea; one did not wait for the other. And you would have seen lances lowered onto lance rests there, and many a fine lance-blow dealt! I am not seeking to add details of my own invention, but the women really had the worst of it, because without arms, many of the maidens were bare-handed.

Two sisters, maidens of very great quality, heard the noise of the battle. They were called Menalipe and Hyppolite, and they were very distressed about this. They were sisters of the queen Sinope and were of very noble origin. They armed themselves most grandly and prepared for battle, mounted on rich war-horses, well positioned in the stirrups, lances in hand. Menalipe attacked Hercules at a full gallop. Hyppolite, who took great pleasure in feats of arms, fought with Theseus. And they should have had great honor from this fight, to tell the truth, because they made the best in the whole world fall in a heap, horse and all, and threw them down with the first blow that they dealt.

13779–13803
The knights, both of whom were knocked down, were shamed. They also knocked the women down, but they quickly jumped to their feet, which made the fight perilous. It seems astonishing that Hercules could be struck down by a woman, because never had anyone been born with as much strength as he, aside from the powerful Samson.[182] But it could well have had to do with the horse, unable to stay on its feet against the maiden's blow, causing Hercules to fall without emptying the saddle. What else will I tell you about it? They battled for a long time, and there was very fierce fighting. But in the end, I have no doubt, the ladies who had done marvels with weapons were taken. That was not at all surprising, because never has anyone heard with his own ears of two stronger, more powerful, and prouder knights than those two. There were many women dead there.

13804–13834: *The Greeks having taken the port, the remaining Amazons retreated into the city. The queen offered ransom for the two women taken hostage. In lieu of ransom, Hercules requested only arms, war-horses, and a promise that the Amazons would never attack the Greeks.*

---

182. Biblical figure whose story is told in Judges 13–16.

13835–13884

It was very joyous news to the queen that she would have the two maidens back. The queen readied herself to go toward the sea, in great celebration, to confirm the agreement. Then in very beautiful array, the richly adorned and very nobly fitted-out ladies left with the queen, heading toward the sea. The Greeks received them with great honor as soon as they saw them, and they made peace in a proper manner. Menalipe was returned to the Amazons, and Theseus took Hyppolite, whom he loved and esteemed, as his wife. He later had a renowned son with her, called Hyppolitus. When they had agreed on the treaties, the Greeks departed. There was great joy throughout Greece when they returned from that voyage through such a good accord. It was said that they had succeeded, because the Greeks had been more fearful and concerned about the Amazons than about any other people.

Thus, as you can see, the queenship of Amazonia was passed from heir to heir. When Orithyia died, her daughter, the valiant Penthesilea, was very distressed by it. Penthesilea was so noble, valiant, wise, and filled with great courage that never has any woman like her been born. They crowned that maiden, who later accomplished many great feats. Deeds of arms pleased her so much that she never did another activity. And as she did not deign to know any man, she was a virgin all her life. She wanted nothing but to carry arms. Later on, in a certain place, you will be told about her at greater length.[183] But for now we will be quiet about her, and talk about another topic. Thus this kingdom where there were only women was founded and advanced, and was greatly renowned for a long time.

III. *Here is told of Hercules and his death*

13885–13918

As for what happened with Hercules, who rested little in his life, I will tell you briefly what I took from the wall of the room where I saw many stories, just as it comes to my memory. Hercules was a Greek knight of astonishing strength, greater than that of any man ever, aside from the one they called Samson. Hercules surpassed all living people in his time, and pursued arms as long as he lived. He vanquished frightening and powerful giants, snakes, and kings. And because he was so inclined toward superhuman deeds, the people, seeing his marvelous feats, said he was the son of Jupiter. Jupiter was their great god at the time they said this. Hercules conquered many foreign places. Because he fought against monsters with strange forms, people said that he went as far as Hades to strike down all the gods of hell. The poets who knew of him related his deeds in poetry. Ovid recounts some of them; he speaks through metaphor in accord with true history. I do not intend to repeat it all now!

---

183. Book 6, chapters 30–33.

13919–13946

Hercules was crowned king of a great country and kingdom. He took the beautiful Iole, daughter of a king and a very high lady, as his wife.[184] When he brought her to his country, he came by sea. He hesitated there, because he was having trouble imagining how he would be able to get his wife past the arm of the sea. At that point a centaur descended from a hill and said that he would surely pass there and take care of the trip, provided that Hercules load the lady on his hindquarters; he should think of nothing else. Hercules believed him and loaded the lady on him, and the centaur immediately took off. He jumped into the sea and carried her beyond, which highly amused him. To help you grasp this better, centaurs were deformed monsters, as I understand it, half horse and half man. Many tales tell of them, and poets speak of them in their works. This centaur was called Nessus. He emerged from the sea with the lady, mocking Hercules, and fled at a full gallop.

13947–13978

Hercules was hardly amused by Nessus, who had carried away his wife. He said that Nessus would soon pay dearly. Hercules loaded the bowstring into the nock of the arrow, and drew back on the bow. He did not fail at all—he hit Nessus beside his lady. When Nessus felt himself mortally struck, he thought about how he would be able to avenge his death. Thereupon, he took a white and delicate shirt which he had put in his belt, and addressed the woman, exhorting her thus: "Lady! I know well that you hold your husband very dear. And you must love him, because surely he well deserves it, but he will make many different forays around the world. Do not think for a minute that he will not have another beloved besides you. He will forget you and love another lady. And since I have pity for you, who will die of anger because of him, I will surely show you how you will get him back." Then he gave her the poisonous shirt and said: "No lady aside from you will ever be loved or remembered by him, as long as he has put on this shirt." She believed him, and very fondly put the shirt aside. Soon after, the centaur died because of the blood he shed.

13979–14024

Hercules came and took his wife away from there to his kingdom and demesne. Then Hercules went by hill and dale on various labors. After a certain time, he had a relationship with the very beautiful maiden Deianira, who held him strongly in her bond. He stayed with her for a long time. The two of them were lovers, lying

---

184. In the mythological story, it is not Iole who is married to Hercules, but Deianira, referred to below; the two women switch places in Christine's text. On this episode and the account of the death of Hercules, see Liliane Dulac, "Le chevalier Hercule, de l'*Ovide moralisé* au *Livre de la mutacion de Fortune* de Christine de Pizan," in "Lectures et usages d'Ovide," ed. Emmanuèle Baumgartner, thematic issue, *Cahiers de recherches médiévales et humanistes* 9 (2002): 115–30 <https://crm.revues.org/68>.

beside each other. She, who had him in her bond, armed herself with weapons and a small sword, and carried a bow and quiver for amusement. And she dressed her lover, gentler than a ewe toward her, in her women's clothing; he did not resist her at all. Thus the two of them carried on joyfully and led a happy life.

After a long time, Iole heard about that situation, and you should know that she was very pained by it and wanted to remedy it. She remembered the shirt that Nessus had given her. Then she came to one of her messengers and gave the shirt to him. She told him to go to Hercules, greet him on her behalf, and request that since he was involved with another lover, out of love for Iole, he should at the very least be willing to wear this shirt that she had spun with her own hands. If he did not want to leave the one with whom he was enjoying himself, at least he could wear the shirt. The messenger did not delay. He quickly gave Hercules the gift from the lady who intended no tricks. Hercules, who did not think about evil, quickly donned the shirt. But once his naked flesh had been in contact with the shirt for a short time, the venom, which burned him all over like fire, raged through his body.

14025–14058

In fury, Hercules thought he would tear up the shirt, but with the shirt he tore away his flesh, all livid with venom, to which the shirt had already adhered. Hercules was now seized by fire. Everything seemed to him to be burning. He ran over mountains; he ran through valleys. Like a wild man, he did not know any way to alleviate his ills. Fortune, who often changes her appearance, who had given him such honor, now led him to a very cruel place! In his violent furor, he knocked down and broke up big trees with the strength of his arms, trying to pull himself out of this painful situation, because he could not die nearly as quickly as he wanted to. He had a big fire prepared to hasten his miserable death. He made great complaints and laments, and many bequests. To his loyal squire and true good friend Philoctetes, he left his bow and arrows, which had vanquished many battlements. Never again will arrows be drawn by such a hand or shot in such a place. Then Hercules threw himself into the fire in great madness. Thus died the proud and strong Hercules; it was a shame. His lover, out of great affliction, killed herself with her own sword, which she struck through her breast.

IV. *Here begins the history of Troy and first the genealogy of the Trojan kings*[185]

14059–14074

In the room that I described, I saw written, along with images well portrayed in gold and blue, the history of Troy, the harm the Greeks and Trojans did to each

---

185. On Troy in this work, see Catherine Croizy-Naquet, "La ville de Troie dans le *Livre de la Mutacion de Fortune* de Christine de Pisan: vv. 13457–21248," in *Actes du colloque Troie au Moyen Age: Univer-*

other, and how they did it. The writing underneath the images recounted all of it. I will relate a short version of it, because it would be difficult to tell it at length, even though this story is very pleasing, true, and well known. And one can learn a great deal about the ways of Fortune from it, if one pays attention to how she frequently changes direction and turns the high to low.

14075–14094: *Friga, grandson of Noah, was the first to inherit the land that Troy would occupy. He named it Phrygia.*[186] *He founded the city, but it would be improved and built up by others. Next came Dardanus, followed by Tros, for whom the city was named.*

14095–14126

Tros had two sons of great renown: one was named Ganymede and the other was called Ilus. In this time, Tantalus reigned in Mycenae, a city in Greece.[187] By necessity or by will, he attacked Troy without seeking peace. The two kings did each other great harm before it came to an end. Ganymede was killed in a violent battle. From there began the roots of the very mortal hatred between the Trojans and the Greeks, who did each other many wrongs after that. King Tantalus, as I read in the history, was the father of the powerful King Pelops. After him, King Pleisthenes reigned in great glory. He was the father of King Agamemnon, the brother of Menelaus, who later had a great deal of trouble because of his wife, lady Helen.[188] It was because of her that Troy was later destroyed and the people killed or put to flight. From King Tros on, the Greeks and Trojans did not like each other, and they did not stop until they destroyed each other, as I find in their history. Many people became serfs and captives as a result, and I told you the cause of it.

14127–14152: *After Tros, Ilus reigned, followed by his son Laomedon. Both successors continued to expand and strengthen the city. At that time, Pelias, whose lineage Ulysses would share, was king in Greece.*

---

sité Charles de Gaulle—Lille III, 24 et 25 septembre 1991, Bien dire et bien aprandre 10 (1992): 17–37; Dulac, "Entre héroïsation et admonestation"; and Marc-René Jung, *La légende de Troie en France au Moyen Age: Analyse des versions françaises et bibliographie raisonnée des manuscrits* (Basel: Francke Verlag, 1996), 629–31.

186. On Phrygia, see Book 3, chapter 6.

187. In Greek mythology, Tantalus ruled the city of Lydia; he was killed by Agamemnon, king of Mycenae, who married Tantalus's wife, Clytemnestra.

188. In most versions of this story, Agamemnon and Menelaus were the sons of Atreus, not Pleisthenes.

V. *Here is told how King Pelias exhorted Jason to go to Colchis to win the golden fleece*[189]

14153–14178

History tells us that King Pelias, of whom I speak, had a nephew named Jason, who was the son of Pelias's brother Aeson. Jason was chosen to be a captain in many armies. There was much talk of him. As Pelias was jealous of his nephew, he wanted to cut his life short, if he could, for fear that Jason would be elected king and he himself dismissed. For that reason, he often undertook to have Jason engage in dangerous feats of arms, so that Jason might die by some means. But Jason always quickly returned victorious. Jason believed that great love moved his uncle to send him for his honor, because his uncle paid him handsomely, without sparing anything, to keep him occupied with voyages. And thus, in spite of Pelias, Jason grew in glory. That troubled Pelias.

14179–14218

King Pelias heard about an island where many went, but from which they were later unable to return. It was commonly held that a sheep with a fleece all of gold was always there. But the gods had placed their guard over the sheep, in a strange way, because an ever-vigilant serpent, and two very marvelous bulls who threw fire and flame at the same time, guarded the sheep night and day. The very famous place was named the Isle of Colchis. Pelias wanted to send Jason to the island, because he thought that if Jason set foot there, he would not return; there was no way to come back.

One day King Pelias summoned Jason and graciously addressed him in front of his barons, praising him enthusiastically for being noble and strong above all living knights. He said that Jason's prowess would be complete if he were able to win the golden fleece. Jason then said that he would go very willingly, and he wished more than anything else to undertake this voyage. There was no journey that he would so want to take! The king, firmly believing that he was rid of Jason, was joyful. Thus he quickly gave Jason whatever he would need to prepare. He quickly had a handsome ship readied, big and well equipped, and furnished with

---

189. Ruth Morse discusses Christine's use of the Jason and Medea story in *The Medieval Medea* (Cambridge, UK, and Rochester, NY: D. S. Brewer, 1996), 97–102. On Medea in Christine's works, see also Patrizia Caraffi, "Medea sapiente e amorosa: Da Euripide a Christine de Pizan," in Hicks, Gonzalez, and Simon, *Au champ des escriptures*, 133–47; Caraffi, "Il mito di Medea nell'opera di Christine de Pizan," in *Magia, gelosia, vendetta: Il mito di Medea nelle lettere francesi, Gargnano del Garda: 8–11 giugno 2005*, ed. Liana Nissim and Alessandra Preda (Milan: Cisalpino, 2006), 57–70; as well as John Jay Thompson, "Medea in Christine de Pizan's *Mutacion de Fortune*, or How To Be a Better Mother," *Forum for Modern Language Studies* 35 (1999): 158–74.

everything necessary for a long voyage by sea. The ship was called Argo, for Argus, who had smoothed it with a plane.[190]

14219–14262: *A number of noble young men, Hercules among them, set off with Jason. They stopped at the port of Troy for rest and provisions. Laomedon, king of Troy, was uncomfortable with their presence and demanded that they leave. That angered Hercules, who threatened to return one day and cause harm.*

14263–14300

The Greeks departed very angry. They sailed, making their way as best they could toward the land where Jason wanted to seek the fleece. They arrived at the port quite quickly, because no opposing wind hindered them. King Aeëtes, the lord of this land, got word of their arrival. He received them with great honor, because he already knew well who they were. He celebrated them very grandly. He inquired about the reason for their trip and who led them. And it was told to him. But "they had gone to this trouble in vain" (the king said this) "because in no way could the fleece be taken by the force of any living man. Anyone who strives for it commits foolishness and confronts his death, because death is the only thing gained by anyone who sets out to take it. Many renowned knights have tried, out of folly, and died in great suffering." He pleaded with Jason and counseled him not to wish to destroy his beautiful youth so foolishly, dying this way for no reason. Thus the king reproached him for the undertaking, saying that whoever sent him there did not love him, because he had sent Jason to his death. But Jason responded that because he had undertaken the voyage, he would in no way be reproached for cowardice, whatever one might say to him, because he would rather die in pain than turn away in vile shame.

14301–14353

King Aeëtes had a daughter, above all other women adroit, wise, learned, and educated in the seven arts. And always, early and late, she studied more magic than the science of logic. Thus she had experience in it and knew the art fully. It was not impossible for her to do anything that one could do with science. She was beautiful of body and face, courtly and well skilled in speaking. But she was so strong-willed that there was no king from any family so high that she would deign to take as a husband, so much did she value the virtue of learning.

One day after dining, to celebrate the foreign guests, the king sent for his lovely daughter. He wanted them to see the one who had no duplicate or equal in the land. She was unparalleled among women! At his command, she came to the king in very noble array. She seemed very much like an honored queen. Her

190. Renowned as a craftsman, Argus built the ship with the help of the goddess Athena. He is not to be confused with Argus, the hundred-eyed giant of myth.

clothing, all golden, was studded with pearls and select precious stones. Her long reddish hair hung down to her heels. She had a crown upon it which was worth a great deal. And she seemed even more beautiful and pleasing than usual. Leading a very great company of ladies, she came before the king. She knelt and became red in the face when she lowered herself before the king, who kissed her. She, in whom knowledge dwelt, was red because of the strangers. Nonetheless, she quickly, courteously, and beautifully greeted them, and they greeted her as well. She seemed to them very gracious and beautiful. Medea was her name. The king, whom she loved, told her to address the strangers and give them some of her jewels, because they were well worth it. At that point they descended toward her, and she toward them, in fine ceremony. Because they were sons of kings, she honored them very greatly.

14354–14378: *She conversed with them at length, and Jason explained his mission. Medea found him pleasing in every way.*

14379–14436

Medea looked at Jason attentively. And then Love, who took notice of it, fired a sharp arrow through a look; the arrow lodged in her heart. He severely wounded Medea. The wound, which would cause her great suffering, would not easily be healed! She would even find herself saddened by it! It was bad for her to have met Jason! She pitied his situation greatly, because it was for his own demise that he came in quest of something no one could gain by chivalry or force. At that point, she tried very hard to dissuade him from it, saying that there was no man in the world powerful, chivalrous, or strong enough to acquire it through any effort. She said that it was an enchanted thing; if he were ever to win the fleece, it would have to be by magic. She informed him of this. She said that he should not wish to sully himself by persevering in a foolish undertaking, and that he would still be able to do a lot of good. But he said that nothing would dissuade him from this adventure. Surely he had to go there, even if he would have to die!

Medea greatly valued his tremendous courage, but lamented the regrettable situation. They left their conversation at that point in order not to arouse suspicion. They then took their leave and went to their rooms, where for several days Medea was very dejected, went pale and changed color, for the love of Jason. She was so severely afflicted that she never had any respite. She sighed and wept, alarmed by what was happening, because she had never paid attention to love. Now it was necessary for her to love a stranger, in spite of herself! Love knew well how to get revenge against the woman whom he had found so rebellious! Then, as a person who understood so much science, she blamed and reprimanded herself for this foolishness. She said that considering her great knowledge and all of the intelligence she possessed, it was not right for her to let Love mislead her heart or for her to be taken by surprise this way. She reproached herself very harshly for it.

But no grumbling had any value, because at the same time, Love gripped her so intensely that, her heart forced, she was obliged to obey him. No reprimand from anybody would matter.

14437–14453: *The tormented Medea tried in vain to fight her "malady" (14439) by avoiding Jason. Meanwhile, the king remained unsuccessful in dissuading Jason from his mission.*

14454–14484
No one could hold Jason back any longer. One day Medea addressed him, saying: "Your pleasing person impels me to speak foolishness. Love is doing this. He binds me in your love, maiden though I may be. It is a great misfortune that I do not have the power to hide it. I have now been pushed to this point. I have never loved anyone, in any instance, even if I may have had compassion for his situation. But Love is your advocate now, and he will not tolerate my letting you offer yourself up to death, beloved Jason. If you are willing to promise me, with your hand on your heart, that from here on you will be mine and you will indeed marry no other or have any other lady or lover, fear not—I will do so much by the art of my magic that you will quickly capture the fleece for which you took this journey. You will not have it by any other means. Now watch what you do. If you deceive me, you will sin so greatly that the vengeance will be a grave misfortune for you. Do not promise me anything without keeping it, if you do not want to die in shame."

14485–14561: *Feigning to be overwhelmed by love, Jason swore his fidelity to Medea. Blinded by love, Medea believed him. Her prudent trepidation overwhelmed by her passion, Medea summoned Jason to her chamber the following night.*

14562–14613
She said to him: "I want to bind you by an oath, beloved! Take care that I never find you deceitful, because that would bring great ill upon you. It would be better for you to say it now." He assured Medea that she could always trust in him. She thereupon opened the little ivory door of a very rich and nobly adorned oratory, where there was a statuette of their great god Jupiter in fine pure gold. Then and there, Jason swore to the gods in a solemn oath that he would always be her beloved, just as he had promised her. He said plenty more to her, but I believe that he would be a perjurer before long, and would think of another love.

Reassured, Medea now had to teach him how to take possession of the golden fleece. At that point, she went to seek a small casket. She gave him writings and charms. He did not need any other weapons. And she told him clearly what he had to do. When she had arranged the whole thing, they kissed each other joyously. And they went to bed and gave each other pleasure at their leisure, I do not doubt it a bit, as lovers do.

In the morning, he took leave of her, thoroughly prepared with what he had learned he had to do. On the day set by Jason, he took leave of his friends to go in quest of the fleece. They all begged him not to seek death that way, and to give up a conquest that was too difficult. But he took no heed of that. He then got into a small boat, armed, and rowed himself because there was no one else. He needed to pass beyond the arm of the sea. He came to the island, stripped completely naked, and rubbed his entire body with an ointment. From that point on he did not have to concern himself about being burned by fire, with which the whole island was inflamed.

14614–14667

He then secured a small image to the crest of his helmet. In his palm he held a ring that had the power to magically destroy anything in an instant. He went confidently toward the bulls, who intended to attack him, growling very menacingly. Jason, without becoming frightened, drove two big balls coated with sticky and inconspicuous glue into their mouths, which immediately stuck their jaws together, putting them entirely at his mercy. He immediately turned toward the serpent. He read a spell, putting the serpent in such a state that it immediately fell dead right there. Then, for fear of displeasing the god, Jason did his oblations with very great devotion.

When he had finished and fulfilled the order of his lady, leaving nothing out, he went toward the sheep, joyous and happy. But the sheep shone so strongly from the sun shining on the gold that the whole island gleamed from it; he was blinded by the sight of it. He took the fleece and left the sheep. At that point he departed, but first he lowered himself to the ground to render thanks to the goddess Venus, to whom the lady who helped him had spoken on his behalf.

Thus Jason left from there, very joyful, along with the fleece, which had the value of a great many treasures. He returned to his boat. From atop towers and belfries, his dear friends, who had feared greatly for him, watched in wait. They immediately sounded the alarm bell when they saw him returning. They began to express great joy. They all ran before him. The king and everyone went forward to watch this marvel. Everyone was astonished that Jason was able to successfully accomplish such a difficult undertaking, by any means. They valued him and praised him greatly, recognizing his tremendous bravery. They said that he had no peer on earth.

14668–14692

They believed that Jason could be the son of the gods who helped him with this; surprisingly, they spoke of that. Hercules, Pirithous, and Theseus did not keep quiet about it at all. They all were marveled by it, and kissed and congratulated

Jason. I do not believe that it pleased the king, whatever he may have shown, for such a treasure to be transported and carried away from his kingdom. But there was nothing he could do about it, so he did himself honor by keeping quiet. Medea could not keep herself from coming to meet up with Jason, and she received him with such joy that it would hardly go unnoticed. Thus one takes note of how Love changes the ways of even the learned. He blinds and deceives so much that the wisest person does not perceive the foolishness that results from loving too much. Therefore the simple one should not be criticized for taking leave of his senses in such a situation, when the wisest does not see a thing.

14693–14734
Jason was bathed, cleaned, and grandly celebrated. He rested there for a whole month. Medea had little repose, and she did not keep it private. The two lovers were so unbridled by the ardor of loving, that several indeed began to criticize Medea and Jason for conversing together too much. Jason heard about that, and said to her: "My beautiful lady! We must leave here, because we could greatly regret the time spent here if the king heard about it. Let us think about the voyage to Greece, where you will be joyfully received when you arrive." Medea said: "My love! My treasure! Your pleasure is entirely mine." The ship was quickly readied. They remained there no longer. Rather, they left by dark of night, without the king hearing any rumor of it. Medea carried off the king's whole treasure, playing and amusing herself over something that would later make her sad. Love[191] excited her very strangely. He knew so well how to wound her that he made her leave her country, kingdom, heritage, and her dear father and family, for a foreign knight who would be able to change his heart quickly, leaving her abandoned and separated from her friends. When they arrived in Greece, there was no stranger or friend who did not celebrate and express joy for Jason's return from the noble voyage. Pelias himself greeted them cheerfully, even though he did not hold their arrival very dear.

VI. Here is told of the destruction of the first Troy

14735–14759: *Still outraged that Laomedon had chased them from his domain, Hercules enlisted the aid of his fellow princes in pursuing revenge.*

14760–14786
They all granted him their aid, without hesitating. There were fifteen strong and well-built ships from Greece and the region. Many a baron came to this army, equipped most grandly. Jason, of whom I told above, and whom Medea had kept from death, was not at this assembly. He had tormented Medea greatly, and was

191. That is, the god of love.

never loyal to her. Rather, the unfaithful, deceitful one exchanged her for another woman and left her. He took the daughter of a king as his wife, whom he loved. Medea was so inflamed when she learned of the marriage that, filled with rage, she killed him and two children that she had had with him. No one saved them. Some say that she then killed herself and others say she did not. And thus it ended badly, despite the fleece of fine gold. May whoever wants to see himself in this do so, as this is one time when a doctor treats the illness of another, and then kills himself!

More of the same

14787–14814

The Greek barons arrived at the port of Troy and anchored there by night, in secret. One part of the army went to lie in ambush in the countryside around Troy, to play a deceitful trick. In the morning, rumor of the Greeks was soon heard. The people of the country were not very happy when they noticed the army, and the news spread quickly through the city. More than a thousand ran to arms. Laomedon was very angered by it. He quickly armed himself and sped toward the fleet, along with as many people as possible. Be they sergeant or knight, all rushed there, shouting hunting cries at the Greeks. People hastened there from everywhere, and even the people who worked the land came in great numbers. They struck without letting up with such weapons as they had. The Greeks, who saw them coming, protected themselves in all parts of the ship, because so many attacked them. And indeed they made the Greeks pull back, and some jumped into the river.

14815–14894: *Through fierce battle, the Greeks managed to enter the city. Hercules found Laomedon and cut his head off. The Greeks annihilated the Trojans, pillaging and setting fire to the city. Telemon Ajax, a Greek baron,[192] took the king's daughter and other maidens in tribute. The Greeks arrived home to great celebration.*

VII. Here is told of King Priam and his fine lineage

14895–14950

Laomedon had a valiant and noble son, chivalrous and renowned, who knew a great deal. He was called King Priam. He was the heir after his father's death, but he had gone away on a long voyage. He was very far from the country of Troy when this misfortune occurred there. It did not end immediately; rather, it was the beginning of great suffering and grave murders. Priam had brought his wife and children with him outside the kingdom for the long time he had to be away, at

---

192. Greek hero, father of Ajax.

the time the Greeks committed this offense against him. He had a very handsome family of children. I do not believe that any king or prince has had such a fine brood since, or ever will—all so powerful, strong, handsome, and sensible. Nor would any be so renowned around the world and considered so good. Priam had eight children with his wife Hecuba, who was a very high lady of noble lineage, courageous, valiant, courtly, and wise.

The eldest child was named Hector, who was so noble and famed that there will forever be memory of his fine condition, endowed with all nobility, and of his very high prowess. No knight more perfect in word and deed has ever been born. Next was the handsome Paris. Never since has there been a young man in the world more perfect in beauty—he had that distinction—courtly, well put-together, and elegantly dressed. But he did not have one one-hundredth the prowess of his brother Hector. Rather, he fired feathered arrows well with a bow, with true aim, whether in battle or in a hunting park. The third one was named Helenus. He was never armed because he was a priest in their religion, and he affirmed for the Trojans the truth of many important things that occurred. It was bad for them when they did not take his counsel as certain and true! He was highly learned. He knew the entire science of astrology and he was well educated in science.

14951–14994

The fourth was named Deiphobus. He was a brave and strong knight, more nimble than any leopard. There was no bow, however strong, that he did not fire. He knew well how to fire an arrow and to attract people with appealing speech. The youngest son was named Troilus. I do not believe that a youth of such great worth has been born since, because he was very handsome, with no faults. And he would have had almost as much power as his brother, the strong Hector, if he had lived. But he was so filled with prowess in his youth that until the day he died, he outdid everyone but Hector. He was joyous, always singing and laughing.

King Priam had three daughters. They were more beautiful than anything ever born. The eldest was named Andromache, who was even wiser than she was beautiful. She was married to her brother Hector; according to their religion at that time, one could do that without sinning. The second was named Cassandra; no woman ever since has been renowned for such wisdom. She lived in a community of devoted women at the temple of sacred Minerva, and she was so learned, educated, and filled with great science that she often had fore-knowledge of what would happen. No one knew more than she did. The youngest was named Polyxena, and her utterly perfect beauty will be renowned forever. Nature had made her entirely in such a way that she was schooled in all honor, courtly, wise, and very well instructed. Priam had thirty other bastard sons, all knights, whom he must have loved because their reputations were very great. For the sake of brevity, I will not tell their names.

VIII. *Here is told of Priam's grief at the death of his father, and of the destruction of the first Troy*

14995–15044: *Devastated by the news of his father's death and the destruction of Troy, Priam rushed home. His grief only grew as he saw his city pillaged and the great castle Ilion in ruins. He lamented that his sister Hesiona had been taken by the Greeks. He wanted both to seek vengeance and rebuild Troy.*

IX. *Here is told how Troy was rebuilt*

15045–15086

King Priam sent word far and wide, seeking laborers to dig the earth. He wanted to make his city so beautiful that there would be no other like it in the entire world. He had large and deep foundations made of marble, to situate the walls at the base. He surrounded the enceinte with a stretch of land that could be worked with three good days' labor. He had the outer walls made of natural grayish-brown and white marble. They would be about as high as an arrow flight when they were done. They were very marvelously thick, and the marble was so polished and made with such beautiful workmanship that the sight of it dazzled when the sun shone down on it. The great, tall, and solid towers were extremely pleasing, as were the many grand fortresses of fine, lustrous marble. He had the noble castle of Ilion erected on a rock stronger than steel; it never had an equal. He had sturdy chisels strike so much that the foundations were made with very strong fittings. The high castle was finished (none so beautiful has ever been made since!), and the city rebuilt in such a way that never was another as good or lovely erected on earth. There was a great deep river below. And the city was built of such construction that the whole world could never harm it. The city had nothing to fear but treachery. It was very rich and well populated, overflowing with all abundance, but I will resist describing it because I would devote too much space to it.

More on this

15087–15144: *Now Priam wanted to attack his enemies. The elders counseled against it because of a prophecy that Troy would be destroyed as a result. The younger people, aside from Helenus, did not share the elders' respect for the ancient texts, and wanted to attack. Priam's focus turned to getting Hesiona back from the Greeks.*

X. Here is told how King Priam sent to Greece, requesting that his sister Hesiona be sent to him

15145–15173: *Priam sent Antenor to Greece to negotiate Hesiona's return. The Greeks refused. Antenor returned to Troy with the bad news, which greatly angered Priam and his sons.*

15174–15214

Hector grieved over this shame. He decided that they should go to Greece with a great army, as Hercules had once done in their land, and destroy it through combat. Paris offered different counsel, saying that he had seen a true sign and vision in his sleep, because the goddess Venus, who has control over lovers, had come to him in a dream. She promised him the beautiful Helen as a sure prize, if he were valorous enough to go to Greece to seek her. As long as he kept the reason for his voyage to Greece well hidden, he would be able to kidnap her, whomever he might displease. He would go if the king consented to the expedition, because he knew and sensed that he would then surely bring Helen to Troy. He did not believe that they would fail to achieve their goal of getting his aunt Hesiona back. The Greeks would surrender lady for lady and would no longer hold Hesiona.

Although the king was in agreement, the elders were against undertaking this, because they said that by taking Helen they would be destroyed, as their prophecies said. They therefore pleaded with the king for Paris not to go there, or they would be destroyed. Helenus, who advised against it, knew it well, but Troilus advised in favor. In short, Paris had presented so many arguments, it was ordered that he would go. He left quite quickly. They arranged a good ship for him, well equipped and nicely fitted out. He brought noble people with him.

XI. Here is told how Paris carried off Helen

15215–15262

Paris traveled so much by sea that he came to a shore in Greece. He descended on an island where more than a thousand people had gathered to celebrate a solemn feast; that number of people had not come all year. It was at the temple of the great Venus, who grants joy and sadness to lovers, on the eve of her feast day. The island where Venus was invoked was called Cythera, and beautiful Helen had come there to the celebration. She had a crown of green leaves, in reverence to the goddess who gives lovers hope. Helen was so beautiful that there was no lady like her in the entire world, more pleasing or less sullied with pride. She was courtly and well taught. She had brought pleasing company along, like the queen she was. Her condition showed it. King Menelaus had married her. She settled in at the temple. She had already heard that Paris, the son of the king of Troy, had come to the area by ship with very noble company. She wanted to see his beauty, because never had anyone observed a man more handsome in every way.

Paris had heard similar words spoken about Helen, which made him strongly desire to see her. He entered the temple and prayed to the goddess to keep her promise to him. He devoutly said his prayers and vows, as was right. Then he turned back around to go from the temple. And thus, as he turned, he soon noticed Helen, and she him. Such a powerful love was conceived between them that it was neither suppressed nor extinguished. By a clever trick, Love very severely wounded him with a look.

15263–15291

Paris made his way around the place, until he was able to speak to Helen. He addressed her with courtly and gracious words, as one who knew better than anyone how to do that. I believe that he forgot nothing that would be fitting to say. He revealed to her his passionate love, and how Venus had promised him that he would have her. That was why he had gone to this trouble. He begged her to accept his overtures favorably, because there was nothing he wanted so badly. In short, Paris pursued her and strove so much for her, with promises, pleas, his courtly ways, and his peerless beauty (with Love alongside counseling him) that Helen granted him all of her love. She agreed to go with him to Troy. But in order to better keep her honor, she wanted him to kidnap her by force at the temple at night, without waiting any longer. She did not want people to believe that there was such sin in her that she would have previously agreed to it. The affair was delayed no further. Paris then took leave of Helen, and joyfully made his way through the temple and departed.

15291–15336

At the specified time, without delay, he had all of his men very well armed. There was a highly notable band of knights and barons among them. They went to the temple furtively like thieves by night, in secret, ready to fight. In little time, the temple was put on alert, and no one who was sleeping failed to wake up very quickly indeed, shaking harder than any leaf when they perceived the armed men heading toward the women. They cried "Alarm! Alarm!," at which point Paris took his lady. He wrapped her in his arms and stole her away. She lamented loudly and pretended that it troubled her very much. There was terrible slaughter and great uproar from those who wanted to run there to rescue her. Thus the Trojans exerted enough effort to get on the ships with the ladies they were taking away, who were very despondent.

They arrived in Troy in little time, where they found a great celebration. They were received with joy and honor. The wisest were nevertheless very grieved by it, however, because they found in their ancient texts and writings that they would surely perish because of this act. Cassandra, the wise and learned woman, daughter of the king, knew well by her great wisdom that things would go badly in the future because of this. And she announced to them, out loud, the suffering, grave losses, and severe trouble that would befall them because of lady Helen's coming. They paid dearly for it later. Helenus was very chagrined because of it, for he knew well the evil that was to come!

XII. *Here is told how all of Greece was provoked by the abduction of Helen*

15337–15388

The news traveled throughout Greece of how Paris had taken the beautiful Helen away to Troy. Two of her brothers, renowned knights named Castor and Pollux,[193] very hastily set off on a journey to come to her aid. No one knows how it happened, but they failed to come to an accord then.[194] King Menelaus, Helen's husband, was intensely angered by this. He was not in his land when it happened. Sad and distraught, he went to all of the kings, princes, and dukes to request their help in avenging this shameful affair. All said that they would not fail him. All of Greece was roused. They would attack Troy to avenge this shame and destroy the Trojans.

On a certain day, as it is told, the barons assembled in the city of Athens. There was no friend in the environs of Greece who did not raise his mast at sea. The gathering of lords in this vast army of knights and sergeants was so great, I do not think that more people had ever assembled on a shore to set off to war by sea. They made a high baron of Greece their leader and put him in charge of the army. This man was named King Agamemnon. He was the brother of King Menelaus, who had readied this great army. There were approximately two thousand ships, with many sails and many oars, completely filled with knights and high barons accustomed to suffering pain in war and to arming themselves. For brevity's sake, I will pass on naming them. On a given day, this great ordered army departed, taking up a lot of space on the sea. The masts and the high sails looked like a perilous forest crossing the sea.

193. Twins whom Zeus later turned into stars and placed in the constellation Gemini.

194. The wording here is puzzling. Christine writes "mais puis ne tournerent en perche" (15344), which could literally mean "but then they did not return to the perch," therefore, figuratively, "home." Solente, however, proposes that "perche" be read as "pache," or accord, leading us to this translation. Further complicating the interpretation of this line is that no existing version of the Greek myth refers to Castor and Pollux having gone to Troy (there are, however, tales of a foray to Athens to negotiate Helen's release from Theseus in a separate kidnapping); my thanks to Nicolle Hirschfeld for this insight.

15389–15420: *They reached the castle Tenedos[195] near Troy, where they spent a year strategizing about how to enter the city. The baron Palamedes[196] arrived. Critical of the delay, he pushed them to get on with the mission.*

XIII. Here is told how the Greeks attacked the port of Troy

15421–15490: *When the Greeks arrived, the Trojans battled as fiercely to defend the port as the Greeks battled to enter. Ultimately, the Greeks prevailed and pushed the Trojans back. But their good fortune would not long last long.*

XIV. Here is told how Hector came to the battle with a great army

15491–15543: *Hector rushed into battle. Protesilaus[197] ran to face him and was quickly killed, making the Greeks fully aware of Hector's prowess. Night fell, separating the armies. In the morning, the Trojans rushed to arms, but Christine decides not to go into detail at this point.*

15544–15584

It suffices for me to tell the outcome of this story in brief, as it appeared to me on the remarkable wall. The tale is there for whoever wants to read it, but may my abridgment be adequate here.

A handsome array of troops issued forth, the gold on the banners and shields shining. The Greeks, who were so renowned, did not consider themselves vanquished. Their leader had well equipped them in magnificent battalions. There were recognizable emblems of gold and colors, and banners of many different kinds. The first battalion was led by a baron well skilled at arms. His name was Patroclus, and he was a renowned prince. He and Achilles loved each other more than anything and called themselves brothers. Their love was so great, people of all sorts asserted that there was a vile sin between them.[198] The marvelously courageous Achilles was the most valiant of all the Greeks. He possessed strength and boldness over all men, aside from Hector, who surpassed the good ones in all points. Some, however, said that their worth was nearly equal. I do not believe that, because histories all over praise Hector in every way, not Achilles. Still, Achilles was adroit, marvelously valiant and strong, and had such great power that he made the Trojans tremble when he came to the battle, putting them all into a fright if the valiant Hector was not there.

---

195. An island in the Aegean Sea, now part of Turkey.

196. Greek prince.

197. A hero of myth, he is the first to leap ashore in the invasion of Troy and to die in the conflict.

198. That is, that they were lovers; see also the section starting at line 16057 below.

15585–15631

These brave, strong, and well-armed people were called Myrmidons.[199] They performed many fine deeds and sustained great hardships in this war. Hector, so filled with courage, had assembled the best from the city along with his thirty brothers—they were of several mothers and he knew them to be very bold—and a number of others as well. Hector wanted to be the chief of this squadron, leading his proud and formidable troops forward. There were fine officers in it!

The two armies quickly entered the fray, and many men had their bones broken. Patroclus, whom Hector had noticed, was eager to engage in one-on-one combat, but he did so out of great foolishness. I believe he made an unfortunate choice. The two knights came together, and were not reluctant to kill each other. Hector did not shy away or yield ground. He pierced Patroclus's liver. A cubit of his lance was visible on the other side; he threw horse and all in a heap. Now the handsome Patroclus was dead, for which there would be great mourning. The Greeks were alarmed by it. Hector killed great numbers in the short time he was among them. The hate began right then, as more than twenty thousand vowed to put Hector to death.

No one would be able to describe Achilles's grief and pitiful lamenting when he learned that Patroclus had been killed. Never had a man suffered more greatly at the death of another. He swore to his gods that he would avenge this offense, and that Hector would have to die in pain. Achilles said that the one who was responsible for his mourning would indeed die by Achilles's own hand, and that he would watch for Hector, morning and night, to catch him vulnerable. Then no one would be able to protect Hector well enough to keep Achilles from striking him dead on the spot.

15632–15659

Thus Achilles harshly threatened Hector, who slaughtered Greeks one after the other. Everyone there would have gone far away if he could, because Hector was greatly feared, and the people who helped him were very worthy. But to make the story short, I will tell you that the Greeks comported themselves so well that they surely brought many of the Trojans to the ground, striking with lances and sword-blades. This conflict lasted all day, with people enduring a great deal. When some squadrons were worn out, others came back, and the tired ones went to rest. You would see the fresh troops coming to keep the battle going at all times, without weakening. Often, when Hector and his whole battalion went back to the city from the battle, the Trojans were chased away by Achilles's people or other Greeks. Thus they drove them back often. As a result, they chased each other from the battle a number of times and by many turns. I do not know what else to tell you about it!

---

199. A Thessalian people known for their warlike ways.

15660–15786: *The Trojans were victorious, thanks to the dauntless Hector. They would have won everything had Mischance and Fortune not turned against them. A strange thing happened—one of the Greeks pursued by Hector begged for mercy, saying that they were of the same lineage. That man's mother was Hector's aunt Hesiona. His father was Telemon Ajax, and his name was Ajax. At his request, Hector sounded retreat. Hector entered Troy, where he was joyously received. Priam granted the Greeks a truce of two months to bury their dead. Cassandra called for an end to the war, but her warning was dismissed as folly.*

XV. Here is told of the other battles that followed between the Trojans and Greeks

15787–15950: *The battle resumed. Achilles and Hector fought each other fiercely a number of times. The Trojans prevailed. A truce was called so the two sides could bury their dead. The Greeks determined that they could not win as long as Hector was alive. They made him a target, but he battled so fiercely that they resorted to projectiles in their unsuccessful attempt to kill him. The fighting continued for ten full years. Several times, the Greeks were inclined to give up the siege, but Calchas[200] dissuaded them from doing so, as he had learned from the Oracle at Delphi[201] that the Greeks would prevail in five years. In spite of hardships, storms, and famine, the Greeks always had enough help from allies to keep sufficient numbers of fresh and rested men.*

15951–15982

The Greeks had many barons of high nobility whose prowess is well recounted in history. For brevity, however, I did not talk about it. The principal barons among them, those who were the most valiant, were: the courageous and strong Achilles; the very powerful Palamedes; Agamemnon, their leader; the wise and temperate Ulysses, who did more with his wisdom than all the others by prowess; Diomedes; and several others. Of the Trojans, the best were: Hector and his brother Troilus, who at his young age unfailingly surpassed all the Trojans except Hector in feats of battle; King Memnon[202] and Polydamas, who was never brought down by the Greeks; and Aeneas and Deiphobus, who made many a Greek's head fly over his chest. The king's bastard sons earned praise for their great prowess. It was a shame when such nobility was thus lost because of Fortune, because no kingdom or city ever had a more gallant body of knights than those spoken of here! There were so many other good ones there that to tell of the whole lot would be a trial!

---

200. A famous Greek seer.

201. See note 171.

202. In the *Iliad*, Memnon is an Ethiopian warrior king who comes to the aid of the Trojans.

XVI. *Here is told how Greeks and Trojans assembled for a conference to discuss peace, and how Achilles went to see Hector*

15983–16039: *High-level Greeks and Trojans convened in a conference, but could not come to any agreement. Priam consented to return Calchas's daughter, Briseida, to him.*[203] *Meanwhile, Achilles sought Hector out, as he had never met him unarmed. Hector received Achilles graciously, and Achilles studied the powerful Hector intently.*

16040–16056
Achilles then said to Hector, not softly, that he had had a great desire to see him, unarmed and at leisure, because of the strength that Hector possessed. Hector had been very fierce against him and made him suffer often. He wanted very much for Hector to know that he would make him pay dearly, if he could, for the pain Hector had caused him over his dear friend Patroclus. And even if it meant that Achilles would have to stay right there, Hector would die by no other hands. Achilles said that he had already watched Hector for many days and would not stop watching him until he could eventually strike him dead. And he said it would be difficult for Hector to get away; Achilles needed to catch him.

16057–16084
Hector responded that a great threat erases the glory of a knight. He said that since Achilles hated him so very intensely for killing Patroclus (the companion whom Achilles held so dear, and with whom he wanted so shamefully to sleep several times, according to a very base rumor that spread about him), Achilles could better seek revenge another way, without harming so many people: those two would battle man-to-man. Hector said that the two sides should swear and agree that if Achilles were victorious, Hector would promise to leave Troy and the entire domain and kingdom for Achilles to do with as he wished, and to hand over hostages for it. If Hector were to defeat Achilles, then the Greeks would go away to their land with opposition from no one. Thus the war would end. Achilles said that it pleased him well, and he left from there with no further discussion. He told it to the Greek barons, but not one of them agreed with it. And the affair was left that way, which weighed heavily on Hector.

---

203. For more on the figure of Briseida, see Kara Doyle, "Beyond Resistance: Azalais d'Altier, Christine de Pizan, and the 'Good' Female Reader of Briseida," *Exemplaria* 20 (2008): 72–97, and Douglas Kelly, "The Invention of Briseida's Story in Benoît de Sainte-Maure's *Troie*," *Romance Philology* 48 (1995): 221–41.

XVII. *Here is told how Briseida was returned to her father Calchas*

16085–16174: Troilus *was distraught when Priam sent Briseida back to her father, because he loved her passionately. The couple was wrenchingly separated when she was handed over. The Greeks comforted her, especially Diomedes, who soon made her forget about Troy by becoming her new lover. There was much fighting between Troilus and Diomedes, but in the name of brevity, Christine opts not to discuss it any further.*

XVIII. *Here is told how many battles there were during the war, and what they and their barons were like*

16175–16206: There were twenty main battles, with truces in between to dispose of the putrid remains of the dead and to allow the injured to heal.*

16207–16238

I am not looking to make a long story of it, because my intention is to tell only the principal facts pertinent to the subject matter, to show how Fortune changes and is not the same at all times. Therefore, I will tell you briefly that the brave knights, scattered among both sides, performed many acts of prowess everywhere. These four mainly stood out for fighting: the Trojans Hector and his brother Troilus, and Achilles and Diomedes from the Greeks. I will be quiet about the rest now, for the sake of brevity. But Hector fought so powerfully there that just as small birds flee before the merlin[204] or the falcon seeking prey, the Greeks fled from his path, because he killed all of them without stopping. But it is now time for me to start telling of his pitiful death, to bring the matter of this sad story to an end. Hector was killed in the tenth and harshest battle; Fortune had set it that way. I will tell you how, as I saw on the wall.

XIX. *Here is told of the battle in which Hector was killed, and of his wife Andromache's dream*

16239–16370: In the fifth year of the wars, in the tenth battle, Hector would be killed. The night before, his wife Andromache had an ominous dream, in which she saw the god Mars[205] face to face. She also saw Venus and Minerva, who exhorted her to keep Hector from going to battle that day. With Hector furious at her pleas that he not go, Andromache implored her father Priam to intervene. Trembling with rage, Hector acceded to Priam's request. Hearing the cries of the Trojans struggling against the Greeks, Hector climbed up on the city wall to see the battlefield. He could hold*

---

204. A small species of falcon.

205. God of war.

back no longer. He gathered a retinue of distinguished men, sounded the horn, and headed toward the fray.

16371–16395

Alas! Now the valiant Hector, so often the one to save his people, went to die! It was a great shame for such a brave and peerless man to die this way, because of Fortune and misfortune, and in such a singular event! But before the next day arrived, a thousand would die by his hand. At that point, Hector resembled a wolf devouring ewes. If he was impetuous, he showed it then. He overturned men and horses at the same time. Whoever could escape fled from him, but anyone he could catch met his death. He had a path made in front of him. Trojans gathered in a band around him, as a litter would typically gather around its mother. The Trojans were cured of their bitter pain! They recovered the courage and the boldness that had been taken from them when they were told that Hector would not go into battle that day. All would surely have been lost.

16396–16424: Hector quickly pushed the Greeks back from the position they had gained.

16425–16460

I do not know what more to say about it! If I wanted to relate all the deeds accomplished by Hector, I would not conclude for a long time. Therefore, I pass on it in brief. On that day, he did greater harm to the Greeks than ever before. They feared him so much that they all fled before him. No one who did not want to die dared to wait for him. Achilles, who always tried to kill Hector, went alongside him. That was to his bad fortune. Hector injured him twice that day and would have killed him without delay, but Achilles's people very quickly came to his aid. Achilles's heart was very haughty toward Hector, but he feared him greatly. Hector killed many kings, dukes, and barons that day; we will leave out their names, for the sake of brevity. Rather, now I must tell of Hector's great suffering when he died, and of the conditions of his demise. Tears of pity nearly make my heart tremble when I remember and reflect upon the value of such a noble man, so strong and valiant. I think about how deceitful and harsh Fortune is, bringing an end to him by such a misadventure. He feared no one man-to-man. There is no knight in memory whose bravery could compare to Hector's, and who was destroyed this way by Mischance.

XX. *Here is told how Hector was killed*

16461–16490

Hector went running through the battle lines, cutting through the men he encountered, ventail[206] and all. Unfortunately for King Polibetes, he met Hector there. Hector struck him with a blow so tremendous that it was not typical of a man, because he split Polibetes clear through. Polibetes fell, stretched out completely dead. Achilles loved this king very much, and even though he feared Hector, the intense rage growing within him made him bold. He attacked Hector at full speed, striking him with such a very great blow that it would have killed anyone else. Hector suffered because of it, and rose up with such violence that if Achilles had not moved out of the way just then, nothing would have protected him from being split open by Hector. But out of fear, Achilles moved to dodge the blow. It broke his shield in two, and Hector cut deep into Achilles's thigh. Achilles was held up so that he did not fall. He was pulled back from the press. He had his wound bound tightly, so that it would be dry. He would die of grief if he did not avenge himself, so he returned to the battle. Hector kept a keen eye on this return.

16491–16530

The king named Polibetes was armed with the richest weapons that a man had ever worn. Because Hector coveted them (just as Fortune, who was troubled by his advantages, wanted it), he lowered himself over Polibetes's body and started to rob him. At that point, Achilles took a sharp spear and approached Hector. He now saw his moment; he would not have traded it for one hundred thousand gold marks! He advanced his step. When he saw Hector lowered, he threw the spear at Hector with all his might, from the back, where there was a gap in the armor. The spear went completely through Hector's liver and lung. Hector fell dead, ghastly in color. Now the flower of the best who ever lived in the world, either there or elsewhere, was dead! It was great pain to his friends and great joy to his enemies!

    When Achilles struck the blow, Hector's loyal cousin and friend, Memnon, jumped on Achilles like a mad wolf. He so loved Hector and held him so dear that he was ready to die to avenge him. And they fought so much that both of them remained in that spot, worn out. Whatever they might have pretended, neither was far from death. Those who were despondent over Achilles took him away, because they truly believed he would die. He passed out a hundred times en route, which deeply disheartened the Greeks. Memnon's people took him away, in great grief. He was barely breathing.

---

206. The movable lower part of a medieval helmet, fitting over the nose and mouth.

XXI. Here is told of the Trojans' mourning of Hector's death, and of the rich tomb they made for him

16531–16662: *Devastated by Hector's death, the Trojans were in disarray. Hector's family grieved piteously, while "Paris cursed his destiny, and Helen the hour she was born" (16565–67). Christine had never seen such mourning depicted in writings. Hector's friends prepared a massive and richly adorned tomb for him, where his body was brought in a great procession. Above his tomb was inscribed "Here lies Hector the strong, the proud, the flower of all knights, whom Achilles killed without reason, in trickery and in treason" (16641–44). A truce held for a time.*

XXII. Here is told of the battles in the year after Hector's death

16663–16690: *The fighting picked up again. Priam armed himself in spite of his age, keen to avenge his son's death. Troilus and his brother Deiphobus demonstrated their prowess. The battle went on for a year.*

XXIII. Here is told of the funeral rites at the end of the year of Hector's death, and how Achilles was in love with the beautiful Polyxena[207]

16691–16724: *During a truce, the anniversary of Hector's death was magnificently celebrated. Many Greeks attended, including Achilles.*

16725–16769

The lovely Polyxena was there. There was no such maiden in the world. She was fair beyond all creatures, lovely in body and manner, sweet, courtly, and pleasing. Achilles, who saw her coming, chose her before all others. The tears, falling in big drops on her shining face, illuminated it even more. There was no lady in that place of similar beauty, besides Helen. Polyxena was even rosier, fresher, and prettier, because she was in the flower of her youth. Achilles watched her very intently. At that moment, Love, who knows how to capture hearts in surprising ways, whatever it takes, wanted to avenge the death of the valiant Hector, whom Achilles had killed. And I believe he knew how to sell it to him at a high price.

At that point, without delay, Love fired the bow called Sweet Simplicity, whose arrow pricks and injures. He injured Achilles with it, sticking him through the heart and putting him in such a state that he had no power to spend any of his time elsewhere. He would not tire of looking at Polyxena if he were to spend his whole life at it, and that would not seem like enough to him. Looking admiringly at her beauty, he was taken like a fly to a candle. He marveled greatly at

207. As stated in chapter 7 above, Polyxena was Hector's sister, the youngest daughter of Priam and Hecuba.

her appearance, because he had never seen a similar beauty. He amused himself there, looking attentively. He made his enemy into his doctor. Love shot Achilles so much that he surrendered to the woman who hated him. He gave himself over completely and submitted, subjugating himself to her. Now the state of things was quite different, in that the one who had no peer in pride was in the service of his enemy, and found himself so taken by a young little maiden.

16770–16809: *Hopelessly gripped by love, Achilles regretted the pain he had caused Polyxena. After the ceremony, a sad and pensive Achilles was determined to win her heart, at any cost.*

16810–16854

He said that he would never arm himself against Trojans, however things might go. Rather, he wanted to arrange for the battle to end and to last no longer, provided that Polyxena be given to him as his wife. He said by his soul that if he could, he would do whatever it took to undo the entire siege. He sent one of his trusted and very wise messengers to the queen. He transmitted some very amiable and honorable letters to her, recommending himself to her. He said that he loved her daughter so much that if the king would be willing to give her to him as his wife, he promised, by his soul, to bring an end to the war and have the Greeks return to their lands. He would indeed not fail at it. He told her to be assured that he would now be as valuable to Polyxena as he had previously been harmful to her! It troubled Achilles that he had had the heart to afflict her so! But he pleaded for her mercy for everything, promising that never in his life would he desire to arm himself against Trojans. And for God, he would strive so that he would have her daughter, of the fair face, with the consent of the king and through a good accord.

Hecuba, the wise queen, looking at the terrible ruin of her people and her whole city, greatly feared the end. Notwithstanding that she found it very painful for her daughter to marry the one who had saddened her so much that she readily wept, she turned toward the messenger. She told him to return another day. She would surely talk to the king about this affair, but the messenger should go now, and come back later on. "And may God grant that peace come here!"

16855–16882

The messenger headed back. He relayed the response to Achilles, who was pensive. And then Achilles was happy, because he had feared the response. At that point it seemed to him that it would be easy to get the Greeks to consent to leaving the siege, if God wanted to carry out his desire. Even though the queen trembled all over because of it, she did not forget for a minute to tell the king about this matter. But the king said that it would be a great shame for him, and he could never turn his heart toward it, at any cost. But the queen spoke to him and exhorted him so much that he came around to her will, as long as it could be accomplished in such a way that it would be the end of the affair and the war. However badly he might have felt about it, he could indeed consent to this marriage. The queen told the messenger this news when he returned. The messenger went back from there, and made Achilles very happy. Now Achilles firmly believed that joy was his. He never thought he would in fact fail to bring an end to the battle.

16883–16962: *At a gathering of the leaders, including Agamemnon, Achilles declared that since it was foolish to lose this many men over one woman, they should end the war and go home. The others felt that after all the struggle, it would be shameful to abandon the siege. Achilles was at odds with them for over a year because of his promise, and he refused to take up arms. Meanwhile, Troilus wreaked havoc on the Greeks.*

XXIV. *Here is told how Agamemnon, emperor of the Greeks, exhorted Achilles until he agreed to let his people go into battle*

16963–17064: *Agamemnon told Achilles that if he did not wish to fight, he should at least allow his men to do so. Achilles consented. Troilus and his men fought like fierce lions against the Greeks. When Achilles saw the blood of his own men, he forgot his vow and became impervious to Love. He regretted having idled, and wanted to make the Trojans suffer. Achilles and Troilus fought, and Achilles was badly wounded. There was a truce for one month. Priam was enraged that Achilles had broken his vow, and believed it had been a trick all along.*

XXV. *Here is told of the very painful seventeenth battle, in which Troilus was killed*

17065–17129: *The fighting resumed. Achilles, still weak from the injury Troilus had inflicted on him, ordered his men to find and surround Troilus so he could kill Troilus himself. When at one point Troilus became separated from his men, Achilles's men surrounded him, and Troilus defended himself valiantly.*

17130–17176
A battle of one knight against a thousand, far from his people and his city, cannot last long! It was a pity for such a young man to die that way, having defended himself with such vigor that he slaughtered everything in front of him and well avenged his death. Achilles, who saw the youth under attack, took a sword of well sharpened steel. They had taken Troilus's war horse from him, so he was on foot, injured and worn out. Achilles killed him there. Alas! it was a shame and a great loss, and obviously a disgraceful act for Achilles. The cruel one aggravated his shame even more, as the account tells it, because he attached Troilus's body

to a horse's tail, and dragged him back and forth in front of the city. More than ten thousand saw all this and believed they would die of grief. The text says that nothing as pitiful has ever been seen as those people running through the fields vanquished.

They did not try to defend themselves. You would have seen them split through in great numbers, and their cries were well heard. They fled from there completely disarmed. The king, the queen, and his sisters, whose hearts must have been broken by this, surrendered in great torment into the hands of the enemy, whose hearts were scarcely softened by the tears they shed. One history tells it this way, but no other affirms it. Another writes that Troilus was not dragged; rather, as I read it, Hector was the one who was thus dragged, because of the rage that so inflamed Achilles.[208] (Whichever of them Achilles treated that way, he did great wrong in dragging the son of a king, certainly one like him, who surpassed all others. Truthfully, it is fitting for Achilles to be greatly reproached for it!)

17177–17201

I will tell you how the body was saved, because it was by an exchange of many blows, which left many tainted with blood. The noble and valiant Memnon, who never fell short, rushed in against Achilles like a madman. To put it briefly, they fought each other so hard that that Achilles was carried to his tent by his men, as if dead. On the other side, Memnon was not deprived of his share. Troilus's body was carried away by his men, who were despondent over it. No one would be able to write of the weeping, regrets, and plaints that overcame all the men and women. I believe that the grief over Hector was hardly worse, because now their hope was gone, and they all considered themselves ruined; they did not know where to find any more inspiration in this war. Troilus was their entire hope; now it was lost because they no longer had him, and they were very low.

17202–17240: *The queen furiously lamented the deception perpetrated by Achilles's messenger and vowed to avenge the death of the three sons she had lost in the fighting.*

XXVI. *Here is told how the valiant knight Memnon was killed*

17241–17290: *The battles continued. Memnon and Achilles sought to kill each other every day. Achilles ultimately prevailed. The Trojans still believed that they could rout the Greeks, and would have if Fortune were not against them.*

---

208. As depicted in the *Iliad*.

XXVII. *Here is told how Achilles was killed*

17291–17320
At this point the queen, lying in her bed ill and unhappy, did not stop thinking about how she could avenge herself, and betray the traitor whom she hated so mortally. She came up with a good idea. She dictated a letter to her very wise secretary and secretly sent it to Achilles by messenger. She told him that in robbing her of her loved ones, he had poorly upheld the oath he had sworn. Nonetheless, if he would be willing to refrain from that now and wished to become their friend, she would pardon him, even though her son's death grieved her greatly. If he wanted to go to Troy by night, covertly and in secret, she would go to Apollo's temple to speak with him, in spite of her grave affliction. She would bring no one with her, aside from her lovely daughter Polyxena. If he wanted that, he should prepare quickly and go there the next night, without any living soul knowing of it. And they would carry out the wedding. She told him to send his wish by the messenger.

17321–17360
When Achilles saw the letter, all his blood stirred. Love awakened in him once again, with a whispered reminder of the beauty of the maiden for whom he had lost all hope (there was none similar to her in the world!). All at once he seemed completely beside himself, repenting for the great misdeed that he had committed against her and her people. But he felt joy beyond measure at this news. He sent the messenger back to the queen, beseeching her to be willing, for God, to spare him her great hatred. And he said that if she were willing to give her incomparably beautiful daughter to him as his wife, he would serve her forever after. He would never render her anything but grace and service, and she would never find vice in it. He repented for having done her wrong and made himself her captive servant. He would go to Troy the next day, without waiting, because he longed for the moment. He thanked her for her pardon, and asked God to keep him in his grace. He gave the messenger great gifts, and then left from there, staying no longer.

Now you see how all sense abandoned this very foolish simpleton, when he believed that the queen pursued his well-being and did his pleasure, after he had committed such grievous offenses against her, such as killing her children! And he trusted this. He was very stupid, presumptuous, and blind. Foolish is he who thinks he is loved by the one against whom he has committed an offense!

17361–17382: *The queen enlisted Paris to carry out her planned revenge.*

17383–17412
At the instigation of his mother, whom he saw suffering bitterly, Paris sat in ambush at the temple of Apollo. He had ten very well armed knights with him. They

readied themselves at the temple. Achilles, who was anxious for the moment and did not believe he had anything to fear, did not forget what he had promised. When night fell, he and one of his companions set off. The messenger accompanied him as well, and directed them to the temple of Apollo. He said he would tell his mistress to come to him quickly. He then left, telling Achilles to stay there. Paris, who was sitting in ambush near Hector's tomb, lifted his head and said to his companions: "Let us not lack courage, because now, by a cunning ruse, we will kill the deceitful traitor." And they got up and went toward the ones who thought they were all alone. Paris called loudly to Achilles: "Ah! Deceitful traitor! You will be paid for your offense! Your death has been arranged right here! You will pay too much for your broken promise! Foolishness has brought you here! You have acted rashly!"

17413–17442

At that point Achilles was aware that he had been betrayed. The knights violently attacked him from all sides. He dealt them many great blows, defending himself with tremendous strength. He killed three or four of them. If he had been armed, they would not have been able to harm him easily, but he carried nothing aside from his sword. His companion was killed, and in the end, he was as well. Thus was the demise of Achilles, who had done so much harm to the Trojans! Love was the instrument of his death.

The Trojans were very joyous about this death and all came running. Those who did not hold Achilles in great esteem wanted to cut him up completely, but Helenus came to stop them, saying that they could be made to pay dearly for it. When the Greeks learned what had happened, they expressed greater mourning than had ever been seen before. But the grief would have been much worse if Achilles had died differently, because it deeply displeased the Greeks that he had turned toward Troy that way. His men mourned terribly for him. They had the body, but they did not end it there. Some of them took it upon themselves to put him in a very rich tomb.

XXVIII. *Here is told how the Greeks sent to Delphos*[209] *to learn from the god Apollo what they should do*

17443–17488: *The battle-weary Greeks sent messengers to Delphos to seek advice from Apollo. They were told to find the son of Achilles*[210] *and that the only way to take the city was by treachery. Ulysses located Achilles's son, who closely resembled his father in every way, and the Greeks were joyous at his coming. Meanwhile, the eighteenth battle between the Greeks and Trojans raged.*

209. The Oracle at the Temple of Apollo in Delphi; see note 171.

210. Pyrrhus, otherwise called Neoptolemus; he is identified by name in line 17784.

XXIX. *Here is told of the eighteenth battle, in which Paris was killed*

17489–17522

The unfortunate eighteenth battle was painful because there was a high number of dead. But to make my account shorter, I will tell you that Ajax and Paris killed each other; they were not saved. Out of great pride, Ajax, who was not much loved, went into battle with one bare arm. He caused suffering to many a Trojan. Paris noticed him and drew, silently firing an arrow at him, in such a way that it passed through his arm and pierced him near the heart. Ajax, who felt himself mortally struck, immediately attacked Paris. He mocked him in a very evil way, saying: "I believe that love is now finished for you and for Helen. It is unfortunate that she was ever born!" And then he struck Paris with such violence that he knocked him dead to the ground at that moment. The Trojans were distressed. Paris was carried away in great mourning. The Trojans, suffering terribly, went after the Greeks. The deep pain was very bitter for Paris's father, the king, and for his mother! They had lost all their handsome sons there and were demoralized from then on. It was done for; they had no more power! The heirs of Troy were lost! They were so despondent that they wished to kill themselves.

17523–17560

But no one mourned Paris as lady Helen did. She doubled over in pain, crying out. She struck herself, shouted, and wailed. She greatly lamented her lover Paris, whom she loved so completely. She said that she was the cause of his death, and cursed death for not taking her. She made a very pitiful declaration! She would have killed herself on his body, but they took her away from it by force. Surely no creature could be more despondent or carry more painful grief than she.

I will now keep quiet about their sorrows, because it is troubling to talk about it so much. Still, I am not recounting the half of what I found in the accounts. A rich and perfectly beautiful sepulcher was made for Paris. Like a spouse, the king put a gold ring on his finger, then he was placed in the tomb. The king put the crown on Paris's head, to signify that he had no more of the handsome sons who should have held the inheritance. It was a shame! Now there were no more. They were all dead, which caused the Trojans woeful sorrow. The Trojans' pause lasted for several days, even though there was no truce. That is because the king, suffering so intensely, did not want them to go out until fresh help could come and provide security, as his people were very weary. He also did not have enough men. The Greeks cried out and demanded battle, but the Trojans did not heed it.

XXX. *Here is told how the valiant Penthesilea went to the aid of the Trojans*[211]

17561–17592

It happened that right then, very significant aid was coming to the Trojans from the Orient. It was the exceedingly valiant, honorable Penthesilea, queen of Amazonia, with her troops. She was so powerful and brave that no man in all the world was known to have such prowess. Penthesilea knew the art of arms completely. She had ten thousand maidens with her, all of whom she knew to be trained in warrior ways and skilled at carrying arms. There were many noble women, whom she held dear, and a good two thousand archers who were masters at shooting arrows.

Penthesilea of the blonde tresses, in whom there was nothing to criticize, had heard about Hector's prowess, his ways and noble deeds, and how perfect he was, because of his great fame which had spread throughout the world. She wanted to see him more than anything else, and for that reason she prepared herself to come to Troy in aid. The way there was not short. Rather, it was far, at the end of the earth. This woman, who had no peer or equal in valiance, came to Troy. It took her more than twenty days.

17593–17640

The king received this lady, who knew all goodness, with great honor. There was very little joy there, however, because they were deprived of it! The king and queen honored Penthesilea, yet they wept the entire time for the memory of their deceased children, and for the grievous offenses that the Greeks had committed against them. They complained and lamented the Greeks' great misdeeds. Penthesilea comforted them, but did not hold back her tears at the fact that Hector, whom she had wanted to see, was no longer alive. She lamented him greatly, and was deeply grieved by it. She said that she would not be slow in avenging him. She would show the Greeks whether women knew anything about carrying arms!

They led her to the temple, where Hector was lying on a litter. In a humble manner, she genuflected before the oratory. When the tabernacle was opened, the balm filled the temple with its odor. Weeping, the lady then began to utter piteous plaints. As if the body were alive, she said: "Lord! Your enemies have put my heart in great pain because of your death. I so wanted to see you that I undertook a long voyage for it. Your famed prowess put me on this route. But since Fortune wants it this way, I swear by the sun and moon that I will avenge you well, if God protects these arms of mine!" This queen pronounced such laments, highly praising Hector, saying that his exalted valiance showed clearly in his appearance. She esteemed and praised him greatly. She could not pull herself away from the place.

211. On Penthesilea in this work, see Brownlee, "Hector and Penthesilea."

In the end, she kissed his hand, with which he held his sword night and morning, and left from there with tears in her eyes. Strongly menacing the Greeks, she returned to the palace, surrounded by kings and dukes.

XXXI. *Here is told how Penthesilea fought against the Greeks*

17641–17770: *Penthesilea and her beautiful, fearsome, richly arrayed troops readied for battle. They fought so fiercely that they chased the Greeks all the way back to the sea and burned their ships. But Diomedes arrived with a great assembly, and the battle redoubled. He and Penthesilea dealt each other lance-shattering blows, and Diomedes had to be rescued from her by his people. Penthesilea also knocked Ajax to the ground, stunning and nearly killing him. The beaten-down Greeks fled, marveling at the women's prowess. Penthesilea was received triumphantly in Troy. The Greeks were granted a truce for one month.*

XXXII. *Here is told of the help that came to the Greeks*

17771–17788: *The battles resumed. This time the Greeks were bolstered by Ulysses and Achilles's son Neoptolemus, known as Pyrrhus, along with twenty thousand men.*

XXXIII. *Here is told of the valiant Penthesilea's brave acts and how she was killed*

17789–17828
When the truces were over, the armies moved on both sides. Agamemnon joyfully made the young men new knights. He exhorted each to carry himself well in the fray, and to avenge the death of their fathers, friends, and brothers. They emerged from the city. Trumpets and horns sounded. The courageous Penthesilea was there, and quickly engaged in the battle. She handled herself so well in the charge that she knocked down a knight and horse—he did not get up again—and it seemed as if nothing bothered her. Her valiant and wise maidens performed such great acts of courage that they were nothing but marvels. They well increased their renown there. The newly armed young men also conducted themselves nobly, demonstrating that they would be brave, not cowardly.

Several times, when the queen held the field, the Greeks were defeated. When she was not there, the Greeks drove the Trojans back. And thus their fighting went on for several days continuously, which resulted in so many dead that the tally was unknown. Pyrrhus conducted himself marvelously there. And just as the father had battled, the son brought down whatever he encountered before him. Whether it was virtue or vice, he fought with cleverness. The Myrmidons were joyous at his presence and helped him greatly.

17829–17856

Fierce hatred arose between Pyrrhus and Queen Penthesilea, because they fought each other in the fray several times. The queen battered him severely, beating him down. She hated him because of his father and was intent on avenging Hector against him. She would have shaken him very gravely if he had not been rescued from her. She injured him very badly, and would have killed him, but his people took him away from her. They carried him away as if dead, for which they were very despondent. I do not know what else to tell you about it! The mighty Penthesilea made the Greeks fear her so much that they all said she would surely subjugate them from every angle, if a solution were not found. They all vowed her death (it would be difficult if this were to last long!). The battle went on for several days, making the laments grow on both sides. But even though force may delay it, Fortune ensures destruction. For the Trojans, the delay was worth nothing, because anything Fortune hates labors in vain!

17857–17896

One day the battle was perilous. The queen performed marvelous deeds there. But this day was the end of Penthesilea and the end of the battles, because she was overwhelmed by the ones who hated her. Ultimately, Pyrrhus's people pursued her so much that they drew her in between them, and she was surrounded. Surrounding her would not have done them much good, but Ajax had come there. She handled herself so mightily against Pyrrhus and Ajax that she made them bleed in great streams. But Ajax and Pyrrhus, who had such power and force, attacked her and forcibly caused her to fall from her war-horse. It was a distressing thing to see! Two knights against a lady. They struck her so much that they made her soul leave her body! Ha! Good God! How pitiable a thing it was, because never had a maiden of such prowess been born! She had such a high and noble heart that as long as she lived, she did not want to know any man, on any account. Her people's pain was indescribable. They all endured great suffering to avenge her, and got themselves cut to pieces. In the end, all the Trojans took off in flight, and were chased and shouted at. Those who escaped rushed to get into their city. They would never arm themselves again, but they would still have many troubles! They barred the gates, and closed and locked them tight. Throughout the city, they were in great mourning because of their extraordinary misfortune.

XXXIV. *Here is told how Troy was taken and destroyed*

17897–17980: *The Greeks praised the gods for the victory, but they were still not sure how they would take the city. Fortune would make it so. Meanwhile, Antenor, Aeneas, Anchises, and Polydamas*[212] *reproached Priam for the bad state of affairs,*

---

212. Leaders among the Trojans.

and said that they should end the siege by handing Helen over and paying tribute to the Greeks. Although Priam sensed treachery afoot, in hopes of peace he allowed them to pursue their plan. The men climbed up on the walls of the city and offered an olive branch to the Greeks. Antenor then offered to hand the city over to the Greeks in exchange for being crowned a king himself.

17981–18024

In short, the traitors arranged things in such a way that they established a fake peace agreement. The Greek barons came to Troy. The king granted them everything they wanted. They pretended to be good friends to the Trojans. But they said that they had promised a gift to the warlike Minerva, and they wanted to assure the goddess that the gift was coming. So they had a marvelous wooden horse built. They said it should be brought to her temple, as a sign that their great victory would be remembered forevermore.

But now listen to the marvelous signs foretelling of a perilous day soon to come for the Trojans, which alarmed and deeply troubled them. They were alarmed for good reason! At the temple, they saw great offerings, vows, and devotions made. They made sacrifices and oblations of bulls and heifers, but the priests performing the services were never able to make a fire on the altar, and could not light it. So they used oil and resin, along with tinder and fibers, to start the fire. But this ominous sign appeared to them: they were never able to light the fire. This rendered them utterly hopeless. The people ran to the temple in great throngs, very frightened. It was soon completely full. At that point, in full view, a great eagle came flying, and as he passed, he took the entrails of the beasts that they were going to use as a sacrifice. That could signify great misfortune for them. The eagle who had taken the entrails devoured every last bit of them amid the Greek army.

18025–18074

They went to the wise Cassandra to ask her for the true meaning of the sign. She gave them an ambiguous response, because she feared angering the gods too much if she were to say more. The worthless traitors spoke with the highest priest of their faith and corrupted him with gifts, to the point that he gave the statue of Pallas over to them. Through all adversity, that statue had protected the strong castle Ilion and the city from being taken by any means. As long as the statue was in Troy, they could not meet their end, as it was destined. (Those devils, fired up by great treason, knew this well!) The traitors well and truly hid the statue and then took it to the army, which brought the Greeks great joy. Then nobles and bourgeois alike were taken and killed, and Troy, where there was once so much honor and joy, was burned!

The wooden horse was completed, but they had made it so big and tall that it was necessary to break a section of the gate for the false offering. The king did not want to bring it in, but the insolent traitors said that no ill could come of it and that he should not be upset. Very reluctantly he consented. Thus the apparatus, in which more than fifty well armed knights were enclosed, entered into Troy. Deceitfully, they led it to the temple in a great procession. Then the Greeks pretended to leave. Upon their departure, they put fire to their lodgings, and then they got into their barges and hoisted the sails of their ships. They appeared to head toward Greece. The Trojans, who from that point believed they were safe, climbed up on the walls. They greatly celebrated the Greeks' departure, but Troy would soon be afflicted!

18075–18130

The Trojans went to bed and slept like people who feared no more. When midnight had passed, the Greeks, who had other ideas, turned back to the port. They exited the ships and all went away from the port. Antenor, knowing the hour, had the bridge lowered. The Greeks entered through the gap, without encountering a soul. The knights inside the horse got down and opened the broken gate, and the entire band entered. They went to the castle and knocked down the doors in little time. The citizens yelled and shouted: "Betrayed! Betrayed!" The Greeks attacked the palace, killing one after another. The king, hearing the carnage, saw that he had been bitterly betrayed. He became blacker than ink. He ran from there to the temple of Apollo. What can I tell you, brief and short? He was killed there, along with all his people, and their property was stolen and pillaged.

There was terrible killing. The cries were horrible. The noble ladies were taken away, the others condemned to death. The Greeks struck fire throughout the city. Blood ran in great streams. Why would I go on telling you about it? The Greeks were there for an entire month and even more, until they had stripped the city of everything and left. Pyrrhus took the noble and cultivated maiden, Polyxena, who was found at the home of Aeneas, who thought he had saved her. To avenge his father, and so that it would be visible there forevermore, Pyrrhus beheaded her on the tomb.[213] Her mother was so distressed by it that she went mad. She crushed the eyes of more than twenty Greeks by throwing rocks at them. And the noble, wise, and good Hecuba, a queen among all women, made herself cry out like a madwoman. Some say that she so wanted death that she willingly pretended to be insane, so she would be killed and not taken away. And she who had been so honored was stoned to death.

---

213. The tomb of Achilles.

XXXV. *Here is told how the traitors were hunted, and of the Greeks' ills upon their return to Greece*

18131–18182

Now I have briefly told you the story of which I took great heed as I looked at the wall of Fortune, she of evil ways. It is certainly good to note it, considering that Fortune can quickly take away the good things that she gives to any mortal person. Whoever relies on her too much is very foolish, because she quickly strikes without provocation. The oath-breaking traitors who put the plan together believed they would reign in Troy and run their domains there because, as you find in history, their castles were not destroyed. Their part of Troy was protected from the suffering because, as it is told, the wicked traitors had a big section of the city under them. But their own people pursued them in shame. As history tells it, if the traitors had not left quickly, the people would have put them in a very bad state (and they had well earned it). The traitors, who were rightly hated, left their land in great haste.

They left from there by sea, along with great treasure and many people of their choosing. They had many great fortunes after that, as you find in history. We read that large numbers of the royal Trojans escaped, and dispersed with many people to a number of places around the world. Long ago, the French came from the sons of Priam, as I understand it. Helenus, who did not like war and anything that went along with it, went to Greece along with many people, well supplied with gold and silver. He then founded numerous cities there and lived in tranquility. As I understand from texts, the great Alexander came from him, after a long time, as the lineage went on. And they multiplied like vines in many foreign regions, about which one reads glowing accounts.

18183–18244

But listen to how Fortune took revenge against the Greeks. She did it this way: at the time they left the port, in joy and pleasure, they had hardly progressed when a great wind arose from the east. It came up in such a way and blew so violently that it sent them hither and yon. It took them to many different countries for several winters and summers, without slowing and without their being able to pull into harbor. They threw the plunder into the sea because they were too loaded down. Many of their ships sank, and others encountered people who robbed and killed them. And thus it was not possible for the Greeks, who had destroyed the Trojans, to return to Greece. The renowned barons, who later arrived there in poverty, were very badly received. Even the emperor Agamemnon's wife, by mistake or fully willingly, had him killed when he came to his empire. Diomedes was refused by his wife and driven away, and never, by force of war, could he do enough to regain his land. So he went to conquer elsewhere; it was necessary to leave that one be.

Others had to win their land by force from their kin who, while they were voyaging at sea, had taken legal possession of it. And they killed each other, and thus few were left of those who had held the siege. Ulysses traveled by sea for a long time, under various winds, so that he could return to Greece. But Fortune made him turn toward Italy, where Rome was located, after which he had many troubles. Circe the enchantress arrived at the port and put many knights-errant into great distress. Whoever stopped there was shamed! Ulysses stayed there for two years. Circe had a child by him who, in a bizarre circumstance, later killed his father (it was a harsh thing!).[214] Ulysses went back toward Greece, and his wife did not turn her back to him at all. Rather, the noble and calm Penelope received him in great joy. Never was there a finer or more honorable woman. And thus was the end of the Greeks. The Trojans hardly had better!

Explicit the story of Troy and the sixth part of The Book of the Mutability of Fortune.

Here begins the seventh part of The Book of the Mutability of Fortune, *which tells the abridged history of the Romans and of Alexander, etc.*

I. *The first chapter, that tells of Aeneas*

18245–18296

Aeneas left the ravaged Troy and set off by sea along with 3,300 men and a great load of treasure. Before they had been journeying for long, it became evident that their torment was not over. Fortune struck them, shaking them so brutally with storms that they had little hope for their lives. They often lost many of their possessions, ships, and people. Sailing for a very long time at sea, roaming here, then there, they went so far that they arrived at the port of Africa, where Dido was the queen of the land.[215] Aeneas had lost his way and landed there. Dido of Carthage knew it. She conceived great joy in her heart, because she had heard many good things about the Trojans. She went toward the fleet. She was very beautiful and

214. This refers to Telegonus. Circumstances would bring the adult Telegonus to his father's homeland, where he would kill Ulysses in a fight, each unaware of the other's identity until it was too late. On Circe and Ulysses, see Book 1, chapter 11.

215. This is probably El Mahdia (Solente, *Mutacion*, 4:114, entry for "Auffrique, port d'"), on the coast of Tunisia. On Dido in Christine's works, see Marilynn Desmond, "Christine de Pizan's Feminist Self-Fashioning and the Invention of Dido," in *Reading Dido: Gender, Textuality, and the Medieval* Aeneid (Minneapolis: University of Minnesota Press, 1994), 195–224.

well accompanied, because she esteemed that lineage greatly. She met Aeneas on the path, and received him very joyfully. Now he would be out of adversity.

She took him to Carthage, her great city, where she did many good things for him, honoring him and his people. They needed that very badly, because they could never conceive of a solution to their situation, having been driven so by storms, and their ships destroyed. And they were nearly dead from hunger, for lack of bread and provisions. Now the sufferers were at ease after the distress. But harm can come from the guest to whom one gladly gives lodging. This lady gave everything she had to Aeneas, putting heart and body in his hands, because he swore to her that he would marry her and never have another in his life. But he lied to her, and left without taking his leave. Dido was in such a state over it that she pitifully killed herself out of grief. And thus perished the radiant Dido, who had been so honorable and wise that no other woman surpassed her! But Love deceives the wise and the foolish alike!

18297–18327
Aeneas, who rejected her, later excused himself for having left her that way, saying that the gods had admonished him to go to Italy and marry a woman there. The Sibyl, who had guided him through burning hell and shown him the soul of Anchises,[216] had prophesied it. She told him that he would engender lineages that would extend throughout the world. And he sailed so far by sea that he reached the shore of Italy. He sent gifts to King Latinus, who was then lord of the place. The king sent back gifts of his own and gave Aeneas permission to disembark on his land. That gave Aeneas great joy and pleasure. With Latinus's permission, Aeneas built a strong castle there, where he took lodging. Then the king gave Aeneas his beautiful, wise, and renowned daughter in marriage. Her name was Lavinia. But once the king had affianced her, Turnus, to whom the king had already promised her, assembled thousands of people from his land and others (I do not know how many), and went to war against Latinus.

18328–18388: Aeneas killed Turnus and married Lavinia. Within three years, he died, leaving Lavinia pregnant with Silvius, who would reign next. Eight more kings came from the lineage, leading to Procas, with whom the history of Rome would begin.

II. Here is told of Romulus, who founded Rome

18389–18446
As I saw it in the room, King Procas of Italy had two sons: Numitor was the name of the elder, Amulius the younger. Amulius, who possessed great vice, maliciously

---

216. Father of Aeneas; Aeneas is guided through the underworld to meet with his soul.

chased his brother away because he knew that Numitor was to reign after their father. Numitor had a daughter. Not satisfied at having exiled her father, Amulius had the daughter taken and made a nun. He did that so no heir by her would have a claim to the kingdom. But it happened otherwise. Not even twenty years had passed when the educated girl had two children from one pregnancy. The foolish people believed that they were fathered by Mars, the god of war, whom they greatly feared.

The children, one named Romulus, the other Remus, were very handsome. The man who had forced Numitor to flee also had the girl buried alive because of this. He ordered his messengers to throw the handsome children, fresh as a rose, into the river, but the messengers did not obey the command. Instead, they put the children side by side and left them on the bank of the Tiber, without harming them. And as one finds in many accounts, these children were nursed by a she-wolf who fed them and saved them from the peril of death. But to tell the truth accurately, a shepherd named Faustus, who lived in the area, took them away from there and his wife nursed them.[217]

As they grew up, they believed they were the shepherd's children. But they were marvelously handsome and noble. Notwithstanding that they led ewes to pasture, under the leaves, they possessed a regal nature and were very proud. The other shepherds held them in esteem, even though the two boys were hard on them, contentious and superior. Those two indeed established the structure and practice of authority. Romulus especially wanted to be master over his brother and all of them, by force if necessary.

18447–18472

The king heard an account of how those children lorded over shepherds in the manner of princes. The king and others marveled at that. The king and then called for Faustus, and asked Faustus for the truth. The king saw the boys and wanted to keep them, but the shepherd quickly took them away from the king and brought them back home with him. When they were grown, they armed themselves and gathered all the most hated thieves and robbers in the land, with Romulus, who led them, as their captain. Thus his dominance began at that time, and it later grew tremendously. He made himself greatly loved by his people, because he gave away so much that he did not keep the gold, silver, or other spoils he acquired. It would be difficult to hate such a captain! Romulus already had many men, because soldiers from all over came to him for the good shares that he gave. And he was considered better than anyone as a keeper of justice.

217. Cf. the story of Cyrus, a king's son raised by a shepherd, in Book 5, chapter 4.

18473–18506

At that time, they did not yet have a fortress or a tower. Rather, for as long as he stayed there, the surrounding forests were their refuge and residence. He armed himself from the age of fifteen. He had already been informed of how his uncle had chased his grandfather away and pursued his death, and had killed their mother. That troubled him deeply. He said that in no way would he let it be. He did not delay an hour, or a half, before he saw his moment and attacked his uncle, who was greatly hated. Romulus took the city of Alba Longa from him,[218] because Romulus had many good people with him. Romulus harassed his uncle so much with fighting that he killed him and conquered the land. Thus Romulus, who was more proud than a bull, put his grandfather Numitor on the throne.

He then set out on the Tiber, where he founded a very fine looking city. When he saw the first tower finished, he said that the seat of his reign would be there. He had the city built well, so he could be proud of it. He named the city, which would be so renowned later, "Rome" after his own name. Although it was well built as far as the houses were concerned, the surrounding wall was, truth be told, not very high. That would cost him dearly later, without a doubt!

III. *Here is told how Remus and Romulus were in conflict about which one of them would possess Rome*

18507–18548

The brothers were in a bit of contention over the city. In the end, they agreed that whoever saw the most birds fly in the morning would have it to himself. The next morning, they set out. In no time, Remus was the first to see six kites fly quickly, and he showed them to his brother. Romulus looked again and saw twelve more of them. At that point Remus said nothing more about fighting over the city. They immediately returned from there, with Romulus holding the authority over Rome.

One day, Remus made fun of the walls of the city, saying that it was a wretched and poor fortress, where one could surely jump the walls. That was told to Romulus, and he vowed by his character, his faith, and his oath that if anyone at all were to jump the walls, he would surely have him killed. Whosoever it may be, he would be destroyed. Romulus had this edict announced everywhere. Once, to take a risk or out of foolishness, Remus jumped the walls; he did not fail at it in the least. He did not think it would be a grave offense, or he did not remember the prohibition. But Romulus did not forget his oath, and he quickly had his brother Remus killed. No one could save him. Romulus was very greatly feared for having made such a harsh judgment. And he had the walls made much higher. Romulus began to advance greatly in force and power, fearing no harm.

---

218. Ancient city of Latium, central Italy.

18549–18587: *Wishing to build the population to sustain his army, Romulus announced a great tournament in Rome to attract women spectators. The Sabines attended.*[219] *At the end of the games, Romulus sounded a signal.*

18588–18608

At that point, the knights, mounted on war-horses, took the ladies. The ladies were very frightened and wretched because they were being taken away by force. The Sabines were deeply disheartened, but power was not on their side at all. Romulus chose a beautiful lover, the daughter of the king, whom he greatly valued. Each one took off with his prize, and they left, quickly fleeing to Rome. The Sabines who fled were not worth an apple. They returned from there sorrowful and ashamed. They would make up for it when they could, and summon their allies. The ladies were very despondent. The knights comforted them, saying that above all else, the ladies would be mistresses over themselves and their possessions. The women were comforted by that. As they could do nothing else about it, they supported each other.

IV. *The war of the Sabines and Romans and how the ladies made peace*

18609–18637

The Sabines assembled a vast army and attacked the Romans as soon as they could. The Romans quickly came forth and violently attacked them. They thus engaged in battle several times, on specified days. Many men were killed there, and even greater ill came of it. But a solution presented itself thanks to the ladies' great prudence. One day, the queen gathered the ladies in conference. She exhorted them that there would be peace, if she was able, provided that they were willing to believe her. The well-spoken woman said to them that since the situation had gone that way, there was no solution for it. It was reasonable for them to love their friends and relatives, who were very saddened, and also not to hate their husbands. It must have been a great outrage and pity for them to see them kill each other. That is why the queen wanted very much to remedy it, and she said all the women should do as she did. Then they all willingly agreed.

18638–18666

They delayed no longer. One day when the great armies were already on the battlefield and about to engage in fighting, the queen came forth with all the women; there were many beautiful ladies among them. Some were pregnant, and many had already given birth, and they carried their children in their arms. With downcast faces, disheveled, they came onto the field. Then, weeping in their torment, they went in between the armies and knelt, crying for the men to make peace for

219. An ancient people of central Italy.

God's sake, and saying that now was the time to stop savagely killing each other. Moved by great pity and affection, the princes made peace. Thus the Sabines and Romans were at peace and took each other by the hands. In great celebration, they entered Rome without trouble. Romulus greatly honored the king for as long as he stayed there. A large part of the city was granted for the residence of more than a thousand of them, so that Rome would have more people. But as I understand it, and as I found in the writings, the cohabitation later proved to be a bad thing.

18667–18702

I have now told you briefly about the establishment of Rome, which went on to be such an important city that it held the whole world in its power. Rome's great authority lasted a long time, without being brought down, because Fortune, of whom I speak, was sweet and gentle toward it for many years. She later changed for the worse and turned good into bad for Rome, to the extent that it lost almost all its glory. Nothing of it remains but the record, through the texts recalling the Romans' great and noteworthy deeds. Such are Fortune's perpetual turns—she does plenty of this!

Regarding my topic, I would indeed like to write more than the history, but I do not intend to describe all of the Romans' ceremonies and deeds, because my topic would never be exhausted. Nor do I intend to describe the terms of their high speech, which things signified harm for them,[220] what they called signs, auspices, omens, and auguries, as one finds in their works, or their games, finery, theaters, gods, or idolatrous temples. Nor will I tell of all the specific feats that their knights accomplished. It suffices for me to recite their principal deeds. It is good to read about their army, to find a good example in it and to learn a great deal. Therefore I will speak beyond the history as it comes to my mind.

V. *Here is told how Romulus organized the senators of Rome*

18703–18728

Romulus installed one hundred senators in Rome. He gave them oversight, as a council, of the city, all civil cases, and all other jurisdiction. He established many fine, noble, and highly valuable ordinances, because he was very wise and learned. Soon after, as one finds in texts, he was carried off from beside a river. No one knew what became of him. The foolish and miscreant people held that he had been taken away to the sky. Thus ended the time of Romulus, who had founded Rome and who lived to the age of thirty-six. According to what is written, he was seventeen when he decided to establish Rome. Three years later he took the

---

220. Solente indicates here that what would have been line 18689 of the poem is missing from all of the manuscripts (*Mutacion*, 3:186).

204 CHRISTINE DE PIZAN

courtly Sabines, with whom they made their lineage. There is no record of Romulus having left an heir of his own. The senators held Rome for fifty years.

18729–18850: *The wise Numa Pompilius then reigned in peace for forty-five years. He built Rome up, establishing the first temples for worship, and added two months to what had been a ten-month calendar. He was followed by the violent Tullus Hostilius, who started a war against Alba Longa. He enclosed the Roman hills within the walls of the city. After thirty-two years, he was killed by lightning. Next came Ancus Marcius who incorporated the Aventine Hill into the city. Tarquin the Elder succeeded him. He installed one hundred senators, fortified the Capitol, expanded Rome, and defeated the Sabines in war. He was murdered by the sons of Ancus Marcius. Next reigned Servius Tullius, who further expanded Rome and imposed a system of taxes and farm rent. The wicked Tarquin the Proud killed him and went on to govern for thirty-four years.[221] His immoral son Tarquin (Sextus Tarquinius) took the married Lucretia by force, for which she killed herself.[222]*

18851–18864

Thus these seven kings reigned in Rome, governing for 244 years. Sometimes they met with good, sometimes with bad. But then the wise and learned senators decided to do things differently. They said they would no longer elect kings, but would govern by themselves instead. Each year, they would elect consuls to govern the city. To prevent them from growing prideful, each year new ones would be elected at the will of all. No longer would kings do whatever they wished there.

VI. *How Rome began to govern itself by consul*

18865–18918: *The wise and noble Brutus, father of Lucretia,[223] was the first elected consul. Brittany was named for him. The praetor and the Capitol guard were also established at this time. Thus began 712 years of Rome being ruled without a king. Tarquin attacked Rome, and he and Brutus killed each other upon their first blow, "as Fortune wanted it" (18910). Rome prevailed, but Brutus was greatly mourned.*

---

221. These are the second through seventh (and last) kings of Rome: Numa Pompilius (reigned 715–673 BCE); Tullus Hostilius (673–642 BCE); Ancus Marcius (642–617 BCE); Tarquin the Elder (616–579 BCE); Servius Tullius (578–535 BCE); Tarquin the Proud (534–510 BCE).

222. The rape of Lucretia, a Roman noblewoman, is considered a spark for the Roman revolution which marked the shift from leadership by kings to leadership by consul.

223. Solente points out that Lucius Junius Brutus, consul of Rome in 509 BCE, was a relative of Lucretia, but not her father (*Mutacion*, 4:118).

VII. *Here is told how the Romans made war with Duke Brennus,*[224] *who laid them low for a time*

18919–19000: *Duke Brennus, of the nearby settlement of Sena Gallia,*[225] *attacked Rome, killing many Romans and laying waste to the city. When he left with a large ransom, the remaining beaten-down Romans wanted to abandon the city.*

VIII. *Here is told how the Romans, who wanted to depart and leave Rome behind, were held there and comforted*

19001–19070: *The noble consul Camillus,*[226] *previously exiled from Rome for little cause, took it upon himself to attack and kill Brennus. Having recovered the ransom that Brennus had taken, Camillus returned to Rome in triumph and rebuilt the city, earning the name "the second Romulus" (19042). Christine chooses not to describe a number of famines, wars, and other misfortunes that befell the Romans after Camillus's death, citing her interest in brevity.*

IX. *Here is told of the beginning of the war between Taranto and the Romans*

19071–19132: *Intent on conquering many lands, the Romans took to the sea. Passing by Taranto, they were attacked on the waters and grievously harmed by the Tarantines. The surviving Romans returned home, amassed a great army even though their forces were already dispersed far and wide, and attacked Taranto.*

X. *Here is told how King Pyrrhus came to the aid of the Tarantines against the Romans*

19133–19338: *Pyrrhus, king of Macedonia,*[227] *came with a great army to the aid of Taranto. The elephants he brought with him terrified the Romans, causing them to flee. Some of the remaining Romans were killed by lightning. After destroying Campania,*[228] *Pyrrhus proposed peace on the condition that he keep the land he had conquered, but the Romans refused. Having figured out how to rout the elephants with fire and other tricks, the Romans defeated Pyrrhus's men in the next round of battles. Pyrrhus was injured. The Roman consul Fabricius*[229] *told Pyrrhus that Pyr-*

224. Gallic military leader who defeated the Romans in the battle of Allia, 390 or 387 BCE.

225. The word in the original is "Sienne," which Solente identifies as Sienna, Tuscany. It should be "Sena Gallia" (now Senigallia), on Italy's Adriatic coast.

226. Marcus Furius Camillus (ca. 446–365 BCE).

227. Reigned as king of Epirus (306–302, 297–272 BCE) and of Macedonia (288–284, 273–272 BCE).

228. A region of southern Italy.

229. Gaius Fabricius Luscinus, consul in 282 and 278 BCE.

rhus's own doctor had offered to poison Pyrrhus. An appreciative Pyrrhus ended his fighting with Rome. He went on to Sicily, from where he was chased to Taranto after being attacked. Pyrrhus carried on his warring ways, but Fortune turned against him. He ultimately perished near Argos.

XI. Here is told of the beginning of the wars between the Romans and Carthage[230]

19339–19404: *After ominous signs occurred in Rome—three wolves dragging a cadaver into the city, great lightning bolts crumbling the walls of a city nearby—the Romans and Carthaginians waged a massive battle. The Romans prevailed, but at great cost. The Carthaginians promised never to attack the Romans again if the Romans would just return their prisoners. The promise would not last.*

XII. Here is told of the signs that appeared in Rome

19405–19458

Fully four-hundred and eighty years after the founding of Rome—its power sometimes high, sometimes low—frightening signs appeared, terrifying the Romans greatly. Blood gushed out through underground galleries. Several springs flowing with blood completely reddened the mire. And pure white milk rained from the sky in big drops, completely covering the rocks and green leaves of the trees with white. At this time, the Carthaginians broke their vow and scorned the Romans by giving substantial support to the king of Syracuse[231] against the people of Messina. The Messinians had not abandoned the Romans; thus Messina was an ally of Rome. The Romans were hostile because of that affront.

The great war started again. It was deadly at sea and on land, and it lasted for a very long time. I do not intend to tell all of it, but will pass on it in the name of brevity. Many lands were destroyed, burned, and ruined, and people were killed and displaced by the lion-like battles and violent combat between the two sides. Sometimes it was the Romans in Carthage, sometimes the Carthaginians on the riverside against Rome, the fighting so great that the land overflowed with it. It was evident how Fortune is able to betray the ones she truly wants to attack, because first they win, and then they lose again, by surprising degrees, indeed whether they are doing well or badly. So as not to put so much time into it, I will pass on naming the princes who were the chiefs and principal leaders of the battles. But it is very reasonable that I speak of the main one from Carthage, well proven in arms, supreme and wise. Fortune was a friend to him for a time, but ultimately his great enemy, in all his undertakings. (And she well knew how to do that!)

230. The three Punic Wars, 264–146 BCE.

231. In the original (line 19422), the word here is "Sarragoce," which Solente identifies as Zaragoza, Spain (*Mutacion*, 3:211 and 4:171, respectively). It should be Syracuse (Siracusa), in Sicily.

XIII. *Here is told of Hannibal, prince of Africa and Carthage*

19459–19503

After the wars and troubles had already been going on for a long time, the valiant and noble warrior Hannibal was made king of Carthage, as he should have been by heritage. He was the prince and emperor of Africa, where there were very violent people. Hannibal was such a powerful warrior that he directed his armies and great wars in many countries and lands. The histories say that he had many notable victories against the Romans, who had already conquered a large part of Spain with their troops. Ultimately, by their great efforts, they conquered all of it in a very short time, a year. But they suffered many tribulations there.

Hannibal battled with the Romans in Spain. He defeated and routed them several times, winning many victories. The Romans also had several notable victories over him. They fought a number of times in hand-to-hand combat. Sometimes it went in their favor, other times against, as it happens in such events. (Those who carry the burden know this!) The very powerful King Hannibal greatly tormented the Romans. Still, he wanted to meet them in their land, to harm them even more. So he crossed the sea with a fleet. Never before had a king, in his life, ever led more people in an army than he wanted to lead against Rome, because indeed the Romans were very mighty. As I understand it, they had acquired more than six distant countries by the time he arrived. By his great force and power, and with an abundance of people, he crossed the Alps of Italy.

19504–19552

He did not cross them quickly, however. They first had to break and smash the hard rocks with very strong chisels of steel and picks as sharp as spikes, because no man had ever passed through there. Hannibal was so focused that there was nothing in feats of war that he did not know and wish to pursue. The great host passed through there. They could not be quick, because there were so many beasts, horses, and wagons that the mountains and valleys everywhere were completely full of them. There were elephants completely loaded up, and an abundance of savage beasts. The cold winter season and the snow in the mountains killed great numbers of them, as well as many a bold knight. Hannibal lost an eye there.

Thus he crossed the Alps. But he had barely advanced when the Romans, who were underway with an intimidating army, were in front of him. But the Romans were routed, without a doubt, because Hannibal had too great a band. The second time, to avenge that misfortune, the Romans quickly sent a very big army. It was quickly defeated, and the Romans lost many good people. For a third time, they again levied an army, which was defeated nonetheless. All there were ill-treated, for which Hannibal was very proud of himself, because his power greatly grew and wore down that of the Romans. Large parts of Italy surrendered to him out of fear, rebelling against the Romans and siding with Hannibal. Many strange signs appeared in Rome, causing great lament. The Romans were afraid and believed in the bad signs, because their deeds met with such misfortune and things were going so badly.

XIV. Here is told of the battle of Cannae[232]

19553–19566: *Rome had endured for 540 years. The Romans prepared for another battle against Hannibal.*

19567–19602

The armies were in Apulia, in front of Cannae, fiercely engaged in battle. Whatever I may say about it could drag it out! Ill fortune and defeat went against the Romans, for whom it was more important to die right there than for anyone to leave. Hannibal lost great numbers of his people, but he gave it back to the Romans well. They all died there except a few who were taken prisoner. And we read that with such a vast throng of Romans, the rings from their hands amounted to such sums that Hannibal sent three full bushels of them to Carthage in souvenir, along with an abundance of other treasure. He was very pleased by that.

The Romans were so low, they would not have been able to defend the city if Hannibal had wanted to enter it at that point. But first he wanted to burn his friends' bodies to ashes and take care of the great spoils. He said he would attack Rome after all that, as he did not believe in the least that he would fail against his enemy, whenever he wanted to get to it. But he was not yet practiced in the tricks meted out by Fortune, who, in a short span of time, sometimes works and then abruptly turns. Thus it is sensible to pursue one's undertaking for as long as she stays favorable.

19603–19624

The Romans were at their lowest point. At that time, they had no hope of ever bringing themselves up again. Because of all this they considered themselves done for, which made them want to leave the city, although it grieved them greatly. They were indeed at the point of leaving, but a very valiant, wise consul of Rome, of very high lineage, did not want to consent to it. He was Cornelius Scipio,[233] an official much loved by the knights. He strongly admonished them to stay, saying that the battle would go against them if anyone were to leave. He said that Fortune changes often, giving him hope for their return to glory. It was more important to die with honor than to flee and run in shame.

---

232. Key battle between the Romans and Carthaginians which took place in southeastern Italy on August 2, 216 BCE.

233. Publius Cornelius Scipio, Roman statesman and general, consul in 218 BCE.

19625–19710: *With Rome so depleted, Scipio resorted to the novel approach of cobbling together an army of serfs, prisoners, and debtors, and turning them into a military force. They surprise-attacked Hannibal and emerged victorious. That victory was followed by three more, against Macedonia, against Hasdrubal[234] in Spain, and in Sardinia. Thanks to Fortune, Rome was again a dominant force.*

XV. Here is told of how a great storm came when the armies of Rome and Carthage intended to engage each other

19711–19774: *After ten years in Italy, Hannibal again sought to attack Rome. As the armies were about to face each other, a great storm halted the battle. Hannibal, believing that the gods were protecting Rome, abandoned Italy. Rome continued to prosper.*

XVI. Here is told of how Scipio went to Spain, which he partially conquered

19775–19850: *Scipio,[235] son of Cornelius Scipio who had defeated Hannibal, headed to Spain to avenge his father's death, which had occurred there. With Hasdrubal engaged in battles elsewhere, Scipio easily took Cartagena, where Hasdrubal's treasure was held. He freed the prisoners held there as well. He sent treasure and prisoners to Rome, and in an act of bravado, returned hostages, who had been held by Hannibal, to Spain. Hasdrubal returned, but Scipio kept his victory.*

XVII. Here is told of how the Romans took Taranto

19851–19886: *During this time, the Romans conquered Taranto, where Hannibal's treasure was held, and brought the treasure back to Rome. A part of Italy that had broken from Rome came back. Meanwhile, Scipio subjugated eighty Spanish towns in three years.*

XVIII. Here is told of how Hasdrubal, who had come to the aid of Hannibal, was killed in Italy by the Romans

19887–19942: *Hannibal, again fighting the Romans in Italy, summoned his brother Hasdrubal for aid. Hasdrubal arrived with a great army, but the Romans were waiting for him at the foot of the Alps. The Romans slaughtered many men and elephants. Hasdrubal was killed and his head sent to Hannibal. Hannibal, fearful*

---

234. Brother of Hannibal.

235. Publius Cornelius Scipio (236–183 BCE), known as Scipio Africanus ("Scipio the African") after his defeat of Hannibal in the Battle of Zama (described below).

of Fortune, retreated to Sicily, which was thereupon attacked by pestilence. A year of peace followed.

XIX. Here is told of Scipio's fine deeds in Spain and how he defeated Hanno,[236] duke of the Punic peoples, and killed him

19943–19976: *Having conquered all of Spain, Scipio returned to Rome in glory and was made a consul. Soon he returned to Carthage, where Hanno, duke of the Punic peoples, went to battle against the Romans and was killed. Meanwhile, the Romans were defeated by Hannibal in Italy, and the consul Tiberius Sempronius Longus[237] fled.*

19977–20012

At this time, the Carthaginians—the Punic peoples and the Numidians[238]—united against Scipio. But they redoubled their foolishness because the very wise Scipio had their lodgings set on fire, in such a way that they did not know who had done it. He thus surprised them and put all of them to the sword. Many heads were cut off. Syphax, king of the Numidians,[239] and Hasdrubal, duke of the Carthaginians,[240] who was related to Hannibal (who was in Italy then), were soon killed and burned with fire. The Carthaginians were then attacked by arms from all sides. There were forty thousand dead and five hundred taken. Soon after that misfortune, however, they entered right back into very serious combat again. To put it briefly, Scipio, proud as a lion, had the victory. King Syphax was taken right there, along with other worthy barons. Many had fled to the city of Cirta,[241] lamenting deeply. Their great defenses notwithstanding, Scipio vanquished them. He acquired vast wealth there and took important prisoners. They and their king were all sent in chains to Rome, by ship, along with a tremendous quantity of treasure, for which the Romans greatly celebrated.

XX. Here is told how the Africans wrote to King Hannibal so that he would return to his country

20013–20099: *The Africans entreated Hannibal to return to contend with Scipio. Despondent at leaving Italy after eighteen years without conquering Rome, Hannibal headed home. He sent one of the sailors up on the mast to look for the closest city,*

---

236. Hanno II the Great of Carthage, aristocrat and military leader in the third century BCE.

237. 260–210 BCE.

238. People of a kingdom in the region of present-day Algeria and Tunisia.

239. Died ca. 203 BCE.

240. A Carthaginian general, not to be confused with Hannibal's brother.

241. Capital of the Numidian kingdom.

and was deeply disturbed when the sailor saw nothing but a tomb, which Hannibal considered an ominous sign. He disembarked at a castle and placed his treasure there. Hannibal's arrival was met with joy throughout the land, but he insisted upon meeting with Scipio before continuing on to Carthage. Scipio demanded that the Carthaginians pay tribute to Rome, and Hannibal refused those terms. A fierce battle ensued.

20100–20132

As I find in the history, the Carthaginians were all defeated there in the end. So many of their people perished, it was nothing if not a marvel. Hannibal, wishing for death, did not know how to help himself. He had such great pain and rage that he nearly killed himself. But he had such a proud heart that he stayed there alone for a while, not deigning to flee. He lamented over Fortune, who had treated him this way. Ultimately, through great effort, he fled from there to Carthage, where he had not returned in the thirty-six years since he had left there with his father, King Hamilcar Barca.[242] That made this entry bitter and sad, as the educated people say.

Scipio went into the king's tents. There was a tremendous amount of plunder, as history informs us, and the Romans were all rich from the treasure of gold, silver, bejeweled objects, vessels, and other items. They took five hundred high men of renown as prisoners, fearful as does, and there were eighty elephants taken if there was one. That was some victory! I know of none more notable for one day! Now the Romans were well on top! Mischance was far away from them!

XXI. *Here is told of how the Carthaginians subjugated themselves to the Romans and made peace*

20133–20178

Hannibal, who had fled to Carthage, lamented his great loss. He spoke to the senators of the city, saying that clearly Fortune's hostility was against them, so they needed to make peace. Otherwise, he knew they would be entirely destroyed, if they did not take the necessary measures. They were in agreement. And in spite of themselves, they sorrowfully agreed that Africa and Carthage would be forevermore under the lordship of the Romans and they would render great tribute. They would thereby be granted peace. This peace was agreed, but do not believe that it pleased or suited Hannibal. Rather, he went out of the city saying that he would not be present for that shameful treaty, and it would be done in his absence.

Filled with rage, Hannibal went to King Antiochus of Syria,[243] who received him gladly. Because Antiochus knew Hannibal to be wise, he made him prince of

242. 275–228 BCE.

243. Antiochus III the Great (242–187 BCE).

his knights and master in his province. Scipio received the homage from the Africans. He had their ships and barges burned, and dictated that they would not have a ship or barge to put to the sea, except for only thirty ships, no more. At the point when he had thus entirely subjugated and acquired Africa for the Romans, the valiant Scipio departed, like a gallant warrior, along with great sums of wealth and prisoners, and gray African horses. He was joyously received in Rome. After this campaign he was called Scipio "the African." He was greatly loved by the Romans. Thus the second Punic war ended in its twentieth year.[244] The Carthaginians had undertaken it, and it ended badly for them.

XXII. *Here is told of King Philip of Macedonia*[245]

20179–20218: *With Philip having rashly transgressed his peace agreement with Rome,[246] the Romans attacked and defeated him. A new covenant was reached, which included Philip turning his son Demetrius over to the Romans as a hostage and returning all the Roman prisoners whom Hannibal had sold to Greece. The Roman consul Titus Quinctius Flamininus[247] arrived triumphantly in Rome with the prisoners and great treasure.*

XXIII. *Here is told how Antiochus, on Hannibal's advice, waged war against the Romans*

20219–20350: *Antiochus wanted to fight against the Romans. At this time, Spain also rebelled against them, but the Romans quelled the rebellion after several ill-fated attempts. When Antiochus snubbed the Romans' proposal of peace, the Romans gathered their army, enlisting the help of Philip of Macedonia, returning his son Demetrius to him in exchange. The Roman forces separated into two parts—one on land, one at sea. In the battle against Antiochus, the Roman land troops struggled, but when night came, they wreaked havoc against the enemy as they slept. Hannibal's sea battle against the Romans was similarly fierce, and Hannibal lost many men. Distraught, he fled by boat before daybreak. Antiochus, whose entire hope had been placed in Hannibal, was obliged to arrange peace. Europe and Asia would now*

244. The second Punic war actually lasted from 218 BCE to 201 BCE.

245. Philip V (238–179 BCE), who was defeated by the Romans at the Battle of Cynoscephalae in 197 BCE.

246. Philip had come to the aid of Hannibal against the Romans, in spite of an earlier agreement after Rome had defeated Macedonia in battle. Christine alludes to that battle in Book 7, chapter 14, among the battles that followed Cannae: "the second in Macedonia, whose king, who held Hannibal as a friend, came to Hannibal's aid" (19688–70).

247. Flamininus (ca. 229–ca. 174 BCE) had defeated Philip V at Cynoscephalae.

be subject to the Romans and pay annual tribute. When the Romans eventually learned of Hannibal's escape to Bithynia,[248] *they wanted to take him at any cost.*

20351–20374

The miserable Hannibal no longer knew where to run. He said he would prefer to die than to fall to the cruelty of the Romans, or into their ruthless hands. He then fell into despair and promptly drank poison. Thus his painful life was brought to an end by his own hand. It is very fitting to note how, when Fortune wants to remove someone from all good fortune, she makes him fall little by little, by meeting often with misfortune. This king was so hard-working, so feared, so wise and valiant, so powerful and chivalrous, and more fortunate at arms for a time than any other man in his lifetime. He so often went to battle and had so many beautiful victories, greater and more notable than I described. When such a king thus dies pitifully and painfully, it is a great example to the proud who do not fear perilous Mischance!

XXIV. *Here is told how the Roman army was so devastated at the Spanish frontier that no one remained to come tell the news*

20375–20432: *Fighting a rebellion at the Spanish frontier, the Romans were so soundly defeated by the Lusitanians*[249] *that none remained to bring the news back to Rome. After a long time, word made its way to Rome via Marseilles. The Romans conquered Mount Olympus, but were then defeated by the Ligurians.*[250] *Meanwhile, the great Scipio Africanus died unspectacularly, exiled in a castle, with Christine unable to explain why he had been sent there.*[251] *A volcanic island appeared in Sicily.*[252] *The Romans waged more campaigns in Spain, ultimately gaining 150 towns and castles.*

XXV. *Here is told how Perseus, king of Macedonia,*[253] *rebelled against the Romans after his father's death*

20433–20496: *Perseus, son of King Philip, rebelled against the Romans. He stirred up the Bastarnae*[254] *to fight the Romans as well, but their army plunged through*

248. A region in Asia Minor on the Black Sea.

249. People of the western Iberian peninsula.

250. People of a region of northwestern Italy.

251. Harassed by political opponents in later life, Scipio Africanus retired to a country estate in Laternum, where he died.

252. Mount Etna.

253. 213–ca. 165 BCE.

254. Germanic tribe of eastern Europe.

the frozen Danube en route. After several defeats, the Romans ultimately prevailed against Perseus. The Romans returned home with two kings and four of the kings' sons, whom they beheaded as an offering of thanks to the god Mars.

XXVI. *Here is told how Spain again rebelled against the Romans*

20497–20552: *Spain rebelled against Rome, prompting the consul Scipio Emilianus, the wise and valiant adoptive grandson of Scipio Africanus,*[255] *to rush there. He encountered the Celtiberians.*[256] *After Scipio defeated "a big, strong, and hideous barbarian" (20515–16) in a joust, the Romans prevailed in the battle. Meanwhile, Servius Sulpicius Galba*[257] *defeated the Lusitanians in Spanish territory, but committed a damnable offense by killing unarmed emissaries. That act cost the Romans, because other groups who would have surrendered did not. While Scipio returned to Rome in great honor, Servius Sulpicius Galba was harshly blamed for stooping to such treachery.*

XXVII. *Here is told how the city of Carthage was completely destroyed*

20553–20598

Soon after, a dispute arose between Rome and Carthage. I do not know the cause, but it was something insignificant. The Romans, saying that this land caused them more harm than gain, no longer wanted their tribute arrangement. This third time, the Romans wanted to destroy Carthage because it troubled them too much.[258] They dispatched two consuls, along with a great number of people, who journeyed there by sea. Their loyal friend Publius Scipio was sent with them. When they arrived at the port in Africa to accomplish their mission, they sent messengers to Carthage. They said that the Romans had a shortage of armaments because of the military expeditions they had undertaken. Therefore the Carthaginians should quickly hand over theirs. The Carthaginians soon obeyed, doing what the Romans commanded of them.

Then the Romans ordered the Carthaginians to leave their city at once, and to make their lodging at ten thousand paces from the sea, because the Romans no longer wanted Carthage to be in the Carthaginians' hands. When the Carthaginians heard this, they grieved and repented greatly for what they had done. They realized too late how they had been deceived. They decided, young and old, that they would rather die in the ruins of their city than leave it in such a despicable

---

255. Scipio Emilianus lived 185–129 BCE. Christine identifies him as a nephew of Scipio Africanus in line 20504; Solente points out the error (*Mutacion*, 4:172).

256. A people of Spain.

257. Praetor in 151 BCE, consul in 144 BCE.

258. In other words, this is the beginning of the third and final Punic war.

way. They would never leave it; rather, they would defend it to the death. They quickly had arms made of gold, silver, iron, and copper. They climbed up on the walls, which were very secure because this city was stronger than any other. There was many a tall tower, many a perfectly beautiful and high gate. Since I would put too much into describing its beauty and design, I will now pass on it and say no more.

20599–20627

It had been nine hundred years since Carthage was founded by the woman who faced harsh recompense for loving Aeneas too much. That was Dido, when Aeneas sailed the sea from Troy. That lady had founded Carthage. It was quite fitting that it would be destroyed and hounded by the lineage of Aeneas, whose mistress was the first one dead; I spoke of how.[259] But it was a great pity to destroy such a city, which radiated in all beauty and richness, and in power, worth, and nobility.

When the Romans saw that the Carthaginians were not responding to them, they violently attacked without warning. The Carthaginians defended themselves very vigorously for a long time. They killed great numbers of Romans by throwing large stones. But the fact that they were meagerly armed was their downfall. This fighting served little purpose for them, because the Romans had a siege engine made, with which they could destroy the walls. That was not done in a day, because the Carthaginians were very entrenched. But in the end, the Carthaginians had to surrender.

20628–20676

The Romans had the whole city set on fire. The better part of the Carthaginians willingly came out toward the flames. Hasdrubal, their king, surrendered, and admonished everyone to do the same. His wife, who would hate life in the hands of the Romans, threw herself and two of her children into the fire. And thus, by fire and ruin, the last queen died just as the first one had. Carthage, the noble city that had endured for nearly a thousand years, was thus destroyed in terrible torment. The Romans took great treasure from it, and they sold all the lamenting, despondent people as slaves. Thus they destroyed the whole country, and then they left.

They had been there for three years. They named Publius "Scipio the African."[260] They gave him that name because Africa was completely conquered by his power and good sense. In Rome, all those who had journeyed were received with great joy. In the same year that Carthage was destroyed, the Romans did great damage in Greece and Macedonia. They destroyed the land that was useless to them, as well as the noble city of Corinth, which was so fertile, good, and

259. Book 7, chapter 1.

260. He was known as Scipio Africanus the Younger to distinguish him from Scipio Africanus, the conqueror of Hannibal.

renowned that several great and noble armies had come from there. They set fire to it and completely burned it. It was a great pity to see misfortune fall that way upon such a city. Thus the Romans had three very notable victories in one year: Corinth, Africa, and Macedonia, where they took many a rich chalcedony[261] and pillaged many magnificent items, as they laid waste to the whole country. I will leave out plenty of other events that occurred in that time, because it would be a long story if someone wanted to tell it all.

XXVIII. Here is told of Viriatus,[262] a shepherd who was later head of an army

20677–20866: *Viriatus, a shepherd in his childhood, amassed a formidable army of brigands and murderers in Spain, and repeatedly caused trouble for the Romans. Ultimately he was killed by his own people to gain Rome's favor.*

Rome faced a number of misfortunes, including several defeats at the hands of the Galicians.[263] Fearing that the gods had turned against them, they threw an armed nobleman into the sea as a gesture of appeasement. That proved futile, as it was soon followed by an epidemic that killed many. Further, the Romans suffered losses against the city of Numantia in Spain.[264] The Romans, led by Scipio, ultimately prevailed because the people of Numantia, preferring death to servitude, burned themselves and their city. Still, the Romans lost more than they gained in the effort. From there, they went on through Spain, destroying the country.

During this time, a number of ominous signs—an eight-limbed child born to a slave, Etna violently erupting—pointed to imminent misfortune for Rome. The signs were soon followed by a widespread slave rebellion, which ended when the Romans drove the slaves into hiding in the mountains, where they died of starvation.

XXIX. Here is told of the great battles that Aristonicus arranged against the Romans

20867–20908: *When Rome had existed for 622 years, King Attalus of Pergamon[265] left his kingdom to the Romans. His displeased son and heir, Aristonicus,[266] assembled four powerful kings to attack Rome—Nicomedes of Bithynia, Mithridates of*

---

261. A variety of quartz; its name probably derived from the ancient town of Chalcedon, in Bithynia (the region to which Hannibal fled after his defeat in the Second Punic War; see chapter 23, above).

262. Leader of the Lusitanians against Rome; died 139 BCE.

263. People from the northwest corner of the Iberian peninsula.

264. An ancient Celtiberian city in northern Spain.

265. Attalus III, who reigned 138–133 BCE. Pergamon was a city in ancient Greece.

266. Aristonicus claimed to be the half-brother, not the son, of Attalus (Solente, *Mutacion*, 4:110).

Armenia, Ariarthes of Cappedocia, and Pylaemenes of Paphlagonia.[267] *The Romans defeated them. Christine hints that she will be treating Mithridates in greater detail.*

XXX. Here is told of the locusts that destroyed the grain, and of many other things

20909–20958: *Ptolemy, king of Egypt,*[268] *died. Etna erupted so violently that land, sea, and population were catastrophically harmed in Sicily. Locusts devoured grain and trees in Africa. Animals, birds, and scores of Romans died of pestilence. The stench of death overtook the land.*

XXXI. Here is told how the city of Carthage was rebuilt

20959–21004: *The Romans decided that it would be useful to them to rebuild Carthage to guard the entry to the province of Africa. In spite of difficulties, such as wolves coming in several nights and destroying the measurement markers, they succeeded, and populated the city with Romans. Additional conflicts occurred and bad omens frightened the Romans.*

XXXII. Here is told of King Bituitus of Gaul,[269] **who attacked the Romans**

21005–21070: *The people of the Balearic Islands*[270] *tried to attack Rome, but were promptly subjugated. That same year, King Bituitus attacked the Romans, intending to conquer Italy. He scorned the Romans when he saw them, thinking that they looked weak. He was soon proven wrong, and in his army's haste to flee over a bridge he had built over the Rhone river, the weight caused the bridge to collapse. Thus he lost more men to drowning than to the battle. King Bituitus was taken. A band of his soldiers, who had already made their way into Italy, killed each other rather than be taken prisoner.*

XXXIII. Here is told how the Romans were sent against King Jugurtha

21071–21202: *Five hundred and thirty-five years after the founding of Rome, the Romans set out to attack King Jugurtha, who had taken Numidia from his cousins, the*

---

267. Nicomedes III of Bithynia (reigned 127–94 BCE); Mithridates VI (the Great) of Pontus (reigned ca. 120–63 BCE); Ariarthes VI of Cappadocia (reigned 130–116 BCE); Pylaemenes II of Paphlagonia (reigned ca. 140–130 BCE). Mithridates appears again in chapters 37–42, below.

268. Ptolemy I Soter, who reigned as pharaoh ca. 306–ca. 285 BCE. He is also referred to in Book 7, chapter 52.

269. King of the Averni tribe in what is now central France (reigned in the second century BCE).

270. In the western Mediterranean, near Spain.

rightful heirs, upon the death of King Micipsa.[271] *Through gifts and flattery, Jugurtha tricked the Romans into believing that he did not want war with them. He was so charming that he was brought to Rome, where through deceptive maneuvers he instigated discord among the Roman barons. Scorning the Romans as easily manipulated, he went on to wage war against them in Africa, took over their kingdom there, and shunned their authority. The Romans set out to retaliate. Jugurtha was not perturbed, as he believed he would simply corrupt the army with gifts. Instead, he was defeated twice. As of the third battle, he negotiated a peace which he soon broke by amassing a huge army in the land of his ally King Bocchus.*[272] *Once the battle raged, Bocchus saw that defeat was imminent. To regain peace, he handed Jugurtha over to the Romans and promised that he would never go to war against them. Jugurtha, two of his children, and many prisoners were taken to Rome and paraded about, alongside the victorious Gaius Marius,*[273] *who entered the city in a golden chariot called Triumph.*

XXXIV. Here is told of the people of the city of Tongeren[274]

21203–21248: *Lucius Cassius Longinus*[275] *led the Romans against the troublesome people of Tongeren, who defeated the Romans three times. To save his own life, a consul negotiated a peace that the Romans found disagreeable, resulting in his exile. The Romans went on to take Toulouse and the marvelous treasure held at the Temple of Apollo. The treasure was stolen en route to Rome, and many suspected that the consul in charge was behind it.*[276]

XXXV. Here is told of the people of Gaul and Germania who won against the Romans

21249–21294

The people of Gaul and Germania joined together in a mustered army, saying they would destroy the Romans and Rome, without leaving a man. A great army was

---

271. Jugurtha lived 160–104 BCE; Micipsa died ca. 118 BCE. Numidia was a Berber kingdom in North Africa.

272. Bocchus I of Mauritania, Numidia's western neighbor. He reigned ca. 110–ca. 80s BCE, and handed Jugurtha over to the Romans in 106 BCE.

273. Roman general and consul; lived 157–86 BCE.

274. In present-day Belgium.

275. Roman consul in 107 BCE.

276. The anonymous consul who negotiated the unsatisfactory peace may have been Gaius Popillius Laenas, who took over command when Lucius Cassius Longinus was killed in an ambush during the Battle of Burdigala (Bordeaux) in 107 BCE. The consul associated with the stolen treasure was Quintus Servilius Caepio, proconsul of Cisalpine Gaul in 105 BCE, who was exiled as a result of this suspected theft. Christine does not refer to him by name.

sent against the Gauls, but it was badly led. A good eighty thousand-plus Romans were killed and taken, which caused great mourning. The Romans were afraid of being finished off by that number of people, who did so much damage to them. The victors did something very surprising—I do not believe that anyone has heard of such a thing since. Without going any further, they took all the Romans' jewels and possessions, but they deigned to keep none of it. They shattered the riches into pieces and threw them into the Rhone. They had the Romans' war-horses tied to posts and drowned. And not a penny's worth of their fortune remained.[277]

The Romans took serious note of that great pride and disdainful arrogance, and it alarmed them terribly. You should understand that the Romans feared them no less than they had once feared Hannibal, who had gravely mistreated them. It was no wonder that they were afraid, because there were five kings united against them, vowing to destroy them and bring down all their power. The vast armies had already crossed the Alps and gathered in Campania. The Romans dispatched a great mustered army against them. The Romans, wise warriors and good battle organizers, took the advantage on the field. To keep the enemy from going to the nearby banks of the river, the Romans lodged themselves away from the plain, between the river and the enemy, whom they would render dejected and anguished.

21295–21328

They battled for three full days. The Romans suffered greatly, but they carried themselves vigorously nonetheless. It went badly for the Gauls, because they were constrained by very severe thirst. To tell you briefly, the thirst and heat caused them to die in suffering. On the fourth day, they could not bear it. If you saw the way their sweat ran down, you would say you were seeing them melt into water. One of their kings was killed; all who fought there were defeated. Two hundred thousand were struck down dead. Few escaped. The Romans killed all before them. These maltreated people had brought women, children, and friends with them, because they believed that before the conflict was over, they would take Rome and set fire to it all. But it went quite differently.

When the ladies saw the great torment that had come upon their people, they went to the consul, suffering greatly. They beseeched him to have pity on them, out of kindness. They said that they would pray for them forever to the gods whom the women would serve, provided that they be protected from shame. Despairing because the consul took no account of it, the women killed themselves and their children.

---

277. A reference to the Romans' defeat in the Battle of Arausio, 105 BCE.

21329–21358

The Romans did not return to Rome. Rather, they turned against the Cimbri and Teutons, who had come against them earlier.[278] With great help that came to them from Rome, they defeated a number of those people, who had completely filled the mountains and plains. The throngs of their women did not go into their houses. Instead, they made a very risky decision. After that defeat, the women assembled all the carts and wagons, such that it seemed like a fortress around them. Then they quickly armed themselves. Like madwomen, they were going to sell their dead friends for a high price. Then, without delay, they inflicted great harm on the Romans. In battle, they knocked several down dead over the stirrups and broke many a ventail. In the end, to make the story short and without recounting all of their deeds, the Romans killed all the women and children, every one there. They never emerged from there. And the Romans won great plunder, all of which they brought back to Rome.

XXXVI. *Here is told of how Italy rebelled against Rome and of the signs that appeared*

21359–21418

The Romans had existed for 649 years at the time that Pompey, who could never be reproached for idleness, was already consul.[279] At that time, the Romans suffered a bad turn because all of Italy rebelled against them. Just before that, frightening signs had appeared. They noticed a great shining coming from the north, taking up a large space, like fire. When bread was sliced, blood came out, sullying people and tables. At that time, fragments of pots fell from the clouds in great quantities, covering all the paths and the green wheat. Domestic animals fled to the woods and abandoned man. The earth split and opened up, and a great flame came out, covering more than ten feet of ground.

At this time, the old Drusus was murdered in his house. He was the reason the cities rebelled.[280] Now it was necessary to go into Italy. The Romans were so intensely sad about it that they abandoned the robes they wore as regalia, and they ceased all joy. That was their custom and their way—when great displeasure arose for them, they set aside all their adornments and noble decoration, and donned robes of mourning until their will was accomplished. Then they took up their finery again.

---

278. This paragraph recounts the victory of the consul Gaius Marius over these Germanic tribes in the battles of Aquae Sextiae and Vercellae in 102–101 BCE.

279. On Pompey, see note 119.

280. Marcus Livius Drusus, an elected official whose assassination in 91 BCE sparked a number of Italian cities to rebel against Rome.

The Romans dispatched great armies of their people, and devoted resources toward the effort. They did not spare body or possessions. The Romans did their duty so well that they could not be faulted. Pompey, whom they should esteem, battled a great deal against Sulla.[281] They won and lost a lot. Julius Caesar certainly earned honor in many battles there. One time, the Romans were defeated; the next time, they won. What am I telling you? It would be tedium to say so much about it! These wars, in which the Romans endured so much, lasted seventeen whole years. They considered themselves very mistreated, because, having used up their wealth, they had to sell some of their own possessions to prevent greater suffering.

XXXVII. *Here is told of the civil war*

21419–21446
Thus was born the vile conflict that caused the Romans to lose so many of their barons and their people. They were seriously harmed by the prolonged unrest. This was the civil war, when they killed each other out of intense rage. This dispute, which resulted in grave harm, came about because Lucius Cornelius Sulla, a valiant Roman prince, brave and exceedingly bold, was chosen and called to go to Asia, in great array. He was to go against the rich and very powerful King Mithridates, who caused the Romans considerable torment.[282] But the distinguished knight was not in Rome when he was chosen for this; he was still in Italy, where he was making many conquests. The war was not over. Italy was then defeated by him. He would hand Italy over to the Romans subjugated, taken, and under their power. To put it briefly, he could not go to Asia immediately.

21447–21496
Gaius Marius, another renowned prince, asked for this expedition.[283] Sulla was so grieved and enraged by Gaius Marius's attempt to take this mission to Asia over him that Sulla went to battle against him. At the start, Sulla killed Gaius Marius's constable and went into the city. In great fury, he killed and slaughtered everyone in more than twenty places. He did not let Gaius Marius's people go. He also set fire to his residences. Sulla killed and badly maltreated Gaius Marius's women, children, and heirs. Gaius Marius, for his part, also put people on Sulla's side to death. In full-on battle, the two sides killed each other in the forum of Rome, in grief and sin.

Why tell it to you in detail? In short, this conflict lasted so long between the Romans, with brothers and cousins heedlessly killing each other, that before it was

---

281. Lucius Cornelius Sulla, Roman general and statesman (ca. 138–78 BCE).

282. King of Pontus and an old enemy of Rome; see note 267.

283. Victor in the Battle of Vercellae; see note 278.

over, among the dead and maltreated Romans were all the highest barons, twenty-three consuls, powerful lords, more than one hundred senators, other nobles, many great governors, and fifty thousand other citizens and people of the city, not counting others who helped them and tormented the Romans. That is just as it is seen in writings. Sulla tormented Gaius Marius in every way, however. He had the feet, fists, and all limbs torn from a son who was very dear to him, which was certainly great cruelty! When Gaius Marius saw that he thus had the worst of the battle, out of despair or fear of falling abruptly into Sulla's cruel hands, he had his own head cut off by one of his people. That was ultimately the end of Gaius Marius. And the war, in which many had suffered hardship, thus came to an end.

XXXVIII. *Here is told of Sulla's victory over King Mithridates*

21497–21630: *Sulla, now governor of Rome, reestablished order there, and then set out against Mithridates. Archelaus, an officer of Mithridates, invaded Greece and took Athens by siege. Sulla battled successfully against Archelaus, who fled, and whose son was killed. Archelaus's next attempt also failed, and his defeated men took refuge in a swamp, only to be killed when hunger forced them to reemerge. Archelaus fled to Mithridates, whose own cities were rebelling against him because of his cruelty, and they refused to join him in war. Mithridates was obliged to ask Sulla for peace, and the country came under Roman authority. After yet another round of war, the Romans laid waste to all of Asia. In the course of the battles, Ilion, the castle of Troy, was destroyed, but Sulla had it rebuilt. Mithridates fled toward Constantinople. His fleet was battered by a great storm, but Mithridates was rescued by a pirate and took refuge in a castle.*[284]

XXXIX. *Here is told how Lucullus, the consul of Rome,*[285] *pursued King Mithridates*

21631–21738: *Lucullus set off for the city where Mithridates had taken refuge. Mithridates was no longer there, and the guards that he had left in charge had pillaged and burned the city. Lucullus took over and put the fires out. Seeing that the person whom they feared would harm them was actually bringing them peace, the country turned itself over to Lucullus. Mithridates fled to the land of the fierce King Tigranes,*[286] *beyond the Tigris River. Lucullus headed that way to do battle, which the Romans won. Mithridates and Tigranes both fled. Messengers came from far and wide to turn their countries over to Lucullus. Lucullus went on to lay waste to*

---

284. Solente identifies this unnamed city as the port of Sinop in Turkey (*Mutacion*, 4:82, note to lines 21497–630). It was the birthplace of Mithridates.

285. Lucius Licinius Lucullus, Roman general and political figure (118–ca. 56 BCE).

286. Tigranes II (the Great), king of Armenia, son-in-law of Mithridates (140–ca. 55 BCE).

Armenia and besiege a city in Mesopotamia where Mithridates's vast treasure was held.[287] *The Romans took everything. Lucullus returned to Rome in triumph.*

XL. *Here is told how Pompey liberated the seaports and then immediately attacked King Mithridates*

21739–21768

At this time, the sea was so full of thieves that everyone who traveled by sea was robbed. That made it difficult to pass through the Mediterranean and Aegean seas. The pirates, who took cities and castles, were Mithridates's people. The worthy and meritorious Pompey set to sea with many people, and went against the thieves. Wherever he found them, he destroyed them. Thus he freed the passage, and sold the thieves into servitude at the end of the war. He rid the seaports and the land of thieves and evildoers, bandits and robbers.

Metellus[288] was also sent to the isle of Crete, where he and his men fought with such effort that they conquered it by force. In the end he imposed the Roman laws. Land there was good and well situated. King Minos[289] had reigned there in the past, and the people still governed themselves by his laws and edicts. But the conquerors took that law away from them, and all men were brought under the law of Rome.

XLI. *Here is told how Pompey conquered great lands from King Mithridates*

21769–21796

Pompey, accompanied by a very noble and powerful army of Romans, was sent back to Armenia to go against King Mithridates. Mithridates, who was well aware of their coming, did not hold his army and people back any longer. They went toward the Romans. Camped along a river, he thought he would catch them with a ruse. By night, when the moon was bright, he believed he could surprise them unprepared. But the Romans, who had a way to find out about it, were warned of the plan and quickly came against Mithridates with a very great army. The wretched king was defeated. He fled immediately. All alone, he did not look like a lord of a kingdom, because the path that he crossed was so narrow and tight that he had to lead his horse by the reins. He fled to King Tigranes, who rejoiced little because of it. Pompey, who had conquered a great deal, stayed there for so

---

287. The unnamed city would have been Nisibis (Solente, *Mutacion*, 4:83, note to lines 21631–738).

288. Quintus Caecilius Metellus Creticus, Roman political figure (ca. 135–late 50s BCE).

289. Cretan king who fed people to the Minotaur in Greek mythology; see Book 5, chapter 28.

long that he founded the beautiful city Nicopolis,[290] and the many Romans in the country retreated there.

21797–21822: *Pompey turned against Tigranes, who immediately surrendered his land to the Romans. Pompey allowed him to retain his crown, on the condition that he remain loyal to Rome. Before returning to Rome, Pompey went on to conquer Caucasian Albania[291] and the Orient. Christine notes that it would take a long time to recount it all.*

XLII. Here is told of King Mithridates's death and of Pompey's fine deeds

21823–21862

At the time when Pompey was in the Orient with his fierce army, Castor, a very notable knight and officer of Mithridates, rebelled against his lord.[292] He said that he no longer wanted to be one of his people, because Mithridates was too filled with rage. Castor and his troops sided with the Romans. He took cities from King Mithridates. The king, who had fled from there, fell into despair when he heard this news. He saw clearly that he had no more power! Four of his sons shared Castor's sentiment, because, thanks to his treacherous disposition, Mithridates had killed two of their brothers in a great rage. And he would have done the same to them, but they fled.

They burned castles and set them afire if they opposed them. But I find in the writing that Pharnaces,[293] one of Mithridates's sons, took refuge in a very strong castle. The father, who was not happy about it, besieged his son there. Pharnaces knew so well how to entreat his father's people, however, that they sided with him, and he turned them away from the rightfully crowned king of their land and kingdom. With a great number of people, Pharnaces went to besiege his father. Mithridates, who saw that he could not hold firm any longer, believed he would go violently mad. Mithridates went up on the wall, pleading with his son to allow him to hold his kingdom peacefully for his lifetime.

21863–21906

But the son entertained no discussion of this with him. Rather, Pharnaces said that if he could hold the kingdom, Mithridates would die in a way befitting his

---

290. Not to be confused with Nicopolis in western Greece, founded by Octavian after his victory over Antony and Cleopatra.

291. An ancient territory of the eastern Caucasus, not to be confused with modern-day Albania.

292. A reference to Castor of Phanagoria, an ancient Greek city on the Taman peninsula. It is said that Castor, having been mistreated by one of Mithridates's eunuchs, killed the eunuch and stirred an uprising against Mithridates.

293. Pharnaces II of Pontus (ca. 97–47 BCE).

cruelty. But Pharnaces would do his father the kindness of letting him choose how he would die, without opposing. The father had great grief at this word, and his eyes began to well with copious tears. Very sadly, he said words such as these: "O you! Gods, in whom we have faith! If you are true gods as we believe, and you have the force to avenge a wrong, I beg that my son Pharnaces may hear threats from his children such as I have heard from him, with no comfort from anyone." At that point, he got down and went to his wife and the more than twenty other women he kept. He had them all killed by poison whether they were in favor or not.

He had the same drink made for himself, but he had taken too many remedies against poison in order to avoid being stricken by any means. And then the tower was taken. He came to a knight whom he beseeched to kill him, and the knight granted it. The knight then cut Mithridates's head off. This great and mighty king thus died in grief and misfortune. He had lived in power and strength to sixty-two years of age. For thirty-two of those years, he had fiercely warred against the Romans, with a proud heart, causing great harm and torment. When Pharnaces had achieved all this, he searched until he found Pompey and surrendered to him. He waited no longer. And Pompey, who never found himself deceived by Pharnaces in any way, received him gladly.

21907–21960: *Pompey, who had conquered Asia up to the entry to India, went toward Arabia, Syria, and Phoenicia, and conquered all. He crossed the river Jordan into Judea, and then attacked Jerusalem. The Romans killed thirteen thousand Jews and destroyed the city. Having gone on to conquer Judea, and with several kings and many great lords as prisoners, he returned to Rome.*

XLIII. Here is told of the dispute between Julius Caesar and Pompey, and how Julius Caesar was crowned[294]

21961–21993
Now it is necessary to finish my story. To tell you briefly, Julius Caesar and Pompey, who had conquered so much by the sword, did not like each other very much at all because each of them considered himself very important. So there was great envy between the two of them, which lasted all their lives. But Pompey was more powerful in Rome. Julius Caesar, with a great number of people, went to Germania. There, before the war was finished, he conquered the whole land. There were great battles, and he laid waste to the country. Then he left for Gaul, and covered so much ground there that he conquered it all for the Romans. He simi-

---

294. On this episode, and Caesar in Christine's works more generally, see Bernard Ribémont, "La figure de Jules César chez Christine de Pizan," in "La figure de Jules César au Moyen Age et à la Renaissance," ed. Bruno Méniel and Bernard Ribémont, part 1 of special issue, *Cahiers de recherches médiévales et humanistes* 13 (2006): 127–47 <http://crm.revues.org/854>.

larly attacked the Bretons, but they defended themselves mightily. The Bretons defeated the Romans in battle. But in the end, whatever he may have had to put into it, Julius Caesar subjugated them to the Romans. I do not know what more tell you about it! Julius and his brave men journeyed so much by mountain and valley, enduring battles and struggles, that in ten years' time they conquered a large block of the West, as far as the sea called the Atlantic. He made many a noble conquest there. Once he had done that, he prepared to return to Rome.

21994–22058

It seemed right to him, having done such a vast number of good things, that great and small owed him tremendous honor. But it played out for him in a completely different way! When he found himself in front of Rome, he believed he would enter with his cohort. But the gates were closed to him and he was told to send his great army away from there. He would not enter, either sooner or later. He was sad and consumed by anger. In fact, he attacked Rome, and strove so much that he took it. He went to the treasury of the city, broke it, and shared what he found among his knights. To put it briefly, he worked things in such a way that he indeed had himself crowned. He occupied the throne, and made the kingdom of Rome into an empire. He was emperor, in fact, by both force and love.

Pompey then immediately went from there to Greece. He assembled so many kings and princes that it was a marvel to see. Without delay, Julius Caesar attacked him with a mustered army. There was such an extraordinary battle that everyone on Pompey's side was put to the sword. Pompey was obliged to flee, gripped by great grief. In misery, he fled to Asia on a merchant ship, via Cyprus. He came to Egypt, where Ptolemy, the king at that time, believing very much that he would please Julius, had Pompey killed.[295] Julius was very sad over it, because he did not wish for Pompey's death.

Then the emperor returned to Rome, where he reigned for a time. But in the end, he was put to death at the council, by the hatred of Pompey's relatives who killed him there. After that, his good nephew Caesar Augustus Octavian reigned,[296] and held the whole kingdom justly. And the whole world made Rome rich. At the beginning, Mark Antony[297] ruled with Octavian, but then Caesar Augustus governed alone for forty-three years' time. Rome had lasted, as I understand it, 712 years. As you can read, the Romans were not idle in this period. They were helped by Fortune, who had elevated them so highly and later forgot them! Jesus Christ was born at this time. The world had peace as long as he lived.

---

295. Ptolemy XIII (ca. 62–47 BCE).

296. See note 7.

297. 83–30 BCE.

XLIV. *Here is told of the four greatest powers in the world*

22059–22090: *There are many histories portrayed in the room, but Christine has focused on the four greatest: Assyria, Carthage, Macedonia, and Rome.*

XLV. *Here begins the abridged story of Alexander*[298]

22091–22148: *Christine turns her attention back to Alexander, son of Philip of Macedonia. Some claimed that Alexander was the son of Nectanebus,[299] a banished king who had fled from Egypt to Macedonia. According to that account, Nectanebus, having read in the stars that a child begotten at a certain time would be destined to conquer the world, succeeded in impregnating Philip's wife, Olympias. Olympias, for her part, believed she was pregnant by the god Ammon. Christine rejects both of those versions of Alexander's story.*

22149–22174

The valiant and wise Alexander was very small in size. He had a very strange physiognomy. He had one eye situated lower than the other on his face. He had a very fierce look in his eye and a loud way of speaking. King Philip was very joyous at Alexander's birth, and sent for wise men to teach him well. He wanted Alexander, in every circumstance, to fulfill what was in his nature. Alexander did not fail in this, because knowledge was a friend to him, as was chivalry, for which he was talented. He was driven by those two. Philosophers introduced him to knowledge in his childhood and in his earliest development, which made it even more valuable. The wise and old Aristotle was his master, and he taught Alexander well. Alexander took up arms at exactly fifteen years old. His great pride already showed, and it was foretold that many kingdoms would submit to him. King Philip was advised of it. I will recount his first deed to the best of my ability, and I will proceed in order.

22175–22242

King Philip had long held a great dispute with King Nicholas,[300] lord of the Aridians. To appease the ire and dispute between these two kings, Alexander went to Nicholas, with a very great company, to pursue peace. The affair went otherwise, because Nicholas harshly slandered and insulted Alexander. They were so hostile

---

298. On Alexander in this work, see Glynnis M. Cropp, "Christine de Pizan and Alexander the Great," in Campbell and Margolis, *Christine de Pizan 2000*, 125–34; Catherine Gaullier-Bougassas, "Histoires universelles"; and Gaullier-Bougassas, "La vie d'Alexandre le Grand dans *Renart le contrefait* et le *Livre de la mutacion de Fortune*," *Bien dire et bien aprandre* 17 (1999): 119–30.

299. Nectanebo II (reigned 360–343 BCE). He is also referred to in Book 5, chapter 18.

300. King of Armenia and Turkey.

with each other that they challenged each other to battle. In the battle, Alexander strove mightily and vanquished the beaten-down and miserable Nicholas. He killed Nicholas with his own hand. I read that in the end, they elected Alexander king, because they considered him valiant and worthy.

Thus Alexander's worth already grew, and he returned to his father. He fitted himself out very handsomely. But as he approached the palace, from quite far away, he heard instruments sounding and the festivity that King Philip had prepared in order to marry a new wife. He wanted to leave Alexander's mother and take another. Alexander, who was able to learn of it, told his father that he did wrong in marrying another woman. When a knight wanted to discuss it, Alexander immediately killed him. That pained the king, although he later calmed down, keeping his first wife and relinquishing the latter.

At this time, the messengers of King Darius[301] came to seek the tribute that Philip owed. Alexander, who had a heart more fierce than a lion's, responded that they should go away. They would have none of it, because he had come of age, and would well forbid that tribute. The messengers marveled at the sense and pride that they found in Alexander. They thereupon headed back to their lord and did not stay any longer.

The news came to King Philip at that time that cities and castles which were accustomed to rendering him tribute were rebelling against him. In Armenia, they renounced and refuted his authority. Alexander promptly went there. He reconquered it quite quickly, by force or by love. During the time Alexander was there, few people remained in Macedonia to guard the country. The king was greatly hated by many of his neighboring kings for the outrages and disorder he inflicted, because he was a very rapacious man, violent and harmful to others.

22243–22284

Then the king of Bithynia, who very much wanted Philip dead because he passionately loved Philip's wife, assembled a great number of people, whom he had rebel against Philip. They eventually engaged in battle. The Macedonians certainly appeared to be valiant people, because they were very few and very nobly defended themselves against their enemies. In the end, Pausanias[302] had greater strength in numbers. He dealt such a blow to King Philip that Philip swooned and did not say a word. When his people saw him on the ground, they believed him dead, at which point they fled in haste. King Pausanias, who saw them flee beaten down and defeated, did not go after them. Rather, he stopped and turned immediately toward the city, where Olympias the queen was. He soon entered it.

---

301. Darius III (ca. 380–330 BCE), last king of the Achaemenid dynasty of Persia.

302. Solente notes that although Pausanias is identified as a Bithynian king, he was actually one of Philip's guards (*Mutacion*, 4:160).

The queen had retreated into a tower, where she had brought all the people she could for defense, along with possessions and wealth. Pausanias assailed her there, and did not find her feeble. It happened that Alexander arrived on the same day that this occurred. He had returned victorious, bringing a great many people back with him. He soon battled King Pausanias, and in the end, he knocked Pausanias down dead. They defeated all his people. Their defense did not benefit them much! Alexander came to the battlefield and found Philip almost dead. That grieved him terribly. Alexander lifted him up, but Philip died a short time later, for which Alexander wept greatly. He had a sepulcher made for Philip with rich engraving.

XLVI. *Here is told how Alexander was crowned and undertook to conquer the world*

22285–22327: *Alexander succeeded his father. He set out with a great host to conquer the world. As he neared Rome, the Romans beseeched him to leave them in peace in exchange for sumptuous provisions, which he accepted. He passed into Africa, and conquered it.*

22328–22382
Then he went on to an island where the temple of the god Ammon was located. Many believed that the god was Alexander's father. On the island, Alexander went down to the temple, where he held great sacrifices and solemn ceremonies. In a great park, Alexander killed a stag with an arrow, which no one else was able to do. The island was therefore called Sagittarius.[303] He conquered it and brought it into his hands. He departed from there one morning and went through Egypt (a land replete with fine rivers), where he subjugated the entire population before leaving.

His next mission was to go to a temple. He made his devotion and prayed to the god Serapis to hold nothing back, and to tell him what would mark the end of his deeds. The god replied that Alexander could no more carry the weight of a mountain than he should concern himself about his works living on. Then Alexander asked the god to please tell him how he would die. Serapis told Alexander plainly, without dissimulation, that he would die of poison. But he would finish his undertaking first. Alexander reflected deeply on that answer, but he was very troubled about his death.

He had a very beautiful city founded. But before it was complete, great hordes of birds carried poison there in their beaks. Alexander despaired over it, because that vision wiped away his hope for lasting peace in the city. But the

---

303. Named for the constellation and zodiac sign, "the Archer." This would appear to be a reference to the Siwa Oasis in western Egypt.

priests reassured him, saying that the place would have good fortune. It would be well populated and filled with all riches. He called his beloved city Alexandria after his own name. When it was complete, he had the bones of the prophet Jeremiah[304] placed on top of the walls, so that, by God's grace, the place would be safe from a great influx of snakes. And so it was, because after that there was no snake or crocodile in the city.

22383–22401: *From there, Alexander went on to conquer Syria, Sidon, Damascus, Tyre, and Sicily.*

22402–22462

He turned toward Jerusalem. The bishop of the Jews surely feared his coming. They performed oblations to God for three days, very devoutly, because he wanted to protect and defend his people from King Alexander. It was revealed to the bishop what he should do. At that point, almost everyone emerged in a procession, dressed in white, along with the bishops dressed in priestly vestments. When Alexander saw their great devotion, he immediately got down off his horse. He praised the name of God and greatly honored the bishop, for which the Jews, great and small, shouted out very willingly and with firm desire, "Long live Alexander the great emperor! May all follow him!" Alexander very devoutly entered the city, with all the people in that great procession.

Alexander's people were amazed by his genuflecting before the bishop, and that he had deigned to do the bishop such an honor. At that point, one of the princes wanted very much to know why he did it. And indeed he asked him. Alexander responded that he had gotten down from the horse that way in reverence to the god that is worshipped in this place. Alexander had seen their god in a dream, and knew of him. The god had promised Alexander that if he spared his people, he would grant Alexander victory against Darius. Therefore, for him and in his memory, Alexander honored the god's servants, his bishop, and his people.

Alexander came to the temple, comporting himself devoutly. He gave offerings and lovely gifts. The bishop, who was a very worthy man, brought him the book of the prophet Daniel. There, Alexander learned how Daniel had perfectly prophesied that a king from Greece would come there, and would take the priests by the hand; his path would lead him there. Alexander was joyous, because he believed he was the one. The priests received great and noble gifts from him. He then left, as I found in the writings. Wanting to take up a mission against Darius, the king of Persia, he set off for that place.

304. Hebrew prophet (died ca. 570 BCE).

XLVII. *Here is told how Alexander defeated King Darius*

22463–22502
Alexander's very great sense and valor were reported to Darius, the king of Persia. Darius saw Alexander's image in a portrait. When he noticed Alexander's small form, he was troubled that such a man, so ugly of body and face, would be so superior to all others that everyone chose him as their lord, the common and the greatest alike. Darius felt tremendous contempt in his heart over it. By his messengers, he immediately sent Alexander a rancorous and ugly letter with a very nasty inscription. In mockery and derision, Darius also sent him a ball to play with, along with a cat o' nine tails, as if he were a young and doltish child. He said that they were fitting because childish folly made Alexander think that he could fight Darius. Alexander should return to his domain, without so foolishly attacking him!

When Alexander saw the letter, he was deeply saddened. But notwithstanding that Darius was putting him to the test, Alexander was well disposed to it all, the ball and the whip alike. According to his interpretation, this was not to be taken badly. Rather, it was all in line with his intention, because the ball, which was round, signified the whole world. And he understood by the whip that he would not delay in correcting the world under his authority, whomever it may trouble or please. Alexander hardly waited before going to Persia to attack King Darius.

22503–22538: *After some acrimonious correspondence, Alexander was eager to see Darius's army. Pretending to be a messenger, he made his way to Darius's city and met the king.*

22539–22578
Night had fully fallen by that hour. Darius promptly took Alexander by the hand. He led him to his palace, and took pains to honor him, because that was how he showed respect to strangers. He greatly feted Alexander's messengers when Alexander had sent them to him. When they were seated at supper, four to six golden vessels were brought in front of him. When he had drunk, he immediately set the vessel on his chest. He was asked why he did that. He wisely responded that it was the custom in Alexander's home. Any man who wanted to take away the vessel that was put before him could do so, and no one would be reprimanded for it. The knights who heard this said it was a very good practice.

Thus they sat at this supper. Several noticed Alexander and recognized him, because they had seen him before. They went to quietly inform Darius. When Alexander saw them come forward, he got up from the table. His departure was so quick that it was not known what had become of him. Thus he went away free and clear. Darius was very sad because of it, and repented for his foolishness. At that moment, a magnificent golden statuette fell right in front of the table. Darius began to cry. He was very frightened and considered it a bad sign, because he had faith in the statuette.

22579–22668: *Alexander had already made headway in conquering Darius's land. When they ultimately came together in battle, Alexander prevailed. Darius turned to Porus, king of India,*[305] *for aid. Meanwhile, an enemy tried unsuccessfully to have Alexander poisoned. Alexander took a fortress where ladies and great riches were kept. Alexander did not entertain Darius's plea that he return the women, telling Darius that he would have to take them back by force.*

22669–22710

Porus sent aid to Darius, and they set off to battle. But first Darius's mother, grieving bitterly, declared to him that he attacked Alexander in vain and fought for nothing. He should make peace or surely he would be destroyed by such a battle, because Alexander was too clever and wise, and imbued with noble qualities. She said that Fortune was in favor of Alexander, and set the stage for all his deeds. Darius did not believe his mother at all, and he rejoined the battle. The Persians were defeated. Darius almost went out of his senses. He fled as best he could, to save his life and find safety. He lost many of his people.

Nearly the entire country surrendered to the emperor Alexander, who went all over taking castles and cities. Now the king of Persia was destroyed, his land taken, ravaged, and burned! Now the tables had surely turned for him, because hardly had there been a man born on earth who had his level of nobility. Now Fortune opposed him, and would quickly drive him to his end. He took two of his closest knights with him. And he fled, wretched and miserable, to seek help elsewhere. The wicked knights almost killed their lord there even though he cried to them for mercy, because they well believed that in killing King Darius, they would please Alexander and earn great recompense. Without further delay, the cruel traitors, who did Darius such a terrible turn, left him for dead.

22711–22762

The news was soon known everywhere. It was revealed to Alexander. It troubled him deeply, and he wept because of it. He made a firm promise that if he could get hold of the traitors, he would bring them to a very bad end. He immediately got on his horse and searched so much, high and low, that he found King Darius nearly dead amid the battlefields, which pained him. Alexander immediately descended, spread his cloak on the ground, and helped to lift Darius, gently saying to him: "King Darius! Do not be disheartened, friend! You will be restored and installed in your lordship, to which you are accustomed. Have a manly heart! And get well, because it pains me to see you in such a bad state." Alexander himself

---

305. Ruler of Pauravas, an ancient kingdom on the Indian subcontinent, from 340–317 BCE.

helped carry Darius to a castle, but he died during the ascent, hardly delaying any longer. Alexander wept copiously because of it. Alexander had him buried nobly, as he reasonably should have.

The whole country waited no longer to surrender to Alexander. He had his laws established everywhere. To elevate his greatness more and more, he granted graces and gifts, and sent everywhere to restore wealth to the people. All told, he did so much by his liberality that everyone turned themselves over to him entirely, because they could never have had a more benevolent lord. All loved him, to tell the truth, for the great good that was in him. Because of this he conquered the whole country, as there was no authority as peaceful and intelligent as his. He took the sweet and tranquil daughter of Darius as his wife, for which the country was overjoyed. All the people would have worshipped him in fact, but he did not want to allow it. He said that no one should offer a living, mortal man such high praise or honor.

XLVIII. *Here is told how Alexander conquered the Orient, and of the queen of Amazonia and King Porus of India*

22763–22786: *Alexander headed off to conquer India and the Orient. In India, the heat was so oppressive that his men talked of leaving him there. Alexander persuaded them to stay.*

22787–22828
Porus sent his messengers to Alexander with insulting words, as Darius had done in the past. Alexander was hardly alarmed by it, saying that by no means would Porus or his threat make him leave that place. He took castles and cities all over, filled with treasure, all of which he gave away. He defeated Porus in battle several times. When Porus would venture out, he would quickly encounter an army ready with very fearsome people and strong resistance. The whole country gave itself over to Alexander, doing whatever he wished. He ordered whatever pleased him.

During this time, Alexander sent word to the queen of Amazonia to come and surrender to him or he would launch a mighty attack against them and entirely destroy her land. She sent word back to him, by her women, saying that they had never been conquered by a prince through force of arms, nor placed into any other subjugation. She sent him many beautiful and noteworthy gifts. At that point, the queen set out and nobly went to him. And he, who possessed all courtliness, very honorably received the queen and her maidens, among whom there was a throng of lovely ones. After that, Alexander went through the country of India, where he found terrible frightening snakes. But with his people very capable of defending themselves, he destroyed them. He found terrifying lions and pigs, many strange ports, and unfavorable rivers with dangerous banks. But he accomplished everything well, even though he might have had trouble and misfortune.

XLIX. *Here is told how Alexander killed King Porus and went to see Queen Cleophis*[306]

22829–22871

King Porus retreated to a fortified city. There were many deserts to traverse. Never could he have thought that Alexander would go there, because bears, lions, leopards, and frightening numbers of serpents made the passing perilous. But Alexander indeed went there. The two armies engaged in combat, where there was great killing. Under a new stipulation, Porus wanted to fight against Alexander, if he were willing to agree to it. Looking at Alexander's small size, Porus said that he would not be concerned about Alexander if they were to fight man-to-man; it would be easy to beat him. Porus sent word to Alexander by messenger, saying it was a pity and a shame for so many people to die because of their conflict. He said that the two of them should fight, with the defeated one becoming the subject of whoever had the better of it between them; each one would swear to it.

Alexander was in agreement. They came to the field, without delay. They fought for a long time, so much that they felt the pounding in their flesh. In the end, Porus dealt such a blow to Alexander that all at once he fell to his knees. His people were distraught over it and cried out, very agitated. Likewise, the others shouted with joy. Porus turned to see what was happening, at which point Alexander came and landed a blow on Porus, laying him out dead in a stream. Thus the battle was over. In the end, the country gave itself entirely to Alexander.

22872–22942: *Continuing his conquests, Alexander made his way toward the city of Queen Cleophis. He rescued the wife of one of the queen's sons from a prince who had taken her. The grateful son invited him to meet the queen. Although Alexander disguised himself for this meeting, the queen recognized him from a vivid portrait that her artist had painted. When she told Alexander that she knew his identity, he was not pleased (one of Cleophis's sons happened to be married to a daughter of Porus). Cleophis reassured Alexander that there would be no ill will toward him. They exchanged handsome gifts, and Alexander departed.*

22943–22958

Alexander went on conquering through hills, valleys, and many towns, through foreign lands and islands. No great king dared to attack him. Rather, they came morning and night to surrender into his hands. He encountered various savage peoples, whom he found fierce and hostile, but in the end, there was not one who

---

306. Queen of the Assacenians, also called Candace, from the region of present-day Pakistan.

did not come to surrender to him. He often attacked fearsome monsters, various beasts, and horrible serpents with large spines. But with the great help of his people, he saw everything through, even though he might have had trouble and misfortune.

L. *How Alexander went to the trees of the sun and moon, who told him when he would die*

22959–22990
Alexander passed back and forth at the Columns of Hercules. He climbed up a hill. He found a great temple, beautiful and very rich, where an old man lay, living on nothing but balm. He had a long white beard on his face. He graciously led Alexander to an utterly beautiful orchard. There, the old man who guided Alexander showed him the two trees of the sun and moon. The old man said that if Alexander wanted to know something, he would immediately hear the truth if he humbly made a request to the trees. Alexander thereupon addressed the trees, entreating them to make known whether he would have a long life, and for how long he would remain in place after being crowned by the world and finishing his journey. The response he heard was painful to him. It was that his life would be short and brief, and he would die by poison. As soon as he was crowned, one of his underlings, full of rage, would give him the fatal drink. Alexander left from there, sad and crying with a breaking heart. It pained him greatly to live such a short time after completing his conquest.

LI. *How Alexander had himself carried into the air and then put at the bottom of the sea*

22991–23044
The valiant and wise Alexander cleverly had a cage made. He had six griffins well attached to the cage, and then, without delay, he got into it. He attached raw meat to a rod, so it would not fall, and held the rod tightly in his hand. The griffins immediately flew, ever higher, believing they would get at the meat. They brought Alexander up so high that they rose above the whole world, such that Alexander felt that the world was nothing but a round ball. The sea surrounding it was so inconspicuous, it seemed to him no more than the course of a small running stream. He already feared that the heat would cause him to die in suffering when he turned the rod back downward. At that point, the cage turned over, and he immediately descended from it to the ground. He thanked God with a glad heart. He found his people very angry and fearful, and those who loved him reproached him for the undertaking. He did not encounter them quickly because he had descended at ten days' distance from the army. But in the end, the valiant lord found them.

He wanted to do even more, because he felt it necessary to know what was enclosed in the sea. He then had a barrel made of thick glass, with a chain, along with burning lamps. Alexander got inside. He had himself lowered into the sea on iron chains, and wanted to go deep enough to reach the sandy bottom. Then he wanted to observe everything. He saw a whale, and fish of many different kinds. There were some among them that seemed like us, as if they could have been women and men. They went on the sandy surface on two feet, and supported themselves upright. When he had seen all that he pleased, he pulled on a chain, without stopping. That is to say, he was pulled up. At that point, without further discussion, his people took him out, and he was joyously welcomed back from that voyage.

23045–23072

Soon after, his noble horse Bucephalus died. Bucephalus had carried him through hill and valley, and in many wars (there was none like him on earth!). That pained Alexander greatly. He took note of this death and reflected on it. Now that he had been separated from his horse, it was clear to Alexander that he would not live any longer. That brought great sadness to his heart. He founded a magnificent city there, in the eastern land,[307] and called it Bucephala. He wandered hither and yon, conquering all, and then went to the great Babylon without delay. He was joyously received. A little while later, tribute was brought to him from all over the world, far and near, which he received honorably. Thus Fortune had put him very high. She was his friend for a long time. Could she now harm him, she who wanted to save him so many times, and from such great perils? Would he be killed by her? Yes, I believe, the tricky rapacious one would soon break her faith with him!

LII. *Here is told of Alexander's death*

23073–23146: *Having conquered the entire world, Alexander wanted to be crowned in the presence of all the powerful princes from far and wide. He sent word to his mother Olympias, who was joyous at the news, but who warned him to be wary of Antipater, one of his lieutenants, because she had a bad feeling about him. Antipater was in fact planning treachery. He charged his son Cassander with delivering poison to his other son Jobas, who was in Alexander's service. Antipater and Cassander arrived for the celebration. Jobas refused to take part in the crime.*

23147–23194

Now listen to how Fortune, who had already turned angry toward the prince whom she had so elevated, would now do him harm. One day, by misfortune, Alexander happened to become angry with Jobas. I do not know why. Alexander

307. India.

lifted his palm and struck Jobas, which upset him. Jobas no longer refused to take the drink from his brother and give it to Alexander.

Princes and kings from all over, in great finery and great array, assembled in Babylon. You can be sure that never had a creature born seen such a number of princes together in one day. They were very joyful. Alexander was crowned in such great honor and glory that never in memory had a man been enthroned in such triumph. But there were mortal enemies there. It well seemed so, in light of the harm that befell him.

At dinner, the perfidious Jobas did not fail to give Alexander the drink. As soon as Alexander swallowed it, it went toward his heart. He felt great pain, but he did not want to show the ill from which he was suffering, so as not to trouble the assembly (but in a short time, it was very troubled!). He left from there as quickly as he could, because his heart was nearly leaving him. He asked the traitor for an apple to bite into and commanded Jobas to seek it for him quickly. He believed he would get rid of the poison that way. But the treacherous, wicked traitor put worse poison into the apple than the first, and gave it to Alexander. He ate it, doing himself great harm. He felt such pain that he was convinced he was burning, and he had no power to get it out of him. The great pain that he felt made him want to kill himself at that moment.

23195–23250

But the queen (who well wished to be dead!) comforted him. She said to him: "Very noble emperor! Do not seek to commit such a horror as to kill yourself! What could one say of you, who had seen such suffering in the past, if you were to finish yourself off that way now? Come to your bed, although you will have no pleasure there. Call your people and speak with them. Order them to do what you wish to be done, and find steadfast courage in yourself!" The emperor, by the good counsel of his wife, got into bed, filled with grief. He called for his barons and began to exhort them very gently to keep themselves in peace after him, and to comport themselves well, without doing harm to any soul.

He entrusted his dear mother and wife to them, sighing and suffering terrible pain. Great grief was expressed. Everyone seemed to be mad with pity and torment. They dearly lamented the loss of Alexander's great worth! He divided the land among them, giving each one his part. If they had troubled themselves for him, he compensated them well now, making them kings and powerful princes. He made the very wise Ptolemy the king of Egypt.[308] He likewise made princes of others, but I do not intend to say how or where, because it would be tedious to write it. He even made the proven traitor who had killed him, showing himself to be disloyal, a great lord of great kingdoms and empires. Alexander died in their hands, which grieved them terribly.

308. Ptolemy I Soter; see note 268.

Thus ended King Alexander, whom Fortune had made aim so high that he had the whole world under him. But as I perceive it, she threw him down very quickly when it pleased her. And she completely broke apart what he had put together. He lived for thirty-two years, no more, and in twelve he had surely conquered the whole world, through intelligence or war. But he possessed it for a very short time, and enjoyed his accomplishment little!

LIII. *How the princes of Alexander were in discord after his death, and how his mother Olympias was pitiably killed*

23251–23276
After Alexander's death, all the princes were in such great discord that within fourteen years they had all killed each other and destroyed themselves. Alexander's mother, who had been so honored, also remained very tormented. Ultimately, Fortune, who hated her very much and was eager to destroy her, led her to such a harsh end that she was chased from Macedonia. Cassander had pursued her to such an extent that she no longer knew where to go. To put it briefly, he caused her to die a cruel and shameful death. He had her limbs and head cut off. And so that there would be no sepulcher, he had them thrown, in great baseness, to dogs and savage birds. Thus the hateful traitor killed son and mother, but the vengeance for it was bitter. Oh, every man in whom vainglory lives, look at yourself, look in this story, and see that perverse Fortune, who turns things upside down in little time, knocks one down from very high!

LIV. *Here are told some other stories from around the time of the person who compiled this book*

23277–23320
I saw these stories, and many others, depicted and painted in the room that I described, where Fortune dwells. I would not be able to recount the whole lot; for the sake of brevity, I pass on it. I spoke of the old ones at greater length than I did the newer ones, because one would not have talked about them as much as the latter, which are more common and ordinary. Now it is fitting that I tell of the kings, princes, and great counts of my time, whom I saw serving at the abode of she who knocks many down from their seats. When I was placed at this court, I was soon keenly aware of representations of princes' and kings' stories, fairly recently portrayed on the walls. The men were deceased, although not necessarily because of violence. She who caused them many a vexation had them depicted there.

I saw the good king of Cyprus[309] portrayed there, of whom so many positive things are said that one could not say more good things about any man, in any empire. I saw how Fortune loved him. She glorified him throughout the world, leading him to many places where he did a great number of admirable deeds. He pleased everybody with his largesse; his goodness made him loved. He stayed for a time in Italy, where he was greatly honored, and then in France, where he jousted. He stopped for a short time in Paris. Then he went to the Holy Father, who spoke gently to him. The lord of Lesparre[310] had a dispute with him, but as one who possesses all honor, the king of Cyprus emerged with Lesparre's praise and esteem.

23321–23356
That good king, who deserves to be loved, prayed for the Christian princes' crusade, because it saddened him deeply to see Saracens in such power. That pained him! He did not meet with great success on that voyage, but then, by his valiance, he took Alexandria by force. He had a noble heart when he undertook to do that, because Alexandria was a marvel to look at. He could not keep it, however, because he had few people. He caused the Saracens great harm. He hated them intensely, as long as he lived. But the very perfidious Envy, who took over his very family, caused his death (it was a shame!); his own brother killed him by his hand. Bitter Fortune thus did him in, after she had put him very high. That is how she treats her friends!

I also saw Spain's great misfortune entirely portrayed in images. I read in the inscription about the great battles of King Peter and the fight he had with his brothers, whom he hated.[311] I saw how Fortune protected him for a while, and then did not hesitate to make him die shamefully, with no one able to help him. I saw plenty other such deeds, freshly portrayed, but I will pass on them because rhyming everything would be a process with no end.

LV. *Here she tells what she saw come to pass*

23357–23384
At that time, at the lady's home where I reside, I saw with my own eyes the good king of Hungary,[312] whom Fortune helped as long as he lived. He reigned for a long time, governed his country well, led his wars wisely, and left two beautiful and very kind daughters behind him. The older one was engaged to the good

309. Peter I (1328–69); see note 50.

310. Florimond de Lesparre, a noble from the Aquitaine region.

311. Peter I the Cruel (1334–69), king of Castile and León 1350–69. He was involved in the murders of three of his siblings, and was ultimately killed by his half-brother, who became Henry II of Castile.

312. Louis I the Great (1326–82), king of Hungary (1342) and Poland (1370).

Louis of France, but the violence of death undid that marriage.[313] The other then married a wise, valiant knight, who was noble and good and had gained great fame for his illustrious deeds. He was willingly made king of the place.[314] I am not discussing many others I saw, who reigned toward the south, in Aragon and Spain, and elsewhere, even in Germany. They were led first high, then low by the lady to whom I was then a servant. Under her authority, I saw the power of the Saracens very strangely exercised and carried out among them. But I do not think I will bother with them. May evil death knock them down!

23385–23428

In Italy, I saw very ill-fated and harsh misfortunes. I saw many a marquis and many lords desiring to be greater than one another, and one brother betraying the other. I saw them hate each other and even attack one another. I saw the queen of Naples[315] in high standing, I promise you, at my lady Fortune's court. There was no woman in the world whom my lady honored more, and, seemingly, loved as much! I saw two of her husbands portrayed on the wall, taken to death by violence,[316] but Fortune protected her for a long time, keeping her in high status. Then very suddenly, Fortune cruelly turned her back on her. Charles de la Paix, in great hostility and not in peace, pursued the queen so much that he captured and killed her, committing a great fault.[317] Thus she who was perched so high was knocked down! The one who had done this ugly deed later met a violent death.[318] Alas! I have since seen the noble land badly ravaged by long war. And the esteemed city of Naples is poor because of harsh adversity, which is still in its midst. Its pain will not diminish quickly!

Did I see God's church at all in this castle, in a bad situation? Of course I did! And I saw it mistreated. But I believe that that was arranged by God, because Fortune would have no power against the church if God did not grant it. He saw the pastors governing too badly, and I believe that it was by his will that the church suffered grief.

313. Catherine of Hungary, betrothed to Charles V's son Louis, died in 1378 at the age of seven.

314. There were actually two other daughters—Hedwig (Jadwiga), who married Władysław II Jagiełło of Poland, and Marie, spouse of Sigismund of Luxembourg, later Holy Roman emperor. Solente notes that Christine confuses Hedwig and Catherine (*Mutacion*, 4:87–88, note to lines 23359–72).

315. Joanna I, who reigned from 1343 until her assassination in 1382.

316. Of Joanna's four husbands, three predeceased her. The first to die violently was Andrew of Hungary, assassinated in 1345. As for the second to whom Christine refers here, Solente proposes that it is Louis of Taranto, dead in 1362 (*Mutacion*, 4:90, note to lines 23393–418).

317. Charles of Durazzo, Charles III of Naples (1345–86). The exact circumstances of Joanna's death are unclear.

318. He was assassinated by order of Elizabeth of Bosnia, dowager queen of Hungary and widow of Louis I (see note 312).

23429–23492

Good God! How I saw the great authority of two knights, who were brothers, climb high, then nearly disappear. No one, I believe, will ever hear of people more favored or led to such a high place! Their uncle was the source of all their advancement. This uncle was the archbishop of Milan,[319] I was told, who was so clever and wise that while he was still alive, he bestowed their inheritances upon them. One had Milan, the other Pavia, very renowned cities. Along with those, they possessed several other fortified cities in Lombardy. Fortune held them in grace, and they kept their cities so powerful and growing that they seemed to be the rightful lords of the country, by lineage. They were obeyed and feared because they kept their subjects on a short leash. As far as one knows, few princes held a more noble court.

One brother was named Galeazzo, the other Bernabò, and they were more feared than loved.[320] They conquered surrounding lands, putting them under their authority. To put it briefly, they grew so powerful that they had alliances with the greatest princes of the world and marriages to their high-hearted children. From those marriages came handsome and noble offspring in France and elsewhere, let us not doubt it. There is no question at all about that. Fortune was thus their friend for a time. She was later extremely hostile toward them. That is why no one should have great faith in her.

A noble and very powerful duke was also born to Galeazzo.[321] He later conquered many lands, more by his great sense than by arms. There was no doubt that he was very strong in his deeds and very fortunate. He therefore defeated many armies. Had he lived a long time and continued to advance in the way he had started, he would perhaps have conquered a large part of Italy. But death destroyed him. Since then, and up to now, Fortune has not kept a proper accord with his children, because it seems to me that a number of cities and great lands, conquered by their father through wars, rebelled. Many are anguished over that. I do not know what more to say about it at this point. I do not know at all whether Fortune will be better or worse for them, because sometimes she sleeps, sometimes she is awake.

LVI. *Here is told of England and other countries*

23493–23534

I saw King Edward of England there, in very grand array.[322] Fortune was such a friend to him all his life that he did not fall in the slightest. She gave his son, the

319. Giovanni Visconti (1290–1354).

320. Bernabò (1319–85) and Galeazzo II (ca. 1320–78) Visconti.

321. Gian Galeazzo Visconti (1351–1402), Duke of Milan as of 1395.

322. Edward III, who reigned 1327–77.

prince, many great and notable victories over a number of kings and princes in many different provinces.[323] I saw King Richard[324] and several dukes descended from their lineage. Ha! Fortune the disloyal! How harmful you were to King Richard, to whom you had been a friend for a long time. You did not fail to destroy him, very shamefully! It is indeed unnecessary for me to give an account of the event. Everyone knows it, which is a pity! He did not have malice in him, but you often harm the good ones more than the bad. Those are your gifts!

In my time, I saw two kings in France overcome a great deal thanks to their fortitude. King John, son of King Philip of Valois,[325] toward whom Fortune was harsh and contrary at the outset, was a wise prince of good character, and very chivalrous. But he was not very fortunate in his deeds, because harsh Fortune did him too many bad turns. As it was sometimes said, he had several disloyal and untrustworthy people in his entourage, and he was worse off for such company! He faced very wicked rebellions and deadly, hostile wars, but he sustained them wisely, and conducted himself very nobly. No one would be able to ignore Fortune when she wants to harm him, but it is sensible to know how to pull oneself out of a hostile fate.

23535–23594

King John's son Charles, the fifth of that name,[326] faced nothing if not misfortune and very wicked attacks in his young age. But he made the leap from bad to good by his very great sense and prudence, because he had such fine foresight and judgment that he chased the enemies around him out of the entire area of his kingdom. And he strove so much that he built himself up greatly. I saw his son, King Charles VI,[327] crowned in the highest glory at the age of twelve. He would surely have finished as a prince in all grace if Fortune, turning a blind eye to that, had not burdened him with an illness. But regardless of what anyone says (thank God!), the kingdom was never more at peace or more free of enemies who had long taken pains to harm it, nor have the people ever obeyed their prince better than they now do (it is right! May God soon grant him a cure!). And I do not believe that any lordship has seen finer chivalry than presently exists in the kingdom of France, where all are ready to put up a defense or attack, if the need were to arise.

I saw his noble brother, Duke Louis of Orléans,[328] well treated by Fortune, who held him dear. Indeed, thanks to her he could not fall! Until now, he has

323. Edward, the Black Prince (1330–76).

324. Richard II (1367–1400).

325. John II the Good (reigned 1350–64).

326. Reigned 1364–80; subject of Christine's laudatory biography.

327. Reigned 1380–1422; he suffered from bouts of insanity starting in 1392. Charles was actually eleven when he became king, crowned a month before his twelfth birthday.

328. Christine's patron and protector, who lived 1372–1407.

had no cause to lament (thank God!). Rather, he becomes ever greater. It is fitting that he be esteemed, because he embodies many good things. The truth is enough evidence for me that the noble dukes of Berry, Burgundy, and Bourbon have good fortune among them (thank God!).[329] Although they had plenty of adversity in times past, at present they are in peace and quiet. Good deeds, good words, good intentions, and their good counsel, if it please God, will protect France from grief.

I saw with the most clear-seeing eyes all these princes in my mistress's home, sometimes in joy, sometimes in distress. And I saw so many other ones there that it would be tedious to explain. The list of people lesser than princes would be long if I wanted to name all whom I saw at the castle expressing joy, and others grief because they had fallen from a high seat.

LVII. *Here is told the conclusion of the book*

23595–23636

Now I have explained enough about what I found, saw, and understood in all my past days, at the place that harmed many. I am still there today. I am presently serving my mistress Fortune in the same way. But I am ever the object of her hatred, and she pays me in great suffering. I cannot gain anything good no matter how much I offer myself up to serve and do my duty, because her treacherous arm destroys whatever I build and whatever I embrace. But she does this turn to many.

You, princes in the high tower, consider for at least a moment whether humans who serve in such danger are very safe. Can one live there in security? Considering the things recounted, are Fortune's transformations small? Should men therefore be proud of such good things, which can quickly fail? Certainly not, because there is no sure thing aside from sadness. Saint Paul speaks of this castle in his epistle for several reasons, saying that "there are many dangers in all conditions: on land, at sea, in solitude, with other people, and in study. The banners of Peril are raised in every kind of situation; nothing is sure."[330]

In order to be disturbed less—since Mischance goes everywhere, and even though he may be ubiquitous—I have chosen as my sole joy (whatever joy someone else may have, this is mine): peace, voluntary solitude, and a secluded, solitary life.

Explicit the seventh and last part of The Book of the Mutability of Fortune. *Thanks be to God.*

---

329. John, Duke of Berry (1340–1416); Philip II, Duke of Burgundy (1342–1404); and Louis II, Duke of Bourbon (1337–1410). They served as regents for their nephew, Charles VI.

330. Reference to 2 Corinthians 11:26–27 (Solente, *Mutacion*, 4:95, note to lines 23621–29).

Appendix

This Appendix contains eleven extended bibliographical discussions that would have overwhelmed the footnote apparatus if included in the main text.

1. Overviews of Christine's Life, Works, and Historical Context

Studies of Christine de Pizan date as far back as Jean Boivin de Villeneuve's "Vie de Christine de Pisan, et de Thomas de Pisan son père," in *Mémoires de littérature tirez des registres de l'Académie royale des Inscriptions et belles-lettres*, 2:762–74 (Paris: Imprimerie royale, 1717) <http://gallica.bnf.fr/ark:/12148/bpt6k5721885d /f1.image>. Two particularly useful such studies are Nadia Margolis, *An Introduction to Christine de Pizan* (Gainesville: University Press of Florida, 2011) and Charity Cannon Willard, *Christine de Pizan: Her Life and Works* (New York: Persea Books, 1984). Christine's own descendant, Françoise (or "Mme Etienne") du Castel penned two: *Damoiselle Christine de Pizan, veuve de M. Etienne de Castel: 1364–1431* (Paris: Picard, 1972) and *Ma grand-mère Christine de Pizan* (Paris: Hachette, 1936). Nineteenth-century studies include Friedrich Koch, *Leben und Werke der Christine de Pizan* (Goslar am Harz: Ludwig Koch, 1885); E.M.D. Robineau, *Christine de Pisan: Sa vie et ses œuvres* (Saint Omer: Fleury-Lemaire, 1882); Raymond Thomassy, *Essai sur les écrits politiques de Christine de Pisan* (Paris: Debécourt, 1838).

Later examples include Françoise Autrand, *Christine de Pizan: Une femme en politique* (Paris: Fayard, 2009); Diane Bornstein, *Ideals for Women in the Works of Christine de Pizan* (Ann Arbor: Medieval and Renaissance Collegium, 1981), 1–28; Marguerite Favier, *Christine de Pisan: Muse des cours souveraines* (1967; Geneva: Edito-Service, 1984); Helen Ruth Finkel, "The Portrait of the Woman in the Works of Christine de Pisan," *Les bonnes feuilles* 3 (1974): 138–51; Astrik L. Gabriel, "The Educational Ideas of Christine de Pisan," *Journal of the History of Ideas* 16 (1955): 3–21; Enid McLeod, *The Order of the Rose: The Life and Ideas of Christine de Pizan* (Totowa, NJ: Rowman and Littlefield, 1976); Gianni Mombello, "Quelques aspects de la pensée politique de Christine de Pizan d'après ses œuvres publiées," in *Culture et politique en France à l'époque de l'humanisme et de la Renaissance*, ed. Franco Simone (Turin: Accademia delle Scienze, 1974), 43–153; Ernest Nys, *Christine de Pisan et ses principales œuvres* (The Hague: Martinus Nijhoff, 1914); Régine Pernoud, *Christine de Pisan* (Paris: Calmann-Lévy, 1982); Marie-Josèphe Pinet, *Christine de Pisan, 1364–1430: Etude biographique et littéraire* (Paris: Champion, 1927); Daniel Poirion, "Christine de Pisan," in *Le Moyen Âge II: 1300–1480* (Paris: Arthaud, 1971), 203–10; Poirion, "Christine de Pisan," in *Le poète et le prince: L'évolution du lyrisme courtois de Guillaume de Machaut à Charles d'Orléans* (Paris: Presses Universitaires de France, 1965), 237–54; Simone Roux, *Christine de Pizan: Femme de tête, dame de coeur* (Paris: Payot, 2006); Suzanne Solente, *Christine de Pisan* (Paris: Imprimerie Nationale and C. Klincksieck, 1969); Solente, ed., *Le Livre des fais et bonnes meurs du sage roy Charles V par Christine de Pisan*, 2 vols. (Paris: Champion, 1936–1940), 1:i–xxxvi; and Charity Cannon Willard, "The Franco-Italian Professional Writer Christine de Pizan," in *Medieval Women Writers*, ed. Katharina Wilson (Athens: University of Georgia Press, 1984), 333–63.

Unpublished dissertations on this topic include George H. Bumgardner, "Tradition and Modernity from 1380 to 1405: Christine de Pizan," PhD diss., Yale University, 1970; Helen Ruth Finkel, "The Portrait of the Woman in the Works of Christine de Pisan," PhD diss., Rice University, 1972 <http://scholarship.rice.edu/handle/1911/14833>; and Margaret S. Wilson, "A Revaluation of Christine de Pisan as a Literary Figure," PhD diss., Stanford University, 1952.

2. Christine's Self-Construction as a Gendered Authorial Persona

For Christine's strategies of self-presentation, see Barbara K. Altmann, "L'art de l'autoportrait littéraire dans les *Cent ballades* de Christine de Pizan," in Liliane Dulac and Bernard Ribémont, eds., *Une femme de lettres au Moyen Age: Etudes autour de Christine de Pizan* (Orléans: Paradigme, 1995), 327–36; Altmann, "'Trop peu en sçay': The Reluctant Narrator in Christine de Pizan's Works on Love," in *Chaucer's French Contemporaries: The Poetry/Poetics of Self and Tradition*, ed. R. Barton Palmer (New York: AMS, 1999), 217–49; Renate Blumenfeld-Kosinski, "Christine de Pizan et l'(auto)biographie féminine," *Mélanges de l'Ecole Française de Rome* 113 (2001): 17–28; Kevin Brownlee, "Christine de Pizan: Gender and the New Vernacular Canon," in *Strong Voices, Weak History: Early Women Writers and Canons in England, France, and Italy*, ed. Pamela Joseph Benson and Victoria Kirkham (Ann Arbor: University of Michigan Press, 2005), 99–120; Brownlee, "Discourses of the Self: Christine de Pizan and the *Rose*," *Romanic Review* 78 (1988): 199–221; Brownlee, "The Image of History in Christine de Pizan's *Livre de la mutacion de Fortune*," in "Contexts: Style and Values in Medieval Art and Literature," ed. Daniel Poirion and Nancy Freeman Regalado, special issue, *Yale French Studies* (1991): 44–56; Brownlee, "Le projet 'autobiographique' de Christine de Pizan: Histoires et fables du moi," in Eric Hicks, Diego Gonzalez, and Philippe Simon, eds., *Au champ des escriptures: IIIe Colloque international sur Christine de Pizan, Lausanne, 18–22 juillet 1998* (Paris: Champion, 2000), 5–23; Brownlee, "Rewriting Romance: Courtly Discourse and Auto-Citation in Christine de Pizan," in Jane Chance, ed., *Gender and Text in the Later Middle Ages* (Gainesville: University Press of Florida, 1996), 172–94; Brownlee, "Widowhood, Sexuality, and Gender in Christine de Pizan," *Romanic Review* 86 (1995): 339–53; Jacqueline Cerquiglini-Toulet, "L'Etrangère," *Revue des langues romanes* 92 (1988): 239–51; Marilynn Desmond, "Christine de Pizan's Feminist Self-Fashioning and the Invention of Dido," in *Reading Dido: Gender, Textuality, and the Medieval Ae-neid* (Minneapolis: University of Minnesota Press, 1994), 195–224; Sylvia Huot, "Seduction and Sublimation: Christine de Pizan, Jean de Meun, and Dante," *Ro-mance Notes* 25 (1985): 361–73; Nadia Margolis, "The Rhetoric of Detachment in Christine de Pizan's *Mutacion de Fortune*," *Nottingham French Studies* 38 (1999): 170–81 <http://www.euppublishing.com/doi/abs/10.3366/nfs.1999-2.008>; Mar-golis, "Christine de Pizan: The Poetess as Historian," *Journal of the History of Ideas* 47 (1986): 361–75; Jennifer Monahan, "Authority and Marginal Status: Authorial Stance in Christine de Pizan's *Livre du corps de policie* and *Livre de la paix*," in Hicks, Gonzalez, and Simon, *Au champ des escriptures*, 41–49; Ana Pairet, "Sub-jectivité poétique et discours historique dans l'œuvre narrative de Christine de Pi-zan," in *Histoires d'historiennes*, ed. Nicole Pellegrin (Saint-Etienne: Publications de l'Université de Saint-Etienne, 2006), 145–55; Anne Paupert, "Le 'je' lyrique féminin dans l'œuvre poétique de Christine de Pizan," in *"Et c'est la fin pour quoy sommes ensemble": Hommage à Jean Dufournet, Professeur à la Sorbonne Nouvelle*, ed. Jean-Claude Aubailly et al. (Paris: Champion, 1993), 3:1057–71; Paupert, "'La narracion de mes aventures': Des premiers poèmes à l'*Advision*, l'élaboration d'une écriture autobiographique dans l'œuvre de Christine de Pizan," in Hicks, Gonzalez, and Simon, *Au champ des escriptures*, 51–71; Maureen Quilligan, "The Name of the Author: Self-Representation in Christine de Pizan's *Livre de la cité des dames*," *Exemplaria* 4 (1992): 201–28; Earl Jeffrey Richards, "Rejecting Essentialism and Gendered Writing: The Case of Christine de Pizan," in Chance, *Gender and Text*, 96–131; Geri L. Smith, "De Marotele au 'Lai mortel': La subversion discursive du code courtois dans deux ouvrages de Christine de Pizan," in Hicks, Gonzalez, and Simon, *Au champ des escriptures*, 651–61; Smith, "Christine de Pizan's *Dit de la pastoure*: A Feminization of the Pastourelle," *Romance Notes* 39 (1999): 285–94; Andrea Tarnowski, "Christine's Selves," in Liliane Dulac, Anne Paupert, Christine Reno, and Bernard Ribémont, eds., *Desireuse de plus avant enquerre ... Actes du VIᵉ Colloque international sur Christine de Pizan: Paris, 20–24 juillet 2006: Volume en hommage à James Laidlaw* (Paris: Champion, 2008), 181–88; Lori J. Walters, "Fortune's Double Face: Gender and the Transformations of Christine de Pizan, Augustine, and Perpetua," *Fifteenth–Century Studies* 25 (2000): 97–114; and Mar-garete Zimmermann, "*Amour d'estude* und *doulx goust de savoir*: neue Konno-tierungen von Weiblichkeit bei Christine de Pizan," *Lendemains* 61 (1991): 28–37.

On the role of Christine's audience in establishing her authorial identity, see Deborah McGrady, "Authorship and Audience in the Prologues to Christine de Pizan's Commissioned Poetry," in Hicks, Gonzalez, and Simon, *Au champ des escriptures*, 25–40. On Christine's self-presentation through images, see Liana De Girolami Cheney, "Christine de Pizan's Collection of Art and Knowledge," in

Angus J. Kennedy, Rosalind Brown-Grant, James C. Laidlaw, and Catherine M. Müller, eds., *Contexts and Continuities: Proceedings of the IVth International Colloquium on Christine de Pizan, Glasgow 21–27 July 2000: Published in Honour of Liliane Dulac,* 3 vols. (Glasgow: University of Glasgow Press, 2002), 1:257-86; Mary Weitzel Gibbons, "Christine's Mirror: Self in Word and Image," in Kennedy et al., *Contexts and Continuities,* 2:367-96; and Maria Giusepina Muzzarelli, "Anatomia e fisiologia di una *mise*: La 'divisa' di Christine de Pizan," in Patrizia Caraffi, ed., *Christine de Pizan: La scrittrice e la città / L'écrivaine et la ville / The Woman Writer and the City: Atti del VII Convegno Internazionale "Christine de Pizan": Bologna, 22–26 settembre 2009* (Florence: Alinea, 2013), 259–69.

3. *The Debate of the* Romance of the Rose

The *Débat sur le Roman de la Rose,* ed. and trans. by Eric Hicks (Paris: Champion, 1977) has long been considered the standard edition of the debate documents; see also the recent Andrea Valentini edition, *Christine de Pizan: Le livre des epistres du debat sus le* Rommant de la Rose (Paris: Garnier, 2014). For a modern French translation, see the translation of Virginie Greene, *Le débat sur le Roman de la Rose* (Paris: Champion, 2006); for English, see Christine McWebb, ed., *Debating the* Roman de la Rose: *A Critical Anthology,* with Introduction and Latin translations by Earl Jeffrey Richards (New York: Routledge, 2007).

Among the numerous studies concerning Christine's involvement in the debate are Pierre-Yves Badel, *Le Roman de la Rose au XIVe siècle: Etude de la réception de l'œuvre* (Geneva: Droz, 1980), 411–89; Rosalind Brown-Grant, *Christine de Pizan and the Moral Defence of Women: Reading Beyond Gender* (Cambridge: Cambridge University Press, 1999), 7–51; Brown-Grant, "Christine de Pizan as a Defender of Women," in Barbara K. Altmann and Deborah L. McGrady, eds., *Christine de Pizan: A Casebook* (New York: Routledge, 2003), 81–100; Brown-Grant, "A New Context for Reading the 'Querelle de la *Rose*': Christine de Pizan and Medieval Literary Theory," in Hicks, Gonzalez, and Simon, *Au champ des escriptures,* 581–95; Kevin Brownlee, "Discourses of the Self: Christine de Pizan and the *Rose,*" *Romanic Review* 78 (1988): 199–221; Brownlee, "Le projet 'autobiographique' de Christine de Pizan: Histoires et fables du moi," in Hicks, Gonzalez, and Simon, *Au champ des escriptures,* 5–23; Marilynn Desmond, "The *Querelle de la Rose* and the Ethics of Reading," in Altmann and McGrady, *Christine de Pizan: A Casebook,* 167–80; Eric Hicks and Ezio Ornato, "Jean de Montreuil et le débat sur le *Roman de la Rose,*" *Romania* 98 (1977): 34–64, 186–219; David F. Hult, "The *Roman de la Rose,* Christine de Pizan, and the *querelle des femmes,*" in *The Cambridge Companion to Medieval Women's Writing,* ed. Carolyn Dinshaw and David Wallace (Cambridge: Cambridge University Press, 2003), 184–94; Hult, ed. and trans., *Debate of the "Romance of the Rose"* (Chicago: University of Chicago

Press, 2010); Sylvia Huot, "Seduction and Sublimation: Christine de Pizan, Jean de Meun, and Dante," *Romance Notes* 25 (1985): 361–73; Enid McLeod, *The Order of the Rose: The Life and Ideas of Christine de Pizan* (Totowa, NJ: Rowman and Littlefield, 1976), 62–72; Christine McWebb and Earl Jeffrey Richards, "New Perspectives on the Debate about the *Roman de la Rose*," in Dulac et al., *Desireuse de plus avant enquerre*, 103–16; Jennifer Monahan, "*Querelles*: Medieval Texts and Modern Polemics," in Kennedy et al., *Contexts and Continuities*, 2:575–84; Régine Pernoud, *Christine de Pisan* (Paris: Calmann-Lévy, 1982), 104–34; Marie-Josèphe Pinet, *Christine de Pisan, 1364–1430: Etude biographique et littéraire* (Paris: Champion, 1927), 64–87; Helen Solterer, "Christine's Way: The *Querelle du Roman de la Rose* and the Ethics of a Political Response," in *The Master and Minerva: Disputing Women in French Medieval Culture* (Berkeley: University of California Press, 1995), 151–75; Anna Suranyi, "A Fifteenth-Century Woman's Pathway to Fame: The *Querelle de la Rose* and the Literary Career of Christine de Pizan," *Fifteenth-Century Studies* 23 (1996): 204–21; and Willard, *Life and Works*, 73–89.

4. Christine's Involvement in the Production of Her Works

See *Christine de Pizan: The Making of the Queen's Manuscript: London, British Library, Harley MS 4431*, website of University of Edinburgh project <http://www.pizan.lib.ed.ac.uk>. Also Sandra Hindman, "The Composition of the Manuscript of Christine de Pizan's Collected Works in the British Library: A Reassessment," *British Library Journal* 9 (1983): 93–123 <http://www.bl.uk/eblj/1983articles/article9.html>; Fabienne Joubert, "L'appropriation des arts visuels par Christine de Pizan," in *Poètes et artistes: La figure du créateur en Europe au Moyen Age et à la Renaissance*, ed. Sophie Cassagnes-Brouquet, Geneviève Nore, and Martine Yvernault (Limoges: Presses Universitaires de Limoges, 2007), 103–20; James Laidlaw, "Christine and the Manuscript Tradition," in Altmann and McGrady, *Christine de Pizan: A Casebook*, 231–49; Laidlaw, "Christine de Pizan—An Author's Progress," *Modern Language Review* 78 (1983): 532–50; Laidlaw, "Christine de Pizan—A Publisher's Progress," *Modern Language Review* 82 (1987): 35–75; Laidlaw, "Christine's Lays—Does Practice Make Perfect?" in Kennedy et al., *Contexts and Continuities*, 2:467–81; Laidlaw, "Christine de Pizan: The Making of the Queen's Manuscript: London, British Library, Harley 4431," in *Patrons, Authors and Workshops: Books and Book Production in Paris Around 1400*, ed. Godfried Croenen and Peter Ainsworth (Louvain: Peeters, 2006), 297–310; Gilbert Ouy, "Une énigme codicologique: Les signatures des cahiers dans les manuscrits autographes et originaux de Christine de Pizan," in *Calames et cahiers: Mélanges de codicologie et de paléographie offerts à Léon Gilissen*, ed. Jacques Lemaire and Emile van Balberghe (Brussels: Centre d'étude des manuscrits, 1985), 119–31; Ouy and Christine M. Reno, "Le catalogue des manuscrits autographes et originaux de Christine de Pizan," in Bernard Ribémont, ed., *Sur le chemin de longue étude ... Actes du colloque d'Orléans, juillet 1995* (Paris: Champion, 1998), 127–33; Ouy and Reno, "Les hésitations de Christine: Etude des variantes de graphies dans trois manuscrits autographes de Christine de Pizan," *Revue des langues romanes* 92 (1988): 265–86; Ouy and Reno, "Identification des autographes de Christine de Pizan," *Scriptorium* 34 (1980): 221–38; Ouy, Reno, and Inès Villela-Petit, *Album Christine de Pizan* (Turnhout: Brepols, 2012); Gabriella Parussa, "Autographes et orthographe: Quelques considérations sur l'orthographe de Christine de Pizan," *Romania: Revue trimestrielle consacrée à l'étude des langues et des littératures romanes* 117 (1999): 143–59; Parussa and Richard Trachsler, "*Or sus, alons ou champ des escriptures*: Encore sur l'orthographe de Christine de Pizan: l'intérêt des grands corpus," in Kennedy et al., *Contexts and Continuities*, 3:621–43; Christine Reno, "Autobiography and Authorship in Christine's Manuscripts," *Romance Languages Annual* 9 (1997): xxi–xxiv; and Reno and Gilbert Ouy, "X + X' = 1: Response to James C. Laidlaw," in Kennedy et al., *Contexts and Continuities*, 3:723–30. For an argument that Christine was not responsible for all the work attributed to her, see Mark Aussems, "Christine de Pizan et la main X: Quelques questions," in Dulac et al., *Desireuse de plus avant enquerre*, 209-19.

5. *Gender Transformation in Christine's* Mutability

See Giovanna Angeli, "Christine de Pizan et la métamorphose," in *Pour acquérir honneur et pris: Mélanges de moyen français offerts à Giuseppe Di Stefano*, ed. Maria Colombo Timelli and Claudio Galderisi (Montreal: CERES, 2004), 61–68; Joël Blanchard, "Christine de Pizan: Les raisons de l'histoire," *Le Moyen Age: Revue d'histoire et de philologie* 92 (1986): 419–21; Renate Blumenfeld-Kosinski, "Christine de Pizan and Classical Mythology: Some Examples from the 'Mutacion de Fortune,'" in Margarete Zimmermann and Dina de Rentiis, eds., *The City of Scholars: New Approaches to Christine de Pizan* (Berlin: De Gruyter, 1994), 3–14; Blumenfeld-Kosinski, "Christine de Pizan: Mythographer and Mythmaker," Chap. 5 in *Reading Myth: Classical Mythology and its Interpretations in Medieval French Literature* (Stanford, CA: Stanford University Press, 1997), 179–84; Kimberly Koch Fonzo, "The Three Genders of Prophetic Authority in Christine de Pizan's *La Mutacion de Fortune*," in Caraffi, *Christine de Pizan: La scrittrice e la città*, 63–74; Judith L. Kellogg, "Transforming Ovid: The Metamorphosis of Female Authority," in Marilynn Desmond, ed., *Christine de Pizan and the Categories of Difference* (Minneapolis: University of Minnesota Press, 1998), 185–89; Didier Lechat, "Christine de Pizan, 'Dire par ficcion le fait de la mutacion,'" Chap. 4 in *"Dire par fiction": Métamorphoses du je chez Guillaume de Machaut, Jean Froissart et Christine de Pizan* (Paris: Champion, 2005), 371–83; Nadia Margolis, "Christine de Pizan: The Poetess as Historian," *Journal of the History of Ideas* 47 (1986): 367–70; Julia A. Nephew,

"Gender Reversals and Intellectual Gender in the Works of Christine de Pizan," in Hicks, Gonzalez, and Simon, *Au champ des escriptures,* 517–31; Earl Jeffrey Richards, "Rejecting Essentialism and Gendered Writing: The Case of Christine de Pizan," in Chance, *Gender and Text,* 108–10; Richards, "Sexual Metamorphosis, Gender Difference, and the Republic of Letters, or Androgyny as a Feminist Plea for Universalism in Christine de Pizan and Virginia Woolf," *Romance Languages Annual* 2 (1991): 148–50; Richards, "Somewhere Between Destructive Glosses and Chaos: Christine de Pizan and Medieval Theology," in Altmann and McGrady, *Christine de Pizan: A Casebook,* 43–55; Richards, "Virile Woman and Woman-Christ: The Meaning of Gender Metamorphosis in Christine," in Jean-Claude Mühlethaler and Denis Billotte, eds., *Riens ne m'est seur que la chose incertaine: Etudes sur l'art d'écrire au Moyen Age offertes à Eric Hicks par ses élèves, collègues, amies et amis* (Geneva: Slatkine, 2001), 239–52; Gabriela Tanase, "La métamorphose du corps chez Christine de Pizan: Masque viril et naissance d'un *je* poétique," in *Le corps romanesque: Images et usages topiques sous l'Ancien Régime: Actes du XXe colloque de la SATOR,* ed. Monique Moser-Verrey, Lucie Desjardins, and Chantal Turbide (Quebec: Presses de l'Université de Laval, 2009), 231–43; Lori J. Walters, "Fortune's Double Face: Gender and the Transformations of Christine de Pizan, Augustine, and Perpetua," *Fifteenth-Century Studies* 25 (2000): 97–114; Walters, "Metamorphoses of the Self: Christine de Pizan, the Saint's Life, and Perpetua," in Ribémont, *Sur le chemin,* 159–81; Walters, "*Translatio Studii*: Christine de Pizan's Self-Portrayal in Two Lyric Poems and in the *Livre de la mutacion de Fortune,*" in Earl Jeffrey Richards, *Christine de Pizan and Medieval French Lyric* (Gainesville: University Press of Florida, 1998), 160–62.

6. Discussions of Fortune in Medieval Literature

See Catherine Attwood, ed., "Fortune and Women in Medieval Literature," special issue, *Nottingham French Studies* 38, vol. 2 (September 1999) <http://www.euppublishing.com/toc/nfs/38/2>; Attwood, *"Fortune la contrefaite": L'envers de l'écriture médiévale* (Paris: Champion, 2007); Glynnis M. Cropp, "Fortune and the Poet in the Ballades of Eustache Deschamps, Charles d'Orléans and François Villon," *Medium Aevum* 58 (1989): 125–32; Barbara Falleiros, "Fortune, force d'ordre ou de désordre chez Christine de Pizan," *Camenulae* 5 (June 2010): 1–11 <http://www.paris-sorbonne.fr/IMG/pdf/Barbara_Falleiros.pdf>; Howard R. Patch, *The Goddess Fortuna in Mediaeval Literature* (New York: Octagon Books, 1967; orig. 1927); and Friedrich Wolfzettel, "La Fortune, le moi et l'œuvre: Remarques sur la fonction poétologique de Fortune au Moyen Age tardif," in Douglas Kelly, ed., *The Medieval Opus: Imitation, Rewriting, and Transmission in the French Tradition: Proceedings of the Symposium Held at the Institute for Research in Humanities, October 5–7, 1995, University of Wisconsin-Madison* (Amsterdam: Rodopi, 1996), 197–203.

On the figure of Fortune in Christine's works more specifically, see Catherine Attwood, "Fortune et le 'moi' écrivant à la fin du Moyen Age: Autour de la *Mutacion de Fortune* de Christine de Pizan," in *Le moi: Essays on Jean de Joinville, Christine de Pizan, La Bruyère, Rousseau, Romain Rolland, Céline, Beckett*, ed. Russell King (Nottingham: Department of French, University of Nottingham, 1999), 25–43; Carole Ann Buchanan, "The Theme of Fortune in the Works of Christine de Pizan," PhD diss., University of Glasgow, 1994; Miranda Griffin, "Transforming Fortune: Reading and Chance in Christine de Pizan's 'Mutacion de fortune' and 'Chemin de long estude,'" *Modern Language Review* 104, vol. 1 (January 2009): 55–70; Carole Kiehl, "Christine de Pizan and Fortune: A Statistical Survey," in Kennedy et al., *Contexts and Continuities*, 2:443–52; Miren Lacassagne, "La figure de Fortune dans *Le livre de la mutacion de Fortune* de Christine de Pizan et la poésie d'Eustache Deschamps," in Hicks, Gonzalez, and Simon, *Au champ des escriptures*, 219–30; Wolfzettel, "La Fortune, le moi," 203–9; Wolfzettel, "Spätmittelalterliches Selbstverständnis des Dichters im Zeichen von Fortuna: Guillaume de Machaut und Christine de Pizan," *Das Mittelalter* 1 (1996): 111–28. Sergio Cigada examines Christine's depiction of Fortune's castle with respect to Arthurian tradition in "Il tema arturiano del 'Château tournant': Chaucer e Christine de Pisan," *Studi medievali,* 3rd series, 2 (1961): 576–606.

7. Christine's Use of Ovid

Studies include Suzanne Conklin Akbari, "Metaphor and Metamorphosis in the *Ovide moralisé* and Christine de Pizan's *Mutacion de Fortune*," in *Metamorphosis: The Changing Face of Ovid in Medieval and Early Modern Europe*, ed. Alison Keith and Stephen Rupp (Toronto: Centre for Reformation and Renaissance Studies, 2007), 77–90; Renate Blumenfeld-Kosinski, "Christine de Pizan and Classical Mythology: Some Examples from the 'Mutacion de Fortune,'" in Zimmermann and de Rentiis, *City of Scholars,* 3–14; Kevin Brownlee, "Ovide et le moi poétique 'moderne' à la fin du moyen âge: Jean Froissart et Christine de Pizan," in *Modernité au moyen âge: Le défi du passé*, ed. Brigitte Cazelles and Charles Méla (Geneva: Droz, 1990), 153–73, especially 164–69; Liliane Dulac, "Le chevalier Hercule, de l'*Ovide moralisé* au *Livre de la mutacion de Fortune* de Christine de Pizan," in "Lectures et usages d'Ovide," ed. Emmanuèle Baumgartner, thematic issue, *Cahiers de recherches médiévales et humanistes* 9 (2002): 115–30 <https://crm.revues.org/68>; Judith L. Kellogg, "Transforming Ovid: The Metamorphosis of Female Authority," in Desmond, ed., *Christine de Pizan and the Categories of Difference*, 181–94; Jean-Claude Mühlethaler, "Entre amour et politique: Métamorphoses ovidiennes à la fin du Moyen Age: La fable de Céyx et Alcyoné, de l'*Ovide moralisé* à Christine de Pizan et Alain Chartier," in "Lectures et usages d'Ovide," ed. Emmanuèle Baumgartner, thematic issue, *Cahiers de recherches médiévales et hu-*

manistes 9 (2002): 143–56 <http://crm.revues.org/76>; and Mühlethaler, "La poé-
tique de la fragmentation ou de la bonne utilisation des figures exemplaires: Enée
dans *Le chemin de long estude* de Christine de Pizan," in Dulac et al., *Desireuse de
plus avant enquerre*, 249–64. A more general overview is Blumenfeld-Kosinski,
"Christine de Pizan: Mythographer and Mythmaker," Chap. 5 in *Reading Myth:
Classical Mythology and its Interpretations in Medieval French Literature* (Stan-
ford, CA: Stanford University Press, 1997). On Christine as a critic of Ovid, see
Earl Jeffrey Richards, "Rejecting Essentialism and Gendered Writing: The Case of
Christine de Pizan," in Chance, *Gender and Text*, 113–18.

8. Christine's Use of Allegory

On allegory in the *Mutability of Fortune*, see Stéphane Gompertz, "Le voyage al-
légorique chez Christine de Pisan," in *Voyage, quête, pèlerinage dans la littérature
et la civilisation médiévales, Sénéfiance* 2 (Aix-en-Provence: Cahiers du Centre
Universitaire d'Etudes et de Recherches Médiévales d'Aix-en-Provence, 1976),
195–208 <http://books.openedition.org/pup/4332? lang=en>; Ana Pairet, *Les
mutacions des fables: Figures de la métamorphose dans la littérature française du
Moyen Age* (Paris: Champion, 2002), 159–65; and Earl Jeffrey Richards, "Chris-
tine de Pizan and Sacred History," in Zimmermann and de Rentiis, *City of Schol-
ars*, 21–25. On Christine's use of allegory more generally, see, for example, Daisy
Delogu, *Allegorical Bodies: Power and Gender in Late Medieval France* (Toronto:
University of Toronto Press, 2015), 68–84; and Armand Strubel, "Le style allé-
gorique de Christine," in Dulac and Ribémont, *Une femme de lettres*, 357–72.

9. The Reception of Christine's Works

Useful studies of the reception of Christine's works include Cynthia J. Brown,
"The Reconstruction of an Author in Print: Christine de Pizan in the Fifteenth
and Sixteenth Centuries," in Desmond, ed., *Christine de Pizan and the Catego-
ries of Difference*, 215–35; William Kemp, "Dame Christine chez les premiers im-
primeurs français, 1488–1536: Vérard, Pigouchet, Hubert et Janot," in Juliette Dor
and Marie-Elisabeth Henneau, eds., *Christine de Pizan: Une femme de science, une
femme de lettres* (Paris: Champion, 2008), 305–23; Nadia Margolis, "Christine at
600: The State of Christine de Pizan Studies for the Second Millennium," in John
Campbell and Nadia Margolis, eds., *Christine de Pizan 2000: Studies on Chris-
tine de Pizan in Honour of Angus J. Kennedy* (Amsterdam: Rodopi, 2000), 31–45;
Margolis, "Modern Editions: Makers of the Christinian Corpus," in Altmann and
McGrady, *Christine de Pizan: A Casebook*, 251–70; Glenda McLeod, ed., *The Re-
ception of Christine de Pizan from the Fifteenth Through the Nineteenth Centuries:
Visitors to the City* (Lewiston, NY: Edwin Mellen Press, 1991); Christine M. Reno,
"Anne Malet de Graville: A Sixteenth-Century Collector Reads (and Writes)

Christine," *The Profane Arts* 7 (1998): 170–82; Charity Cannon Willard, "The Manuscript Tradition of the *Livre des trois vertus* and Christine de Pizan's Audience," *Journal of the History of Ideas* 27 (1966): 433–44; Willard, *Life and Works*, 211–23; Margarete Zimmermann, "Christine de Pizan et les féminismes autour de 1900," in Ribémont, *Sur le chemin*, 183–204; and Zimmermann, "L'œuvre de Christine de Pizan à la croisée des cultures," in Dulac et al., *Desireuse de plus avant enquerre*, 427–39.

On Christine's early reception in Italy, see Gianni Mombello, "Pour la réception de Christine de Pizan en Italie: *L'Arte del rimare* de Giovanni M. Barbieri," in Campbell and Margolis, *Christine de Pizan 2000*, 263–81. Mombello also examines Christine's manuscripts owned by the House of Savoy: "Christine de Pizan and the House of Savoy," in Earl Jeffrey Richards, Joan Williamson, Nadia Margolis, and Christine Reno, eds., *Reinterpreting Christine de Pizan* (Athens: University of Georgia Press, 1992), 187–204.

On Christine's reception in England, see Percy G. Campbell, "Christine de Pisan en Angleterre," *Revue de littérature comparée* 5 (1925): 659–70; Stephanie Downes, "Debating Christine in Victorian England," in Dulac et al., *Desireuse de plus avant enquerre*, 373–84; Hope Johnston, "How *Le livre de la cité des dames* First Came to be Printed in England," in Dulac et al., *Desireuse de plus avant enquerre*, 385–96; and Dhira B. Mahoney, "Middle English Regenderings of Christine de Pizan," in Kelly, *Medieval Opus*, 405–27. On this poem as a possible source for the fifteenth-century *Sir Gawain and the Green Knight,* see John Eadie, "A New Source for the Green Knight," *Neuphilologische Mitteilungen: Bulletin de la Société néophilologique de Helsinki/Bulletin of the Modern Language Society of Helsinki* 87 (1986): 569–77.

On Christine's attention to inscribing herself into cultural memory, see Bernard Ribémont, "'Quand écrire est se remémorer' ... Le motif du souvenir comme déclencheur de l'écriture chez Christine de Pizan," in *Das Schöne im Wirklichen, das Wirkliche im Schönen: Festschrift für Dietmar Rieger zum 60. Geburstag,* ed. Anne Amend-Söchting, Kirsten Dickhaut, Walburga Hülk-Althoff, Klaudia Knabel, and Gabriele Vickermann (Heidelberg: Winter, 2002), 263–64; and Margarete Zimmermann, "Christine de Pizan: Memory's Architect," in Altmann and McGrady, *Christine de Pizan: A Casebook,* 57–77.

10. *Manuscripts Containing All or Part of* The Mutability of Fortune

- B (Brussels, Bibliothèque royale de Belgique 9508, 190 ff.);
- M (Chantilly, Musée Condé 493) is a collection of works in Christine's hand;
- O (Paris, Bibliothèque nationale f. fr. 604), is a later copy of M;

- H (The Hague, Koninklijke Bibliotheek 78 D 42), originally for John of Berry, is single-text, partially in Christine's hand;
- C (Chantilly, Musée Condé 494) is single-text, amended by Christine;
- E (Munich, Bayerische Staatsbibliothek Cod. gall. 11) is single-text, amended by Christine; Book VII is missing;
- F (Paris, Bibliothèque nationale f. fr. 603), also amended by Christine, contains the *Mutability of Fortune* and the *Deeds of Arms and of Chivalry;*
- U (Paris, Bibliothèque de l'Arsenal 3172), containing only Books 1–5, dates from the sixteenth century;
- P (Paris, Bibliothèque nationale f. fr. 25430), also from the sixteenth century, contains only Books 4 and 5;
- V (Paris, Bibliothèque nationale nouv. acquis. fr. 14852) is a later fragment of two folios;
- S (ex-Phillipps 207), single-text, is privately owned, for which see Laidlaw, "Christine and the Manuscript Tradition," 243.

In her edition of the *Mutacion de Fortune,* Solente describes all but manuscript V (*Mutacion,* 1:xcix–cxlii). For detailed descriptions of the manuscripts produced by Christine's workshop, see Ouy, Reno, and Villela-Petit, *Album Christine de Pizan,* 174–76, 184–85, 202–12, 294–306, and 413–75. See also Gilbert Ouy and Christine M. Reno, "Identification des autographes de Christine de Pizan," *Scriptorium* 34 (1980): 221–38; and Reno, "Les *nota bene* dans trois manuscrits de présentation de la *Mutacion de Fortune,*" in Hicks, Gonzalez, and Simon, *Au champ des escriptures,* 781–87. On manuscript illustration, see chapter 4 in Marie-Josée Marquis, "'Une image vaut bien mille mots': Recherche sur l'iconographie des textes allégoriques de Christine de Pizan," PhD diss., University of Connecticut, 2014 <digitalcommons.uconn.edu/dissertations/632>; Millard Meiss, "Christine de Pisan: *La mutacion de Fortune,*" in *French Painting at the Time of Jean de Berry: The Limbourgs and Their Contemporaries* (New York: Pierpont Morgan Library, 1974), 1 ("Text"): 8–12; 2 ("Illustrations"): figures 1–2, 14–16, 19–34; John F. Moffitt, "*Le livre de la Mutacion de Fortune:* Picturing the Art of Memory in Christine de Pisan's Hall of Fortune," *Pantheon: Internationale Jahreszeitschrift für Kunst* 57 (1999): 178–81; Olga Vassilieva-Codognet, "Les illustrations des manuscrits du *Livre de la mutacion de Fortune,*" in Danielle Buschinger, Liliane Dulac, Claire Le Ninan, and Christine Reno, eds., *Christine de Pizan et son époque: Actes du Colloque international des 9, 10 et 11 décembre 2011 à Amiens. Médiévales* 53 (Amiens: Presses du Centre d'Etudes Médiévales, Université de Picardie, 2012), 210–25; Vassilieva-Codognet, "'Mais toudis va en tournoyant': Le motif de la Roue de Fortune dans le *Livre de la Mutacion de Fortune* et dans les illustrations de quelques manuscrits contemporains: Pétrarque, Gerson, Boccace," in Caraffi, *Christine de Pizan: La scrittrice e la città,* 301–22; and Barbara Wagner, "Tradition or Innovation? Research on the Pictorial Tradition of a Miniature in the *Mutacion:* 'Le plus hault siège,'" in Kennedy et al., *Contexts and Continuities,* 3:855–72. On a lost manuscript of Book 7 and its possible link to manuscript P, see Angus J. Kennedy, "The Châtellerault Manuscript of Book VII of Christine de Pizan's *Mutacion de Fortune* and the *Epistre a la Reine,*" in Mühlethaler and Billotte, *Riens ne m'est seur,* 25–36; Kennedy, "Le manuscrit de Châtellerault: Un manuscrit perdu du VIIe livre de *La Mutacion de Fortune,*" in Zimmermann and de Rentiis, *City of Scholars,* 107–15; and Kennedy, "Christine de Pizan, Victor de Saint-Genis et le manuscrit de Châtellerault," *Romania: Revue trimestrielle consacrée à l'etude des langues et des littératures romanes* 109 (1988): 540–60.

11. Christine's Use of Language

Studies include Fabienne Baider, "Christine de Pizan: Femme de lettres, femme de mots," in Dor and Henneau, *Christine de Pizan: Une femme de science,* 271–88; Rosalind Brown-Grant, "Christine de Pizan: Feminist Linguist *avant la lettre?*" in Campbell and Margolis, *Christine de Pizan 2000,* 65–76; Charles Brucker, "Aspects du vocabulaire politique et social chez Oresme et Christine de Pizan: Une nouvelle conception de l'Etat et de la société," *Cahiers de recherches médiévales et humanistes* 8 (2001): 227–49 <http://crm.revues.org/408>; Brucker, "Elévation, gloire et renommé dans quelques œuvres de Christine de Pizan," in Ribémont, *Sur le chemin,* 45–64; Jan Gerard Bruins, *Observations sur la langue d'Eustache Deschamps et de Christine de Pisan* (Amsterdam: De Dordrechtsche Drukkerij, 1925); Lucy M. Gay, "On the Language of Christine de Pisan," *Modern Philology* 6 (1908–1909): 69–96; Monique Lemieux and Christiane Marchello-Nizia, "L'analyse quantitative en diachronie: L'évolution de l'ordre des mots," in *Le moyen français: Philologie et linguistique: Approches du texte et du discours: Actes du VIIIe colloque international sur le moyen français, Nancy, 5-6-7 septembre 1994,* ed. Bernard Combettes and Simone Monsonégo (Paris: Didier Erudition, 1997), 529–39; Nadia Margolis, "Les terminaisons dangereuses: Lyrisme, féminisme et humanisme néologiques chez Christine de Pizan," in *Autour de Jacques Monfrin: Néologie et création verbale: Actes du colloque international Université McGill, Montréal, 7-8-9 octobre 1996,* ed. Giuseppe Di Stefano and Rose M. Bidler (Montreal: CERES, 1997), 381–404; Ernst Müller, *Syntax der Christine de Pisan* (Greifswald: Julius Abel, 1886) <http://babel.hathitrust.org/cgi/pt?id=uc1.b2621498 ;view=1up;seq=13>; Gabriella Parussa, "*Rimoier* et *exposer*: Quelques remarques sur la syntaxe de Christine de Pizan," in *Le moyen français,* 573–93; Michel Quereuil, "Le verbe *mander* dans la *Mutacion de Fortune* de Christine de Pizan," in *Actas do XIX Congreso Internacional de Lingüística e Filoloxía Románicas, Universidade de Santiago de Compostela, 1989,* ed. Ramón Lorenzo (Coruña: Fundación

"Pedro Barrié de la Maza, Conde de Fenosa," 1992), 2:625–30; and Solente, *Christine de Pisan*, 82–84.

Lexicons based at least in part on the *Mutability of Fortune* are Joël Blanchard and Michel Quereuil, *Lexique de Christine de Pizan* (Paris: Klincksieck, 1999); *Christine de Pizan: The Making of the Queen's Manuscript*; *DMF: Dictionnaire du Moyen Français, 1330–1500: Analyse et traitement informatique de la langue française* (Paris: Centre National de la Recherche Scientifique; Nancy: Université de Lorraine) <http://www.atilf.fr/dmf/>; and "Christine de Pizan Database Release 2 (July 2006)" <http://www.christine.llc.ed.ac.uk/>.

Bibliography

The Mutability of Fortune

Manuscripts containing all or part of The Mutability of Fortune

Brussels, Bibliothèque royale de Belgique 9508, 190 ff. (B)

Chantilly, Musée Condé 493, ff. 232r–427r (M)

Chantilly, Musée Condé 494, 177 ff. (C)

Hague, The, Koninklijke Bibliotheek 78 D 42, 170 ff. (H)

Munich, Baycrische Staatsbibliothek, Codices gallici 11, 140 ff. (E)

Paris, Bibliothèque nationale de France, Arsenal 3172, 301 ff. (U)

Paris, Bibliothèque nationale de France, fonds français 603, f. 81r–242r (F)

Paris, Bibliothèque nationale de France, fonds français 604, f. 160v–314r (O)

Paris, Bibliothèque nationale de France, fonds français 25430, 181 ff. (P)

Paris, Bibliothèque nationale de France, nouvelles acquisitions françaises 14852, 2 ff. (V)

Private collection (ex-Phillipps 207), 178 ff. (S)

Modern Edition of The Mutability of Fortune

Le Livre de la mutacion de Fortune par Christine de Pisan. Edited by Suzanne Solente. 4 vols. Société des anciens textes français. Paris: Picard, 1959 (vols. 1 and 2) and 1966 (vols. 3 and 4).

English Translations of The Mutability of Fortune (extracts)

Brownlee, Kevin, trans. "From *The Book of Fortune's Transformation.*" In *The Selected Writings of Christine de Pizan,* edited by Renate Blumenfeld-Kosinski, translated by Renate Blumenfeld-Kosinski and Kevin Brownlee, 88–109. New York: Norton, 1997. Translation of Book 1 and final chapter.

Hult, David F. "From Christine de Pizan, *Book of Fortune's Transformation (Livre de la mutacion de Fortune,* November 1403)." In *Debate of the "Romance of the Rose,"* edited and translated by David F. Hult, 233–34. Chicago: University of Chicago Press, 2010. Translation of lines 5537–5602.

Margolis, Nadia, trans. "From *The Book of the Mutation of Fortune.*" In *The Writings of Christine de Pizan,* edited by Charity Cannon Willard, 109–36. New York: Persea Books, 1994. Selected excerpts.

McWebb, Christine, ed. *Debating the* Roman de la Rose: *A Critical Anthology,* 381–87. New York: Routledge, 2007. Translation of lines 5537–5642.

Other Cited Works by Christine de Pizan ("Pisan")

The Book of the City of Ladies. Translated by Earl Jeffrey Richards. New York: Persea Books, 1982. Revised edition, 1998.

The Book of Deeds of Arms and of Chivalry. Translated by Sumner Willard. Edited by Charity Cannon Willard. University Park: Pennsylvania State University Press, 1999.

The Book of the Deeds and Good Conduct of the Wise King Charles V (excerpt). In *The Selected Writings of Christine de Pizan,* edited by Renate Blumenfeld-Kosinski, translated by Renate Blumenfeld-Kosinski and Kevin Brownlee, 113–16. New York: Norton, 1997.

Le chemin de longue étude. Edited and translated by Andrea Tarnowski. Paris: Livre de Poche, 2000.

Ditié de Jehanne d'Arc: Christine de Pisan. Edited by Angus J. Kennedy and Kenneth Varty. Oxford: Society for the Study of Mediaeval Languages and Literature, 1977.

Le livre de l'advision Cristine. Edited by Christine Reno and Liliane Dulac. Paris: Champion; Geneva: Editions Slatkine, 2001.

Le livre de la cité des dames. Edited and translated by Thérèse Moreau and Eric Hicks. Paris: Stock, 1992.

Le livre des fais et bonnes meurs du sage roy Charles V par Christine de Pisan. Edited by Suzanne Solente. 2 vols. Paris: Champion, 1936–1940.

Œuvres poétiques de Christine de Pisan. Edited by Maurice Roy. 3 vols. Paris: Firmin Didot, 1886–1896.

The Vision of Christine de Pizan. Translated by Glenda McLeod and Charity Cannon Willard. Cambridge: D. S. Brewer, 2005.

Other Primary Sources

Cecco d'Ascoli. *L'Acerba.* Edited by Pasquale Rosario. Lanciano: R. Carabba, 1916. <https://archive.org/details/lacerbao00ceccuoft>.

Deschamps, Eustache. *Œuvres complètes de Eustache Deschamps.* Edited by le Marquis de Queux de Saint-Hilaire. 11 vols. Paris: Firmin Didot, 1878–1903.

Fear, A. T., ed. and trans. *Orosius: Seven Books of History against the Pagans.* Liverpool: Liverpool University Press, 2010.

Fenster, Thelma S., and Mary Carpenter Erler, eds. and trans. *Poems of Cupid, God of Love: Christine de Pizan's* Epistre au dieu d'Amours *and* Dit de la rose, *Thomas Hoccleve's* The Letter of Cupid. Leiden: Brill, 1990.

Gaullier-Bougassas, Catherine, ed. *L'histoire ancienne jusqu'à César, ou, Histoires pour Roger, châtelain de Lille, de Wauchier de Denain; L'Histoire de la Macédoine et d'Alexandre le Grand.* Turnhout: Brepols, 2012.

Greene, Virginie, trans. *Le débat sur le Roman de la Rose.* Paris: Champion, 2006.

Herodotus. *The Landmark Herodotus: The Histories.* Edited by Robert B. Strassler; translated by Andrea L. Purvis. New York: Pantheon Books, 2007.

Hicks, Eric, ed. and trans. *Le débat sur le Roman de la Rose.* Paris: Champion, 1977.

Hult, David F., ed. and trans. *Debate of the "Romance of the Rose."* Chicago: University of Chicago Press, 2010.

Isidore of Seville. *The Etymologies of Isidore of Seville.* Translated, with introduction and notes, by Stephen A. Barney, W. J. Lewis, J.A. Beach, and Oliver Berghof. Cambridge: Cambridge University Press, 2006. <http://pot-pourri.fltr.ucl.ac.be/files/AClassftp/TEXTES/ISIDORUS/Etymologie/B1N8PW-GetQy.pdf>.

Latini, Brunetto. *The Book of the Treasure: Li livres dou Tresor.* Translated by Paul Barrette and Spurgeon Baldwin. Garland Library of Medieval Literature 90. New York: Garland, 1993.

Leo, Archipresbyter. *The History of Alexander's Battles: Historia de preliis: The J¹ Version.* Edited and translated by Roger Telfryn Pritchard. Toronto: Pontifical Institute of Medieval Studies, 1992.

Machaut, Guillaume de. *Œuvres de Guillaume de Machaut.* Edited by Ernest Hoepffner. 3 vols. Paris: Firmin Didot, 1908–21. <https://archive.org/details/oeuvresdeguillau02guiluoft>.

McWebb, Christine, ed. *Debating the* Roman de la Rose: *A Critical Anthology.* Introduction and Latin translations by Earl Jeffrey Richards. New York: Routledge, 2007.

Prior, Oliver H., ed. *L'image du monde de Maître Gossouin: Rédaction en prose.* Lausanne and Paris: Payot, 1913.

Ribémont, Bernard, ed. *Nicole de Margival: Le Dit de la Panthère.* Paris: Champion, 2000.

Valentini, Andrea, ed. *Christine de Pizan: Le livre des epistres du debat sus le Rommant de la Rose.* Paris: Garnier, 2014.

Visser-van Terwisga, Marjike de, ed. *Histoire ancienne jusqu'à César: Estoires Rogier.* Tome I: *Assyrie, Thèbes, le Minotaure, les Amazones, Hercule.* Orléans: Paradigme, 1995.

Secondary Sources

Abray, Lorna Jane. "Imagining the Masculine: Christine de Pizan's Hector, Prince of Troy." In *Fantasies of Troy: Classical Tales and the Social Imaginary in Medieval and Early Modern Europe,* edited by Alan Shepard and Stephen D.

Powell, 133–48. Toronto: Centre for Reformation and Renaissance Studies, 2004.

Adams, Tracy. *Christine de Pizan and the Fight for France.* University Park: Pennsylvania State University Press, 2014.

———. "Christine de Pizan, Isabeau of Bavaria, and Female Regency." *French Historical Studies* 32 (2009): 1–32.

———. "Isabeau de Bavière dans l'oeuvre de Christine de Pizan: Une réévaluation du personnage." In Dor and Henneau, *Christine de Pizan: Une femme de science,* 133–46.

———. "Isabeau de Bavière et la notion de régence chez Christine de Pizan." In Dulac et al., *Desireuse de plus avant enquerre,* 33–44.

———. "A Re-assessment of the Relationship between Christine de Pizan and Louis of Orléans." In Caraffi, *Christine de Pizan: La scrittrice e la città,* 17–27.

Akbari, Suzanne Conklin. "Metaphor and Metamorphosis in the *Ovide moralisé* and Christine de Pizan's *Mutacion de Fortune.*" In *Metamorphosis: The Changing Face of Ovid in Medieval and Early Modern Europe,* edited by Alison Keith and Stephen Rupp, 77–90. Toronto: Centre for Reformation and Renaissance Studies, 2007.

Altmann, Barbara K. "L'art de l'autoportrait littéraire dans les *Cent ballades* de Christine de Pizan." In Dulac and Ribémont, *Une femme de lettres,* 327–36.

———. "Last Words: Reflections on a 'Lay Mortel' and the Poetics of Lyric Sequences." *French Studies* 50 (1996): 385–99.

———. "'Trop peu en sçay': The Reluctant Narrator in Christine de Pizan's Works on Love." In *Chaucer's French Contemporaries: The Poetry/Poetics of Self and Tradition,* edited by R. Barton Palmer, 217–49. New York: AMS, 1999.

Altmann, Barbara K., and Deborah L. McGrady, eds. *Christine de Pizan: A Casebook.* New York: Routledge, 2003.

Angeli, Giovanna. "Charité et pauvreté chez Christine de Pizan." In Hicks, Gonzalez, and Simon, *Au champ des escriptures,* 425–38.

———. "Christine de Pizan et la métamorphose." In *Pour acquérir honneur et pris: Mélanges de moyen français offerts à Giuseppe Di Stefano,* edited by Maria Colombo Timelli and Claudio Galderisi, 61–68. Montreal: CERES, 2004.

———. "Figure della povertà da Boezio a Christine de Pizan." *Rivista di letterature moderne e comparate* 49 (1996): 143–60.

Arden, Heather. "Her Mother's Daughter: Empowerment and Maternity in the Works of Christine de Pizan." In Kennedy et al., *Contexts and Continuities,* 1:31–41.

Attwood, Catherine, ed. "Fortune and Women in Medieval Literature." Special issue, *Nottingham French Studies* 38, vol. 2 (September 1999). <http://www. euppublishing. com/toc/nfs/38/2>.

_____. "Fortune et le 'moi' écrivant à la fin du Moyen Age: Autour de la *Mutacion de Fortune* de Christine de Pizan." In *Le moi: Essays on Jean de Joinville, Christine de Pizan, La Bruyère, Rousseau, Romain Rolland, Céline, Beckett,* edited by Russell King, 25–43. Nottingham: Department of French, University of Nottingham, 1999.

_____. *"Fortune la contrefaite": L'envers de l'écriture médiévale.* Paris: Champion, 2007.

_____. "The 'I' Transformed: The Poetic 'I' in the Works of Christine de Pizan." Chap. 5 in *Dynamic Dichotomy: The Poetic "I" in Fourteenth- and Fifteenth-Century French Lyric Poetry.* Amsterdam: Rodopi, 1998.

Aussems, Mark. "Christine de Pizan et la main X: Quelques questions." In Dulac et al., *Desireuse de plus avant enquerre,* 209–19.

Autrand, Françoise. *Christine de Pizan: Une femme en politique.* Paris: Fayard, 2009.

Badel, Pierre-Yves. *Le Roman de la Rose au XIVe siècle: Etude de la réception de l'oeuvre.* Geneva: Droz, 1980.

Baider, Fabienne. "Christine de Pizan: Femme de lettres, femme de mots." In Dor and Henneau, *Christine de Pizan: Une femme de science,* 271–88.

Beer, Jeanette M. A. "Christine et les conventions dans *Le livre de la mutacion de Fortune:* 'abriger en parolles voires.'" In Dulac and Ribémont, *Une femme de lettres,* 349–56.

_____. "Stylistic Conventions in *Le livre de la mutacion de Fortune.*" In Richards et al., *Reinterpreting Christine de Pizan,* 124–36.

Bell, Susan Groag. "Christine de Pizan (1364–1430): Humanism and the Problem of the Studious Woman." *Feminist Studies* 3 (1976): 173–84.

Berriot-Salvadore, Evelyne. "La *Mutation de Fortune* de Clément Marot." In *Clément Marot: à propos de l'Adolescence Clémentine: Actes des quatrièmes Journées du Centre Jacques de Laprade tenues au Musée national du château de Pau les 29 et 30 novembre 1996,* edited by James Dauphiné and Paul Mironneau, 89–101. Biarritz: J and D Editions, 1996.

Blanchard, Joël. "Christine de Pizan: Les raisons de l'histoire." *Le Moyen Age: Revue d'histoire et de philologie* 92 (1986): 417–36.

Blanchard, Joël, and Michel Quereuil. *Lexique de Christine de Pizan.* Paris: Klincksieck, 1999.

Blumenfeld-Kosinski, Renate. "Christine de Pizan and Classical Mythology: Some Examples from the 'Mutacion de Fortune.'" In Zimmermann and de Rentiis, *City of Scholars,* 3–14.

_____. "Christine de Pizan and the Political Life in Late Medieval France." In Altmann and McGrady, *Christine de Pizan: A Casebook,* 9–24.

_____. "Christine de Pizan et l'(auto)biographie féminine." *Mélanges de l'Ecole Française de Rome* 113 (2001): 17–28.

———. "Christine de Pizan: Mythographer and Mythmaker." Chap. 5 in *Reading Myth: Classical Mythology and its Interpretations in Medieval French Literature*. Stanford, CA: Stanford University Press, 1997.

Boivin de Villeneuve, Jean, "the Younger." "Vie de Christine de Pisan, et de Thomas de Pisan son père." In *Mémoires de littérature tirez des registres de l'Académie royale des Inscriptions et belles-lettres*, 2:762–74. Paris: Imprimerie royale, 1717. <http://gallica.bnf.fr/ark:/12148/bpt6k5721885d/f1.image>. Reprinted in *Collection des meilleurs ouvrages français, composés par des femmes, dédiée aux femmes françaises*, by Louise Félicité Guinement de Kéralio, 2:109–29. Paris: Lagrange, 1787.

Bornstein, Diane. *Ideals for Women in the Works of Christine de Pizan*. Ann Arbor: Medieval and Renaissance Collegium, 1981.

Brabant, Margaret, ed. *Politics, Gender, and Genre: The Political Thought of Christine de Pizan*. Boulder, CO: Westview, 1992.

Brown, Cynthia J. "The Reconstruction of an Author in Print: Christine de Pizan in the Fifteenth and Sixteenth Centuries." In Desmond, *Christine de Pizan and the Categories of Difference*, 215–35. Minneapolis: University of Minnesota Press, 1998.

Brown, Patricia Fortini. *Venice and Antiquity: The Venetian Sense of the Past*. New Haven: Yale University Press, 1996.

Brown-Grant, Rosalind. *Christine de Pizan and the Moral Defence of Women: Reading Beyond Gender*. Cambridge: Cambridge University Press, 1999.

———. "Christine de Pizan as a Defender of Women." In Altmann and McGrady, *Christine de Pizan: A Casebook*, 81–100.

———. "Christine de Pizan: Feminist Linguist *avant la lettre?*" In Campbell and Margolis, *Christine de Pizan 2000*, 65–76.

———. "Les exilées du pouvoir? Christine de Pizan et la femme devant la crise du Moyen Age finissant." In *Apogée et déclin*, edited by Claude Thomasset and Michel Zink, 211–23. Paris: Presses de l'Université de Paris-Sorbonne, 1993.

———. "A New Context for Reading the 'Querelle de la *Rose*': Christine de Pizan and Medieval Literary Theory." In Hicks, Gonzalez, and Simon, *Au champ des escriptures*, 581–95.

Brownlee, Kevin. "Christine de Pizan: Gender and the New Vernacular Canon." In *Strong Voices, Weak History: Early Women Writers and Canons in England, France, and Italy*, edited by Pamela Joseph Benson and Victoria Kirkham, 99–120. Ann Arbor: University of Michigan Press, 2005.

———. "Discourses of the Self: Christine de Pizan and the *Rose*." *Romanic Review* 78 (1988): 199–221. Reprinted in *Rethinking the* Romance of the Rose, edited by Kevin Brownlee and Sylvia Huot, 234–61. Philadelphia: University of Pennsylvania Press, 1992.

_____. "Hector and Penthesilea in the *Livre de la mutacion de Fortune:* Christine de Pizan and the Politics of Myth." In Dulac and Ribémont, *Une femme de lettres,* 69–82.

_____. "The Image of History in Christine de Pizan's *Livre de la mutacion de Fortune.*" In "Contexts: Style and Values in Medieval Art and Literature," edited by Daniel Poirion and Nancy Freeman Regalado, special issue, *Yale French Studies* (1991): 44–56.

_____. "Ovide et le moi poétique 'moderne' à la fin du moyen âge: Jean Froissart et Christine de Pizan." In *Modernité au moyen âge: Le défi du passé,* edited by Brigitte Cazelles and Charles Méla, 153–73. Geneva: Droz, 1990.

_____. "Le projet 'autobiographique' de Christine de Pizan: Histoires et fables du moi." In Hicks, Gonzalez, and Simon, *Au champ des escriptures,* 5–23.

_____. "Rewriting Romance: Courtly Discourse and Auto-Citation in Christine de Pizan." In Chance, *Gender and Text,* 172–94.

_____. "Widowhood, Sexuality, and Gender in Christine de Pizan." *Romanic Review* 86 (1995): 339–53.

Brucker, Charles. "Aspects du vocabulaire politique et social chez Oresme et Christine de Pizan: Une nouvelle conception de l'Etat et de la société." *Cahiers de recherches médiévales et humanistes* 8 (2001): 227–49. <http://crm.revues.org/408>.

_____. "Elévation, gloire et renommé dans quelques œuvres de Christine de Pizan." In Ribémont, *Sur le chemin,* 45–64.

_____. "Mouvement et fragilité humaine dans quelques œuvres de Christine de Pizan." In Mühlethaler and Billotte, *Riens ne m'est seur,* 161–80.

Bruins, Jan Gerard. *Observations sur la langue d'Eustache Deschamps et de Christine de Pisan.* Amsterdam: De Dordrechtsche Drukkerij, 1925.

Buchanan, Carole Ann. "The Theme of Fortune in the Works of Christine de Pizan." PhD diss., University of Glasgow, 1994.

Bumgardner, George H. "Tradition and Modernity from 1380 to 1405: Christine de Pizan." PhD diss., Yale University, 1970.

Buschinger, Danielle, Liliane Dulac, Claire Le Ninan, and Christine Reno, eds. *Christine de Pizan et son époque: Actes du Colloque international des 9, 10 et 11 décembre 2011 à Amiens. Médiévales* 53. Amiens: Presses du Centre d'Etudes Médiévales, Université de Picardie, 2012.

Callahan, Leslie Abend. "Filial Filiations: Representations of the Daughter in the Works of Christine de Pizan." In Hicks, Gonzalez, and Simon, *Au champ des escriptures,* 481–91.

Campbell, John, and Nadia Margolis, eds. *Christine de Pizan 2000: Studies on Christine de Pizan in Honour of Angus J. Kennedy.* Amsterdam: Rodopi, 2000.

Campbell, Percy G. "Christine de Pisan en Angleterre." *Revue de littérature comparée* 5 (1925): 659–70.

_____. *L'epitre d'Othéa: Etude sur les sources de Christine de Pisan*. Paris: Champion, 1924.

Caraffi, Patrizia, ed. *Christine de Pizan: La scrittrice e la città / L'écrivaine et la ville / The Woman Writer and the City: Atti del VII Convegno Internazionale "Christine de Pizan": Bologna, 22–26 settembre 2009*. Florence: Alinea, 2013.

_____. "Medea sapiente e amorosa: Da Euripide a Christine de Pizan." In Hicks, Gonzalez, and Simon, *Au champ des escriptures*, 133–47.

_____. "Il mito di Medea nell'opera di Christine de Pizan." In *Magia, gelosia, vendetta: Il mito di Medea nelle lettere francesi, Gargnano del Garda: 8–11 giugno 2005*, edited by Liana Nissim and Alessandra Preda, 57–70. Milan: Cisaplino, 2006.

Cerquiglini-Toulet, Jacqueline. "L'étrangère." *Revue des langues romanes* 92 (1988): 239–51.

_____. "Le goût de l'étude: Saveur et savoir chez Christine de Pizan." In Hicks, Gonzalez, and Simon, *Au champ des escriptures*, 597–608.

_____. "Sexualité et politique: Le mythe d'Actéon chez Christine de Pizan." In Dulac and Ribémont, *Une femme de lettres*, 83–90.

Chance, Jane, ed. *Gender and Text in the Later Middle Ages*. Gainesville: University Press of Florida, 1996.

_____. "Gender Trouble in the Garden of Deduit: Christine de Pizan Translating the *Rose*." *Romance Languages Annual* 4 (1993): 20–28.

Cheney, Liana De Girolami. "Christine de Pizan's Collection of Art and Knowledge." In Kennedy et al., *Contexts and Continuities*, 1:257–86.

"Christine de Pizan." Les Archives de littérature du Moyen Age (ARLIMA) <http://www.arlima.net/ad/christine_de_pizan.html>.

"Christine de Pizan Database Release 2 (July 2006)." <http://www.christine.llc. ed.ac.uk/>.

Christine de Pizan: The Making of the Queen's Manuscript: London, British Library, Harley MS 4431. Website of University of Edinburgh project <http://www. pizan. lib.ed.ac.uk>.

Cigada, Sergio. "Il tema arturiano del 'Château tournant': Chaucer e Christine de Pisan." *Studi medievali*, 3rd series, 2 (1961): 576–606.

Colish, Marcia L. *The Stoic Tradition from Antiquity to the Early Middle Ages*. Leiden: Brill, 1990.

Croizy-Naquet, Catherine. "La ville de Troie dans le *Livre de la Mutacion de Fortune* de Christine de Pisan: vv. 13457–21248." In *Actes du colloque Troie au Moyen Age: Université Charles de Gaulle—Lille III, 24 et 25 septembre 1991*. *Bien dire et bien aprandre* 10 (1992): 17–37.

Cropp, Glynnis M. "Boèce et Christine de Pizan." *Le Moyen Age* 87 (1981): 387–417.

_____. "Christine de Pizan and Alexander the Great." In Campbell and Margolis, *Christine de Pizan 2000,* 125–34.

_____. "Fortune and the Poet in the Ballades of Eustache Deschamps, Charles d'Orléans and François Villon." *Medium Aevum* 58 (1989): 125–32.

_____. "Philosophy, the Liberal Arts, and Theology in *Le Livre de la mutacion de Fortune* and *Le Livre de l'advision Cristine.*" In Green and Mews, *Healing the Body Politic,* 139–59.

Delany, Sheila. "'Mothers to Think Back Through': Who Are They? The Ambiguous Example of Christine de Pizan." In *Medieval Texts and Contemporary Readers,* edited by Laurie A. Finke and Martin B. Schichtman, 177–97. Ithaca, NY: Cornell University Press, 1987.

Delogu, Daisy. "*Advocate et moyenne:* Christine de Pizan's Elaboration of Female Authority." In Dulac et al., *Desireuse de plus avant enquerre,* 57–67.

_____. *Allegorical Bodies: Power and Gender in Late Medieval France.* Toronto: University of Toronto Press, 2015.

Desmond, Marilynn, ed. *Christine de Pizan and the Categories of Difference.* Minneapolis: University of Minnesota Press, 1998.

_____. "Christine de Pizan's Feminist Self-Fashioning and the Invention of Dido." In *Reading Dido: Gender, Textuality, and the Medieval* Aeneid, 195–224. Minneapolis: University of Minnesota Press, 1994.

_____. "The *Querelle de la Rose* and the Ethics of Reading." In Altmann and McGrady, *Christine de Pizan: A Casebook,* 167–80.

DMF: *Dictionnaire du Moyen Français, 1330–1500: Analyse et traitement informatique de la langue française.* Paris: Centre National de la Recherche Scientifique; Nancy: Université de Lorraine. <http://www.atilf.fr/dmf/>.

Dor, Juliette, and Marie-Elisabeth Henneau, eds. *Christine de Pizan: Une femme de science, une femme de lettres.* Paris: Champion, 2008.

Downes, Stephanie. "Debating Christine in Victorian England." In Dulac et al., *Desireuse de plus avant enquerre,* 373–84.

Doyle, Kara. "Beyond Resistance: Azalais d'Altier, Christine de Pizan, and the 'Good' Female Reader of Briseida." *Exemplaria* 20 (2008): 72–97.

Du Castel, Françoise (or "Mme Etienne"). *Damoiselle Christine de Pizan, veuve de M. Etienne de Castel: 1364–1431.* Paris: Picard, 1972.

_____. *Ma grand-mère Christine de Pizan.* Paris: Hachette, 1936.

Dudash, Susan J. "Christine de Pizan and the 'menu peuple.'" *Speculum* 78 (2003): 788–831.

_____. "Christine de Pizan's Views of the Third Estate." In Kennedy et al., *Contexts and Continuities,* 2:315–30.

_____. "Christinian Politics, the Tavern, and Urban Revolt in Late Medieval France." In Green and Mews, *Healing the Body Politic,* 35–59.

Dulac, Liliane. "Le chevalier Hercule, de l'*Ovide moralisé* au *Livre de la mutacion de Fortune* de Christine de Pizan." In "Lectures et usages d'Ovide," edited by Emmanuèle Baumgartner, thematic issue, *Cahiers de recherches médiévales et humanistes* 9 (2002): 115–30. <https://crm.revues.org/68>.

_____. "Entre héroïsation et admonestation: La matière troyenne chez Christine de Pizan." In *Conter de Troie et d'Alexandre: pour Emmanuèle Baumgartner,* edited by Laurence Harf-Lancner, Laurence Mathey-Maille, and Michelle Szkilnik, 91–113. Paris: Presses de la Sorbonne Nouvelle, 2006.

Dulac, Liliane, Anne Paupert, Christine Reno, and Bernard Ribémont, eds. *Desireuse de plus avant enquerre ... Actes du VIᵉ Colloque international sur Christine de Pizan: Paris, 20–24 juillet 2006: Volume en hommage à James Laidlaw.* Paris: Champion, 2008.

Dulac, Liliane, and Bernard Ribémont, eds. *Une femme de lettres au Moyen Age: Etudes autour de Christine de Pizan.* Orléans: Paradigme, 1995.

Dziedzic, Andrzej. "A la recherche d'une figure maternelle: L'image de la mère dans l'oeuvre de Christine de Pizan." *Neophilologus* 86 (2002): 493–506.

Eadie, John. "A New Source for the Green Knight." *Neuphilologische Mitteilungen: Bulletin de la Société néophilologique de Helsinki/Bulletin of the Modern Language Society of Helsinki* 87 (1986): 569–77.

Falleiros, Barbara. "Fortune, force d'ordre ou de désordre chez Christine de Pizan." *Camenulae* 5 (June 2010): 1–11. <http://www.paris-sorbonne.fr/IMG/pdf/Barbara_Falleiros.pdf>.

Favier, Marguerite. *Christine de Pisan: Muse des cours souveraines.* 1967. Geneva: Edito-Service, 1984.

Fenster, Thelma. "The Fortune of the Jews in the *Mutacion de Fortune.*" In Buschinger et al., *Christine de Pizan et son époque,* 80–87.

Finkel, Helen Ruth. "The Portrait of the Woman in the Works of Christine de Pisan." PhD diss., Rice University, 1972. <http://scholarship.rice.edu/handle/1911/14833>.

_____. "The Portrait of the Woman in the Works of Christine de Pisan." *Les Bonnes feuilles* 3 (1974): 138–51.

Flutre, Louis-Fernand. "Eustache Deschamps et Christine de Pisan ont-ils utilisé les *Faits des Romains?*" *Cultura neolatina* 13 (1953): 229–40.

Fonzo, Kimberly Koch. "The Three Genders of Prophetic Authority in Christine de Pizan's *La Mutacion de Fortune.*" In Caraffi, *Christine de Pizan: La scrittrice e la città,* 63–74.

Gabriel, Astrik L. "The Educational Ideas of Christine de Pisan." *Journal of the History of Ideas* 16 (1955): 3–21.

Gaullier-Bougassas, Catherine. "Histoires universelles et variations sur deux figures du pouvoir: Alexandre et César dans l'*Histoire ancienne jusqu'à César, Renart le Contrefait* et le *Livre de la mutacion de Fortune* de Christine de Pizan." In "La Figure de Jules César au Moyen Age et à la Renaissance (II)," edited by Bruno Méniel and Bernard Ribémont, special issue, *Cahiers de recherches médiévales et humanistes* 14 (2007): 7–28. <https://crm.revues.org/2556>.

———. "La vie d'Alexandre le Grand dans *Renart le contrefait* et le *Livre de la mutacion de Fortune.*" *Bien dire et bien aprandre* 17 (1999): 119–30.

Gay, Lucy M. "On the Language of Christine de Pisan." *Modern Philology* 6 (1908–9): 69–96.

Gibbons, Mary Weitzel. "Christine's Mirror: Self in Word and Image." In Kennedy et al., *Contexts and Continuities*, 2:367–96.

Gilli, Patrick. "Politiques italiennes, le regard français: c. 1375–1430." *Médiévales* 19 (1990): 109–23. <http://www.persee.fr/web/revues/home/prescript/article/medi_0751-2708_1990_num_9_19_1192>.

Gompertz, Stéphane. "Le voyage allégorique chez Christine de Pisan." In *Voyage, quête, pèlerinage dans la littérature et la civilisation médiévales. Sénéfiance* 2, 195–208. Aix-en-Provence: Cahiers du Centre Universitaire d'Etudes et de Recherches Médiévales d'Aix-en-Provence, 1976. <http://books.openedition.org/pup/4332?lang=en>.

Gottlieb, Beatrice. "The Problem of Feminism in the Fifteenth Century." In *Women of the Medieval World: Essays in Honor of John H. Mundy*, edited by Julius Kirshner and Suzanne F. Wemple, 337–64. Oxford: Basil Blackwell, 1985.

Green, Karen, and Constant J. Mews, eds. *Healing the Body Politic: The Political Thought of Christine de Pizan*. Turnhout: Brepols, 2005.

Griffin, Miranda. "Transforming Fortune: Reading and Chance in Christine de Pizan's 'Mutacion de fortune' and 'Chemin de long estude.'" *Modern Language Review* 104, vol. 1 (January 2009): 55–70.

Hicks, Eric, Diego Gonzalez, and Philippe Simon, eds. *Au champ des escriptures: IIIᵉ Colloque international sur Christine de Pizan, Lausanne, 18–22 juillet 1998*. Paris: Champion, 2000.

Hicks, Eric, and Ezio Ornato. "Jean de Montreuil et le débat sur le *Roman de la Rose.*" *Romania* 98 (1977): 34–64, 186–219.

Hindman, Sandra. "The Composition of the Manuscript of Christine de Pizan's Collected Works in the British Library: A Reassessment." *British Library Journal* 9 (1983): 93–123. <http://www.bl.uk/eblj/1983articles/article9.html>.

Holderness, Julia Simms. "Castles in the Air? The Prince as Conceptual Artist." In Green and Mews, *Healing the Body Politic*, 161–75.

_____. "Christine, Boèce et saint Augustin: La consolation de la mémoire." In Dulac et al., *Desireuse de plus avant enquerre*, 279–89.

Holguera Fanega, María Angela. "Manifestaciones autobiográficas en *Le livre de la mutacion de Fortune* de Christine de Pizan." In *Las sabias mujeres: Educación, saber y autoría: siglos III–XVII*, edited by María del Mar Graña Cid, 203–11. Madrid: Al-Mudayna, 1994.

Huber, Franziska. "*L'histoire ancienne jusqu'à César*, source du *Livre de la mutacion de Fortune* de Christine de Pizan: Etude comparative des récits sur Cyrus." In Hicks, Gonzalez, and Simon, *Au champ des escriptures*, 161–74.

Hult, David F. "The *Roman de la Rose*, Christine de Pizan, and the *querelle des femmes*." In *The Cambridge Companion to Medieval Women's Writing*, edited by Carolyn Dinshaw and David Wallace, 184–94. Cambridge: Cambridge University Press, 2003.

Huot, Sylvia. "Seduction and Sublimation: Christine de Pizan, Jean de Meun, and Dante." *Romance Notes* 25 (1985): 361–73.

Johnston, Hope. "How *Le livre de la cité des dames* First Came to be Printed in England." In Dulac et al., *Desireuse de plus avant enquerre*, 385–96.

Joubert, Fabienne. "L'appropriation des arts visuels par Christine de Pizan." In *Poètes et artistes: La figure du créateur en Europe au Moyen Age et à la Renaissance*, edited by Sophie Cassagnes-Brouquet, Geneviève Nore, and Martine Yvernault, 103–20. Limoges: Presses Universitaires de Limoges, 2007.

Jung, Marc-René. *La légende de Troie en France au Moyen Age: Analyse des versions françaises et bibliographie raisonnée des manuscrits*. Basel: Francke Verlag, 1996.

Kellogg, Judith L. "Transforming Ovid: The Metamorphosis of Female Authority." In Desmond, *Christine de Pizan and the Categories of Difference*, 181–94.

Kelly, Douglas. "The Invention of Briseida's Story in Benoît de Sainte-Maure's *Troie*." *Romance Philology* 48 (1995): 221–41.

_____, ed. *The Medieval Opus: Imitation, Rewriting, and Transmission in the French Tradition: Proceedings of the Symposium Held at the Institute for Research in Humanities, October 5–7, 1995, University of Wisconsin-Madison*. Amsterdam: Rodopi, 1996.

_____. "Reflections on the Role of Christine de Pisan as a Feminist Writer." *Substance* 2 (1972): 63–71.

Kemp, William. "Dame Christine chez les premiers imprimeurs français, 1488–1536: Vérard, Pigouchet, Hubert et Janot." In Dor and Henneau, *Christine de Pizan: Une femme de science*, 305–23.

Kennedy, Angus J. "The Châtellerault Manuscript of Book VII of Christine de Pizan's *Mutacion de Fortune* and the *Epistre a la Reine*." In Mühlethaler and Billotte, *Riens ne m'est seur*, 25–36.

_____. *Christine de Pizan: A Bibliographical Guide.* London: Grant and Cutler, 1984.

_____. *Christine de Pizan: A Bibliographical Guide. Supplement 1.* London: Grant and Cutler, 1994.

_____. *Christine de Pizan: A Bibliographical Guide. Supplement 2.* Woodbridge, UK: Tamesis, 2004.

_____. "Christine de Pizan, Victor de Saint-Genis et le manuscrit de Châtellerault." *Romania: Revue trimestrielle consacrée à l'etude des langues et des littératures romanes* 109 (1988): 540–60.

_____. "Le manuscrit de Châtellerault: Un manuscrit perdu du VIIᵉ livre de 'La Mutacion de Fortune.'" In Zimmermann and de Rentiis, *City of Scholars,* 107–15.

_____. "A Selective Bibliography of Christine de Pizan Scholarship, circa 1980–1987." In Richards et al., *Reinterpreting Christine de Pizan,* 285–98.

Kennedy, Angus J., Rosalind Brown-Grant, James C. Laidlaw, and Catherine M. Müller, eds. *Contexts and Continuities: Proceedings of the IVth International Colloquium on Christine de Pizan, Glasgow 21–27 July 2000: Published in Honour of Liliane Dulac.* 3 vols. Glasgow: University of Glasgow Press, 2002.

Kéralio, Louise Félicité Guinement de. "Le livre de la mutacion de Fortune." In *Collection des meilleurs ouvrages français, composés par des femmes, dédiée aux femmes françaises,* 3:111–32. Paris: Lagrange, 1787. <https://archive. org/stream/collectiondesme00keragoog#page/n3/mode/2up>.

Kiehl, Carole. "Christine de Pizan and Fortune: A Statistical Survey." In Kennedy et al., *Contexts and Continuities,* 2:443–52.

Koch, Friedrich. *Leben und Werke der Christine de Pizan.* Goslar am Harz: Ludwig Koch, 1885.

Kosta-Théfaine, Jean-François. "Christine de Pizan et la question des Juifs: Problème d'orthodoxie, d'hétérodoxie ou simple (in)tolérance?" *Speculum medii aevi* 3 (1997): 39–52.

Krueger, Roberta. "Christine's Anxious Lessons: Gender, Morality, and the Social Order from the *Enseignemens* to the *Avision.*" In Desmond, *Christine de Pizan and the Categories of Difference,* 16–40.

Lacassagne, Miren. "La figure de Fortune dans *Le livre de la mutacion de Fortune* de Christine de Pizan et la poésie d'Eustache Deschamps." In Hicks, Gonzalez, and Simon, *Au champ des escriptures,* 219–30.

Laennec, Christine Moneera. "Christine *Antygrafe*: Authorial Ambivalence in the Works of Christine de Pizan." In *Anxious Power: Reading, Writing, and Ambivalence in Narrative by Women,* edited by Carol J. Singley and Susan Elizabeth Sweeney, 35–49. Albany: State University of New York Press, 1993.

Laidlaw, James. "Christine and the Manuscript Tradition." In Altmann and McGrady, *Christine de Pizan: A Casebook,* 231–49.

———. "Christine de Pizan—An Author's Progress." *Modern Language Review* 78 (1983): 532–50.

———. "Christine de Pizan—A Publisher's Progress." *Modern Language Review* 82 (1987): 35–75.

———. "Christine de Pizan, the Earl of Salisbury, and Henry IV." *French Studies* 36 (1982): 129–43.

———. "Christine de Pizan: The Making of the Queen's Manuscript: London, British Library, Harley 4431." In *Patrons, Authors and Workshops: Books and Book Production in Paris Around 1400,* edited by Godfried Croenen and Peter Ainsworth, 297–310. Louvain: Peeters, 2006.

———. "Christine's Lays—Does Practice Make Perfect?" In Kennedy et al., *Contexts and Continuities,* 2:467–81.

———. "Maurice Roy: 1856–1932." In Campbell and Margolis, *Christine de Pizan 2000,* 233–50.

———. "Writing Lives—Christine de Pizan." *New Comparison* 25 (Spring 1998): 25–39.

Laird, Edgar. "Christine de Pizan and Controversy Concerning Star-Study in the Court of Charles V." *Allegorica* 18 (1997): 21–30.

Le Brun-Gouanvic, Claire. "Mademoiselle de Keralio, commentatrice de Christine de Pizan au XVIIIe siècle, ou la rencontre de deux femmes savantes." In Dor and Henneau, *Christine de Pizan: Une femme de science,* 326–41.

Lechat, Didier. "Christine de Pizan, 'Dire par ficcion le fait de la mutacion.'" Chap. 4 in *"Dire par fiction": Métamorphoses du je chez Guillaume de Machaut, Jean Froissart et Christine de Pizan.* Paris: Champion, 2005.

Lemieux, Monique, and Christiane Marchello-Nizia. "L'analyse quantitative en diachronie: L'évolution de l'ordre des mots." In *Le moyen français: Philologie et linguistique: Approches du texte et du discours: Actes du VIIIe Colloque international sur le moyen français, Nancy, 5-6-7 septembre 1994,* edited by Bernard Combettes and Simone Monsonégo, 529–39. Paris: Didier Erudition, 1997.

Le Ninan, Claire. "La veuve et le tyran: L'exemplum de Judith dans l'oeuvre de Christine de Pizan." In Caraffi, *Christine de Pizan: La scrittrice e la città,* 75–82.

Lorcin, Marie-Thérèse. "Mère nature et le devoir social: La mère et l'enfant dans l'oeuvre de Christine de Pizan." *Revue historique* 282 (1989): 29–44.

———. "'Seulete suy et seulete vueil estre….'" In Kennedy et al., *Contexts and Continuities,* 2:549–60.

Lotfi, Sarah R. "La Mutacion de Fortune." Short film (2010). <http://vimeo.com/38158445>.

Mahoney, Dhira B. "Middle English Regenderings of Christine de Pizan." In Kelly, *The Medieval* Opus, 405–27.

Marchand, Prosper. "Christine de Pizan." In *Dictionnaire historique, ou mémoires critiques et littéraires, concernant la vie et les ouvrages de divers personnages distingués, particulièrement dans la république des lettres,* 2:146–50. The Hague: Pierre de Hondt, 1759. <http://gallica.bnf.fr/ark:/12148/bpt6k96497774/f1.item.r=prosper%20marchand%20dictionnaire%20historique>.

Margolis, Nadia. "Christine at 600: The State of Christine de Pizan Studies for the Second Millennium." In Campbell and Margolis, *Christine de Pizan 2000,* 31–45.

――――. "Christine de Pizan and the Jews: Political and Poetic Implications." In Brabant, *Politics, Gender, and Genre,* 53–73.

――――. "Christine de Pizan: The Poetess as Historian." *Journal of the History of Ideas* 47 (1986): 361–75.

――――. "Culture vantée, culture inventée: Christine, Clamanges et le défi de Pétrarque." In Hicks, Gonzalez, and Simon, *Au champ des escriptures,* 269–308.

――――. *An Introduction to Christine de Pizan.* Gainesville: University Press of Florida, 2011.

――――. "Modern Editions: Makers of the Christinian Corpus." In Altmann and McGrady, *Christine de Pizan: A Casebook,* 251–70.

――――. "'Où celestiel chimphonye chante ... ': Voyage encyclopédique d'un terme musical devenu moral de Macrobe à Christine de Pizan." *Cahiers de recherches médiévales et humanistes* 6 (1999): 187–203. <http://crm.revues.org/935>.

――――. "The Poetics of History: An Analysis of Christine de Pizan's *Livre de la Mutacion de Fortune*." PhD diss., Stanford University, 1977.

――――. "The Rhetoric of Detachment in Christine de Pizan's *Mutacion de Fortune.*" *Nottingham French Studies* 38 (1999): 170–81. <http://www.euppublishing.com/ doi/abs/10.3366/nfs.1999-2.008>.

――――. "Les terminaisons dangereuses: Lyrisme, féminisme et humanisme néologiques chez Christine de Pizan." In *Autour de Jacques Monfrin. Néologie et création verbale: Actes du colloque international Université McGill, Montréal, 7-8-9 octobre 1996,* edited by Giuseppe Di Stefano and Rose M. Bidler, 381–404. Montreal: CERES, 1997.

Marquis, Marie-Josée. "'Une image vaut bien mille mots': Recherche sur l'iconographie des textes allégoriques de Christine de Pizan." PhD diss., University of Connecticut, 2014. <digitalcommons.uconn.edu/dissertations/632>.

McGrady, Deborah. "Authorship and Audience in the Prologues to Christine de Pizan's Commissioned Poetry." In Hicks, Gonzalez, and Simon, *Au champ des escriptures,* 25–40.

McLeod, Enid. *The Order of the Rose: The Life and Ideas of Christine de Pizan.* Totowa, NJ: Rowman and Littlefield, 1976.

McLeod, Glenda, ed. *The Reception of Christine de Pizan from the Fifteenth Through the Nineteenth Centuries: Visitors to the City.* Lewiston, NY: Edwin Mellen Press, 1991.

McWebb, Christine, and Earl Jeffrey Richards. "New Perspectives on the Debate about the *Roman de la Rose.*" In Dulac et al., *Desireuse de plus avant enquerre,* 103–16.

Meiss, Millard. "Christine de Pisan: *La mutacion de Fortune.*" In *French Painting at the Time of Jean de Berry. The Limbourgs and Their Contemporaries.* 1 ("Text"): 8–12; 2 ("Illustrations"): figures 1–2, 14–16, 19–34. New York: Pierpont Morgan Library, 1974.

Moffitt, John F. "*Le Livre de la Mutacion de Fortune:* Picturing the Art of Memory in Christine de Pisan's 'Hall of Fortune.'" *Pantheon: Internationale Jahreszeitschrift für Kunst* 57 (1999): 178–81.

Mombello, Gianni. "Christine de Pizan and the House of Savoy." In Richards et al., *Reinterpreting Christine de Pizan,* 187–204.

_____. "Pour la réception de Christine de Pizan en Italie: *L'Arte del rimare* de Giovanni M. Barbieri." In Campbell and Margolis, *Christine de Pizan 2000,* 263–81.

_____. "Quelques aspects de la pensée politique de Christine de Pizan d'après ses œuvres publiées." In *Culture et politique en France à l'époque de l'humanisme et de la Renaissance,* edited by Franco Simone, 43–153. Turin: Accademia delle Scienze, 1974.

Monahan, Jennifer. "Authority and Marginal Status: Authorial Stance in Christine de Pizan's *Livre du corps de policie* and *Livre de la paix.*" In Hicks, Gonzalez, and Simon, *Au champ des escriptures,* 41–49.

_____. "*Querelles:* Medieval Texts and Modern Polemics." In Kennedy et al., *Contexts and Continuities,* 2:575–84.

Morse, Ruth. *The Medieval Medea.* Cambridge, UK and Rochester, NY: D. S. Brewer, 1996.

Mühlethaler, Jean-Claude. "Entre amour et politique: Métamorphoses ovidiennes à la fin du Moyen Age: La fable de Céyx et Alcyoné, de l'*Ovide moralisé* à Christine de Pizan et Alain Chartier." In "Lectures et usages d'Ovide," edited by Emmanuèle Baumgartner, thematic issue, *Cahiers de recherches médiévales et humanistes* 9 (2002): 143–56. <http://crm.revues.org/76>.

_____. "La poétique de la fragmentation ou de la bonne utilisation des figures exemplaires: Enée dans *Le chemin de long estude* de Christine de Pizan." In Dulac et al., *Desireuse de plus avant enquerre,* 249–64.

Mühlethaler, Jean-Claude, and Denis Billotte, eds. *Riens ne m'est seur que la chose incertaine: Etudes sur l'art d'écrire au Moyen Age offertes à Eric Hicks par ses élèves, collègues, amies et amis.* Geneva: Slatkine, 2001.

Müller, Ernst. *Syntax der Christine de Pisan.* Greifswald: Julius Abel, 1886. <http://babel.hathitrust.org/cgi/pt?id=ucl.b2621498;view=1up;seq=13>.

Muzzarelli, Maria Giusepina. "Anatomia e fisiologia di una *mise*: La 'divisa' di Christine de Pizan." In Caraffi, *Christine de Pizan: La scrittrice e la città,* 259–69.

_____. "Louise de Kéralio Reads the Biography of Charles V Written by Christine de Pizan: A Comparison of Two Female Intellectuals who Lived Four Centuries Apart." *Imago temporis: Medium Aevum* 5 (2011): 101–15.

Nephew, Julia A. "Gender Reversals and Intellectual Gender in the Works of Christine de Pizan." In Hicks, Gonzalez, and Simon, *Au champ des escriptures,* 517–31.

Nys, Ernest. *Christine de Pisan et ses principales œuvres.* The Hague: Martinus Nijhoff, 1914.

Oexle, Otto Gerhard. "Christine et les pauvres." In Zimmermann and de Rentiis, *City of Scholars,* 206–20.

Ouy, Gilbert. "Une énigme codicologique: Les signatures des cahiers dans les manuscrits autographes et originaux de Christine de Pizan." In *Calames et cahiers: Mélanges de codicologie et de paléographie offerts à Léon Gilissen,* edited by Jacques Lemaire and Emile van Balberghe, 119–31. Brussels: Centre d'étude des manuscrits, 1985.

Ouy, Gilbert, and Christine Reno. "Le catalogue des manuscrits autographes et originaux de Christine de Pizan." In Ribémont, *Sur le chemin,* 127–33.

_____. "Les hésitations de Christine: Etude des variantes de graphies dans trois manuscrits autographes de Christine de Pizan." *Revue des langues romanes* 92 (1988): 265–86.

_____. "Identification des autographes de Christine de Pizan." *Scriptorium* 34 (1980): 221–38.

Ouy, Gilbert, Christine Reno, and Inès Villela-Petit. *Album Christine de Pizan.* Turnhout: Brepols, 2012.

Pairet, Ana. "'Circes l'enchanteresse': De l'*Epistre Othea* au *Livre de la mutacion de Fortune.*" In Buschinger et al., *Christine de Pizan et son époque,* 108–14.

_____. *Les mutacions des fables: Figures de la métamorphose dans la littérature française du Moyen Age.* Paris: Champion, 2002.

_____. "Subjectivité poétique et discours historique dans l'oeuvre narrative de Christine de Pizan." In *Histoires d'historiennes,* edited by Nicole Pellegrin, 145–55. Saint-Etienne: Publications de l'Université de Saint-Etienne, 2006.

Paris, A. Paulin. *Les manuscrits françois de la bibliothèque du roi: Leur histoire et celle des textes allemands, anglois, hollandois, italiens, espagnols de la même collection.* 5:136–48. Paris: Techener, 1842.

Parussa, Gabriella. "Autographes et orthographe: Quelques considérations sur l'orthographe de Christine de Pizan." *Romania: Revue trimestrielle consacrée à l'etude des langues et des littératures romanes* 117 (1999): 143–59.

———. "*Rimoier* et *exposer:* Quelques remarques sur la syntaxe de Christine de Pizan." In *Le moyen français: Philologie et linguistique: Approches du texte et du discours: Actes du VIIIe colloque international sur le moyen français, Nancy, 5-6-7 septembre 1994,* edited by Bernard Combettes and Simone Monsonégo, 573–93. Paris: Didier Erudition, 1997.

Parussa, Gabriella, and Richard Trachsler. "*Or sus, alons ou champ des escriptures:* Encore sur l'orthographe de Christine de Pizan: l'intérêt des grands corpus." In Kennedy et al., *Contexts and Continuities,* 3:621–43.

Patch, Howard R. *The Goddess Fortuna in Mediaeval Literature.* 1927. New York: Octagon Books, 1967.

Paupert, Anne. "Le 'je' lyrique féminin dans l'oeuvre poétique de Christine de Pizan." In *Et c'est la fin pour quoy sommes ensemble: Hommage à Jean Dufournet, Professeur à la Sorbonne Nouvelle,* edited by Jean-Claude Aubailly et al., 3:1057–71. Paris: Champion, 1993.

———. "'La narracion de mes aventures': Des premiers poèmes à *l'Advision,* l'élaboration d'une écriture autobiographique dans l'oeuvre de Christine de Pizan." In Hicks, Gonzalez, and Simon, *Au champ des escriptures,* 51–71.

———. "Philosophie 'en forme de sainte Théologie': L'accès au savoir dans l'oeuvre de Christine de Pizan." In Dor and Henneau, *Christine de Pizan: Une femme de science,* 39–53.

Pernoud, Régine. *Christine de Pisan.* Paris: Calmann-Lévy, 1982.

Pinet, Marie-Josèphe. *Christine de Pisan, 1364–1430: Etude biographique et littéraire.* Paris: Champion, 1927.

Poirion, Daniel. "Christine de Pisan." In *Le Moyen Âge II: 1300–1480,* 203–10. Paris: Arthaud, 1971.

———. "Christine de Pisan." In *Le poète et le prince: L'évolution du lyrisme courtois de Guillaume de Machaut à Charles d'Orléans,* 237–54. Paris: Presses Universitaires de France, 1965.

Quereuil, Michel. "Le verbe *mander* dans la *Mutacion de Fortune* de Christine de Pizan." In *Actas do XIX Congreso Internacional de Lingüística e Filoloxía Románicas, Universidade de Santiago de Compostela, 1989,* edited by Ramón Lorenzo, 2:625–30. Coruña: Fundación "Pedro Barrié de la Maza, Conde de Fenosa," 1992.

Quilligan, Maureen. *The Allegory of Female Authority: Christine de Pizan's Cité des dames.* Ithaca, NY: Cornell University Press, 1991.

_____. "The Name of the Author: Self-Representation in Christine de Pizan's *Livre de la cité des dames.*" *Exemplaria* 4 (1992): 201–28.

Régnier-Bohler, Danielle. "La tragédie thébaine dans 'La mutacion de Fortune.'" In Zimmermann and de Rentiis, *City of Scholars,* 127–47.

Reno, Christine M. "Anne Malet de Graville: A Sixteenth-Century Collector Reads (and Writes) Christine." *The Profane Arts* 7 (1998): 170–82.

_____. "Autobiography and Authorship in Christine's Manuscripts." *Romance Languages Annual* 9 (1997): xxi–xxiv.

_____. "Christine de Pizan: At Best a Contradictory Figure?" In Brabant, *Politics, Gender, and Genre,* 171–91.

_____. "Les *nota bene* dans trois manuscrits de présentation de la *Mutacion de Fortune.*" In Hicks, Gonzalez, and Simon, *Au champ des escriptures,* 781–87.

Reno, Christine M., and Gilbert Ouy. "X + X' = 1: Response to James C. Laidlaw." In Kennedy et al., *Contexts and Continuities,* 3:723–30.

Ribémont, Bernard. "Christine de Pizan écrivain didactique: La question de l'encyclopédisme." In Dor and Henneau, *Christine de Pizan: Une femme de science,* 71–93.

_____. "Christine de Pizan, Isidore de Séville et l'astrologie: Compilation et 'mutacion' d'un discours sur les arts libéraux." In Dulac et al., *Desireuse de plus avant enquerre,* 303–14.

_____. "La figure de Jules César chez Christine de Pizan." In "La figure de Jules César au Moyen Age et à la Renaissance" edited by Bruno Méniel and Bernard Ribémont, part 1 of special issue, *Cahiers de recherches médiévales et humanistes* 13 (2006): 127–47. <http://crm.revues.org/854>.

_____. "'Quand écrire est se remémorer' … Le motif du souvenir comme déclencheur de l'écriture chez Christine de Pizan." In *Das Schöne im Wirklichen, das Wirkliche im Schönen: Festschrift für Dietmar Rieger zum 60. Geburstag,* edited by Anne Amend-Söchting, Kirsten Dickhaut, Walburga Hülk-Althoff, Klaudia Knabel, and Gabriele Vickermann, 255–64. Heidelberg: Winter, 2002.

_____, ed. *Sur le chemin de longue étude … Actes du colloque d'Orléans, juillet 1995.* Paris: Champion, 1998.

Richards, Earl Jeffrey. "Christine de Pizan and Jean Gerson: An Intellectual Friendship." In Campbell and Margolis, *Christine de Pizan 2000,* 197–208.

_____, ed. *Christine de Pizan and Medieval French Lyric.* Gainesville: University Press of Florida, 1998.

_____. "Christine de Pizan and Sacred History." In Zimmermann and de Rentiis, *City of Scholars,* 15–30.

_____. "Christine de Pizan, the Conventions of Courtly Diction, and Italian Humanism." In Richards et al., *Reinterpreting Christine de Pizan,* 250–71.

_____. "Christine de Pizan, Tolerance and the Plea for Equal Protection under the Law: Revisiting the Question of Her Attitudes toward Hierarchical Justice, the Jews, Widows and Rape Victims: A Close Reading of the *Livre des fais et bonnes meurs du sage roy Charles V*, 1.23." In *Tolérance et intolérance: Actes du Colloque international des 1ᵉʳ, 2 et 3 mars 2011 à Amiens*, edited by Danielle Buschinger, 108–14. Amiens: Presses du Centre d'Etudes Médiévales, Université de Picardie-Jules Verne, 2011.

_____. "The Medieval 'femme auteur' as a Provocation of Literary History: Eighteenth-Century Readers of Christine de Pizan." In McLeod, *Reception of Christine de Pizan*, 101–26.

_____. "Poems of Water without Salt and Ballades without Feeling, or Reintroducing History into the Text: Prose and Verse in the Works of Christine de Pizan." In Richards, *Medieval French Lyric*, 206–29.

_____. "Rejecting Essentialism and Gendered Writing: The Case of Christine de Pizan." In Chance, *Gender and Text*, 96–131.

_____. "Sexual Metamorphosis, Gender Difference, and the Republic of Letters, or Androgyny as a Feminist Plea for Universalism in Christine de Pizan and Virginia Woolf." *Romance Languages Annual* 2 (1991): 146–52.

_____. "Somewhere Between Destructive Glosses and Chaos: Christine de Pizan and Medieval Theology." In Altmann and McGrady, *Christine de Pizan: A Casebook*, 43–55.

_____. "Virile Woman and WomanChrist: The Meaning of Gender Metamorphosis in Christine." In Mühlethaler and Billotte, *Riens ne m'est seur*, 239–52.

Richards, Earl Jeffrey, Joan Williamson, Nadia Margolis, and Christine Reno, eds. *Reinterpreting Christine de Pizan*. Athens: University of Georgia Press, 1992.

Rigaud, Rose. *Les idées féministes de Christine de Pisan*. Neuchâtel: Imprimerie Attinger Frères, 1911.

Robineau, E.M.D. *Christine de Pisan: Sa vie et ses œuvres*. Saint Omer: Fleury-Lemaire, 1882.

Roux, Simone. *Christine de Pizan: Femme de tête, dame de cœur*. Paris: Payot, 2006.

Sasaki, Shigemi. "Fontaine de Pégase et 'chappel' de la poétesse dans *Le livre de la mutacion de Fortune*." In Dulac et al., *Desireuse de plus avant enquerre*, 265–76.

Sigal, Pierre André. "Christine de Pizan et le peuple." In Kennedy et al., *Contexts and Continuities*, 3:811–28.

Slerca, Anna. "L'*Advision Cristine*, Guillaume de Machaut, Boccace et le thème de la rétraction." In Dulac et al., *Desireuse de plus avant enquerre*, 315–26.

_____. "*Le livre de la mutacion de Fortune*, source du *Labyrinthe de Fortune* de Jean Bouchet." In Dulac and Ribémont, *Une femme de lettres*, 509–21.

Smith, Geri L. "Christine de Pizan's *Dit de la pastoure:* A Feminization of the Pastourelle." *Romance Notes* 39 (1999): 285–94.

_____. "De Marotele au 'Lai mortel': La subversion discursive du code courtois dans deux ouvrages de Christine de Pizan." In Hicks, Gonzalez, and Simon, *Au champ des escriptures,* 651–61.

Solente, Suzanne. *Christine de Pisan.* Paris: Imprimerie Nationale and C. Klincksieck, 1969. Also printed as "Christine de Pisan" in *Histoire littéraire de la France* 40 (1974): 335–422.

_____. "Le *Jeu des échecs moralisés,* source de la *Mutacion de Fortune.*" In *Recueil de travaux offerts à M. Clovis Brunel par ses amis, collègues et élèves,* 2:556–65. Mémoires et documents 12. Paris: Société de l'Ecole des Chartes, 1955.

Solterer, Helen. "Christine's Way: The *Querelle du Roman de la Rose* and the Ethics of a Political Response." In *The Master and Minerva: Disputing Women in French Medieval Culture,* 151–75. Berkeley: University of California Press, 1995.

Strubel, Armand. "Le style allégorique de Christine." In Dulac and Ribémont, *Une femme de lettres,* 357–72.

Suranyi, Anna. "A Fifteenth-Century Woman's Pathway to Fame: The *Querelle de la Rose* and the Literary Career of Christine de Pizan." *Fifteenth-Century Studies* 23 (1996): 204–21.

Tanase, Gabriela. "La métamorphose du corps chez Christine de Pizan: Masque viril et naissance d'un *je* poétique." In *Le corps romanesque: Images et usages topiques sous l'Ancien Régime: Actes du XXe colloque de la SATOR,* edited by Monique Moser-Verrey, Lucie Desjardins, and Chantal Turbide, 231–43. Quebec: Presses de l'Université de Laval, 2009.

Tarnowski, Andrea. "Christine's Selves." In Dulac et al., *Desireuse de plus avant enquerre,* 181–88.

_____. "Maternity and Paternity in 'La mutacion de Fortune.'" In Zimmermann and de Rentiis, *City of Scholars,* 116–26.

_____. "Order and Disorder in Christine de Pizan." PhD diss., Yale University, 1991.

_____. "Pallas Athena, la science et la chevalerie." In Ribémont, *Sur le chemin,* 149–58.

Thomassy, Raymond. *Essai sur les écrits politiques de Christine de Pisan.* Paris: Debécourt, 1838.

Thompson, John Jay. "Medea in Christine de Pizan's *Mutacion de Fortune,* or How To Be a Better Mother." *Forum for Modern Language Studies* 35 (1999): 158–74.

Varty, Kenneth. "Christine's Guided Tour of the *Sale Merveilleuse:* On Reactions to Reading and Being Guided Round Medieval Murals in Real and Imaginary Buildings." In Campbell and Margolis, *Christine de Pizan 2000,* 163–73.

Vassilieva-Codognet, Olga. "Les illustrations des manuscrits du *Livre de la mu- tacion de Fortune*." In Buschinger et al., *Christine de Pizan et son époque*, 210–25.

_____. "'Mais toudis va en tournoyant': Le motif de la Roue de Fortune dans le *Livre de la Mutacion de Fortune* et dans les illustrations de quelques manu- scrits contemporains: Pétrarque, Gerson, Boccace." In Caraffi, *Christine de Pizan: La scrittrice e la città*, 301–22.

Videt-Reix, Delphine. "Christine de Pizan et la poétique de la justice." PhD diss., Aix Marseille Université, 2011. <www.theses.fr/2011AIX10006.pdf>.

Wagner, Barbara. "Tradition or Innovation? Research on the Pictorial Tradition of a Miniature in the *Mutacion*: 'Le plus hault siège.'" In Kennedy et al., *Con- texts and Continuities*, 3:855–72.

Walters, Lori J. "Christine's Symbolic Self as the Personification of France." In Dor and Henneau, *Christine de Pizan: Une femme de science*, 191–215.

_____. "The Figure of the *seulette* in the Works of Christine de Pizan and Jean Gerson." In Dulac et al., *Desireuse de plus avant enquerre*, 119–39.

_____. "Fortune's Double Face: Gender and the Transformations of Christine de Pizan, Augustine, and Perpetua." *Fifteenth-Century Studies* 25 (2000): 97–114.

_____. "Metamorphoses of the Self: Christine de Pizan, the Saint's Life, and Per- petua." In Ribémont, *Sur le chemin*, 159–81.

_____. "Signatures and Anagrams in the Queen's Manuscript: London, British Library, Harley MS 4431." *Christine de Pizan: The Making of the Queen's Manuscript* (website, November 30, 2012). <http://www.pizan.lib.ed.ac.uk/ waltersanagrams.html>.

_____. "*Translatio Studii*: Christine de Pizan's Self-Portrayal in Two Lyric Poems and in the *Livre de la mutacion de Fortune*." In Richards, *Medieval French Lyric*, 155–67.

Wandruszka, Nikolai. "Familial Traditions of the *de Piçano* at Bologna." In Ken- nedy et al., *Contexts and Continuities*, 3:889–906.

_____. "The Family Origins of Christine de Pizan: Noble Lineage Between City and 'Contado' in the Thirteenth and Fourteenth Centuries." In Hicks, Gon- zalez, and Simon, *Au champ des escriptures*, 111–30.

Willard, Charity Cannon. "Christine de Pizan as Teacher." *Romance Languages Annual* 3 (1992): 132–36.

_____. *Christine de Pizan: Her Life and Works*. New York: Persea Books, 1984.

_____. "Christine de Pizan: The Astrologer's Daughter." In *Mélanges à la mémoire de Franco Simone: France et Italie dans la culture européenne*, vol. 1, edited by Jonathan Beck and Gianni Mombello, 95–111. Geneva: Slatkine, 1980.

_____. "The Franco-Italian Professional Writer Christine de Pizan." In *Medieval Women Writers,* edited by Katharina Wilson, 333–63. Athens: University of Georgia Press, 1984.

_____. "The Manuscript Tradition of the *Livre des trois vertus* and Christine de Pizan's Audience." *Journal of the History of Ideas* 27 (1966): 433–44.

Wilson, Margaret S. "A Revaluation of Christine de Pisan as a Literary Figure." PhD diss., Stanford University, 1952.

Woledge, Brian. "Le thème de la pauvreté dans la *Mutacion de Fortune* de Christine de Pisan." In *Fin du Moyen Âge et Renaissance: Mélanges de philologie française offerts à Robert Guiette,* 97–106. Antwerp: Nederlandsche Boekhandel, 1961.

Wolfzettel, Friedrich. "La Fortune, le moi et l'oeuvre: Remarques sur la fonction poétologique de Fortune au Moyen Age tardif." In Kelly, *The Medieval Opus,* 197–210.

_____. "Spätmittelalterliches Selbstverständnis des Dichters im Zeichen von Fortuna: Guillaume de Machaut und Christine de Pizan." *Das Mittelalter* 1 (1996): 111–28.

Yenal, Edith. *Christine de Pisan: A Bibliography of Writings by Her and About Her.* Metuchen, NJ: Scarecrow Press, 1982.

Zimmermann, Margarete. "*Amour d'estude* und *doulx goust de savoir:* neue Konnotierungen von Weiblichkeit bei Christine de Pizan." *Lendemains* 61 (1991): 28–37.

_____. "Christine de Pizan et les féminismes autour de 1900." In Ribémont, *Sur le chemin,* 183–204.

_____. "Christine de Pizan: Memory's Architect." In Altmann and McGrady, *Christine de Pizan: A Casebook,* 57–77.

_____. "L'Œuvre de Christine de Pizan à la croisée des cultures." In Dulac et al., *Desireuse de plus avant enquerre,* 427–39.

Zimmermann, Margarete, and Dina de Rentiis, eds. *The City of Scholars: New Approaches to Christine de Pizan.* Berlin: De Gruyter, 1994.

Index

Abel, 120

Abraham, 115, 121, 124, 136n139

Abydos, 142

Achilles, 15, 178–90, 193; versus Hector, 178–81, 183–85, 188; versus Paris, 189–90; love for Polyxena, 185–87, 189–90

Achior, 136

Actaeon, 87

Adam and Eve, 15, 118–20

Adrastus, 154–57

Aeëtes, 167

Aegean (sea), 223

Aegialeus, 148

Aeneas, 85n57, 87n62, 180, 194, 196; and Dido, 198–99, 215

Africa, 82–83, 217, 218, 229. *See also* Carthage; Hannibal; Scipio, Publius Cornelius (Scipio Africanus, "the African")

Agamemnon, 165, 165n187, 177, 180, 187, 193, 197

Ages of the world, 120–21

Agincourt, battle of, 10, 12

Ahasuerus (Artaxerxes II Mnemon, king of Persia), 144–48

Ajax, 180, 191, 193–94

Alba Longa, 201, 204

Alcyone, 46

Aletes (king of Corinth), 124

Alexander the Great (Alexander III of Macedonia), 15, 19, 88–89, 128, 148, 197, 227–38; and Aristotle, 90, 96, 227; conflict with Darius, 148n163, 230–33; forays into sky and sea, 235–36

Alexandria, 230, 239

allegory: Christine's use of, 18, 19, 253

Allia, battle of, 205n224

Amazons, 15, 132–33, 159–62, 233. *See also individual names*

Ammon (god), 227, 229

Ammon (leader of Ammonites), 136

Amphiaraus, 155

Amulius, 199–200

Anacharsis, 97

Anchises, 194, 199

Andromache, 173, 182

Antenor, 86, 175, 194–96

Antigone, 153

Antiochus III the Great (king of Syria), 211–12

Antiope, 160

Antipater, 236

Apis. *See* Serapis

Apollo, 151, 189–90, 196, 218

Apostles, 81

Aquae Sextiae, battle of, 220n278

Arausio, battle of, 219n277

Arbaces, 129

Archelaus, 222

Argo (ship), 167

Argos, 149, 154–57

Ariadne, 158

Aristonicus, 216

Aristotle, 16; and Alexander the Great, 90, 96, 227

Armagnacs. *See* Hundred Years' War

arms and armor, 126–27; Minerva's innovations to, 149

Arphaxad (king of Media), 134–35

Arras, 75

Arses (king of Persia), 148

283